QUEER KOREA

PERVERSE

MODERNITIES *A series*

edited by Jack Halberstam

and Lisa Lowe

Todd A. Henry

QUEER KOREA

Duke University Press *Durham and London* 2020

Designed by Courtney Leigh Baker
Typeset in Arno Pro and Avant Garde Gothic Std by
Westchester Publishing Services

Library of Congress Cataloging-in-Publication Data
Names: Henry, Todd A., [date] editor.
Title: Queer Korea / [edited by] Todd A. Henry.
Description: Durham : Duke University Press, 2020.
Series: Perverse modernities | Includes bibliographical
references and index.
Identifiers: LCCN 2019032736 (print) | LCCN 2019032737 (ebook)
ISBN 9781478001928 (hardcover) | ISBN 9781478002901 (paperback) |
ISBN 9781478003366 (ebook)
Subjects: LCSH: Homosexuality—Korea (South) |
Sexual minorities—Korea (South) | Gays—Korea (South) |
Lesbians—Korea (South) | Homosexuality—Korea. |
Sexual minorities—Korea. | Gays—Korea. | Lesbians—Korea.
Classification: LCC HQ.16.K6 . Q44 2020 (print) | LCC HQ75.16. K6
(ebook) | DDC 306.76/6095195—dc23
LC record available at https://lccn.loc.gov/2019032736
LC ebook record available at https://lccn.loc.gov/2019032737

This work was supported by Core University Program for Korean
Studies through the Ministry of Education of the Republic of Korea
and Korean Studies Promotion Service of the Academy of Korean
Studies (AKS-2013-OLU-2250002).

Cover art: Early South Korean representation of female
homoeroticism in film *Chilt'u* (*Jealousy*, 1960), directed by
Han Hyŏng-mo. Cover photograph compliments of the Korean
Film Archive (donation by Cho Hŭi-mun).

This printing of *Queer Korea* includes a number of changes and
corrections and supersedes the first printing.

Fontispiece: "Chilt'u" (*Jealousy*, 1960). Frontispiece compliments of
the Korean Film Archive (donation by director of photography, Pak
Sŭng-bae).

CONTENTS

ACKNOWLEDGMENTS

Books, especially edited volumes, do not write themselves. This one is certainly no exception, and it has taken many years and much support to make the present volume possible. Replaying that history in reverse makes the point clear. This volume began as an international symposium, film festival, and art exhibition held at the University of California, San Diego (UCSD), in 2014. "Remembering Queer Korea" was the first of its kind to bring together scholars, directors, and artists to rethink the peninsula's history and culture from the perspective of non-normative subjects and queer analytics. As discussants, Jin-kyung Lee, Minjeong Kim, and Han Sang Kim helped reshape the conference papers. Courtney Hibbard and Jennifer Dieli at UCSD's Program in Transnational Korean Studies (TKS) provided endless administrative support. Jaekyung Jung was instrumental in installing the artwork of Siren Eun Young Jung and creating the promotional materials for the exhibition, "Yeosung Gukgeuk Project: (Off)Stage/Masterclass (2013)." I thank the student workers who staffed the exhibition while it was open to the public. The film festival would not have been possible without Han Sang Kim who helped coordinate the screening of several historical films from the Korean Film Archive, including *The Pollen of Flowers* (1972) and *Sabanji* (1988). Brian Hu, the artistic director of the San Diego Pacific Arts Movement and currently a professor at San Diego State University, was a wonderful co-collaborator in reaching a wider audience of Southern Californians who viewed the queer films of South Korea. Lee Ann Kim, the former director of the Pacific Arts Movement, is a true visionary in making this organization one of San Diego's most prominent. Major financial support was provided by the Academy of Korean Studies, which also helped launch UCSD's TKS with a generous grant of $600,000. Additional assistance was offered by UCSD's Division of Arts and Humanities, the Visual Arts Department, the Association for Asian Studies, and Film Out San Diego.

A smaller version of the film festival took place in 2013 at Hanyang University's Research Institute of Comparative History and Culture (RICH). I thank Jie-Hyun Lim for allowing me to curate a film event on Korea's forgotten pasts. It is my firm belief that filmmakers are some of the best historians of queer Korea, and I wanted to showcase their remarkable achievements. I am grateful to have hosted some of these persons in the context of the 2013 (and 2014) event: Kwŏn Chong-gwan, So Chun-mun, Kim Hye-jŏng, and Pak Chae-jo. In screening their films, I benefited from the assistance and hard work of Kang Kim, Yeonbo Jeong, and Seong-hee Hong at RICH. Intellectuals of Korean gender and sexuality joined us for some memorable dialogues; they include Han Ch'ae-yun, Pak Jŏng-mi, Ruin, Kim Chi-hye, and Kim Kyŏng-t'ae.

Since the early 2000s, involvement with activist organizations and community groups dedicated to the protection and well-being of Korean "sexual minorities" has facilitated my knowledge and approach to the issues raised in this volume. I continue to rely on their indefatigable passion and generous guidance. Over fifteen years ago, I was fortunate to befriend Sŏ Tong-jin who, in 1995, created the first LGBT student group, Come Together, at Yonsei University. He would be happy to know that, as of 2019, there are nearly seventy-five such groups scattered across the country. And although he often claims to have "retired" from LGBT studies, a recent reunion over food and spirits convinced me that he is one of many living treasures of South Korea's queer activism. So, too, is Han Ch'ae-yun, whose tireless dedication to sexual minorities is unparalleled. Countless others continue to staff numerous LGBTI organizations that have flourished since the late 1990s. I cannot possibly name all of them here, but a visit to the booths that today populate annual queer pride celebrations, many of them relatively new, will convince any reader of their dynamism. So many inspiring people in these organizations have generously shared their intimate knowledge, deep commitment, and endless passion with me over the years. They include Tari Young-jung Na, Siren Eun Young Jung, Kim Chi-hye, Candy Yun, Ruin, Yi Min-hŭi, Kim/Cho-Kwang-su, Heezy Kim Yang, Yi Ho-rim, Kim Kyŏng-muk, Kim Tae-hyŏn, Heo Yun, Yi Hyŏk-sang, Yi Chong-gŏl, Kim/Yun Myŏng-u, Chung'gangye, Ch'oe Ŭn-kyŏng, Kim Yŏng-min, and Kim Bi. I also thank Stephano Park, Sang Lee, Seung Chang, and their comrades in Los Angeles for showing me what a vibrant Korean gay/queer community looks like in the diaspora.

Largely "outside" of South Korea but always in interactive dialogue with it, a growing coterie of scholars dedicated to scholarship on queer Korea and its diasporas have supported me in my work and done so much themselves to build this field. They are Jesook Song, Ju Hui Judy Han, John (Song Pae) Cho, Sam Perry, Allan Simpson, Dredge Kang, Patty Ahn, Erica Cho, Timothy Gitzen, John Treat, Eunjung Kim, Layoung Shin, Carter Eckert, Rachael Miyung Joo, Anthony Y. Kim, Woori Han, Minwoo Jung, Kyunghee Sabina Eo, Yeong Ran Kim, Chelle Jones, Soo Ryon Yoon, and Ungsan Kim.

In bringing this volume to fruition, I thank Ken Wissoker, my editor at Duke University Press who believed in this project from the beginning and assisted me at all stages to make it a reality. I have learned so much from his wisdom and friendship. Nina Foster, Olivia Polk, and Sara Leone as well as many others at Duke University Press helped polish the manuscript. Two talented reviewers provided criticism that sharpened the prose and made the volume more accessible. I am grateful to Lisa Lowe and Jack Halberstam for including *Queer Korea* in their pathbreaking series, Perverse Modernities. I also thank Anjali Arondekar, Howard Chiang, Janice Kim, Stephen Sohn, and Sonja Kim for reading my own contributions and helping me to make them more compelling. My co-writers endured many editorial demands in making *Queer Korea* cohere. I thank them for putting up with my "crazy love" (*yŏlae*)—coincidentally, the name of one of South Korea's first transgender bars. Kyunghee Sabina Eo and Max Balhorn have done a tremendous service in translating the essays of Korea-based scholars whose important work Anglophone readers have access to for the first time. I hope that more of this translingual labor continues and that the flow of liberating knowledge and praxis moves increasingly in the direction of enlightening those of us on this side of the Pacific. The willingness of so many South Koreans to regularly take to the streets for social change is what keeps me going. So, too, are the many graduate students who continue to produce scholarship on queer subjects without any promise of future employment. All too many of them enter their respective disciplines knowing that their work will likely be misunderstood, devalued, and even shunned. I will not rest until at least one of them gains tenure-track employment at a Korean university. That work is, in short, the basis of my activism.

It brings me great personal pleasure to complete these acknowledgements where this project really began. In 1999, exactly twenty years ago, I arrived in Seoul to begin my journey of studying Korea and the language, and familiarizing myself with its queer communities. A stint working at an It'aewŏn gay bar in 2003–2004 and participation in Seoul National University's LGBTI student group, then called Maŭm 005, allowed me to make my intellectual work more meaningful to the communities about whom I try to think, speak, and write. I am especially grateful for the loving support of my family and Derek Shin who kept me brutally honest about how I can and cannot relate to queer and other marginalized folks. It is to all these peoples—known and unknown . . . from the past, in the present, and into the future—that I dedicate this volume. May individual and collective peace, happiness, and, above all, liberation (however defined) arrive very soon.

QUEER KOREA

TOWARD A FIELD OF ENGAGEMENT

Todd A. Henry

On September 7, 2013, two South Korean men—gaudily clad in shiny, beige-colored tunic jackets with mandarin collars—held a public wedding ceremony in downtown Seoul.[1] Along the Ch'ŏnggye Stream, a site of recreation typically occupied by straight couples and hetero-sexual families, Kim/Cho Kwang-su, a gay activist and filmmaker, and Kim Sŭng-hwan, his longtime boyfriend and cinematic collaborator, professed their love for one another at a Las Vegas–style spectacle. In addition to congratulatory remarks offered by media celebrities, the wedding ceremony included upbeat songs performed by the gay men's chorus and a musical ser-enade comically enacted by the newlyweds themselves. Even more controver-sial, Kim/Cho and Kim vowed to use their symbolic union as a national test case for marriage equality, contributing their wedding donations (ch'ugŭigŭm) to create a private organization in support of other same-sex couples. How-ever, even before the country's judicial system (which ultimately denied them a marriage license in 2016) could deliberate on the legality of their relation-ship, fundamentalist Christians waged an equally spectacular protest by cov-ering the stage with human feces, reminding well-wishers and event onlook-ers of the Bible's purported denunciation of homosexuality as sinful.[2] Since this dramatic confrontation, most progressive politicians have succumbed to ultraconservative constituents who regularly use pride festivals and other queer celebrations to oppose policies aimed at protecting "sexual minorities" (sŏngsosuja). For example, in 2014, just months after being elected to a second term as the mayor of Seoul, Pak Wŏn-sun suggested that South Korea become the first country in Asia to legalize gay marriage, if only as a token gesture of tolerance aimed at proving the country's cosmopolitan credentials to the region and the wider world.[3] But, unfortunately for South Korean proponents of same-sex unions, including Kim/Cho and Kim, Taiwan won that honor in May 2017 when the Constitutional Court passed a landmark ruling establishing the illegality of current marriage laws, a decision that has paved the way for gay and lesbian couples in that Asian nation to wed.

From the vantage point of queer activists who have repeatedly called on government officials to adopt nondiscriminatory policies toward LGBTI citizens and their continued demonization by fundamentalist conservatives who brazenly claim that "anal sex is not a human right" (hangmun seksŭ inkwŏn i anida), it appears that South Korea, like Taiwan, can be located along a teleological, if highly contentious, trajectory of liberal inclusion at whose end point stands the Holy Grail of marriage equality. Indeed, over the past fifteen years, movements advancing marriage equality have quickly gained currency across many parts of the world, with same-sex weddings becoming legal in much of Western Europe and North America, parts of Latin America and Oceania, and one nation in Africa. In this sense, Pak Wŏn-sun's controversial call for South Korea to engage in what might be called "matrimonial one-upmanship" and activists' own citation of global precedents, including the U.S. Supreme Court's 2015 ruling in favor of gay marriage, suggest that the country simply lags behind other parts of the world in this respect.[4] According to this progressive model of "global queering" (on which more later), South Korea will, with the passage of time, eventually join its more advanced counterparts, as the country has since the 1980s in terms of capitalist development and procedural democracy.[5]

However, a closer examination of the sexual minority movement and the conservative heteronationalists who oppose such activism reveal a related but different narrative of queer life in this postcolonial, postauthoritarian society—one that has tended to fall outside the empirical and epistemological purview of a queer studies that continues to privilege North America and Western Europe. Indeed, that most LGBTI-identified South Koreans (for whom marriage equality is ostensibly being advanced) refuse to take a public stance on this fraught issue suggests the need to interrogate the social conse-quences and intimate stakes of making known or visible their non-normative sexuality or gender variance. As in other parts of the world, in South Korea the practice of marriage not only involves two atomized individuals seek-ing legal recognition from the state but also deeply implicates family mem-bers, intimate friends, and co-workers. For most heterosexual couples enter-ing matrimony, these overlapping communities play crucial roles in actively promoting—but, in the case of queer subjects, potentially endangering—their material security and psychological well-being. Even for the most vocal advocates of same-sex marriage, including Kim/Cho Kwang-su, it took several years to convince his partner, Kim Sŭng-hwan—and, by extension, his part-ner's family—to acquiesce to a public ceremony that undoubtedly would cata-pult them into the national limelight. Although ultimately deciding to bless their sons' relationship, participation by the couple's parents at the 2013 wed-ding ceremony, which included an emotional speech by Kim/Cho Kwang-su's mother, subjected them and other relatives to the possibility of what might be called "homophobia (or transphobia) by association," a concept invoked by several authors in this volume.[6] A variant of "guilt by association" (*yŏnjwaje*), a system of collective culpability that was used both before and after the Korean War (1950–53) to punish family members of alleged communists, the phrase refers to a similar stigma that marginalizes sexual minorities and, by extension, their kin.[7] Such homophobic and transphobic associations can even follow queer Koreans into the diaspora. In the U.S., for example, church and other organizations often form the community around which diasporics seek to protect themselves against racial violence and the economic vicissitudes of their host country, but where they also regularly encounter the anti-LGBTI agenda of conservative community groups.[8] In this sense, the visible participa-tion of some parents in support of their "out" children at recent pride festivals and other public events marks a highly controversial dimension of a queer politics that, in South Korea as elsewhere, remains as much family-oriented as individually based.[9]

In recent years, the plight of sexual minorities has become a rallying point for some progressive-minded individuals, particularly among millennial South Koreans who, when compared with their older counterparts, tend to support cultural diversity. But the increased visibility and heightened stakes of same-sex marriage have ironically diverted the attention of many non-normative communities away from public advocacy for liberal forms of inclusion, human rights protection, and identity-based politics. Especially in the current age of neoliberal consumption, the internet and other digital technologies, such as smart phone–based dating applications, have enabled a new generation of South Koreans to pursue a wide range of self-oriented practices of intimacy, but without necessarily creating public personas that subject them to endangering forms of alienation from family, society, or nation. Although a Western-centric lens might simplistically characterize their lives as "closeted," a locally grounded analytic insists that individuals politicized as sexual minorities have deftly carved out an "under-the-radar" presence.[10] Such clandestine sociality in both on- and off-line spaces has allowed LGBTI South Koreans to cultivate intimacies with other gender-variant or sexually non-normative subjects while attempting to shield themselves from the public scrutiny that only a small number of activists, such as Kim/Cho Kwang-su and Kim Sŭng-hwan, are willing to endure. Just as remarkable as the large crowds that gathered along the Ch'ŏnggye Stream in the fall of 2013 to support their symbolic union were many more under-the-radar queers who avoided participating in the celebration precisely because they feared that their presence at that public site would subject them to the kind of legibility they had worked so carefully to avoid.[11] In spite of these efforts, high-ranking military officers have, in recent years, exploited digital technologies to infiltrate gay male subcultures. Subjecting active-duty soldiers to arcane regulations that criminalize same-sex acts (even when consensual and done off base), high-ranking leaders have transformed the private practice of anal sex *(kyegan)* into charged matters of public concern and national security.

Although same-sex marriage poignantly underscores one fraught aspect of queer life in South Korea today, other historical modes of same-sex sexuality, cross-gender identification, and non-normative intimacies—on the Korean Peninsula and in the diaspora, as well as in relation to Asia and the wider world—remain a troubling oversight that the present volume seeks to address. This blind spot not only plagues present debates about acceptable boundaries of hotly debated issues, such as class inequalities, rampant suicide, sexual harassment, and patriarchal domination as well as labor migration and citizenship rights. It also limits how the past is imagined and recounted in terms of similarly contested processes of Korean modernity, which include colonial rule, nationalist politics, and authoritarian development. The problematic occlusion of queerness in the politicized narration of history is perhaps most apparent in the media's power to frame present manifestations of non-normative practices of gender and sexuality in terms of past traditions, especially by highlighting the purported lack thereof. To return to the frenzied fanfare of 2013, mainstream newspapers heralded the union of Kim/Cho Kwang-su and Kim Sŭng-hwan as the country's *first* same-sex wedding.[12] To be sure, efforts to gain official recognition of their relationship marked a turning point insofar as their public ceremony sparked a national debate over legal definitions of matrimony.[13] However, lost in sensational accounts of this recent case is that gay marriage—whether performed as public ceremonies seeking state protection, conducted to dignify queer relationships in the eyes of family and friends, or adopted as a practical mechanism to protect the economic well-being of marginalized individuals—is neither new nor foreign to the peninsula.[14] Indeed, alarmist reports of the 2013 celebration overlooked previous attempts by same-sex couples to secure recognition of their unions. For example, as early as 2004 a lesbian woman tried to sue her ex-girlfriend to have their relationship accepted as a de facto marriage (*sasilhon*), an arrangement that protects most heterosexual partners who do not officially wed one another. In the end, the court refused to rule on this attempt to divide the lesbian couple's assets. But the presiding judge, a young man who had studied European precedents, did respond to the precarious situation of sexual minorities by advocating civil unions as a possible way of protecting their relationships.[15]

Although this progressive proposal remains politically unpopular and has yet to bear legal fruit, South Korea boasts an even longer but largely unknown history of same-sex unions, particularly among working-class women. As my contribution documents, such bonds took root after the Korean War, a deadly conflict that severely disrupted heteropatriarchal kinship practices. In response to gynocentric subcultures that emerged in the wake of this national tragedy, journalists routinely covered female-female wedding ceremonies from the 1950s to the 1980s, if only as an entertaining tactic of profitmaking that minimized the economic struggles of single or abandoned women. Not unlike media accounts of the 2013 celebration, postwar reports repeatedly cited these queer unions as the county's first, even to the point of obvious incredulity. Their accuracy notwithstanding, sensational accounts of same-sex weddings, I argue, sought to accommodate nonconforming practices of kinship into the country's hetero-marital culture. They did so by describing male-dressed women as "husbands" and female-dressed women as their "wives," rather than referencing the subcultural terms *paji-ssi* (Ms. Pants) and *ch'ima-ssi* (Ms. Skirt) used by queer women to express their desires for one another. Underscoring the unsustainability and evanescence of their relationships, such profitmaking reports also functioned as cautionary tales aimed at redirecting subversive forms of homoeroticism toward advancing the (re)productive goals of capitalist accumulation and national loyalty.

In addition to offering historicized accounts that recall such charged moments of social and cultural anxiety, *Queer Korea* examines the ongoing effects of these pasts in "a field of power that seeks to silence, erase, and assimilate all non-normative expressions and desires."[16] To this end, we use interdisciplinary methods such as close reading, archival research, visual analysis, and ethnographic fieldwork to trace the understudied ways in which queerness has been represented and, more often than not, exploited to consolidate idealized notions of family and community, as well as compulsory paths of development and citizenship. By exploring the instrumentalist nature of discourses and practices of non-normative sexuality and gender variance, the volume challenges privileged but limited forms of knowledge that have tended to advance nationalist trajectories and similarly homogenizing operations of power. Like media accounts, most academic narratives of Korea continue to neglect critical insights offered by a sustained focus on queerness, which they often implicitly consider a foreign or threatening presence to collective images of the self, whether defined in national, religious, sexual/gendered, or other terms. To be sure, the number of students interested in LGBTI-related topics at South Korean universities has grown dramatically in recent years. But in a society that discouraged queer subjects from documenting or verbalizing their experiences until at least the 1990s, even the most eager researchers struggle to locate relevant texts to analyze and willing informants to interview. Perhaps more detrimental, many students lack institutional support for their research, forcing some to pursue graduate degrees at overseas universities. Although a small coterie of dedicated scholars have succeeded in publishing pioneering studies on non-normative sexuality and gender variance, few can succeed in an academy that remains disinterested in, if not hostile to, queer studies.[17] For their part, most activists, although often trained in graduate programs, are so occupied with countering LGBTI discrimination that they cannot adequately investigate how past representations of "problematic" bodies endanger their present-oriented tactics of survival.

Such epistemological and political conditions inform the urgent nature of this intellectual project, which began as an international conference, film festival, and art installation at the University of California, San Diego (UCSD), in the fall of 2014. From its inception, the project, then entitled "Remembering Queer Korea," aimed to facilitate a multilingual and multidirectional traffic in textual and visual forms, both from Korean contexts to English ones and vice versa.[18] Unfortunately, readers of this volume no longer have access to the films that UCSD subtitled and screened in partnership with the Pacific Arts Movement, a San Diego–based film organization, or a version of Siren Eun Young Jung's "(Off)Stage/Masterclass (2013)," an exhibition that addressed the nearly forgotten history of South Korea's all-female theater (yŏsŏng kukkŭk).[19] However, that spirit of transnational dialogue appears here in terms of two expertly translated essays by scholars and activists based in South Korea. These essays offer readers unprecedented access to pioneering research on queer Korea produced by intellectuals working in linguistic and cultural environments that differ from, but engage with, those of our English-language authors, many of whom were also raised in Korean and diasporic communities.

As editor, I thus attempted to foreground scholars, filmmakers, and artists based in South Korea on whom many of us based outside the peninsula rely for inspiration. But in the end, many essays published in this volume were written by academics anchored in North America. A critical and geographic distance from Korea likely enabled these authors to approach their subjects without having to negotiate the myriad institutional and cultural barriers that make generating knowledge about queerness on the peninsula so difficult. Such conditions are perhaps most noticeable in the notable absence of work on North Korea, information about which most scholars lack access or interest.[20] However, this apparent dearth does not mean that North Korea fails to impinge on the consciousness of South Korea—or that South Korea fails to impinge on the consciousness of the North. Nor should it signal that North Korea cannot or should not be a part of what is written about the peninsula, which remains dominated by a focus on South Korea. If these rival states succeed in formally ending the Korean War (or eventually reunifying) and opening their borders to one another, silenced histories of non-normative sexuality and gender variance in North Korea will likely teach us much about the lived experiences of this postcolonial authoritarian state, one guided by nationalist-socialist principles and Kim family rule. Indeed, the guiding premise of Queer Korea is that such Cold War geopolitics directly inform the vernacular languages and the local politics of non-normativity on the peninsula and among its diasporic communities. As such, the chapters that follow do not simply explore these trans- and intranational articulations of queerness as recuperative exercises that only aim to locate LGBTI subjects in Korean history. By authenticating their marginalized position in the nation, the resurrection of such "subjugated knowledges" will likely benefit sexual minorities, especially those who embrace identity politics and other forms of liberal inclusion. While encouraging these possibilities, we also explore past expressions of Korean queerness to reveal the regulatory mechanisms and resistant forces foreclosed or enabled by a shifting set of geopolitical conditions and related epistemologies. We aim to support related narratives of and struggles for empowerment—for example, by the disabled, foreign migrants, "half-bloods," single women, and the proletarian classes—that revolve around similar and overlapping dynamics of mystification, obfuscation, and marginalization.

In this spirit, *Queer Korea* problematizes how practices of non-normative sexuality and gender variance have been consistently ignored or thought away, as suggested earlier by the purported novelty and foreignness of same-sex marriage. To counter such popular and academic myths, we attend to pervasive forms of "queer blindness" that surround the peninsula and its inhabitants, typically described in nationalist narratives as the collective victims of Japanese colonialism, civil war, national division, Cold War rivalries, and other tragedies of the twentieth century (and before). Due to these traumatic experiences, scholars have tended to frame Korean society and culture in terms of ethnoracial and heteropatriarchal purities. To be sure, these "survivalist epistemologies" aimed to create living spaces for a community understood as consistently beleaguered by outside forces. However, both nationalist and postnationalist narratives have overlooked critical light that non-normative sexuality and gender variance can shed on the operation of successive and intersecting structures of power, including colonialism, nationalism, capitalism, and neoliberalism. When considered in these expansive ways, queerness emerges as an important dynamic of Korean history and a revealing analytic of its society and culture, rather than appearing as a disruptive force or an internecine form of subversion.

In addition to queering a Korean studies that remains nationalistically heteronormative, our examination of the peninsula contributes to critiques of queer studies that have focused on displacing Euro-American forms of non-normative sexuality and gender variance. Despite its ongoing reputation as the world's "hermit kingdom," the peninsula functioned as a particularly intense site of transnationality during both the colonial and postcolonial periods.[21] Queer studies of Korea thus serve as much more than an Orientalist object of inquiry or a Cold War application of area studies.[22] In the essays that follow, Korea serves as a critical space to examine what Anjali Arondekar and Geeta Patel have called the "geopolitics of queer studies"—in this case, one closely connected to such historical processes as colonial modernity, authoritarian development, and neoliberal familialism.[23] Like much new scholarship on queer Asia, the volume aims to "provincialize" approaches to non-normative sexuality and gender nonconformity that remain anchored in North American and Western European contexts of liberal pluralism and multicultural assimilation. As the example of same-sex marriage mentioned earlier illustrates, some South Korean activists are clearly pushing their state to create the conditions necessary for the political inclusion of sexual minorities as normalized objects of human rights. However, in a postcolonial society that, even after the formal end of authoritarian rule in 1993, continues to exclude them from such protections and regularly exposes them to various forms of cultural alienation, most queer subjects have consciously avoided the kind of public visibility that typically undergirds identity politics. Foregrounding such predicaments, *Queer Korea* shifts our attention to historical junctures when nonliberal regimes have sought to control the purported monstrosity of bodily differences or erase them as threats to organic conceptions of family, society, nation, or empire. In highlighting these politicized moments of the peninsula's past, we strive to formulate new ways to think and act beyond the politics of despair and violence that have come to dominate the present.[24] Although legal arrangements such as same-sex marriage may solve this predicament for some individuals, we should not assume that its liberal and assimilationist tenants will necessarily create conditions of survival and well-being for many others whose life practices relegate them to the fringes of social respectability and cultural acceptability. Perhaps it is only from this uncomfortably queer position, or what Lauren Berlant has called "cruel optimism," that marginalized subjects on the peninsula and in similar sites of abjection can imagine new possibilities for liberation, but ones that do not necessarily rely on a hostile state or a sensationalizing media to promote their economic viability and emotional fulfillment.[25]

Unruly Subjects under Colonial and Postcolonial Modernity

Whether the object of empirical study or the subject of critical analysis, queerness has remained largely invisible in research on the peninsula, buried under male- and elite-centered accounts that have overwhelmingly focused on the tribulations of a modernizing nation. In historical accounts of Korea, the experiences of Japanese rule (1910–45) and, later, of anticommunist or anticapitalist development under postcolonial authoritarianism have tended to dominate, leaving little room for non-normative stories of the past.[26] When mentioned at all, individuals who do not figure as "proper" subjects of these collectivized narratives—including, but not limited to, those engaging in non-normative sexuality or exhibiting gender variance—were made hypervisible as social threats or, worse yet, rendered as pro-Japanese collaborators.[27] Although such labels gained currency during the colonial era, pundits later deployed them as potent tools of subjectification during and after the Korean War.[28] In the ongoing context of Cold War politics, triumphant expressions of heteronormativity and cisgenderism have persisted as powerful ideologies of national security that aim to promote and ensure bodily purity on both sides of the 38th Parallel. In North Korea, for example, media and literary images of reproductive wholesomeness continue to function as a key strategy of collective mobilization in its historic struggle against an allegedly hedonistic south, which, along with the U.S., its patron state, Democratic People's Republic of Korea (DPRK) leaders regularly accuse of fomenting homosexuality and related "perversions."[29] Much the same can be said of South Korea, where in recent years a growing number of fundamentalist Christians boldly charge sexual minorities with harboring pro–North Korean tendencies and spreading the AIDS virus, but without providing evidence to validate their exaggerated and exclusionary claims.[30] In these alarmist formulas, "homophobia (and transphobia) by association" extends far beyond the stigmatizing confines of one's biological family, transforming individual expressions of non-normative sexuality or gender variance into national threats that purportedly demand vigilant surveillance, repeated punishment, and even further marginalization.

Through such instrumentalist discourses of deviance, representations of queerness have aimed to accommodate nonconforming bodily practices to the (re)productive aims of successive regimes on the Korean Peninsula.[31] Although never fully successful, these "epistemological interventions," as I call them in my essay on female homoeroticism (see chapter 6), worked to assimilate the imagined monstrosity of corporal differences, harnessing them to collective ends. When not already denigrated in these ways, nationalist and most postnationalist scholars have largely ignored the subcultures of "perverse" bodies, deeming them insignificant or embarrassing to their respective intellectual agendas, whether feminist, Marxist, or otherwise. By contrast, the authors in this volume actively recall such moments of forgetfulness and denunciation in both historical and epistemological processes of cultural homogenization. Together, they question such heteronormalizing forces as imperialism, nationalism, militarism, and industrialization, focusing on the lived experiences of "unruly" subjects and their subordinated status in archival, visual, literary, and ethnographic registers. Meanwhile, we eschew ghettoized approaches to marginality that treat queerness only in terms of minority or visibility paradigms. As mentioned earlier, this liberal model emerged in South Korea only during the 1990s and still does not include North Korea. Rather than assuming the pervasiveness of a globalized logic of identity politics, we deploy queer analytics to interrogate disciplinary, biopolitical, and necropolitical structures of normalization that have come to weigh on *all* residents of the peninsula, albeit in considerably uneven ways. *Queer Korea* thus seeks to complicate narratives that tend to advance, rather than to question, collective state goals, such as androcentric familialism and capitalist (or socialist) development.

Several decades before Japanese officials managed to forcibly annex the peninsula in 1910, a concerned group of male intellectuals, most trained in the Confucian classics, appointed themselves as the patriarchal guardians of the Chosŏn Court (1392–1910), which, in their view, desperately required "modernization" to retain national autonomy. Although sharing many of the same reformist goals, these elites adamantly opposed the tactics of their lower-class counterparts, including the millenarian ideas advocated by Eastern Learning *(tonghak)* adherents and the antiestablishment agendas of other grassroots movements, including the first generation of Korean feminists.[32] To guide the masses under their tutelage, some nationalist leaders abandoned Confucian praxis in favor of Western- and Japanese-inspired models of "civilization and enlightenment" *(munmyŏng kaehwa)*. However, the epistemic frames of this modernist paradigm tended to replicate those of their imperialist counterparts, thereby undercutting the ability of nationalists to retain Korea's sovereignty.[33] Although couched in familiar terms of Confucian statecraft, even "Eastern values and Western skills" *(tongdo sŏgi)*, an indigenous style of modernization aimed at placating conservative court stalwarts, also foundered as a strategy to protect the Great Han Empire (1897–1910) at a dangerous time of imperialist incursions.[34] After annexation, the nature and pace of reform fell into the hands of Japanese rulers who adroitly hijacked the nation-building efforts of Korean elites while actively resurrecting and idealizing heteropatriarchal traditions as the moral basis of a new colonial modernity, not unlike early Meiji leaders had done at home.

For emasculated leaders now expected to serve a foreign empire, the traumatic experience of Japanese occupation informed which individuals appeared in an increasingly defensive narrative of the nation and how Koreans were positioned, or sought to position themselves, as legitimate subjects of that collective history. For example, patriarchal invocations of women's lowly status as a worrisome barometer of Korea's purportedly lagging "level of civilization" *(mindo)* nationalized the concerns of this marginalized, but increasingly vocal, subpopulation. On the one hand, bourgeois instrumentalizations of illiterate Korean women produced an androcentric view of femininity that ironically converged with imperialist and Christian views of "benighted" and "heathen" subjects in desperate need of education, if only to promote their cultivation as "wise mothers and good wives" *(hyŏnmo yangch'ŏ)*. On the other hand, such male-dominated discourses did encourage a small group of educated New Women *(sinyŏsŏng)* to seek liberation from a refortified system of heteropatriarchy.[35]

Amid this gender warfare, government officials, medical doctors, and other regulatory professionals in colonial Korea came to define "women" and "men" in epistemologically binary and biologically dimorphic terms. In mirrorlike fashion, these terms extended to equally rigid notions of femininity and masculinity. Such powerful categories of sex and gender worked to obfuscate a wide range of queer practices and non-normative life courses adopted by colonized Koreans and Japanese settlers.[36] During the Asia-Pacific War (1937–45), officials adopted the same binary paradigm to categorize "imperial subjects" *(hwang guk sinmin)* as dutifully abiding by or treacherously deviating from bodily norms aimed at maintaining a system of reproductive heterosexuality on which colonial capitalism relied. A lack of empirical traces in colonialist, nationalist, and missionary archives, especially those voiced by queer subjects themselves, have restricted scholars' ability to appreciate how unruly bodies were, like those of so-called New Women, of critical importance to the powerful confluence of imperialism and nationalism, as well as other modes of collective mobilization and individual contestation, such as socialism and anarchism.[37]

In her essay on shamanism, Merose Hwang reveals this important point by demonstrating the understudied role that this folk religion, later described as the quintessential spirit of the Korean people, played in the regulatory imagination of both imperial authorities and colonized nationalists. She locates the queerness of sorcerers, fortunetellers, and female entertainers—a motley group placed under police surveillance by the Government-General and the intellectual scrutiny of native intellectuals—in their ability to disrupt elite- and male-dominated formulas of colonial modernity, both of which treated popular practices of spiritual healing as superstition. For bourgeois nationalists seeking to promote a morally "healthy" society as the foundation of independence, members of the Sowi Church Guild thus figured as an unruly problem of (self-)governance. Although accused by male nationalists as collaborators (a label many would later apply to them), adherents of the guild boldly dressed in the cultural garb of their colonial overlords as devotees of Shintō, the Japanese spirituality used by the Government-General to "assimilate" Koreans.[38] Imagining the marginalized perspective of the guild, Hwang argues that its resourceful members, many of them female masters of ritual performance, donned the disruptive "drag" of spiritual respectability to survive under an increasingly watchful regime, especially in the wake of a major nationalist uprising in 1919. Even as they provided their colonizers with outward compliance, shamans questioned elites' embrace of heteropatriarchy and their concern with controlling the nation's religious traditions. Hwang also shows that colonial-period efforts at regulation followed longer histories of state violence and social displacement, contexts that explain why disaffected Koreans gravitated to these healers.

Rather than being denigrated as a dangerous presence in their colonized nation, shamanic leaders appeared in another politicized guise as heroically resistant, even in their very queerness. Hwang thus reveals that Korean ritualists straddled a narrow space among colonial control, cultural erasure, and nationalist appropriation. Although reviled for not marrying women and accused of engaging in sexual perversion, well-known male intellectuals such as Ch'oe Nam-sŏn (1890–1957) and Yi Nŭng-hwa (1869–1945) exploited the precolonial traditions of these marginalized women to forge a glorious story of the nation, one that re-centered Korea and Manchuria in a larger, continental culture of shamanism. Having elevated this Pan-Korean identity above a Japan-dominated ideology of common ancestry, transgender practices, same-sex unions, and other queer customs now appeared as core attributes of a proud indigenous culture. If masculinized under the guidance of nationalist intellectuals, this culture could, according to their heteronormalizing agenda, serve as a bulwark against colonial assimilation. Demonstrating how shamans negotiated their position and livelihood through archives of official denunciation and cultural appropriation, Hwang highlights the subversive nature of these popular ritualists, exposing the powerful but contradictory dynamics of colonial rule and nationalist politics.

Like Hwang's essay on the regulatory anxieties and disruptive practices of shamanism, John Treat uses the pioneering prose of Yi Sang (b. 1910) to reveal a similarly troubling dimension about this in(famous) writer and his position in the queer temporality of a colonized nation. Since his premature death in 1937, scholarly evaluations of Yi have tended to vacillate widely. Whereas early narratives bemoaned his literary style as embarrassingly individualistic and thus not representative of serious and collective concerns, later accounts championed his writing as admirably avant-garde and thus befitting a Korean modernist of his day. Seeking to transcend nationalist interpretations, Treat adopts José Esteban Muñoz's notion of queer time in a nonidentitarian reading of "Wings," a short story penned by Yi in 1936. Rather than focus on the author's sexual desire or gendered selfhood as the standards by which to assess his conformity (or lack thereof), Treat highlights the disjoined temporality of the work itself, which, he argues, exposes an overdetermined concurrence of postcolonial and queer stylistics. While foregrounding the migratory nature of this modernist's prose, he shows how the straight time of colonial modernity, embedded in public icons like the clock of the Seoul train station, is continually displaced in "Wings," a title that underscores the author's peripatetic movements across the colonial capital of Seoul and the imperial metropolis of Tokyo. Through such unruly practices, the male narrator "I" and his wife manage to deviate from a heteronormative life course of monogamous and reproductive sexuality, a system of power institutionalized by both Japanese colonizers and Korean nationalists. In his nuanced reading of "Wings," Treat also suggests that the queer time of the story should not be understood as a utopian critique of straight time writ large wherein Korean authors are assumed to write only as colonized subjects or in queer time. Rather, he understands Yi's prose as a vexed encounter between the reproductive futurism of a colonized nation and the reality that most subjects in this occupied territory existed on the fringes of an alienating system that made liberation nearly impossible. However, according to Treat's analysis, that alienation also provided unconventional writers like Yi with hope for a more unencumbered future, whether that emancipation arrived on personal or collective terms.

The essential queerness of colonial modernity, defined by seemingly insurmountable structures of domination and the uncanny ability of deviant subjects to reveal its disabling power through utopic expressions, is further developed in Pei Jean Chen's examination of "free love"(*yŏnae; renai* in Japanese; *lian ai* in Chinese) in occupied Korea. Building on studies that have begun to examine the colonial sensibilities and affective underpinnings of Japanese rule, she argues that literary representations of and public debates about non-normative sexuality and gender nonconformity primarily functioned as regulatory mechanisms.[39] In her analysis of queer expressions under colonial modernity, Chen borrows Elizabeth Povinelli's notion of the intimate event, which Povinelli conceptualized as encounters between "autological," or self-authored (and thus free), and "genealogical," or discursive (and thus constraining), forms of knowledge. With this framework, Chen argues that homosexual (and heterosexual) forms of love were dislodged from traditional paradigms of Confucian kinship and subsequently framed as engagements of choice, if risky ones that often ended in tragedy. A transculturated and translated form of liberalism that arrived in Korea from the West via Japan, expressions of romantic freedom were severely hampered by sexological frames disseminated under a modernizing regime of civilization and enlightenment. Often described as laboratories of modernity, Korea and colonies like it became fertile grounds for the dissemination of genealogical modes of knowledge, whose primary function was regulatory and exploitative rather than self-determining and liberatory. To a degree unseen in the metropole, where more liberal forms of love thrived, colonial discourses on queer desires and other non-normative embodiments worked alongside state policies and nationalist ideologies aimed at managing the gendered and sexualized (dis)abilities of Korean bodies.[40]

In her analysis of literary and media representations from the 1910s to the 1930s, Chen also demonstrates that male authors spiritualized same-sex intimacies as a way of circumventing what they came to view as "perverted" under a scientific paradigm of sexology. But whereas these writers framed intimate relationships between men as homoerotic connections of sympathy (*tongjŏng*) and as tolerable expressions of nationalist fervor, they often engaged in voyeuristic practices of narration that sexualized similar bonds between young women. Chen reveals how seemingly liberating (or autological) depictions of female homoeroticism—double suicides committed by schoolgirls, for example—discouraged adult lesbianism, a life course deemed antithetical to the (re)productive goals of colonial modernity. In response to representations of same-sex relations as deviations from "proper" relations of love, Chen reevaluates them as incomplete projects that, even if thwarted expressions of unruly desires, contained within them subaltern traces of a counterdiscourse. Often articulated as a backward-looking nostalgia for their youth or a refusal to transition from homoerotic bonds to heterosexual marriage, this counterdiscourse appeared as personal tragedies that implicitly questioned normalizing "traditions" of feminine love narrowly defined as heterosexual, monogamous, and reproductive in Korean culture.

Launching her analysis where Chen ends her discussion of same-sex sexuality, Shin-ae Ha explores the queer underside of Korea's literary world of the late 1930s and early 1940s. As studies of this period have demonstrated, mobilization for the Asia-Pacific War led Japanese officials to develop new models of governance and citizenship that could compete with those of their enemy Allies while paving the way for a postwar order.[41] Despite increasingly extensive efforts to integrate despised others into an avowedly multiethnic and postracist empire, officials continued to rely on older methods of resource extraction, including heavy industries and munitions and mining, as well as forced sexual labor.[42] As historically marginalized subjects, Koreans and other colonized subpopulations bore the brunt of proving their loyalties to the Japanese emperor.[43] Ha's essay further complicates the uneven effects of and varied responses to "imperial subjectification" (hwangminhwa) by offering a feminist analysis of Korean literature produced during this controversial period. She argues that becoming "Japanese" entailed an added burden for colonized women. As military mothers, they had far more to lose than their male counterparts, whose soldierly service allowed some of them and their families to benefit from self-sacrifice. If the biopolitical concerns of imperial subjectification offered Korean men new possibilities for empowerment, this highly gendered project of mass mobilization further disenfranchised colonized women, whose agonizing "choice" to serve as "wise mothers and good wives" exposed deep and irresolvable fissures in wartime iterations of colonial modernity.

Ha's postnationalist revision of the wartime period addresses changes in the cultural significance of same-sex intimacies between Korean "sisters." Although increasingly despised under the normalizing mandates of mass mobilization, these gynocentric relationships, she argues, shed important light on female domination and subjectivity during the late colonial period. She criticizes unreflective scholars who, like their patriarchal predecessors under Japanese rule, minimized female same-sex relationships as a transitory phase along an inevitable path toward heterosexual matrimony and reproduction. To be sure, these biopolitical imperatives foreclosed liberatory possibilities that modern education hitherto had offered Korea's New Women. Even as mass mobilization reduced same-sex love to antisocial practices deemed unpatriotic, powerful memories of all-female classrooms and dormitories continued to haunt wholesome images of Korean women. Exposing the messy underbelly of propagandistic stories written by two women writers, Chang Tŏk-jo (1914–2003) and Ch'oe Chŏng-hŭi (1912–90), Ha innovatively excavates the internal subjectivities of female subjects by disclosing the gender and sexual norms of imperial subjectification. Furthermore, she reveals the agony of wartime injunctions and the joys of prewar freedoms as a charged threshold at which women entered, if only tentatively, into a hyper-patriarchal regime that trivialized gynocentric expressions of modernity as deviant. Throughout this externalized process of identification, refusals to follow officially sanctioned values quietly reemerged in nostalgic memoires of liberation, which, as entrenched forms of everyday resistance, delayed and disrupted the domination of women under late colonialism.

Upon liberation in 1945, Korean leaders worked to rehabilitate damaged kin networks as the basis of establishing a sovereign nation, but the fragile hegemony of the late colonial period continued into the postliberation period.[44] Amid internecine conflicts that began as outgrowths of decolonization, wartime strategies of military defense quickly merged with new Cold War exigencies that, after 1948, sought to protect a divided nation with two opposing economic systems. Even after the deadly Korean War, rival states employed similar strategies of mass mobilization and ideological suasion, with queerness playing a pivotal role on both sides of the 38th Parallel. As the two chapters on postcolonial journalism and film demonstrate, Cold War geopolitics led to the creation and maintenance of rigid, but not impenetrable, boundaries aimed at demarcating the normative and non-normative qualities of each state's citizens and their participation in such important areas as family life, economic development, and mass culture.

Although given greater license in South Korea than in the north, popular representations of queerness during the period of Park Chung Hee (1961–79) sought to tame unruly subjects and non-normative practices at a volatile time of revolutionary fervor. Addressing cultural productions created and disseminated during this period, Chung-kang Kim and I demonstrate the important role played by the media in the development of what Jie-hyun Lim [Yim Chi-hyŏn] calls "mass dictatorship."[45] Coined in the early 1990s at a time when democracy was rapidly replacing authoritarian societies across the world, this concept aimed to capture the unexpected ways in which nonelites participated in illiberal political formations and, to varying degrees, continued to do so after the formal demise of autocracies. Such dictatorial legacies have been especially pronounced on the peninsula, where the politics of national division continue to subordinate queer individuals and communities to heteropatriarchal and gender-normative dictates. These Cold War conditions and the self-disciplinary habits they produced discourage scholars from addressing questions of same-sex sexuality and gender variance, including otherwise progressive intellectuals who have adopted mass dictatorship theory to explain how authoritarian regimes relied heavily on social cohesion and cultural conformity for their own power. Nor have they devoted adequate attention to the role of the mass media in manufacturing such forms of consent.[46] As Kim and I both demonstrate, popular images of the nation under South Korean dictatorships regularly featured and profited from queer subjects, while disavowing them in efforts to buttress the heteropatriarchal and cisgender bases of anticommunist development.

In her essay on B-grade films from the late 1960s and early 1970s, Kim highlights tensions created by visual representations of gender variance in this popular but understudied genre.[47] Arguing against anatomically binary notions of sexual difference, she posits that non-normative embodiments proliferated during Park's reign—a period typically studied either in terms of political and economic repression by the state and capital or in relation to public protest movements led by students and laborers. Rather than assume the omnipotence of this developmental regime, Kim also shows how female-dressed men (yŏjang namja) in comedy films exposed the antihegemonic underside of mass culture in Cold War South Korea. To be sure, Park's authoritarian government actively regulated the film industry, using the promulgation of laws and censorship codes to propagate images of the nation that idealized conventional gender norms and wholesome sexual roles. However, as in the aftermath of the Korean War, a crisis of patriarchal control and Confucian morality reappeared during the mid-1960s, an era of social dislocation caused by rapid industrialization and intense urbanization.[48] Rather than simply bemoan fissures in the national body, B-grade directors creatively exploited them in producing comedy films that appealed to the sensibilities of various audiences, especially lower-class laborers moving to cities in increasing numbers.

For example, in Sim U-sŏp's *Male Kisaeng* (1969), the focus of Kim's essay, Mr. Hŏ, the male patriarch and a company president, is transformed into an object of derision by his potent wife. Meanwhile, Mr. Ku, a former employee, flees to a *kisaeng* house where he becomes a female-dressed entertainer and engages in what appears as (but is not) a lesbian relationship with a co-worker. However, because the audience assumes that Mr. Ku is a biological man masquerading as a woman, Mr. Hŏ's attraction to him, captured in a scandalous scene where the latter gropes the former and requests that the two men spend the night together, suggests the irrepressibility of queer desires. This homoerotic possibility is perhaps best underscored by a scandalous kiss that Mr. Hŏ bestows on a now gender-normative Mr. Ku, who returns as a male employee at Mr. Hŏ's company. According to Kim's nuanced analysis, what remains for viewers of comedy films such as *Male Kisaeng* is an irresolvable instance of "gender trouble" wherein heteronormative recuperation and queer subversion intermingle uncomfortably.

My contribution on the historical meanings of female homoeroticism in authoritarian South Korea locates a similar tension between normalizing narratives of heteropatriarchy and allegedly disruptive subcultures of gynocentric intimacies. Using newspaper weeklies and other popular accounts published from the 1950s to the 1980s, I argue that media reports about same-sex weddings drew on medicalized notions of sexual and gender dimorphism, producing compelling stories that could entertain a wide range of intrigued readers while simultaneously moralizing them. Repeatedly emphasizing the alarming novelty (rather than the entrenched tradition) of female-female unions, these sensational accounts sought to dissuade women who, although perhaps numerically insignificant, were challenging heteropatriarchy by opting out of this oppressive system, even as they seemed to depend on its most visible symbols. To minimize their cultural protest, media reports and related images underscored that same-sex weddings relied on the sartorial and ceremonial conventions of heterosexual marriage. Refusing to examine the subcultural meanings of these gendered rituals, intrusive journalists strategically deployed them as epistemological interventions aimed at containing their purportedly corrosive effects. To this end, they designated male-dressed partners as "husbands" and their female-dressed counterparts as "wives," a dichotomized pair that indicated the instability of these very categories. In the end, even such heteronormative labels—coincidentally, not the terms that queer women used to refer to their own gendered subjectivities—could not adequately address the challenge of female homoeroticism, which a voyeuristic media was forced to implicitly admit by describing queer women as distinct and even dangerous.

Rather than documenting the subcultural realities of these women, middlebrow forms of mass media combined the narrative conventions of pulp fiction in its secondary exploitation of the female proletariat. In addition to entertaining readers through profitmaking strategies, popular reports functioned as cautionary tales for gendered projects of anticommunist citizen making. Although largely aimed at the libidinal energies of bourgeois men, their misogyny was, according to the desexualizing logic of the mass media, driving mistreated women into the arms of their female and American counterparts. In these alarmist narratives, women who formed symbolic unions with each other predictably appear as destined for unhappy lesbian futures. Accounts about their short and tragic lives thus provided female readers with a moralizing guide for self-regulation and discouraged them from "veering off track" (*t'alsŏn*), an ideological catchword popular during this period. However, when consumed by "shadow readers," even such disparaging texts could offer queer women uncanny ways to imagine a community of like-minded subjects. In an era of limited and censored media, these popular accounts came to function as veritable guides with which the female proletariat and other marginalized readers could carve out spaces of intimacy and pleasure in South Korea's public culture of authoritarian development.

Citizens, Consumers, and Activists in Postauthoritarian Times

Whether appearing on the peninsula or in the diaspora, more recent, postauthoritarian expressions of non-normative sexuality and gender variance among Korean subjects also depart from (neo-)liberal logics of visibility politics, human rights, and multicultural diversity, issues that continue to dominate queer analyses of Western societies. Insofar as our intellectual project focuses on the illiberal underside of Korean modernity and its uneven effects on marginalized subpopulations, this volume resonates with queer-of-color critiques, which have sought to expand the purview of queer studies beyond the privileged vantage point of white, middle-class, gay men. Through transnational and diasporic approaches, queer-of-color critiques have exposed the subordinated status but insurgent agency of racial minorities who inhabit the contradictory cracks of liberal societies in North American and Western Europe.[49] We highlight the historical forces and dissident subjectivities of Korean queers who, although not necessarily articulating their sense of self only in terms of identity politics, similarly struggle for sustenance and survival in their own national and diasporic communites. As in the West, they are currently waging those struggles under global capitalist logics of consumerism and atomization, as well as amid growing threats of vigilante trolls and religious xenophobes who, in both on- and off-line sites, seek to silence, erase, and even injure social minorities, including women, Muslims, and refugees.[50]

In addition to its alignment with queer-of-color critique, this volume draws on insights from the increasingly vibrant field of Asian queer studies. Although encompassing a wide geographical area and disparate methodological approaches, much of this work has also sought to "provincialize" the Western-centric foci and nativist proclivities of queer studies. Moreover, Asian queer studies has questioned the heteronormative assumptions of area studies and, more recently, its ethnonationalist underpinnings.[51] The causes of the emergence of Asian queer studies since the 1990s are multiple and complex. One important undercurrent connecting the region is the nearly simultaneous development of LGBTI organizations, film festivals, and political organizations during a period that witnessed the establishment of democratic institutions across much of Asia and the Pacific. The preconditions for increased visibility of queer, trans, and intersex communities were thus clearly regional and global in scope.[52] Despite obvious transnational connections, scholars trained in anthropology, history, literature, and other humanistic disciplines responded to these transformations by analyzing non-normative sexuality and gender variance in local contexts. Conditioned in part by Cold War traditions of area studies, this research aimed to specify the terminology, temporality, and texture of queer and transgender communities, often in a single nation-state. In recent years, such inquiries have been advancing in increasingly intraregional directions.[53] In addition to countless book chapters and journal articles, one can now find monographic work in almost every national subfield of Anglophone Asian studies, to say nothing of their Asian-language counterparts.[54] These include Japan; the Sinophone states of China, Taiwan, Hong Kong, and Singapore; Indonesia; Thailand; and India.[55] By including Korea within the purview of Asian queer studies, this volume is intended as a preliminary but necessary effort to analyze local manifestations of gender variance and non-normative sexuality. As suggested earlier, we also aim to expand the temporal scope of a small but growing field of Korean queer studies that tends to focus on the recent past (e.g., 1990s forward), often to the detriment of what came before our current age. Rather than treating these faint histories as irretrievable or irrelevant to the present, we seek to draw vital connections between manifestations of unruly bodies during the (post)colonial era and the current struggles of queer subjects on and beyond the peninsula.

Much research on Asian expressions of same-sex sexuality and gender nonconformity has developed in response to Western-centric arguments advocating queer globalization as a model suitable for understanding contemporary developments across the region. Indeed, it has become near de rigueur for critical scholars to challenge Dennis Altman who, in 1997, argued that LGBTI movements in North America and Western Europe were quickly spreading to their counterparts throughout Asia and the Pacific.[56] Although controversial, queer globalization helped spur important studies on the subjectivities of sexual minorities who, in part, embraced visibility politics and human rights. Altman's paradigm also generated productive debates about studying same-sex sexuality and non-normative gender in cross-border and diasporic modes, especially as they relate to migrant subjects residing in white-dominated communities of the West.[57] Taken together, these studies revealed the interpretive difficulties of analyzing Asian and Pacific forms of queerness without over-simplistically adopting either a model of imperialist diffusion or one of nativist resistance.

As in other regions of the global South, alienating processes of foreign intervention, including imperialism/colonialism, military occupation, and transnational capitalism, have encroached on the diverse populations of Asia and the Pacific. As Tze-lan D. Sang has argued about the effects of these processes, "The complexity of translated modernity in the non-West means that, even when a particular non-Western space for inquiry is ostensibly identified as the nation, it is always already shot through with colonial, imperial, transnational, cosmopolitan, global—whatever we call it—presence and valence."[58] Concerns about the specter of Western (and, in pre–World War II Asia, we might also extend this to Japanese) influence on the developing world have similarly preoccupied many postcolonial critics. Searching for liberating ways of narrating knotted histories of dominated peoples, they identified unequal power relationships that had tended to homogenize their own histories. As Dipesh Chakrabarty articulated this intellectual project from the perspective of South Asia, "To 'provincialize' Europe was precisely to find out how and in what sense European ideas that were universal were also, at one and the same time, drawn from very particular intellectual and historical traditions that could not claim any universal validity."[59]

By contrast, some intellectuals, particularly those living and working in Asia and the Pacific, have responded to the historical predicament of postcolonialism and the perceived threat of queer globalization by asserting nativist accounts of gender variance and non-normative sexuality. Although a minority, they argue for the alleged impenetrability of Western categories. Instead, nativists posit the radical difference of Asian queers in a formula that Howard H. Chiang has aptly described as "self- or re-Orientalization."[60] In the field of Chinese studies, for example, Wah-Shan Chou has boldly suggested that "the family kinship system, rather than an erotic object choice, is the basis for a person's identity."[61] Although useful in elucidating local specificities of homoeroticism in Taiwan, China, and Hong Kong, Chou's model tends to treat these societies as socially undifferentiated in terms of sex, class, religion, and generation. By suppressing internal differences, he asserts an unchanging cultural essence. Moreover, Chou frames his argument in terms of the region's isolation from, rather than interaction with, the outside world. In this "hermit kingdom" paradigm, Chinese societies are analytically sealed off from one another and from cross-cultural interactions, as well as from culture areas beyond the Sinophone world.[62]

Even as some scholars adopt nativist models that reject or minimize outside forces, many practitioners of Asian queer studies have sought to reorient knowledge from the West and other dominant locations by subjecting it to a relational and agent-based analytic of translation. Whether conducted as ethnographic fieldwork, textual exegesis, or studies of visual or auditory materials, the translation model recognizes the undeniable power of globalizing structures (i.e., LGBTI identity categories) but emphasizes the ability of local subjects to actively negotiate these transnational forces. For example, Tom Boellstorff has deployed the technological and cultural connotations of dubbing as a framework for understanding the complex subjectivities of lesbian and gay Indonesians who, he argues, are neither fully voluntaristic nor wholly dominated by outside messages. As Boellstorff writes, "Just as the range of possibilities for a dubbed soundtrack is shaped by images originating elsewhere, so a 'dubbed' subject-position, and the persons who occupy that position in some fashion, cannot choose their subjectivities as they please."[63] Focusing on the role of foreign films, television shows, and other mass media, he also addresses the complex issue of authenticity, which nativist studies of queer Asia tend to reduce to a function of unchanging traditions. By contrast, his nuanced ethnography demonstrates how Indonesian consumers resignify the original meaning of cultural products. Through such mediated processes of translation, some (but not necessarily all) individuals, Boellstorff argues, can also experience "gay," "lesbi(an)," or other identity categories as authentic— even as their non-normative subjectivities are connected to fractured but influential discourses emanating from distant societies and cultures including, but not limited to, those of the West.[64]

Using anthropological and other critical approaches to interrogate the place of queer and transgender subjectivities in contemporary South Korea, the concluding three chapters similarly focus on actor-centered and culturally specific analyses of normative politics under neo-liberal capitalism, postauthoritarian democracy, and heteropatriarchal conformism. With the Cold War still impacting everyday life on the peninsula, these cross-cutting dynamics continue to impose collective demands on the population as individual citizens while simultaneously encouraging personal endeavors as consumers and activists. These studies of postauthoritarian South Korea engage with what Michael Warner once termed "homonormativity" in his analysis of assimilationist movements for same-sex marriage in the U.S.[65] For nearly two decades, critiques of heteronormativity in North America and Western Europe have occupied the energy of many intellectuals and activists working in queer studies. As discussed earlier, queer-of-color critiques highlighted the uneven effects of what David Eng calls "queer liberalism."[66] For example, Jasbir Puar's conception of homonationalism challenged unprobed assumptions about whiteness and citizenship privilege by exposing how gender variance and non-normative sexuality disempower terrorist subjects in a globalized world of labor migration, mass displacement, and securitized geopolitics.[67] In his pioneering analysis of Latinx drag performers, José Esteban Muñoz proposed the concept of disidentification to underscore how multiply marginalized subjects transform stigmatized images generated by heteronormativity, white supremacy, and misogyny into an empowering aesthetic of resistance and survival that exudes sexiness and glamour.[68]

While drawing inspiration from these studies, the authors in this volume also adopt provincializing analytics developed in Asian queer studies. We question ahistorical applications of heteronormativity and homonormativity, which tend to assume a high degree of atomization and the hegemony of a rights-based model of LGBTI politics. As Petrus Liu writes, "While US-based queer theory enables a rethinking of the relations between the diacritical markers of personhood—race, gender, class, sexuality, and religion—this queer theory's conception of social differences remains restricted to a liberal pluralist culture of identity politics that is distinctively American."[69] To better capture power dynamics in and between the People's Republic of China and the Republic of China (Taiwan), a divided nation also separated as a result of Japanese imperialism and the Cold War, Liu explores Sinophone intellectuals working in the tradition of what he calls "nonliberal queer theory." While recognizing the modularity of LGBTI politics as identity, visibility, and consumption, this epistemological framework refuses to accept capitalist globalization and human rights as the only dominant logic of contemporary Asian societies. In a similar vein, Yau Ching has problematized culturally specific notions of normativity that often appear in discussions of queer liberalism anchored in Western Europe and North America. As she writes, "Not only does that normativity need to be foregrounded and interrogated as 'variegated, striated, contradictory' . . . , it is also important to remember that normativity as a relative ideal might not be accessible for many people in most parts of the world."[70] Through a subject-centered study, she argues that many inhabitants of China and Hong Kong struggle to approximate idealized but powerful notions of normativity, often as a way of maintaining bonds of sustenance with family, friends, and co-workers. Using ethnographic approaches, Lucetta Y. L. Kam, Elisabeth L. Engebretsen, and other Sinologists have similarly sought to provincialize antinormative critiques by foregrounding the subjectivities of Chinese queers.[71] In pursuing "normal" lives, for example, lesbians express complex desires to sustain the comforting but demanding bonds of kinship, even as they pursue relationships that challenge but do not necessarily destroy entrenched structures of heteropatriarchy.[72] The prevalence of "contract marriages" between gays and lesbians is one instructive example of how East Asian queers, particularly those of the professional classes, navigate this knotty situation, relying on conjugal and filial conventions that privilege men at the expense of women.[73] Another example are *lala* households, new kinship formations located outside natal families wherein young Chinese lesbians "can socialize with each other without the fear of exposure and public scrutiny."[74]

Articulating his ethnography of male homosexuality in terms of successive normativities, John (Song Pae) Cho argues that two contradictory forces of capitalist development have shaped the subjectivities of South Korean gay men since the 1970s: biopolitical familialism and neoliberal individualism. According to this historical account, the heterosexual, nuclear family, a shifting but enshrined pillar of national life, played an important role in circumscribing how men could express same-sex desires and forge non-normative intimacies. Characterizing the 1970s and 1980s as late developmentalist, Cho reveals the centrality of a hypermasculine ideology of capitalist growth during an extended period of military dictatorship. He argues that South Korea's authoritarian development expressed itself in chrononormative terms, prescribing "proper" life courses for citizens based on a dimorphic notion of biological sex. Highly gendered in its assumptions, this Cold War ideology not only demanded that men contribute to the national economy through industrial labor and military service, but also beseeched them to abide by its heteropatriarchal strictures. As a result, men who harbored attractions for one another were ultimately forced to marry women and produce male heirs to carry on family lines. Discouraged from forming long-lasting relationships and homosexual identities, most postwar gays managed to engage only in fleeting practices of "skinship" in military barracks, male dormitories, and movie theaters, public sites that they transformed into temporary cruising grounds. The Korean term *pogal*, an inversion of the word similarly used to denigrate female sex workers of the lower classes (*kalbo*), best captures this (self-)disparaging and bourgeois view of these shadowy men.[75]

During the subsequent decade of political liberalization and economic globalization (the mid- to late 1990s), queer subjects took advantage of new discursive, technological, and spatial networks to promote more autonomous selves. But, according to Cho, gay men—increasingly referred to as *iban* to denote their second-class status—tended to focus on finding an "ordinary" lover rather than engaging in identity politics. These expressions signified a deep-seated desire to create discrete, middle-class lives shielded from hetero-marital and homophobic pressures, including those that might shame the family members of "out(ed)" South Koreans. However, rather than understand their subjectivities as decidedly un-queer, Cho underscores subject-oriented meanings of normativity. For him, the very act of finding one another and creating durable networks of sociality constitute salient dimensions of gay life politics in contemporary South Korea, even if those personal politics have not always transmogrified into the rights-based activism that one might expect from a diffusionist or teleological notion of queer globalization.

Although Cho traces a shift from biopolitical familialism to atomized individualism, his discussion of the early twenty-first century underscores how discourses and practices of heteropatriarchal conformity continue to inflect neoliberal expressions of the self amid new, alienating forces of stigma against queer subjects. Perhaps most illustrative of these contradictory forces is the recent phenomenon of gay "bats." A strategic response to the insecurities of globalization, these neoliberal men have chosen to retreat from same-sex communities and, instead, focused on self-cultivation and financial security. However, rather than using these resources to seek exile from the heteronormative pressures of family life, gay bats, particularly those living in costly cities, have decided to remain within the materially and psychologically comforting confines of consanguineous relations. In sum, the complex imbrication of familial constraints, individual freedom, and political homophobia reveal that the path of South Korean gay men cannot be reduced to a progressive story of increased visibility or enhanced rights, but must be situated within the political, social, and cultural matrix of successive regimes of Cold War capitalism.

Like Cho, Layoung Shin takes a materialist approach in examining the gendered practices and embodied subjectivities of queer female youth, an increasingly precarious sector of South Korea's LGBTI population. Seeking to provincialize Western-centric discussions of gender conformity and homonormative assimilation under neoliberal capitalism, she argues that government-led policies of economic restructuring after the International Monetary Fund crisis of 1997 reenshrined the nuclear family as the basis of personal survival. Shin's ethnography demonstrates how these socioeconomic transformations had a particularly negative impact on lower-class lesbian women, who, when compared with their bourgeois and male counterparts, were forced to rely on family members for material support. To be sure, the rise of the Korean Wave, a state-led response to a downturn in the manufacturing sector by investing in the media activities of large corporations, provided young women new aesthetic styles with which to refashion their gendered sense of self. But individual expressions of female masculinity by queer women, briefly showcased at public sites such as Sinch'on Park, had led by the early 2010s to a homophobic backlash among South Koreans. Through such visible expressions, human rights activism, and exploitative media representations, the public became aware of female homosexuality, which they correlated with the nonconforming bodies of butch lesbians. Thereafter, queer women who harbored desires for one another refashioned themselves in gender-normative ways or, if they were unwilling to "straighten" their outward appearance, actively avoided public visibility through more furtive, online interactions.

Rather than locating these ethnographic observations in a narrative of queer liberalism or homonormative assimilation, Shin explains the notable shift from gender-variant expressions to a heterosexual style of presentation among lesbian youth in terms of associatively homophobic institutions that fail to provide legal protections for LGBTI people. Foregrounding local causes of gender conformity, public displays of queerness subject lesbian women to dangerous forms of familial alienation, stigmatizing gazes of social disapproval, and precarious experiences of economic misery. Rather than reading young women's desire for invisibility as a depoliticized practice marking the emergence of homonormative assimilation or queer liberalism in South Korea, Shin identifies them as a troubling symptom of a postauthoritarian system that continues to neglect the emotional and material well-being of queer people, especially those of the lower classes. Through a subject-centered analysis, she also considers sartorial, tonsorial, and other expressions of normativity as survival strategies necessary to navigate a society that persistently threatens queer women with various forms of harm and loss if they come out or, worse yet, are outed by a friend, relative, or co-worker on whom they must rely for sustenance and support.

While Cho and Shin focus on how financial and emotional insecurity resulting from the neoliberalization of a global marketplace and the hetero-normalization of local life have informed the complex subjectivities of South Korean gays and lesbians, the final chapter emphasizes another important feature of this postauthoritarian democracy, one that also tends to endanger the well-being of queer citizens in the name of national defense and capitalist accumulation. Ruin, a self-identified "transgenderqueer" intellectual and activist, demonstrates the need to route sexual difference and gender variance through the collectivizing dynamics of Cold War geopolitics rather than simply understanding non-normative expressions as an atomizing function of neoliberal identities.[76]

Zhe (Ruin's preferred gender pronoun) examines the biopolitical effects of South Korea's resident registration system while offering liberating ways to deconstruct this alienating institution for the nonconforming citizens it most negatively affects. Tracing the system's origins from the Chosŏn Dynasty through the colonial period, Ruin argues that resident registration took root during the reign of Park Chung Hee and led to state-led violence against individuals accused of harboring communist sympathies. Over time, this omnipotent mechanism of population control became deeply entangled in South Korea's system of military conscription, labor mobilization, family registration, and medical regulation. Insofar as a dimorphic (and, until recently, an immutable) conception of biological sex still structures these national institutions, bodies that do not conform to strict boundaries between men and women face intense scrutiny and various forms of material and psychological suffering.[77] Not unlike the situation of alleged "reds" (ppalgaeng'i) after the Korean War, transgender and intersex South Koreans struggle to survive as internal exiles in a postauthoritarian society that continues to define itself in rigid terms of anticommunist militarism and cisgender heteropatriarchy. The ongoing breakdown of the South Korean family—evidenced in increasing numbers of single women and divorced people as well as a plummeting birth rate, the rise of the LGBTI rights movements, and the influx of foreign brides and migrant workers—has only exacerbated these tensions, with Christian conservatives decrying such demographic changes as an apocalyptic cause for grave concern and hateful protest.

Although sympathetic to efforts aimed at abolishing national identification cards and compulsory fingerprinting, Ruin asks a series of incisive questions that aim to deconstruct the binary logic of South Korea's sex-gender system. The lived experiences of transgender people provide the critical fodder for interrogating the dehumanizing effects this system—even under a democratic system that avows to protect the rights of all citizens but does so in highly uneven and discriminatory ways. For example, military and civil laws have created strict boundaries between men and women while medical professionals take charge of policing the boundaries between them. Meanwhile, transgender and intersex South Koreans who must inhabit sexed and gendered bodies disrupt this politicized binary, if only in subtle and unsanctioned ways. For example, Ruin occupies both male and female positions in how zhe addresses family members with terms of appellation. To survive in a rigid environment of gender policing, transgender activists have sought to change the first digit in the second half of their national identification numbers. Although seeming to accept the sex-gender binary fortified by the resident registration system, Ruin interprets this activist position as one aimed at personal survival and psychological well-being. Considered in this way, efforts to change one's registration number seek to guarantee the rights of transgender people to designate their own sense of self within a sex-gender system already narrowed by Cold War exigencies, while doing so in a manner that does not rely on definitions determined by military, government, and medical authorities.

Conclusion

As Ruin's fiery appeal makes clear, activism remains an essential but insufficient means of ensuring the humanity and livelihood of transgender people, gay soldiers, aspirants to same-sex marriage, and a wide range of other marginalized subjects, including the disabled, the poor, and migrants. Although obviously experienced in different ways based on one's gender, class, sex, orientation, generation, location, and more, LGBTI South Koreans face innumerable obstacles in a society in which homophobia, transphobia, toxic masculinity, misogyny, and other marginalizing pressures cause an alarmingly high number of queers (and other alienated citizens) to commit suicide or inflict self-harm.[78] Even today, when democratic institutions nominally provide a procedural mechanism for voicing one's needs and wants, being LGBTI in South Korea entails much more than visibly manifesting an all-encompassing identity or engaging in a rights-based politics of recognition, especially when such "out and proud" modes of expression endanger one's ability to please kin networks, maintain intimate relationships, and succeed (or even survive) in the labor market. That some HIV-positive South Koreans would—from a pervasive fear of being known as infected to and stigmatized by friends, co-workers, (potential) lovers, and family members—avoid taking anti-retroviral medications known to effectively manage their illness (because treatment requires registration with the national government) indicates the saddening degree to which a mere diagnosis can itself lead to premature and preventable deaths. Although not technically prohibited, public presentations of non-normative sexuality and gender variance in North Korea are anecdotally known to be severely punished for contravening the state's heteropatriarchal credo of socialist nationalism. Fragmentary but inconclusive evidence of the death penalty for such behavior suggests the necropolitical consequences of this extralegal policy.[79]

In the chapters that follow, we address such precarious modes of queer existence by highlighting how nonconforming subjects have disproportionately faced state violence, media scrutiny, social stigma, cultural alienation, and economic poverty. Whether articulated as modern nationalism under colonial rule, anticommunism during the authoritarian period, or national security in the current era of neoliberal globalization and troll vigilantism, repeated struggles for collective survival on both sides of the 38th Parallel and in the diaspora have tended to devalue and dehumanize gender variance, same-sex sexuality, and other non-normative life-forms.[80] If we look beyond behind the liberal rhetoric of tolerance and legal forms of inclusion that aim to promote the happiness and welfare of some LGBTI communities (but often at the expense of other social minorities) in Western Europe and North America, we will also discover highly uneven forms of privilege and accessibility to heteronormative power. Not unlike their queer Korean counterparts, migrants, women, and transgender people continue to experience intense alienation and virulent discrimination, even in societies that boast democratic protections. For example, vulnerable communities living in the United States, often touted as the "land of the free and home of the brave" and held up by some South Korean progressives as an inspiration for their own activism, face the added burden of perpetuators who verbally abuse, physically assault, and brutally murder queer and transgender people, especially women and those of color.[81] The officially sanctioned virulence of the Trump administration has only made this cruel reality all the more apparent. In that sense, the United States and the Koreas share far more in common than most liberals on both sides of the Pacific (and across the 38th Parallel) are willing to admit.

Precisely because violent state mobilizations, objectifying media practices, and alienating cultural norms have seriously jeopardized the livelihoods of queer, transgender, and other socially despised subjects, marginalized communities, where possible, have sought to forge spaces of intimacy, labor, and pleasure to protect and sustain their well-being. Given those basic human needs and their virtual erasure from narratives about the peninsula (and elsewhere), it is worth recalling these forgotten stories of subordination, lest similar ones continue to emerge. Since the late nineteenth century, various and overlapping exigencies of collective survival have, ironically, come to endanger the very existence of "unruly" and "deviant" Koreans who have not fit normative frameworks of imperial resistance, nationalist politics, capitalist power, and other culturally homogenizing systems of domination and development. With this historical hindsight, the time has finally arrived for scholars, students, activists, and other like-minded allies to recognize the distinctively perverse underside of the peninsula's modernity, whether expressed in illiberal or liberal terms or as something in between these two imagined extremes. It is toward this shared goal of disruptive inquiry and the empowering insights it will produce that *Queer Korea* directs its critical energy.

In closing, I propose that the obscured queerness of the peninsula's recent past provides critical insights to overcome the current impasse of both LGBTI activism and neoliberal consumerism, allowing (South) Koreans to forge intergenerational alliances, cross-community collaborations, and a rehabilitated mass politics that looks beyond individualized suffering and state protection. Since the establishment of procedural democracy and the emergence of "sexual minorities" as a putative constituency during the 1990s, efforts to empower LGBTI citizens have understandably focused on eradicating discriminatory conventions, including military penal code 92-6. Given the stronghold of authoritarian-era practices, ridding society of such illiberal institutions are, of course, a necessary first step. However, rather than engage in spirited dialogue or transformative education, these efforts often take the form of angry confrontation, especially with culturally conservative and politically reactionary citizens. Alongside the recent growth of sexual minority activism, fundamentalist movements advancing homophobia, transphobia, and misogyny have also emerged as significant obstacles to a liberal politics of recognition centered on personalized suffering and legalistic remedies. Meanwhile, the seemingly liberatory ability to express one's gender and sexuality in a myriad of consumer spaces (many of them online) has, ironically, created an increasingly atomized, competitive, and antagonistic culture in which most LGBTI people have retreated from public view to enjoy the fruits of economic development in isolated spheres.

By contrast, a more radical and expansive model of intergenerational co-operation and post-identity alliances across class offers a viable alternative to the current milieu of despair and fragmentation. Indeed, lacking in most movements today is a historical appreciation of how non-normative subjects, many of them quite poor, sought to promote their well-being without dependence on an unreliable state or an antagonistic society. Revisiting their past livelihoods and bonds provides one way to transcend activism that is today focused on atomized individuals and state-sanctioned remedies, often to the detriment of collective politics. Confronted by this neoliberal impasse, it is worth recalling how agents from the past took meaningful action in the face of seeming impossibility and overwhelming alienation. Rather than consider these actions as prepolitical or authoritarian-era vestiges that no longer suit the present, their strategies of personal survival and "under-the-radar" alliances offer empowering resources for a diverse range of marginalized individuals to engage and learn from one another as part of an intergenerational, cross-community, and trans-class movement. If *Queer Korea* can somehow aid in that process of radical transformation, the struggle to publish this volume will have been well worth the effort.

Notes

1   Their hybrid ensemble combined Prussian school uniform, Nehru suit, and the outfit worn by a queer character in *The Rose of Versailles*, a Japanese shōjo manga. For insights on the sartorial meanings of their outfits, I thank the respondents to my Facebook post on Koreanists from August 15, 2016.

2   For an analysis of this confrontation, see Joseph Yi, Joe Phillips, and Shin-Do Sung, "Same-Sex Marriage, Korean Christians, and the Challenge of Democratic Engagement," *Culture and Society* 51 (2014): 415–22.

3   I predicted this possibility in my 2013 interview for Arirang Television. To view it, see the clip from 17:30 at https://www.youtube.com/watch?v=vNFXWoi2osU. On Pak's controversial statement, see "Seoul Mayor Park Won-soon Wants Same-Sex Marriage in Korea as First in Asia," *San Francisco Examiner*, October 12, 2014. For more on the ongoing controversy, see "Seoul Mayor Wants South Korea to Legalize Same-Sex Marriage," *KoreAm Journal*, October 13, 2014. On the double-edged sword of exploiting LGBTI-based consumerism for national purposes, see Eng-Beng Lim, "Glocalqueering in New Asia: The Politics of Performing Gay in Singapore," *Theatre Journal* 57 (2005): 383–405.

4   On Korean queer activists' use of foreign powers to promote their cause, see Woori Han, "Proud of Myself as LGBTQ: The Seoul Pride Parade, Homonational-

ism, and Queer Developmental Citizenship," *Korea Journal* 58, no. 2 (Summer 2018): 27–57.

5 On this conception of sexual politics as it relates to the current era of globalization, see Dennis Altman, "Global Gaze/Global Gays," GLQ 3, no. 4 (1997): 417–36. Even progressive media outlets have presented similarly teleological accounts about the "lag" in repealing the military's ban on anal sex, upheld by the Constitutional Courts in 2002, 2011, and 2016. For a narrative of this variety, see "Constitutional Court Upholds Military's Ban on Sodomy," *Hankyoreh*, August 4, 2016.

6 For a co-produced account of their path to marriage, see Jang Hee-Sun, dir., *My Fair Wedding*, documentary (Rainbow Factory, Seoul, 2015). That the South Korean family continues to influence the livelihood of its queer offspring can also be seen in regulations requiring that parents provide consent for their transgender children to undertake gender confirmation surgery, even when they are legal adults: Tari Young-Jung Na, "The South Korean Gender System: LGBTI in the Contexts of Family, Legal Identity, and the Military," *Journal of Korean Studies* 19, no. 2 (Fall 2014): 361.

7 Heonik Kwon, "Guilty by Association," *Papers of the British Association for Korean Studies* 13 (2011): 89–104. For a sanguine narrative about the rise and fall of homophobia by association, see Kim-Cho Kwang-su, dir., *Two Weddings and a Funeral* (Generation Blue Films, Seoul, 2011). See also Kim Su-hyŏn, dir., *Life Is Beautiful* (television series, 2010).

8 On the experience of queer Koreans in the U.S. diaspora, see Jeeyeun Lee, "Toward a Queer Korean American Diasporic History," in *Q & A: Queer in Asian America*, ed. David L. Eng and Alice Y. Hom (Philadelphia: Temple University Press, 1998), 185–212; Ju Hui Judy Han, "Incidents of Travel," in Eng and Hom, *Q & A*, 185–212; Ju Hui Judy Han, "Organizing Korean Americans against Homophobia," *Sojourner* 25, no. 10 (June 2000): 1–4; Margaret Rhee, "Towards Community: *KoreAm Journal* and Korean American Cultural Attitudes on Same-Sex Marriage," *Amerasia Journal* 32, no. 1 (2006): 75–88; Anna Joo Kim, "Korean American LGBT Movements in Los Angeles and New York," in *Asian Americans: An Encyclopedia of Social, Cultural, Economic, and Political History*, ed. Xiaojian Zhao and Edward J. W. Park (Santa Barbara, CA: Greenwood, 2014), 683–85. For a story of a Korean gay man living in Japan, see Nakata Toiichi, dir., *Osaka Story: A Documentary* (First Run/Icarus Films, New York, 1994).

9 For accounts by the parents and families of LGBTI South Koreans, see *Na nŭn sŏngsosuja ŭi pumonim imnida: Tongsŏng'aeja, yangsŏng'aeja, tŭrensŭjendŏ chanyŏ rŭl tun pumodŭl ŭi chinsul han iyagidŭl* (Seoul: Sŏngsosuja Pumo Moim, 2015).

10 When beginning to occupy public spaces for political protests, East Asian queers, like their counterparts in Latin America and elsewhere across the global South, often opted for forms of expression that departed significantly from modes of visibility common in North American and Western Europe but that may have subjected onlookers to even more potent critiques. For studies of these practices of protest, see Fran Martin, "Surface Tensions: Reading Productions of Tongzhi

in Contemporary Taiwan," GLQ 6, no. 1 (2000): 61–86; Katsuhiko Suganuma, "Associative Identity Politics: Unmasking the Multilayered Formation of Queer Male Selves in 1990s Japan," *Inter-Asia Cultural Studies* 8, no. 4 (2007): 485–502; José Quiroga, *Tropics of Desire: Interventions from Queer Latina America* (New York: New York University Press, 2000), esp. 1–29.

11 On the other hand, a survey of more than four thousand LGBTI-identified South Koreans in 2013 conducted by Ch'ingusai, the South Korean gay men's human rights organization, found that nearly 60 percent of those surveyed favored the institutionalization of same-sex unions, while another 36 percent advocated civil unions, but only when posed the *conditional* and *future-oriented* question, "If the following measures regarding same-sex unions were to become possible, which one would you choose?": Ch'ingusai, "The Key Results of the South Korean LGBTI Community Social Needs Assessment Survey," Ch'ingusai, Seoul, 2014, 24.

12 See, e.g., "Han'guk ŭi 'tongsŏng kyŏlhon' hapbŏphwa rŭl wihan ch'ŏt kŏrŭm i sijak toetta!" *Huffington Post Korea*, July 6, 2015; "Gay Couple Sue for Recognition of Their Same-Sex Marriage in South Korea," *The Telegraph*, July 7, 2015.

13 See, e.g., "Same-Sex Couple Seeks to Gain Legal Status," *Korea Times*, December 10, 2013.

14 See, e.g., "Han'guk ŭi 'tongsŏng kyŏlhon' hapbŏphwa rŭl wihan ch'ŏt kŏrŭm i sijak toett!"; "Gay Couple Sue for Recognition of Their Same-Sex Marriage in South Korea."

15 On this case, see Chang Sŏ-yŏn, "Han'guk esŏ tongsŏng kyŏlhap sosong ŏttŏke hal kŏsinga?" Tongsŏng kyŏlhap sosong ŭi ŭimi wa kwaje (2013): 4–40; "Hyŏnjik p'ansa 'tongsŏng kyŏlhon hŏyong ipbŏp koryŏ haeya," *Daŭm*, December 13, 2005. I thank JB Hur for alerting me to this case and the articles about them. For a report on South Korea's first(?) public wedding between two men, see "Uri nara 'pubu' anin tongpanja imnida: Han'guk ch'ŏt namsŏng tongsŏng aeja kong'gae kyŏlhon," *Chosŏn Ilbo*, March 8, 2004.

16 Petrus Liu, *Queer Marxism in the Two Chinas* (Durham, NC: Duke University Press, 2015), 50. For a critical statement of and an intellectual response to this situation, see Todd A. Henry, "In this Issue—Queer/Korean Studies as Critique: A Provocation," *Korea Journal* 58, no. 2 (Summer 2018): 5–26.

17 See, e.g., Kwiŏ Iron Munhwa Yŏn'guso Moim, ed., *Chendŏ ŭi ch'aenŏl ŭl tollyŏra* (Seoul: Saram Saeng'gak, 2008); Kwŏn/Kim Hyŏn-yŏng, Chŏng Hŭi-jin, Na Yŏng-jŏng, Ruin, Ŏm Ki-ho, eds., *Namsŏngsŏng kwa chendŏ* (Seoul: Chaŭm kwa Moŭm, 2011); Kwŏn/Kim Hyŏn-yŏng, Han Ch'ae-yun, Ruin, Yu Chin-hŭi, and Kim Chu-hŭi, eds., *Sŏng ŭi ch'ŏngch'i, sŏng ŭi kwŏlli* (Seoul: Chaŭm kwa Moŭm, 2012); Pak/Ch'a Min-jŏng, *Chosŏn ŭi k'wiŏ: Kŭndae ŭi t'ŭmsae e sumŭn pyŏnt'aedŭl ŭi ch'osang* (Seoul: Hyŏnsil Munhwa Yŏn'gu, 2018); and the essays in *Korea Journal* 58, no. 2 (Summer 2018).

18 Some Korean studies specialists based outside the peninsula have forged close connections to queer activists in South Korea, allowing knowledge produced

through political struggles there to filter into the Anglophone academy. This volume seeks to expand these intellectual connections. For one example, see Na, "The South Korean Gender System." For a foundational text of this sort, see Seo Dong-jin, "Mapping the Vicissitudes of Homosexual Identities in South Korea," *Journal of Homosexuality* 40, nos. 3–4 (2001): 56–79.

19 To read more on the film festival and art installation, see http://festival.sdaff.org /2014/remembering-queer-korea/ and http://kore.am/san-diego-asian-film -festival-remembers-queer-korea. One of the films, *The Pollen of Flowers* (1972), can be viewed with English subtitles at https://www.youtube.com/watch?v =jLvJBBHSRaw. For a bilingual discussion of Siren's work, see Chŏng Ŭn-yŏng et al., *Chŏnhwan kŭkjang: Yŏsŏng kukkŭk p'ŭrojekt'ŭ* (Seoul: P'orŭm Ei, 2016).

20 For one exception, see Haruki Eda, "Outing North Korea: Necropornography and Homonationalism" (master's thesis, London School of Economics, 2012).

21 Yi T'ae-jin, "Was Early Modern Korea Really a 'Hermit Nation'?" *Korea Journal* 38, no. 4 (Winter 1998): 5–35.

22 For a critique of this paradigm, see Bruce Cumings, "Boundary Displacement: The State, the Foundations, and Area Studies during and after the Cold War," in *Learning Places: The Afterlives of Area Studies*, ed. Masao Miyoshi and Harry Harootunian (Durham, NC: Duke University Press, 2002), 261–302.

23 Anjali Arondekar and Geeta Patel, "Area Impossible: Notes toward an Introduction," GLQ 22, no. 2 (2016): 151–71. In the field of Chinese studies, Petrus Liu has similarly advocated for a necessary dialogue between U.S.-based queer theory and Cold War geopolitics: Liu, *Queer Marxism in Two Chinas*.

24 On the consequences of forgoing pain and loss as foundational structures of queer life, see Heather Love, *Feeling Backward: Loss and the Politics of Queer History* (Cambridge, MA: Harvard University Press, 2009).

25 Lauren Berlant, *Cruel Optimism* (Durham, NC: Duke University Press, 2011). For a queer analysis that offers a bold political imaginary, see José Esteban Muñoz, *Cruising Utopia: The Then and There of Queer Futurity* (New York: New York University Press, 2009).

26 On the development of nationalist historiography as a postcolonial by-product, see Henry H. Em, *The Great Enterprise: Sovereignty and Historiography in Modern Korea* (Durham, NC: Duke University Press, 2013).

27 On the question of collaboration in history writing, see Koen De Ceuster, "The Nation Exorcised: The Historiography of Collaboration in South Korea," *Korean Studies* 25, no. 2 (2001): 207–42; Kyu Hyun Kim, "Reflections on the Problem of Colonial Modernity and 'Collaboration' in Modern Korean History," *Journal of International and Area Studies* 1, no. 3 (2004): 95–111. For an account of one prominent woman accused of antipatriotic activities, see Insook Kwon, "Feminists Navigating the Shoals of Nationalism and Collaboration: The Post-Colonial Korean Debate over How to Remember Kim Hwallan," *Frontiers* 27, no. 1 (2006): 39–66.

28 Pak/Ch'a, *Chosŏn ŭi k'wiŏ*; Hŏ Yun, "1950 k'wiŏ chang kwa bŏpjŏk kyuje ŭi chŏpsok: 'Pyŏngyŏkbŏp,' 'kyŏngbŏmbŏp,' ŭl t'ong han sekshuŏllit'i ŭi t'ongje," *Pŏp Sahoe* 51 (April 2016): 229–50.

29 See, e.g., "Koyongbyŏngdŭl ŭi muri," *Nodong Sinmun*, January 24, 2000; "Sesang usŭm kŏri," *Nodong Sinmun*, April 29, 2001; "Kwaei han 'chŏngch'i munje,'" *Nodong Sinmun*, August 21, 2003; "Ingan todŏkjŏk bup'ae pijŏnaenŭn chabonjuŭi sahoe," *Nodong Sinmun*, May 28, 2011; "Miguk esŏ sasang ch'oeak ŭi ch'onggyŏk sakkŏn: 100 yŏ myŏng sasangja palsaeng," *Nodong Sinmun*, June 14, 2016. For a short story on the alleged homosexuality of American soldiers captured during the 1968 Pueblo Incident, see "P'yŏngyang ŭi nun pora," *Chosŏn Munhak* 11 (2000): 1–22. I thank Benoit Berthelier for providing me with these articles. See also "North Korea Slams UN Human Rights Report Because It Was Led by Gay Man," *Washington Post*, April 22, 2014. On nativist accounts of North Korean purity, see B. R. Myers, *The Cleanest Race: How North Koreans See Themselves—and Why It Matters* (New York: Melville House, 2010). For accounts of "queer" life in North Korea, see "Being Gay in the DPRK," NK News.org, November 13, 2013, https://www.nknews .org/2013/11/being-gay-in-the-dprk/; "A Gay NK Defector's Journey to Find Love," *Korea Herald*, May 28, 2015; "North Korean Defector Opens Up about Long-Held Secret: His Homosexuality," *New York Times*, June 5, 2015. For an autobiographical story of living as a gay man in the DPRK, see Chang Yŏng-jin, *Pulgŭn nekt'ai: Chang Yŏng-jin changp'yŏn sosŏl* (Seoul: Mulmangch'o, 2015).

30 On current associations of queerness with communism, see Judy Han Chu-hŭi [Ju Hui Judy Han], "K'wiŏ chŏngch'i, k'wiŏ chŏngchi'ihak," *Munhwa Kwahak* 83 (2015): 62–81. For a documentary critiquing the politicized connections forged between non-normative practices and antinationalist sentiments in South Korea, see Yi Yŏng, dir., *Troublers*, documentary (WOM Docs, Seoul, 2015).

31 On bureaucratic practices of modern rule on the peninsula, see Kyung Moon Hwang, *Rationalizing Korea: The Rise of the Modern State, 1894–1945* (Berkeley: University of California Press, 2015).

32 On the complex intellectual background of the Eastern Learning movement, see, e.g., Susan S. Shin, "Tonghak Thought: The Roots of Revolution," *Korea Journal* 19, no. 9 (September 1979): 204–23; Shin Yong-ha, "Tonghak and Ch'oe Che-u," *Seoul Journal of Korean Studies* 3 (1990): 83–102; George L. Kallander, *Salvation through Dissent: Tonghak Heterodoxy and Early Modern Korea* (Honolulu: University of Hawai'i Press, 2013). For the early feminist movement, see Yung-Hee Kim, "Under the Mandate of Nationalism: Development of Feminist Enterprises in Modern Korea, 1860–1910," *Journal of Women's History* 7, no. 4 (Winter 1995): 120–36; Hyaeweol Choi, *Gender and Mission Encounters in Korea: New Women, Old Ways* (Berkeley: University of California Press, 2009).

33 Andre Schmid, *Korea between Empires, 1895–1919* (New York: Columbia University, 2002). See also Em, *The Great Enterprise*.

34 On these modernizing efforts, see Kim Dong-no, John B. Duncan, and Kim Do-hyung, eds., *Reform and Modernity in the Taehan Empire* (Seoul: Jimoodang,

2006). On other nation-saving endeavors, see Yumi Moon, *Populist Collabora-tors: The Ilchinohoe and the Japanese Colonization of Korea, 1896–1910* (Ithaca, NY: Cornell University Press, 2013).

35   On these politics, see Choi, *Gender and Mission Encounters in Korea*; Hyaeweol Choi, ed., *New Women in Colonial Korea: A Sourcebook* (New York: Routledge, 2012). For the position of Korean women during the immediate precolonial period, see Kim, "Under the Mandate of Nationalism."

36   For a wide-ranging study of this period, see Pak/Ch'a, *Chosŏn ŭi k'wiŏ*.

37   For other studies of the colonial period, not all of which connect queer expres-sions to larger social or intellectual concerns, see Sin Chi-yŏn, "1920–30 nyŏndae 'tongsŏng(yŏn)ae' kwallyŏn kisa ŭi susajŏk maengnak," *Minjok Munhwa Yŏn'gu* 45 (2006): 265–92; Pak Kwan-su, "1940 nyŏndae 'namsŏng tongsŏng'ae' yŏn'gu," *Pigyo Minsokhak* 31 (2006): 389–438. See also Layoung Sin's chapter in this volume.

38   Todd A. Henry, *Assimilating Seoul: Japanese Rule and the Politics of Public Space in Colonial Korea, 1910–1945* (Berkeley: University of California Press, 2014), 62–91, 168–203.

39   For these approaches to Japanese imperialism, see the essays in *Positions: East Asia Culture Critique* 21, no. 1 (Winter 2013), a special issued edited by Jordan Sand. See also Christopher P. Hanscom and Dennis Washburn, eds., *The Affect of Difference: Representations of Race in East Asian Empire* (Honolulu: University of Hawai'i Press, 2016).

40   Theodore Jun Yoo, *It's Madness: The Politics of Mental Health in Colonial Korea* (Berkeley: University of California Press, 2016); Eunjung Kim, *Curative Violence: Rehabilitating Disability, Gender, and Sexuality in Modern Korea* (Durham, NC: Duke University Press, 2017), esp. 42–80.

41   See, e.g., Prasenjit Duara, "The Imperialism of 'Free Nations': Japan, Manchukuo, and the History of the Present," in *Imperial Formations*, ed. Ann Laura Stoler, Carole McGranahan, and Peter C. Perdue (Santa Fe, NM: School for Advanced Research Press, 2007), 211–39; Takashi Fujitani, *Race for Empire: Koreans as Japanese and Japanese as Americans during World War II* (Berkeley: University of California Press, 2011).

42   For a study that follows the nationalist paradigm of cultural erasure *(malsal)* to de-scribe how colonized Koreans experienced the Asia-Pacific War, see Ch'oe Yu-ri, *Ilche malgi singingji chibae chŏng ch'aek yŏn'gu* (Seoul: Kukhak Charyowŏn, 1997).

43   For a subject-oriented analysis of colonized Taiwanese, see Leo T. S. Ching, *Be-coming "Japanese": Colonial Taiwan and the Politics of Identity Formation* (Berkeley: University of California Press, 2001).

44   For related studies of this period, see Bruce Cumings, *The Origins of the Korean War*, vol. 1 (Princeton, NJ: Princeton University Press, 1981); Suzy Kim, *Everyday Life in the North Korean Revolution, 1945–1950* (Ithaca, NY: Cornell University Press, 2013).

45 For an overview of this revisionist concept, see Namhee Lee, "The Theory of Mass Dictatorship: A Re-examination of the Park Chung Hee Period," *Review of Korean Studies* 12, no. 3 (September 2009): 41–69.

46 For a feminist critique of this male-dominated paradigm, see Chŏng Hŭi-jin, "Han'guk sahoe ŭi chisik saengsan pangbŏp kwa taejung tokjaeron," in *Kŭndae ŭi kyŏnggye esŏ tokjae rŭl ikkda: Taejung tokjae wa Pak Chŏng-hŭi ch'eje*, ed. Chang Mun-sŏk and Yi Sang-nok (Seoul: Kurinbi, 2006), 403–19. For an exceptional study of the print media during the Park era, see Yi Sang-nok, "Pak Chŏng-hŭi ch'eji ŭi 'sahoe chŏnghwa' tamnon kwa ch'ŏngnyŏn," in Chang and Yi, *Kŭndae ŭi kyŏnggye esŏ tokjae rŭl ikkda*, 335–76.

47 For another related study, see So Kok-suk, "1960 nyŏndae huban'gi han'guk pyŏngjang k'omidi yŏnghwa ŭi taejungsŏng yŏn'gu: Pyŏnjang mot'ip'u rŭl t'onghan naerŏt'ib'ŭ chŏllyak ŭl chungsim ŭro" (PhD diss., Dongguk University, Seoul, 2003).

48 On the fluidity of postliberation masculinities, see Hŏ Yun, *1950 nyŏndae han'guk sosŏl ŭi namsŏng chendŏ suhaengsŏng yŏn'gu* (Seoul: Yŏnnak, 2018); Charles R. Kim, *Youth for Nation: Culture and Protest in Cold War South Korea* (Honolulu: University of Hawai'i Press, 2017), 43–74.

49 For studies central to queer-of-color critique, see José Esteban Muñoz, *Disidentifications: Queers of Color and the Performance of Politics* (Minneapolis: University of Minnesota Press, 1999); Roderick A. Ferguson, *Aberrations in Black: Toward a Queer of Color Critique* (Minneapolis: University of Minnesota Press, 2004); Jasbir Puar, *Terrorist Assemblages: Homonationalism in Queer Times* (Durham, NC: Duke University Press, 2007); Fatima El-Tayeb, *European Others: Queering Ethnicity in Postnational Europe* (Minneapolis: University of Minnesota Press, 2011).

50 I thank one anonymous reviewer for suggesting the possibility that vigilante trolls may be seeking to compete with or even displace the globalized regime of neoliberalism. If that is indeed the case in South Korea, such forces have appeared at a time that LGBTI subjects are only just beginning to benefit from the fruits of liberal inclusion.

51 The following anthologies mark the vibrancy of this field: Chris Berry, Fran Martin, and Audrey Yue, eds., *Mobile Cultures: New Media in Queer Asia* (Durham, NC: Duke University Press, 2003); Fran Martin, Peter A. Jackson, Mark McLelland, and Audrey Yue, eds., *AsiapacifiQueer: Rethinking Genders and Sexualities* (Urbana: University of Illinois Press, 2008); Raquel A. G. Reyes and William G. Clarence-Smith, *Sexual Diversity in Asia, c. 600–1950* (London: Routledge, 2012). For an overview of this field, see Megan Sinnot, "Borders, Diaspora, and Regional Connections: Trends in Asian 'Queer' Studies," *Journal of Asian Studies* 69, no. 1 (February 2010): 17–31; Evelyn Blackwood and Mark Johnson, "Queer Asian Subjects: Transgressive Sexualities and Heteronormative Meanings," *Asian Studies Review* 36, no. 4 (2012): 441–51.

52 For a manifesto announcing this political position, see Seo, "Mapping the Vicissitudes of Homosexual Identities in South Korea." On the role of film, see Jeongmin Kim, "Queer Cultural Movements and Local Counterpublics of Sexuality: A Case

of Seoul Queer Films and Videos Festival," *Inter-Asia Cultural Studies* 8, no. 4 (2007): 617–733. For accounts that historicize the sexual minority movement more generally, see Youngshik D. Bong, "The Gay Rights Movement in Democratizing Korea," *Korean Studies* 32 (2009): 86–103; Hyun-young Kwon Kim and John (Song Pae) Cho, "The Korean Gay and Lesbian Movement 1993–2008: From 'Identity' and 'Community' to 'Human Rights,'" in *South Korean Social Movements: From Democracy to Civil Society*, ed. Gi-Wook Shin and Paul Chang (London: Routledge, 2011). For a wider, regional account, see Josephine Ho, "Is Global Governance Bad for East Asian Queers?" *GLQ* 14, no. 4 (2008): 457–79.

53 On the development of area studies, particularly of East Asia and its critique, see Miyoshi and Harootunian, *Learning Places*. For work on what might be called "intra-Asian queer studies," see Ara Wilson, "Queering Asia," *Intersections* 14 (November 2006), http://intersections.anu.edu.au/issue14/wilson.html; Tom Boellstorff, *A Coincidence of Desires: Anthropology, Queer Studies, Indonesia* (Durham, NC: Duke University Press, 2007), 181–218; Fran Martin, *Backward Glances: Contemporary Chinese Cultures and the Female Homoerotic Imaginary* (Durham, NC: Duke University Press, 2010); Howard Chiang, "(De)Provincializing China: Queer Historicism and Sinophone Postcolonial Critique," in *Queer Sinophone Cultures*, ed. Howard Chiang and Ari Larissa Heinrich (London: Routledge, 2014), 19–51; Howard H. Chiang, Todd A. Henry, and Helen Hok-Sze Leung, "Trans-in-Asia, Asia-in-Trans: An Introduction," *TSQ* 5, no. 3 (August 2018): 298–310; Todd A. Henry, *Japan's Gay Empire: Sex Tourism, Military Culture, and Memory Making in Postcolonial Asia-Pacific* (forthcoming).

54 Another indication of the growing prominence and institutionalization of this subfield is the creation of a Facebook page for queer East Asian studies in 2012 and the establishment of the Society for Asian Queer Studies in 2015 as an affiliate organization of the Association for Asian Studies. Although not focused on Asian studies, the Association for Queer Anthropology, formerly known as the Society of Lesbian and Gay Anthropologists, was founded in 1988 as a section of the American Anthropological Association.

55 Monographic treatments of Japan include Hideko Abe, *Queer Japanese: Gender and Sexual Identities through Linguistic Practices* (New York: Palgrave Macmillan, 2010); Sharon Chalmers, *Emerging Lesbian Voices from Japan* (London: Routledge, 2014); Gary Leupp, *Male Colors: The Construction of Homosexuality in Tokugawa Japan* (Berkeley: University of California Press, 1997); Jonathan D. Mackintosh, *Homosexuality and Manliness in Postwar Japan* (London: Routledge, 2010); Mark McLelland, *Male Homosexuality in Modern Japan: Cultural Myths and Social Realities* (Richmond, VA: Curzon, 2000); Mark McLelland, *Queer Japan from the Pacific War to the Internet Age* (Lanham, MD: Rowman and Littlefield, 2005); Gregory M. Pflugfelder, *Cartographies of Desire: Male-Male Sexuality in Japanese Discourse* (Berkeley: University of California Press, 1999); James Reichert, *In the Company of Men: Representations of Male-Male Sexuality in Meiji Literature* (Stanford, CA: Stanford University Press, 2006); Jennifer Robertson, *Takarazuka: Sexual Politics*

and *Popular Culture in Modern Japan* (Berkeley: University of California Press, 1998); Katsuhiko Suganuma, *Contact Moments: The Politics of Intercultural Desire in Japanese Male-Queer Cultures* (Hong Kong: University of Hong Kong Press, 2012); J. Keith Vincent, *Two-Timing Modernity: Homosocial Narrative in Modern Japanese Fiction* (Cambridge, MA: Harvard University Press, 2012).

On China, Taiwan, Hong Kong, and Singapore, see Howard Chiang, ed., *Transgender China* (New York: Palgrave Macmillan, 2012); Howard Chiang and Ari Larissa Heinrich, eds., *Queer Sinophone Cultures* (London: Routledge, 2013); Yau Ching, ed., *As Normal as Possible: Negotiating Sexuality and Gender in Mainland China and Hong Kong* (Hong Kong: Hong Kong University Press, 2010); Lynette J. Chua, *Mobilizing Gay Singapore: Rights and Resistance in an Authoritarian State* (Philadelphia: Temple University Press, 2014); Elisabeth L. Engebretsen, *Queer Women in Urban China: An Ethnography* (London: Routledge, 2015); Elisabeth Engebretsen, William F. Schroeder, and Hongwei Bao, eds., *Queer/Tongzhi China: New Perspectives on Research, Activism and Media Cultures* (Copenhagen: Nordic Institute of Asian Studies, 2015); Bret Hinsch, *Passions of the Cut Sleeve: The Male Homosexual Tradition in China* (Berkeley: University of California Press, 1992); Loretta Wing Wah Ho, *Gay and Lesbian Subculture in Urban China* (London: Routledge, 2011); Hans Huang, *Queer Politics and Sexual Modernity in Taiwan* (Hong Kong: Hong Kong University Press, 2011); Lucetta Y. L. Kam, *Shanghai Lalas: Female Tongzi Communities and Politics in Urban China* (Hong Kong: Hong Kong University Press, 2013); Wenqing Kang, *Obsession: Male Same-Sex Relations in China, 1900–1950* (Hong Kong: Hong Kong University Press, 2009); Travis S. K. Kong, *Chinese Male Homosexualities: Memba, Tongzhi and Golden Boy* (London: Routledge, 2012); Helen Leung, *Undercurrents: Queer Culture and Postcolonial Hong Kong* (Hong Kong: Hong Kong University Press, 2009); Liu, *Queer Marxism in Two Chinas*; Martin, *Backward Glances*; Fran Martin, *Situating Sexualities: Queer Representation in Taiwanese Fiction, Film and Public Culture* (Hong Kong: Hong Kong University Press, 2003); Lisa Rofel, *Desiring China: Experiments in Neoliberalism, Sexuality, and Public Culture* (Durham, NC: Duke University Press, 2007); Tze-Lan D. Sang, *The Emerging Lesbian: Female Same-Sex Desire in Modern China* (Chicago: University of Chicago Press, 2003); Matthew Sommers, *Sex, Law, and Society in Late Imperial China* (Stanford, CA: Stanford University Press, 2002); Denise Tse-Shang Tang, *Conditional Spaces: Hong Kong Lesbian Desires and Everyday Life* (Hong Kong: Hong Kong University Press, 2011); Giovanni Vitiello, *The Libertine's Friend: Homosexuality and Masculinity in Late Imperial China* (Chicago: University of Chicago Press, 2011); Cuncun Wu, *Homoerotic Sensibilities in Late Imperial China* (London: Routledge, 2012); Audrey Yue and Jun Zubillaga-Pow, eds., *Queer Singapore: Illiberal Citizenship and Mediated Cultures* (Hong Kong: Hong Kong University Press, 2013); Tiantian Zheng, *Tongzhi Living: Men Attracted to Men in Postsocialist China* (Minneapolis: University of Minnesota Press, 2015).

On Indonesia, see Evelyn Blackwood, *Falling into Lesbi World: Desire and Difference in Indonesia* (Honolulu: University of Hawai'i Press, 2010); Boellstorff, *A*

Coincidence of Desires; Tom Boellstorff, *The Gay Archipelago: Sexuality and Nation in Indonesia* (Princeton, NJ: Princeton University Press, 2005); Michael Peletz, *Gender Pluralism: Southeast Asia since Early Modern Times* (London: Routledge, 2009).

On Thailand, see Peter A. Jackson, *Dear Uncle Go: Male Homosexuality in Thailand* (Bangkok: Bua Luang, 1995); Peter A. Jackson, *Male Homosexuality in Thailand: An Interpretation of Contemporary Sources* (Elmhurst, NY: Global Academic, 1989); Peter A. Jackson, *Queer Bangkok: 21st Century Markets, Media, and Rights* (Hong Kong: Hong Kong University Press, 2011); Peter A. Jackson and Gerard Sullivan, eds., *Lady Boys, Tom Boys, Rent Boys: Male and Female Homosexualities in Contemporary Thailand* (New York: Haworth, 1999); Megan Sinnott, *Toms and Dees: Transgender Identity and Female Same-Sex Relationships in Thailand* (Honolulu: University of Hawai'i Press, 2004).

On India, see Gayatri Gopinath, *Impossible Desires: Queer Diasporas and South Asian Public Cultures* (Durham, NC: Duke University Press, 2005); Serena Nanda, *Neither Man nor Woman: The Hijras of India* (Belmont, CA: Wadsworth, 1999); Gayatri Reddy, *With Respect to Sex: Negotiating Hijra Identity in South India* (Chicago: University of Chicago Press, 2005); Ruth Vanita, *Queering India: Same-Sex Love and Eroticism in Indian Culture and Society* (London: Routledge: 2013).

56 Altman, "Global Gaze/Global Gays." For early critiques of Altman in queer Asian and Asian American studies, see Lisa Rofel, "Qualities of Desire: Imagining Gay Identities," GLQ 5, no. 4 (1999): 451–74; Martin F. Manalansan IV, "Diasporic Deviants/Divas: How Filipino Gay Transmigrants 'Play with the World,'" in *Queer Diasporas*, ed. Cindy Patton and Benigno Sánchez-Eppler (Durham, NC: Duke University Press, 2000), 183–203.

57 For foundational work in this area, see Arnoldo Cruz-Malavé and Martin F. Manalansan IV, eds., *Queer Globalizations: Citizenship and the Afterlife of Colonialism* (New York: New York University Press, 2002); Inderpal Grewal and Caren Kaplan, "Global Identities: Theorizing Transnational Studies of Sexuality," GLQ 7, no. 4 (2001): 663–79; Tithne Luibhéid and Lionel Cantù Jr., eds., *Queer Migrations: Sexuality, U.S. Citizenship, and Border Crossings* (Minneapolis: University of Minnesota Press, 2005); Martin F. Manalansan IV, *Global Divas: Filipino Gay Men in the Diaspora* (Durham, NC: Duke University Press, 2003); Cindy Patton and Benigno Sanchéz-Eppler, eds., *Queer Diasporas* (Durham, NC: Duke University Press, 2000); Elizabeth A. Povinelli and George Chauncey, eds., "Thinking Sexuality Transnationally," GLQ 5, no. 4 (1999): 439–50.

58 Sang, *The Emerging Lesbian*, 9.

59 Dipesh Chakrabarty, *Provincializing Europe: Postcolonial Thought and Historical Difference* (Princeton, NJ: Princeton University Press, 2007), xiii. For a related intellectual project rooted in East Asia, and to a lesser extent in Southeast Asia, see Kuan-Hsing Chen, *Asia as Method: Toward Deimperialization* (Durham, NC: Duke University Press, 2010). On responses in South Korea, see Em, *The Great Enterprise*, esp. 138–60.

60 Chiang, "(De)Provincializing China: Queer Historicism and Sinophone Postco-lonial Critique," 32.

61 Wah-Shan Chou, *Tongzhi: Politics of Same-Sex Eroticism in Chinese Societies* (New York: Haworth, 2000), 1.

62 For a collection of works advancing this notion of a Chinese-speaking world, see Shu-mei Shih, Chien-hsin Tsai, and Brian Bernards, eds., *Sinophone Studies: A Critical Reader* (New York: Columbia University Press, 2012).

63 Tom Boellstorff, "I Knew It Was Me: Mass Media, 'Globalization,' and Lesbian and Gay Indonesians," in Berry et al., *Mobile Cultures*, 25.

64 For another study that underscores the multidirectional sources of queer subjec-tivities, see Lim, "Glocalqueering in New Asia."

65 Michael Warner, *The Trouble with Normal: Sex, Politics, and the Ethics of Queer Life* (Cambridge, MA: Harvard University Press, 1999). For an elaboration, see Lisa Duggan, *The Twilight of Equality? Neoliberalism, Cultural Politics, and the Attack on Democracy* (Boston: Beacon, 2003).

66 David L. Eng, *The Feeling of Kinship: Queer Liberalism and the Racialization of Intimacy* (Durham, NC: Duke University Press, 2010).

67 Puar, *Terrorist Assemblages*, xiv.

68 Muñoz, *Disidentifications*. For other important work in people-of-color critique, see Ferguson, *Aberrations in Black*.

69 Liu, *Queer Marxism in Two Chinas*, 7. Similarly, Puar has suggested the limitations of intersectionality—an analytic predominant in U.S. ethnic studies, but one en-trenched in regulatory (state-centered) models of multiculturalism and diversity. By contrast, she advocates for assemblages as a concept that "moves away from excavation work, deprivileges a binary opposition between queer and not-queer subjects, and, instead of retaining queerness exclusively as dissenting, resistant, and alternative (all of which queerness importantly is and does), . . . underscores contingency and complicity with dominant formations": Puar, *Terrorist Assem-blages*, 205. For another attempt to de-idealize oppositional politics as the basis for queer analytics, see Kadji Amin, *Disturbing Attachments: Genet, Modern Pederasty, and Queer History* (Durham, NC: Duke University Press, 2017).

70 Yau Ching, "Dreaming of Normal while Sleeping with Impossible: Introduction," in Ching, *As Normal as Possible*, 1–14.

71 This problematic resonates with recent debates about the normativity of queer theory. However, to date these important debates remain grounded in the U.S. academy, bracketed from discussions animating the field of Asian queer studies and other non-Western contexts. On these debates, see the essays in *Differences* 26, no. 1 (May 2015), a special issue edited by Robyn Wiegman and Elizabeth A. Wilson. For a critical rebuttal, see Jack [Judith] Halberstam, "Straight Eye for the Queer Theorist: A Review of 'Queer Theory without Antinormativity,'" *Bully Bloggers*, September 12, 2016, https://bullybloggers.wordpress.com/2015

/09/12/straight-eye-for-the-queer-theorist-a-review-of-queer-theory-without
-antinormativity-by-jack-halberstam.

72 Engebretsen, *Queer Women in Urban China.*

73 On this practice, see John (Song Pae) Cho, "The Wedding Banquet Revisited: 'Contract Marriages' between Korean Gays and Lesbians," *Anthropological Quarterly* 82, no. 2 (2009): 401–22; Engebretsen, *Queer Women in Urban China,* 104–23.

74 Kam, *Shanghai Lalas,* 36.

75 *Yangbogal,* a related term that one can still hear in South Korea today, refers to Korean men who historically crossed as women and engaged in sexual relations with white men, often for money or other material rewards. The term bears a close relationship to *yanggongju* (Western whore). In fact, these two figures tended to work in close proximity to each other near U.S. military bases, such as the one next to It'aewŏn in downtown Seoul. For more on this history, see Ruin, "Kaemp'ŭ T'ŭraensŭ: It'aewŏn chiyŏk t'ŭraensŭjendŏ ŭi yŏksa ch'ujŏk hagi, 1960–1989," *Munhwa Yŏn'gu* 1, no. 1 (2012): 244–78.

76 For more on the place of geopolitics in queer studies, see Liu, *Queer Marxism in Two Chinas*; Arondekar and Patel, "Area Impossible."

77 For more on the experiences of transgender South Koreans, see Kim Sŭng-sŏp, *Ap'ŭm i kil i toeryŏmyŏn: Chŏngŭiroun kŏn'gang ŭl ch'aja, chilbyŏng sahoejŏk ch'aegim ŭl mutta* (Seoul: Tong Asia, 2017); Yi Horim and Timothy Gitzen, "Sex/Gender Insecurities: Trans Bodies and the South Korean Military," *TSQ* 5, no. 3 (Summer 2018): 376–91.

78 According to a 2013 survey of four thousand LGBTI-identified South Koreans, 28.4 percent revealed that they had attempted suicide, and 35 percent said that they had engaged in self-harm. Of young respondents (eighteen and younger), 45.7 percent had attempted suicide, and 53.3 percent had inflicted self-harm. In addition, of those who had experienced discrimination or violence due to their sexual minority status, 40.9 percent had attempted suicide, and 48.1 percent had inflicted self-harm. These figures are much higher than those of people who had not experienced discrimination or violence, which were 20.9 percent for suicide attempts and 26.9 percent for self-harm attempts: Ch'ingusai, "The Key Results of the South Korean LGBTI Community Social Needs Assessment Survey," 34–35.

79 "North Executes Lesbians for Being Influenced by Capitalism," *Korea Times,* September 29, 2011.

80 For the most recent documentation of these forms of marginalization, see "Human Rights Situation of LGBTI in South Korea, 2016," Korean Society of Law and Policy on Sexual Orientation and Gender Identity, Seoul, 2017, available at http://annual.sogilaw.org. See also Ch'ingusai, "The Key Results of the South Korean LGBTI Community Social Needs Assessment Survey."

81 On this phenomenon, see Doug Meyer, "An Intersectional Analysis of Lesbian, Gay, Bisexual, and Transgender (LGBT) People's Evaluations of Anti-Queer Violence," *Gender and Society* 26, no. 6 (2012): 8, 49–73.

Works Cited

NEWSPAPERS AND MAGAZINES

Chosŏn Ilbo
Chosŏn Munhak
Daŭm
The Hankyoreh
Huffington Post Korea
Korea Herald
KoreAm Journal
Korea Times
New York Times
Nodong Sinmun
San Francisco Examiner
The Telegraph
Washington Post

KOREAN-LANGUAGE SOURCES

Chang Sŏ-yŏn. "Han'guk esŏ tongsŏng kyŏlhap sosong ŏttŏke hal kŏsinga?" *Tongsŏng kyŏlhap sosong ŭi ŭimi wa kwaje* (2013): 4–40.

Chang Yŏng-jin. *Pulgŭn nekt'ai: Chang Yŏng-jin changp'yŏn sosŏl.* Seoul: Mulmangch'o: 2015.

Ch'oe Yu-ri. *Ilche malgi singingji chibae chŏng ch'aek yŏn'gu.* Seoul: Kukhak Charyowŏn, 1997.

Chŏng Hŭi-jin. "Han'guk sahoe ŭi chisik saengsan pangbŏp kwa taejung tok-jaeron." In *Kŭndae ŭi kyŏnggye esŏ tokjae rŭl ikkda: Taejung tokjae wa Pak Chŏng-hŭi ch'eje,* ed. Chang Mun-sŏk and Yi Sang-nok, 403–19. Seoul: Kurinbi, 2006.

Chŏng Ŭn-yŏng et al., *Chŏnhwan kŭkjang: Yŏsŏng kukkŭk p'ŭrojekt'ŭ.* Seoul: P'orŭm Ei, 2016.

Han, Chu-hŭi [Ju Hui Judy Han]. "K'wiŏ chŏngch'i, k'wiŏ chŏngchi'ihak." *Munhwa Kwahak* 83 (2015): 62–81.

Hŏ Yun. "1950 k'wiŏ chang kwa bŏpjŏk kyuje ŭi chŏpsok: 'Pyŏngyŏkbŏp,' 'kyŏngbŏmbŏp,' ŭl t'ong han sekshuŏllit'i ŭi t'ongje." *Pŏp Sahoe* 51 (April 2016): 229–50.

Hŏ Yun. *1950 nyŏndae han'guk sosŏl ŭi namsŏng chendŏ suhaengsŏng yŏn'gu.* Seoul: Yŏnnak, 2018.

Kim Sŭng-sŏp. *Ap'ŭm i kil i toeryŏmyŏn: Chŏng'ŭiroun kŏn'gang ŭl ch'aja, chilbyŏng sahoejŏk ch'aegim ŭl mutta.* Seoul: Tong Asia, 2017.

Kwiŏ Iron Munhwa Yŏn'guso Moim, ed. *Chendŏ ŭi ch'aenŏl ŭl tollyŏra.* Seoul: Saram Saeng'gak, 2008.

Kwŏn/Kim Hyŏn-yŏng, Chŏng Hŭi-jin, Na Yŏng-jŏng, Ruin, and Ŏm Ki-ho, eds. *Namsŏngsŏng kwa chendŏ*. Seoul: Chaŭm kwa Moŭm, 2011.

Kwŏn/Kim Hyŏn-yŏng, Han Ch'ae-yun, Ruin, Yu Chin-hŭi, and Kim Chu-hŭi, eds. *Sŏng ŭi ch'ŏngch'i, sŏng ŭi kwŏlli*. Seoul: Chaŭm kwa Moŭm, 2012.

Na nŭn sŏngsosuja ŭi pumonim imnida: Tongsŏng'aeja, yangsŏng'aeja, tŭrensŭjendŏ chanyŏ rŭl tun pumodŭl ŭi chinsul han iyagidŭl. Seoul: Sŏngsosuja Pumo Moim, 2015.

Pak/Ch'a Min-jŏng. *Chosŏn ŭi k'wiŏ: Kŭndae ŭi t'ŭmsae e sumŭn pyŏnt'aedŭl ŭi ch'osang*. Seoul: Hyŏnsil Munhwa Yŏn'gu, 2018.

Pak Kwan-su. "1940 nyŏndae 'namsŏng tongsŏng'ae' yŏn'gu." *Pigyo Minsokhak* 31 (2006): 389–438.

Ruin. "Kaemp'ŭ T'ŭraensŭ: It'aewŏn chiyŏk t'ŭraensŭjendŏ ŭi yŏksa ch'ujŏk hagi, 1960–1989." *Munhwa Yŏn'gu* 1, no. 1 (2012): 244–78.

Sin Chi-yŏn. "1920–30 nyŏndae 'tongsŏng(yŏn)ae' kwallyŏn kisa ŭi susajŏk maengnak." *Minjok Munhwa Yŏn'gu* 45 (2006): 265–92.

So Kok-suk. "1960 nyŏndae huban'gi han'guk pyŏngjang k'omidi yŏnghwa ŭi taejungsŏng yŏn'gu: Pyŏnjang mot'ip'u rŭl t'onghan naerŏt'ib'ŭ chŏllyak ŭl chungsim ŭro." PhD diss., Dongguk University, Seoul, 2003.

Yi Sang-nok. "Pak Chŏng-hŭi ch'eji ŭi 'sahoe chŏnghwa' tamnon kwa ch'ŏngnyŏn." In *Kŭndae ŭi kyŏnggye esŏ tokjae rŭl ikkda: Taejung tokjae wa Pak Chŏng-hŭi ch'eje*, ed. Chang Mun-sŏk and Yi Sang-nok. Seoul: Kurinbi, 2006.

ENGLISH-LANGUAGE SOURCES

Abe, Hideko. *Queer Japanese: Gender and Sexual Identities through Linguistic Practices*. New York: Palgrave Macmillan, 2010.

Altman, Dennis. "Global Gaze/Global Gays." GLQ 3, no. 4 (1997): 417–36.

Amin, Kadji. *Disturbing Attachments: Genet, Modern Pederasty, and Queer History*. Durham, NC: Duke University Press, 2017.

Arondekar, Anjali, and Geeta Patel, eds. "Area Impossible: Notes on an Introduction." GLQ 22, no. 2 (2016): 151–71.

Blackwood, Evelyn. *Falling into Lesbi World: Desire and Difference in Indonesia*. Honolulu: University of Hawai'i Press, 2010.

Blackwood, Evelyn, and Mark Johnson. "Queer Asian Subjects: Transgressive Sexualities and Heteronormative Meanings." *Asian Studies Review* 36, no. 4 (2012): 441–51.

Berlant, Lauren. *Cruel Optimism*. Durham, NC: Duke University Press, 2011.

Berry, Chris, Fran Martin, and Audrey Yue, eds. *Mobile Cultures: New Media in Queer Asia*. Durham, NC: Duke University Press, 2003.

Boellstorff, Tom. *A Coincidence of Desires: Anthropology, Queer Studies, Indonesia*. Durham, NC: Duke University Press, 2007.

Boellstorff, Tom. *The Gay Archipelago: Sexuality and Nation in Indonesia*. Princeton, NJ: Princeton University Press, 2005.

Boellstorff, Tom. "I Knew It Was Me: Mass Media, 'Globalization,' and Lesbian and Gay Indonesians." In *Mobile Cultures: New Media in Queer Asia*, ed. Chris Berry, Fran Martin, and Audrey Yue, 21–51. Durham, NC: Duke University Press, 2003.

Bong, Youngshik D. "The Gay Rights Movement in Democratizing Korea." *Korean Studies* 32 (2009): 86–103.

Choi, Hyaeweol. *Gender and Mission Encounters in Korea: New Women, Old Ways.* Berkeley: University of California Press, 2009.

Choi, Hyaeweol, ed. *New Women in Colonial Korea: A Sourcebook.* New York: Routledge, 2012.

Chakrabarty, Dipesh. *Provincializing Europe: Postcolonial Thought and Historical Difference.* Princeton, NJ: Princeton University Press, 2007.

Chalmers, Sharon. *Emerging Lesbian Voices from Japan.* London: Routledge, 2014.

Chen, Kuan-Hsing. *Asia as Method: Toward Deimperialization.* Durham, NC: Duke University Press, 2010.

Chiang, Howard. "(De)Provincializing China: Queer Historicism and Sinophone Postcolonial Critique." In *Queer Sinophone Cultures,* ed. Howard Chiang and Ari Larissa Heinrich, 19–51. London: Routledge, 2014.

Chiang, Howard, ed. *Transgender China.* New York: Palgrave Macmillan, 2012.

Chiang, Howard, and Ari Larissa Heinrich, eds. *Queer Sinophone Cultures.* London: Routledge, 2013.

Chiang, Howard H., Todd A. Henry, and Helen Hok-Sze Leung. "Trans-in-Asia, Asia-in-Trans: An Introduction." *TSQ* 5, no. 3 (August 2018): 298–310.

Ching, Leo T. S. *Becoming "Japanese": Colonial Taiwan and the Politics of Identity Formation.* Berkeley: University of California Press, 2001.

Ching, Yau, ed. *As Normal as Possible: Negotiating Sexuality and Gender in Mainland China and Hong Kong.* Hong Kong: Hong Kong University Press, 2010.

Ch'ingusai. "The Key Results of the South Korean LGBTI Community Social Needs Assessment Survey." Report. Ch'ingusai, Seoul, 2014.

Cho, John (Song Pae). "The Wedding Banquet Revisited: 'Contract Marriages' between Korean Gays and Lesbians." *Anthropological Quarterly* 82, no. 2 (2009): 401–22.

Chou, Wah-Shan. *Tongzhi: Politics of Same-Sex Eroticism in Chinese Societies.* New York: Haworth, 2000.

Chua, Lynette J. *Mobilizing Gay Singapore: Rights and Resistance in an Authoritarian State.* Philadelphia: Temple University Press, 2014.

Cruz-Malavé, Arnoldo, and Martin F. Manalansan IV, eds. *Queer Globalizations: Citizenship and the Afterlife of Colonialism.* New York: New York University Press, 2002.

Cumings, Bruce. "Boundary Displacement: The State, the Foundations, and Area Studies during and after the Cold War." In *Learning Places: The Afterlives of Area Studies,* ed. Masao Miyoshi and Harry Harootunian, 261–302. Durham, NC: Duke University Press, 2002.

Cumings, Bruce. *The Origins of the Korean War,* vol. 1. Princeton, NJ: Princeton University Press, 1981.

De Ceuster, Koen. "The Nation Exorcised: The Historiography of Collaboration in South Korea." *Korean Studies* 25, no. 2 (2001): 207–42.

Duara, Prasenjit. "The Imperialism of 'Free Nations': Japan, Manchukuo, and the History of the Present." In *Imperial Formations,* ed. Ann Laura Stoler, Carole McGranahan, and Peter C. Perdue, 211–40. Santa Fe, NM: School for Advanced Research Press, 2007.

Duggan, Lisa. *The Twilight of Equality? Neoliberalism, Cultural Politics, and the Attack on Democracy.* Boston: Beacon, 2003.

Eda, Haruki. "Outing North Korea: Necropornography and Homonationalism." Master's thesis, London School of Economics, 2012.

El-Tayeb, Fatima. *European Others: Queering Ethnicity in Postnational Europe.* Minneapolis: University of Minnesota Press, 2011.

Em, Henry H. *The Great Enterprise: Sovereignty and Historiography in Modern Korea.* Durham, NC: Duke University Press, 2013.

Eng, David L. *The Feeling of Kinship: Queer Liberalism and the Racialization of Intimacy.* Durham, NC: Duke University Press, 2010.

Engebretsen, Elisabeth L. *Queer Women in Urban China: An Ethnography.* London: Routledge, 2015.

Engebretsen, Elisabeth, William F. Schroeder, and Hongwei Bao, eds. *Queer/Tongzhi China: New Perspectives on Research, Activism and Media Cultures.* Copenhagen: Nordic Institute of Asian Studies, 2015.

Ferguson, Roderick A. *Aberrations in Black: Toward a Queer Color of Critique.* Minneapolis: University of Minnesota Press, 2004.

Fujitani, Takashi. *Race for Empire: Koreans as Japanese and Japanese as Americans during World War II.* Berkeley: University of California Press, 2011.

Gopinath, Gayatri. *Impossible Desires: Queer Diasporas and South Asian Public Cultures.* Durham, NC: Duke University Press, 2005.

Grewal, Inderpal, and Caren Kaplan. "Global Identities: Theorizing Transnational Studies of Sexuality." GLQ 7, no. 4 (2001): 663–79.

Halberstam, Jack [Judith]. "Straight Eye for the Queer Theorist: A Review of 'Queer Theory without Antinormativity.'" *Bully Bloggers,* September 12, 2016. https:// bullybloggers.wordpress.com/2015/09/12/straight-eye-for-the-queer-theorist-a -review-of-queer-theory-without-antinormativity-by-jack-halberstam.

Han, Ju Hui Judy. "Incidents of Travel." In *Q & A: Queer in Asian America,* ed. David L. Eng and Alice Y. Hom, 397–404. Philadelphia: Temple University Press, 1998.

Han, Ju Hui Judy. "Organizing Korean Americans against Homophobia." *Sojourner* 25, no. 10 (June 2000): 1–4.

Han, Woori. "Proud of Myself as LGBTQ: The Seoul Pride Parade, Homonationalism, and Queer Developmental Citizenship." *Korea Journal* 58, no. 2 (Summer 2018): 27–57.

Hanscom, Christopher P., and Dennis Washburn, eds. *The Affect of Difference: Representations of Race in East Asian Empire.* Honolulu: University of Hawai'i Press, 2016.

Ho, Josephine. "Is Global Governance Bad for East Asian Queers?" GLQ 14, no. 4 (2008): 457–79.

Henry, Todd A. *Assimilating Seoul: Japanese Rule and the Politics of Public Space in Colonial Korea, 1910–1945*. Berkeley: University of California Press, 2014.

Henry, Todd A. "In this Issue—Queer/Korean Studies as Critique: A Provocation." *Korea Journal* 58, no. 2 (Summer 2018): 5–26.

Henry, Todd A. *Japan's Gay Empire: Sex Tourism, Military Culture, and Memory Making in Postcolonial Asia-Pacific*. Forthcoming.

Hinsch, Bret. *Passions of the Cut Sleeve: The Male Homosexual Tradition in China*. Berkeley: University of California Press, 1992.

Ho, Loretta Wing Wah. *Gay and Lesbian Subculture in Urban China*. London: Routledge, 2011.

Huang, Hans. *Queer Politics and Sexual Modernity in Taiwan*. Hong Kong: Hong Kong University Press, 2011.

"Human Rights Situation of LGBTI in South Korea, 2016." Korean Society of Law and Policy on Sexual Orientation and Gender Identity, Seoul, 2017.

Hwang, Kyung Moon. *Rationalizing Korea: The Rise of the Modern State, 1894–1945*. Berkeley: University of California Press, 2015.

Jackson, Peter A. *Dear Uncle Go: Male Homosexuality in Thailand*. Bangkok: Bua Luang, 1995.

Jackson, Peter A. *Male Homosexuality in Thailand: An Interpretation of Contemporary Sources*. Elmhurst, NY: Global Academic, 1989.

Jackson, Peter A. *Queer Bangkok: 21st Century Markets, Media, and Rights*. Hong Kong: Hong Kong University Press, 2011.

Jackson, Peter A., and Gerard Sullivan, eds. *Lady Boys, Tom Boys, Rent Boys: Male and Female Homosexualities in Contemporary Thailand*. New York: Haworth, 1999.

Kallander, George L. *Salvation through Dissent: Tonghak Heterodoxy and Early Modern Korea*. Honolulu: University of Hawai'i Press, 2013.

Kam, Lucetta Y. L. *Shanghai Lalas: Female Tongzi Communities and Politics in Urban China*. Hong Kong: Hong Kong University Press, 2013.

Kang, Wenqing. *Obsession: Male Same-Sex Relations in China, 1900–1950*. Hong Kong: Hong Kong University Press, 2009.

Kim, Anna Joo. "Korean American LGBT Movements in Los Angeles and New York." In *Asian Americans: An Encyclopedia of Social, Cultural, Economic, and Political History*, ed. Xiaojian Zhao and Edward J. W. Park, 683–85. Santa Barbara, CA: Greenwood, 2014.

Kim, Charles R. *Youth for Nation: Culture and Protest in Cold War South Korea*. Honolulu: University of Hawai'i Press, 2017.

Kim, Dong-no, John B. Duncan, and Kim Do-hyung, eds. *Reform and Modernity in the Taehan Empire*. Seoul: Jimoodang, 2006.

Kim, Eunjung. *Curative Violence: Rehabilitating Disability, Gender, and Sexuality in Modern Korea*. Durham, NC: Duke University Press, 2017.

Kim, Jeongmin. "Queer Cultural Movements and Local Counterpublics of Sexuality: A Case of Seoul Queer Films and Videos Festival." *Inter-Asia Cultural Studies* 8, no. 4 (2007): 617–733.

Kim, Kyu Hyun. "Reflections on the Problem of Colonial Modernity and 'Collaboration' in Modern Korean History." *Journal of International and Area Studies* 1, no. 3 (2004): 95–111.

Kim, Suzy. *Everyday Life in the North Korean Revolution, 1945–1950.* Ithaca, NY: Cornell University Press, 2013.

Kim, Yung-Hee. "Under the Mandate of Nationalism: Development of Feminist Enterprises in Modern Korea, 1860–1910." *Journal of Women's History* 7, no. 4 (Winter 1995): 120–36.

Kong, Travis S. K. *Chinese Male Homosexualities: Memba, Tongzhi and Golden Boy.* London: Routledge, 2012.

Kwon, Heonik. "Guilty by Association." *Papers of the British Association for Korean Studies* 13 (2011): 89–104.

Kwon, Insook. "Feminists Navigating the Shoals of Nationalism and Collaboration: The Post-Colonial Korean Debate over How to Remember Kim Hwallan." *Frontiers* 27, no. 1 (2006): 39–66.

Kwon Kim, Hyun-young, and John (Song Pae) Cho. "The Korean Gay and Lesbian Movement 1993–2008: From 'Identity' and 'Community' to 'Human Rights.'" In *South Korean Social Movements: From Democracy to Civil Society*, ed. Gi-Wook Shin and Paul Chang, 206–23. London: Routledge, 2011.

Lee, Jeeyeun. "Toward a Queer Korean American Diasporic History." In *Q&A: Queer in Asian America*, ed. David L. Eng and Alice Y. Hom, 185–212. Philadelphia: Temple University Press, 1998.

Lee, Namhee. "The Theory of Mass Dictatorship: A Re-examination of the Park Chung Hee Period." *Review of Korean Studies* 12, no. 3 (September 2009): 41–69.

Leung, Helen. *Undercurrents: Queer Culture and Postcolonial Hong Kong.* Hong Kong: Hong Kong University Press, 2009.

Leupp, Gary. *Male Colors: The Construction of Homosexuality in Tokugawa Japan.* Berkeley: University of California Press, 1997.

Lim, Eng-Beng. "Glocalqueering in New Asia: The Politics of Performing Gay in Singapore." *Theatre Journal* 57 (2005): 383–405.

Liu, Petrus. *Queer Marxism in the Two Chinas.* Durham, NC: Duke University Press, 2015.

Love, Heather. *Feeling Backward: Loss and the Politics of Queer History.* Cambridge, MA: Harvard University Press, 2009.

Luibhéid, Tithne, and Lionel Cantù Jr., eds. *Queer Migrations: Sexuality, U.S. Citizenship, and Border Crossings.* Minneapolis: University of Minnesota Press, 2005.

Mackintosh, Jonathan D. *Homosexuality and Manliness in Postwar Japan.* London: Routledge, 2010.

Manalansan, Martin F., IV. "Diasporic Deviants/Divas: How Filipino Gay Transmigrants 'Play with the World.'" In *Queer Diasporas*, ed. Cindy Patton and Benigno Sánchez-Eppler, 183–203. Durham, NC: Duke University Press, 2000.

Manalansan, Martin F., IV. *Global Divas: Filipino Gay Men in the Diaspora*. Durham, NC: Duke University Press, 2003.

Martin, Fran. *Backward Glances: Contemporary Chinese Cultures and the Female Homoerotic Imaginary*. Durham, NC: Duke University Press, 2010.

Martin, Fran. *Situating Sexualities: Queer Representation in Taiwanese Fiction, Film and Public Culture*. Hong Kong: Hong Kong University Press, 2003.

Martin, Fran. "Surface Tensions: Reading Productions of Tongzhi in Contemporary Taiwan." *GLQ* 6, no. 1 (2000): 61–86.

Martin, Fran, Peter A. Jackson, Mark McLelland, and Audrey Yue, eds. *AsiapacifiQueer: Rethinking Genders and Sexualities*. Urbana: University of Illinois Press, 2008.

McLelland, Mark. *Male Homosexuality in Modern Japan: Cultural Myths and Social Realities*. Richmond, VA: Curzon, 2000.

McLelland, Mark. *Queer Japan from the Pacific War to the Internet Age*. Lanham, MD: Rowman and Littlefield, 2005.

Meyer, Doug. "An Intersectional Analysis of Lesbian, Gay, Bisexual, and Transgender (LGBT) People's Evaluations of Anti-Queer Violence." *Gender and Society* 26, no. 6 (2012): 849–73.

Miyoshi, Masao, and Harry Harootunian, eds. *Learning Places: The Afterlives of Area Studies*. Durham, NC: Duke University Press, 2002.

Moon, Yumi. *Populist Collaborators: The Ilchinohoe and the Japanese Colonization of Korea, 1896–1910*. Ithaca, NY: Cornell University Press, 2013.

Muñoz, José Esteban. *Cruising Utopia: The Then and There of Queer Futurity*. New York: New York University Press, 2009.

Muñoz, José Esteban. *Disidentifications: Queers of Color and the Performance of Politics*. Minneapolis: University of Minnesota Press, 1999.

Myers, B. R. *The Cleanest Race: How North Koreans See Themselves—and Why It Matters*. New York: Melville House, 2010.

Na, Tari Young-Jung. "The South Korean Gender System: LGBTI in the Contexts of Family, Legal Identity, and the Military." *Journal of Korean Studies* 19, no. 2 (Fall 2014): 357–77.

Nanda, Serena. *Neither Man nor Woman: The Hijras of India*. Belmont, CA: Wadsworth, 1999.

Patton, Cindy, and Benigno Sanchéz-Eppler, eds. *Queer Diasporas*. Durham, NC: Duke University Press, 2000.

Peletz, Michael. *Gender Pluralism: Southeast Asia since Early Modern Times*. London: Routledge, 2009.

Pflugfelder, Gregory M. *Cartographies of Desire: Male-Male Sexuality in Japanese Discourse*. Berkeley: University of California Press, 1999.

Povinelli, Elizabeth A., and George Chauncey, eds. "Thinking Sexuality Transnationally." *GLQ* 5, no. 4 (1999): 439–50.

Puar, Jasbir. *Terrorist Assemblages: Homonationalism in Queer Times*. Durham, NC: Duke University Press, 2007.

Quiroga, José. *Tropics of Desire: Interventions from Queer Latina America*. New York: New York University Press, 2000.

Reddy, Gayatri. *With Respect to Sex: Negotiating Hijra Identity in South India*. Chicago: University of Chicago Press, 2005.

Reichert, James. *In the Company of Men: Representations of Male-Male Sexuality in Meiji Literature*. Stanford, CA: Stanford University Press, 2006.

Reyes, Raquel A. G., and William G. Clarence-Smith. *Sexual Diversity in Asia, c. 600–1950*. London: Routledge, 2012.

Rhee, Margaret. "Towards Community: *KoreAm Journal* and Korean American Cultural Attitudes on Same-Sex Marriage." *Amerasia Journal* 32, no. 1 (2006): 75–88.

Robertson, Jennifer. *Takarazuku: Sexual Politics and Popular Culture in Modern Japan*. Berkeley: University of California Press, 1998.

Rofel, Lisa. *Desiring China: Experiments in Neoliberalism, Sexuality, and Public Culture*. Durham, NC: Duke University Press, 2007.

Rofel, Lisa. "Qualities of Desire: Imagining Gay Identities." GLQ 5, no. 4 (1999): 451–74.

Sang, Tze-Lan D. *The Emerging Lesbian: Female Same-Sex Desire in Modern China*. Chicago: University of Chicago Press, 2003.

Schmid, Andre. *Korea between Empires, 1895–1919*. New York: Columbia University Press, 2002.

Seo, Dong-jin. "Mapping the Vicissitudes of Homosexual Identities in South Korea." *Journal of Homosexuality* 40, nos. 3–4 (2001): 56–79.

Shih, Shu-mei, Chien-hsin Tsai, and Brian Bernards, eds. *Sinophone Studies: A Critical Reader*. New York: Columbia University Press, 2012.

Shin, Susan S. "Tonghak Thought: The Roots of Revolution." *Korea Journal* 19, no. 9 (September 1979): 204–23.

Shin, Yong-ha. "Tonghak and Ch'oe Che-u." *Seoul Journal of Korean Studies* 3 (1990): 83–102.

Sinnot, Megan. "Borders, Diaspora, and Regional Connections: Trends in Asian 'Queer' Studies." *Journal of Asian Studies* 69, no. 1 (February 2010): 17–31.

Sinnot, Megan. *Toms and Dees: Transgender Identity and Female Same-Sex Relationships in Thailand*. Honolulu: University of Hawai'i Press, 2004.

Sommers, Matthew. *Sex, Law, and Society in Late Imperial China*. Stanford, CA: Stanford University Press, 2002.

Suganuma, Katsuhiko. "Associative Identity Politics: Unmasking the Multilayered Formation of Queer Male Selves in 1990s Japan." *Inter-Asia Cultural Studies* 8, no. 4 (2007): 485–502.

Suganuma, Katsuhiko. *Contact Moments: The Politics of Intercultural Desire in Japanese Male-Queer Cultures*. Hong Kong: Hong Kong University Press, 2012.

Tang, Denise Tse-Shang. *Conditional Spaces: Hong Kong Lesbian Desires and Everyday Life*. Hong Kong: Hong Kong University Press, 2011.

Vanita, Ruth. *Queering India: Same-Sex Love and Eroticism in Indian Culture and Society*. London: Routledge, 2013.

Vincent, J. Keith. *Two-Timing Modernity: Homosocial Narrative in Modern Japanese Fiction*. Cambridge, MA: Harvard University Press, 2012.

Vitiello, Giovanni. *The Libertine's Friend: Homosexuality and Masculinity in Late Imperial China*. Chicago: Chicago University Press, 2011.

Warner, Michael. *The Trouble with Normal: Sex, Politics, and the Ethics of Queer Life*. Cambridge, MA: Harvard University Press, 1999.

Wilson, Ara. "Queering Asia," *Intersections* 14 (November 2006). http://intersections.anu.edu.au/issue14/wilson.html.

Wu, Cuncun. *Homoerotic Sensibilities in Late Imperial China*. London: Routledge, 2012.

Yi, Horim, and Timothy Gitzen. "Sex/Gender Insecurities: Trans Bodies and the South Korean Military." *TSQ* 5, no. 3 (Summer 2018): 376–91.

Yi, Joseph, Joe Phillips, and Shin-Do Sung. "Same-Sex Marriage, Korean Christians, and the Challenge of Democratic Engagement." *Culture and Society* 51 (2014): 415–22.

Yi, T'ae-jin. "Was Early Modern Korea Really a 'Hermit Nation'?" *Korea Journal* 38, no. 4 (Winter 1998): 5–35.

Yoo, Theodore Jun. *It's Madness: The Politics of Mental Health in Colonial Korea*. Berkeley: University of California Press, 2016.

Yue, Audrey, and Jun Zubillaga-Pow, eds. *Queer Singapore: Illiberal Citizenship and Mediated Cultures*. Hong Kong: Hong Kong University Press, 2013.

Zheng, Tiantian. *Tongzhi Living: Men Attracted to Men in Postsocialist China*. Minneapolis: University of Minnesota Press, 2015.

Part I

UNRULY SUBJECTS
UNDER COLONIAL AND
POSTCOLONIAL MODERNITY

Chapter One

RITUAL SPECIALISTS IN COLONIAL DRAG

SHAMANIC INTERVENTIONS IN 1920S KOREA

Merose Hwang

In July 1920, at a crucial moment in Korea's history when a repressive colonial regime moved to adopt more persuasive strategies of rule in the bloody aftermath of the March 1 Uprising (1919), a man by the name of Kim T'ae-ik unveiled what one newspaper report described as the "mysterious Sowi Church Guild."[1] At that time, shamans, sorcerers, fortunetellers, female entertainers, and so-called flower boys (*hwarang*) were gathering to form a guild, or a labor and cultural union, so their occupations would be recognized as a part of a burgeoning field in "traditional" trades.[2] They recruited students, conducted classes, administered exams, provided apprenticeships, and issued certifications to professionalize "shamanic labor."[3] The guild orchestrated cultural performances and even experimented with avant-garde theater. Their shows attracted all types of audiences, from housewives and intellectuals to colonial officials.[4] These activities were such a successful endeavor that, by the end of the colonial period in 1945, the Sungsinin Chohap (Spirit Worshipers' Guild) had expanded to more than sixty affiliated organizations nationwide.

The Korean media, which had recently reemerged in the early 1920s after a decade of suppression by colonial officials, wasted no time expressing its opinion on this matter. One of the biggest newspapers at the time, the *Tong'a Ilbo*

(East Asia Daily) was determined to get the backstory on how this guild could become so successful at orchestrating and publicizing its grand rituals. It purported that these community-based performances were becoming "wildly popular," promoting superstition and effectively reversing Korea's path to modernity.[5] So what was the colonial government doing about this impending disaster? Not much, the *East Asia Daily* responded, ranting, "Whether it is a truth or a lie, the slogan 'Cultural Rule' (*munhwa t'ongch'i*) can be discovered daily through strange-looking groups like the Sowŏn Sungsinin Chohap."[6]

In this chapter, I introduce the three concepts of "colonial spiritual assimilation," "shamanic nationalism," and "colonial drag" to show a triangulation of colonialist-nationalist-spiritualist actors involved in a battle for cultural representation. Wishing to privilege the vantage point of the spiritual/ritual agents, I propose that shamans, both as imperial subjects and cultural nationalist icons, created an antinormative treasure trove of queer modern possibility. Thinking about their ability to rouse a collective memory and assess a shared consciousness enables me to explore alternative renderings of the politics of shamanic performance. The Sungsinin guild's community theater involved public rituals of transformation and had the potential to change people's perception of truth and reality. What the colonial media saw as hyper- and non-normative sexualized acts may have been acts of resistance as shrine patron impersonators and ethnohistoriographical transgenders operated in an environment of colonial assimilation and national erasure.

This chapter proposes a queer intervention into Korean history to question the common position that colonial cultural projects produced ambivalent effects. My rendition of queer lives in Korean history questions our identitarian politics by considering a range of historical subjectivities based on intensified stratification of power under colonialism. Colonial cosmopolitan dreams of Korea's queer spiritualism have manifest contents in a politically unpredictable era of cultural rule. To help me bend the conversation on the theoretical and historical implications embedded in Korean shamanism of the 1920s, I look to the framework of two important theorists. First, I picture José Esteban Muñoz's interests in postcolonial performativity and mandate of queer futurity to help me see why Sungsinin was conducting a backward glance to a royally shamanic era, using ancient royalty to help enact a future vision to overcome imperialist and patriarchal nationalist oppression.[7] Sungsinin's turn to the past was a way to critique the present and ignite a post-statist futurity. Colonialist and nationalist arguments against shamans were grounded in hateful charges of their sexual abnormality, such as homosexuality, transgenderism, or female-dominant desire, deriving from desires and experiences of mourning, incest, and even homicide.[8] Sungsinin presented an alternative to that colonial bipolarity, moving beyond the civilizing impulses to capture the indigenous subject, venturing into unexpected avenues to overcome colonially contingent representations.

Second, I use Petrus Liu's historical tool of "nonliberal queer theory" to temper seeing the past through a white, queer studies lens of non-normative temporality.[9] Laurel Kendall has established the point that gender and sexual fluidity are part and parcel of Korean shamanic communities.[10] Extending this gender argument to historical subjects, Liu helps me see that their gendered expressions should not be conflated to contemporary Western notions of queer social identity. Following Liu's caution on white homonormative politics, I use Kendall's point on ritual fluidity to argue that during the colonial era, female shamans had the wherewithal to revert to armored symbols of patriarchy to meet public demands for hetero-centrist membership.[11] That said, I aim to reverse the colonial media's misogynistic impressions of shamans by creating a space for their shamanic agency and geopolitical visions. Considering shamanic acts as affect, sentiment, embodiment, and sensation adds a dimension beyond the media's dull loathing of shamanism, creating a space for shamanic magnificence in the form of ritual. I seek to entertain lived colonial experience by finding ingenuity in the methods by which shamans overcame oppression as they donned sumptuous layers of local, regional, and universal gods, daring to conjure an alternative geopolitical order. Queer forms of analysis thus allow me to materialize what has not entered the historical record, the embodied, nonrational, collective experiences that are not yet culturally legible.

Colonial Spiritual Assimilation

Korea's modernization campaign to manage and regulate religious practices preceded colonialism, but the Japanese streamlined government oversight to radically include administering "folk customs." From the turn of the century, religious organizations throughout Korea were compelled to work with various colonial administrations.[12] Starting in 1906, the Japanese resident-general of Korea issued Shūkyō no Gifu ni Kan Suru Kisoku (Regulations on Religious Activities), placing Japanese Buddhist groups in administrative charge of Korean temples. Then, to oversee all religious activity on the Korean peninsula more effectively, the Government-General issued Shūkyō no Senpu ni Kansuru Kisoku (Regulations on Religious Propagation) in 1915. Throughout the period of military rule (a term historians refer to today as representing the first decade of colonial rule in the 1910s), the Government-General worked to destroy shrines, confiscate ritual paintings, disperse neighborhood loiterers, fine, and even incarcerate ritual leaders. Criminalization of decentralized ritual leaders such as shamans was fueled by long-standing discrimination against such people, whom government officials viewed alongside fortune-tellers and female entertainers (*kisaeng*) as morally and ethically inept.[13] However, the colonial administration grew increasingly aware that no quantity of police patrols or punitive fines could eliminate Korea's clandestine network of spiritual patrons and services.[14] Even with the help of civic neighborhood watch campaigns, the police, colonial administration, local intelligentsia, and media all found themselves fighting an impossible battle. By the end of the decade, it had become clear that the colonial administration was gradually loosening its shaman persecution.

Colonial policies of the 1920s presented new challenges and opportunities for Korean shamans. On March 1, 1919, widespread indigenous uprisings to overthrow the Japanese colonial government were quelled through bloody suppression. What escalated into a global spectacle forced Japanese officials to reconsider how they managed Korea and to implement what appeared as a softer form of "cultural rule." In terms of security, they first replaced the old Government-General administration; then they expanded their surveillance and penal systems throughout the peninsula. They also hand-selected members of the native community to advise the new colonial administration and commissioned them to survey preexisting native policies to integrate the most effective social regulations. Finally, the imperial government drastically increased the number of Japanese shrines to be erected in Korea. Nakajima Michio argues that the exponential increase in Shintō shrines "shows how serious the Japanese government was about extending its imperial rule over Korea."[15]

As soon as the Korean printing presses began running again, newspapers complained about how the government's soft hand would allow shamanism and Shintōism to take over society. The *East Asia Daily* was shocked that "the Government-General's cultural politics do not prohibit calling spirits, chanting sutras, calling shamans and sorcerers and conducting rituals." Korean writers were, moreover, outraged by the "lack of administrative control" over shamanic activity, in contrast to its persecution against more "modern" (perhaps referring to Christian) organizations.[16] The *East Asia Daily* accused Japan of "attempting to establish a new culture" in Korea.[17] Korean intellectuals were well aware of the precolonial existence of Shintō in Korea and feared shamanic participation could further colonial assimilation/Japanese religious hegemony against their own nationalist vision.[18] In an article titled "To Get Rid of Shamans," *East Asia Daily* responded by reporting that the police were taking an "irresponsibly noninterventionist policy" toward what it called "superstitious" activities, believing that this policy would adversely affect the Japanese colonial promise to promote public health.[19] The paper expressed its position on the policy shift from prohibiting to conciliating popular ritual leaders by asking the loaded question: "When the police repeatedly feign ignorance while looking at these common people, is this a manifestation of cultural rule?"[20] In fact, the colonial administration ushered in an unprecedented number of regulations to centralize ritual communities under which it compelled "common people" such as shamans to comply.

In this new phase of colonial rule, shamans became "conspicuous indigenes," a term I use to understand why this subaltern community was silent in the mass media and misrepresented in modern ethnographies while they were also subalterns actively pursuing their livelihood through experimental forms of self-representation. Starting with the first colonial papers, the dailies ceaselessly attempted to shame and even plead with the colonial government to maintain its iron fist of legal and penal measures against subalterns, laws that effectively privileged elite, patriarchal religious establishments such as Christian churches. They feared that flourishing conspicuous indigeneity would hinder Korea's "progress" and that the Japanese government would enable a "most backward culture" if shamanic organizations were to be "officially recognized by police." It warned that the guild members had "a bad effect and poison[ed] this society," calling their indigenous rituals "very deeply rooted, ordinary, incidental customs."[21] It also asserted that the colonial government was "allowing Korean society to stagnate and people's laziness to spread into the future."[22] The news dailies reminded their readers that the Japanese were not delivering on their promise to "modernize" Korea and were encouraging the country's destruction instead.

Undoubtedly, drastic changes were on the colonial horizon. Murayama Chijun (1891–1968) became the first scholar to work under the new administration of cultural rule in Korea. Trained as a sociologist with specific emphasis on criminology, he was appointed to investigate and police religious practices, prompting additional research to effectively govern over Korean shamans. For example, Ordinance 386, issued on August 20, 1919, established a Bureau of Academic Affairs to oversee a Department of Religion and Department of

Research on National Treasures.[23] These offices broadened official recognition of decentralized spiritual activities, unifying all religious and spiritual practices under imperial sanction.[24] The colonial government broadened its religious registries to gain mass cooperation in its public health and sanitation policies and worked closely with the colonial police. Murayama was assigned to assess Korean thought and character. He based his studies on previous criminal records of "dissidents" such as shamans to design more effective measures of surveillance and control over the peninsula. This administration further established a Sociology Department and an Anthropology Department at Seoul Imperial University, creating a foundation of imperially trained ethnographers to research Korea's indigenous practices to "pluck the sprouts" of Korean insurgence.[25]

Like the Sungsinin Chohap, religious journals took advantage of the cultural rule environment to self-shape their church identities. Meanwhile, the Japanese administration attempted to counter religious insurgencies by creating "conciliatory policies" and by finding "collaborative persons" in each religious organization.[26] These new religion policies began to generate fervent discussions about which organizations were the most civilized, rational religions. Despite the lack of written self-representation, shamanic ritual specialists were represented under a governing branch of indigenous theism, making them a silent, but important, contender in the religion debate.[27] All faiths and denominations wrote, asserting the modern, rational aspects of their churches and how "un-shamanic" they were.[28] Even *Ch'ŏndogyo Hoewŏlbo* (Heavenly Church Monthly), which stemmed from the Eastern Learning Church, with its shamanic elements (also known as Tonghak, an anti-imperial, nationalistic millenarian political and religious movement, founded in the late 1800s), preemptively forwarded rationalist statements such as, "The nature of religion is superstitious from start to finish, and, many other religions are limited by this, but namely our religion rightly starts and finishes as a true religion."[29] *Kaebyŏk* (Creation), a later manifestation of the journal, criticized that "reactionary forces within society" were fostering an "anti-religious movement."[30] Religious journals, limited by the constraints of colonial structures and instruments, often pitted themselves against one another to gain administrative favor in their pursuit for government favor.

If the colonial government was looking to find and control the most radical organizations, it needed only to turn to these church debates. The unilateral indigenous religious opposition to shamans created certain opportunities for the colonial administration to bring these conspicuous indigenes into their fold. Colonizers co-opting the united opposition to shamans could have been a way for them to diffuse the radicalized momentum of the March 1 Movement. While token agents of indigenous traditions enjoyed privileges that came with government sanction, this "finessed" cultural governance undeniably penetrated levels and modes of oppression by allowing Korea's spiritual communities to pit themselves against one another.[31] Whatever the motive, the Government-General provided administrative oversight to help establish a new Sinhŭng Church that had some sixty different spiritual factions, and the Sungsinin cooperative emerged as one of them. Among conspicuous shamanic factions, the Sungsinin cooperative was most noticeable because its headquarters were in the capital, Seoul, and got on well with the large Japanese settler community in the city.[32] They openly participated in Japanese Shintō festivities—participation the colonial government declared was not a religious but, rather, a civic act.[33] The Korean media exaggerated shamanic engagement with Shintō to argue that Koreans were in danger of becoming Japanese.[34] As Sungsinin appeared amenable to mandates of Shintō worship, Korean intellectuals delegitimized guilds and affinity institutions such as the Sinni Chonggyo (Divinity Church) in their attempt to resist Japan's efforts to create colonial hegemony over Korea's spiritual traditions.

Shamanic political opportunism was not unique to the colonial era. In fact, a discursive subterfuge for indigenous social customs and spiritual exchanges between Japan and Korea dated at least to the late nineteenth century. It would not have been surprising for this shamanic community to drape itself with Shintō symbols and allegedly to frame its rituals more generally as *sindo* (the way of the gods) to break down the barriers between the Chosŏn (1392–1910) and Meiji ritual worlds. For his part, Tae-gon Kim examines how Korean shamans collaborated with Shintō shrines in the late Chosŏn era.[35] Shamanic organizations also incorporated the earliest local developments in Mahayana Buddhist traditions to gain political favor.[36] Traces of political and clerical embrace of shamanism can also be found in ancient Taoist records.[37] The most obvious form of political opportunism can be found in the second half of the Chosŏn Dynasty. Royal edicts from this time show the government effectively regulating household taxes to increase state revenue and to reinforce neo-Confucian ruling ideologies. These regulations directly affected heterodox ritual communities.[38] The Chosŏn government vacillated between ritual practices it deemed proper or improper, including permitting and then disallowing rituals that venerated ancient Chinese Taoist and shamanic deities.[39] For fiscal purposes, nonconforming ritualists

provided a tax collection base for the government and incentivized administrators to enforce shamanic registration and licensure. They allowed shamans
space to organize and tolerated shamans' concentration just outside the gates
of the capital for these reasons.[40] Korean ritual specialists possessed a long,
complicated relationship with government and state religions much before
Japanese annexation.[41]

Once "shamanism" was imported to Korea as a colonial trope, uninstitution-
alized ritual specialists were captured in a new national debate.[42] Colonial-era
intellectuals sustained older neo-Confucian criticisms of heterodox shamanic
practices while they forwarded an elitist rhetoric of modernity. Shamanism
was rendered into a colonial condition and used as a scapegoat for national
demise. Although the Korean media framed shamanic organizations as a new
phenomenon and saw these regulatory practices as a method for the colonial
state to extend its rule, the Japanese administration of the 1920s claimed that
it was simply reviving late Chosŏn-era customary policies.[43] But this administration undoubtedly contributed to further politicizing shamanism. Religious
studies academics working under the colonial administration eagerly married
Korean shamanism to Japanese Shintō through their theory of ancient spiritual
affinities. When the Sungsinin Chohap secured shamanism in the ministerial
category of "folk religion," debates flourished about whether the Government-
General should incorporate this outlier community into its religious policy.[44]
Korean ritual workers registered with Shintō shrines, not as religious affiliates,
but as members of Japanese colonial social "custom" and political philosophy,
granting them high visibility and flexibility to conduct their work as cultural
ambassadors.[45] In so doing, their professions emerged aboveground, validat-
ing their occupations in unprecedented ways and making them a conspicuous
target for nationalist elites.

Shamanic Nationalism

The debate over religion of the 1920s generated academic offshoots into Korean religions and spirituality. The Japanese government commissioned two
men, Ch'oe Nam-sŏn (1890–1957) and Yi Nŭng-hwa (1869–1945), to aid the
Government-General's History Compilation Committee in its creation of a
massive archival project, Chosŏnsa (Korean History).[46] Unlike the highly visible and lowbrow assessments of Sungsinin's public performances, Ch'oe and
Yi sat quietly on the political margins as they broadened the scope of Korean
studies in the 1920s. In 1927, they jointly wrote Treatise on Korean Shamanism,

the first such project to understand Korean history in its entirety through the lens of shamanism. They defined the path that shamanism studies would take in a newly developed folklore studies, which generations later was assumed under anthropology.[47]

I pose a couple of questions in this section to better understand the historical significance of this treatise. What was the purpose of using shamanism to understand Korean history? Whose interests did it serve? To be sure, it benefited colonialists by rendering Koreans as backward and unable to govern themselves, thereby justifying colonial rule. However, I posit that the treatise also produced an underexplored effect insofar as it allowed these writers to *feel* for a nation that the Japanese empire was erasing. These men used shamanism in an unprecedented way to mourn and resuscitate a dying nation. Their treatise was a mode of colonial *hybrid* expression to capture the colony-nation, an inherently fragmentary subject, by traversing new universal models of ethnicity, sexuality, and gender identification.[48] I see this move less as the colonized exercising their Western intellectual pedigree than as their paving new historical paths to better assess their colonial present in the 1920s. In these ways, Ch'oe and Yi's shamanism project was ultimately a product of their colonized being.

While they expressed loss, Ch'oe and Yi were also hopeful, using this highly visible but under-recorded subject to stir nostalgic longings for masculine days gone by, to make colonialism ephemeral, and to spark emotions and activate a call to action for an emancipatory postcolonial future. The prior statement on national loss under colonialism may not be as surprising as this observation about Korea's 1920s futurity. These scholars started with Korea's primordial origins rooted in a spiritually shamanic past.[49] Then, using intensely gendered characterizations, they highlighted Korea's unique, continental, and prehistoric roots. Their project elided the dangers of shaman-induced social regression and colonial assimilation by ingeniously highlighting the nation's ethno-spiritual father, angling the conflicted "conspicuous indigenes" debate toward more fruitful possibilities of what Kim Seong-Nae calls "intellectual nationalist self-consciousness."[50]

This treatise not only echoed precolonial renderings of Korea's mainland affinities but also, more pointedly, offered a new kind of "queer continentalism" in which a transgendered shamanic history marked Korea's continental orientations.[51] To analyze their work as part of "queer studies" may suggest that this approach casts a Western cultural imperialist lens onto yet another Oriental subject. This criticism could easily be made of Ch'oe Nam-sŏn's contribution—how his literature review mostly referenced American social science publications and how generously he peppered his prose with English social taxonomies.[52] This historical experiment had the potential to push Korea out of its colonial "ghetto," to tinker with continental identities, and to venture into unchartered global affinities like Nordic shamanism.[53]

While Ch'oe Nam-sŏn enjoyed conducting these types of thought experiments on universal phenomena, his practical mission was to restore the Korean nation. He was broadly trained in the Chinese classics and Western anthropology. He was also responsible for drafting the Korean Declaration of Independence that spurred the March 1 Movement of 1919. For his role in that uprising, Ch'oe was imprisoned for two years. Upon his release, he continued to push politicized academic boundaries by writing on numerous nationalist projects of which this shamanism project was one. This publication caused an interesting turn of events, as the governor-general commissioned Ch'oe to join Yi Nŭng-hwa and more than a dozen other Korean scholars to work on the Korean History Compilation Committee.[54] Ch'oe appealed to the colonial administration's interest in Korean history and shamanism studies, even if his conclusions on Siberian connections destabilized colonialist notions that Korea shared ethnic origins with Japan.[55]

Ch'oe was able to sever Korea's close association to Japan by suggesting that Korea's historical roots stemmed away from the Japanese archipelago, in the opposite direction, toward the Asian continental interior.[56] Inspired by fieldwork done on a neolithic shamanic tradition that mapped out a northern transcontinental belt, Ch'oe pointed out the sites along this belt that had been discussed to date:

> All the ancient peoples of Asia, from the southern parts (Ainu), Japan, the Ryūkyū Islands, Korea, Manchuria, Mongolia, through Central Asia extending out to Eastern Europe (Eur-Asia)—(stemming from the Northeast division of Siberia, extending to the eastern end of the Paengnyŏng Strait to the western end to the Scandinavian border), lay the basis of spirit worship, through animism. It is popular for a diviner (or shaman doctor) to perform a job that is a kind of primordial religion (natural religion, religious sorcery, ancient faith). This is what scholars call the religion of shamanism.[57]

Blurring shamanism's origins along this belt removed Japan's monopoly on Korea's evolution, placing Siberian polygenetic diffusion in its place. What is more, identifying shamanism in a region indicated that that region was "developing" and not yet "advanced." Tying Japan to this belt meant that Japan could not secure its place ahead of Korea because shamanic places could not already be evolved.

The geographic boundary of shamanism was redrafted to create a northeastern Asian orientation, using a strategy of queer continentalism to counter Japanese imperial diffusionism. Ch'oe considered a particular group of scholarly specialists who had argued that the shamanism they found in some Siberian tribes was the only type. In other words, the shamanism that Siberian ethnographers used as an analytical category to study all indigenous communities should be exclusive to Siberia, and practices outside of these tribes were something else entirely. A good example of broad misappropriation can be found in the Japanese colonial model that followed closely the work of Edward B. Tylor, an English anthropologist who was commonly credited with founding the field of social anthropology. According to Ch'oe, "The shamanism research of northwest Asia follows the influence of all of Tylor's animism theories," and Ch'oe surmised that these scholars "misuse the word 'spirit.'"[58] He questioned the cultural "survival" model that Japanese anthropologists borrowed from Tylor's cultural evolutionism theory to naturalize Japan's colonization.

This new shamanic geography was buttressed with a cultural particularity of transgenderism.[59] Korean roots were supposedly tied to tribes northeast of Mongolia and the eastern coast of Siberia. A Korean-Buryati-Siberian connection was carefully drawn out according to historical societies with ritual specialists that had undergone a "change of sex."[60] Three categories of male shamans based on Buryati shamanism were also found in Korean shamans as "priests," "medicine men," and "prophets." Ch'oe claimed that Korean shamans were originally like Siberian practitioners in that they were both "similar to the holy man or priest." These three regional cultures were connected through their origins as male-dominant traditions.

A more recent predominance of female-to-male shamans signaled a gendered temporal transition from "paleo" (*ku*) to "neo" (*sin*) Siberian practices. Ch'oe highlighted, "As for the people of Siberia, the *change of sex* is found chiefly among Palaeo-Siberians, namely the Chukchee, Koryak, Kamchadal, and Asiatic Eskimo."[61] In a section entitled "Gender Transformations of Shamans," Ch'oe described how later Siberian shamans engaged in transgender practices, using the feminization of men as the first sign of a sovereign nation entering its decline. According to his assessment, certain men fell into spiritual illness for which they had no other cure than to cross-dress and change their gender. These men, "by order of the spirits," entered into homosexual marriages with those male spirits. "These shamans," he continued, "had a duty to change their genital organs through some kind of ceremony."[62] Then, their communities could acknowledge a match between (what some in today's trans* community call) a male-to-female human and a male spirit and enfold this couple as a conjugal union between opposite-sex beings. Transgendered shaman initiates passed as women by dressing, talking, and behaving as women. Under the guidance of spirits and with the support of their communities, they immediately abandoned their manly responsibilities, quickly mastered women's household and communal work, and even entered "female-only spheres." For instance, these "trans spiritualists" played a central role in places where cismen were not permitted, such as the chambers where women gave birth.[63] They acted as midwives before, during, and after labor and were responsible for the well-being of the community at large.

Ch'oe believed that the presence of nonheterosexual practices signaled unhealthy communities, which he then used to map out colonized territories. He saw trans-ritualists less as women than as "soft men," putting himself in the company of other global researchers of sexology while also positioning himself as an outsider to his native community. He remarked on how their communities allowed trans-spiritualists not only to behave as women, but also to lead "homosexual" lives (disregarding opposite-sexed spiritual unions). The archives of Siberian and early American expeditions were duplicated to talk about shamanic homosexuality. Ch'oe highlights what he believes are the most important aspects of the 1755 writings of Kurasenin Nikov in this way: "There was much on these developments but the point is that those records of 'normal homosexualism' and [sex] 'change' (tarŭn) derived from shamanic inspiration."[64] Ch'oe accepted the long-standing ethnographic diagnoses of trans-ritualists as "ill," describing this as a "curious phenomenon, a mystical change of sex" and a "sexual perversion."[65] In addition to pathologizing these communities, Ch'oe emphasized that a predominance of "soft men" and their "feminine habits" constituted recent historical developments, synchronizing them with recent colonial trends.

Yi Nŭng-hwa echoed Ch'oe's masculinist logic to document the nation's masculine origin. Best known for his pro-Buddhism writings, Yi was among the oldest members of the History Compilation Committee.[66] He may have been less globally minded than Ch'oe, but of the two, he was the more archive-driven historian.[67] Starting with Tan'gun Ruler, a figure deemed the legendary founder of Kojosŏn (the first mythical kingdom of Korea), Yi believed that the nation had distinctly male origins because Tan'gun was not just the nation's founder; he was also the first shaman king and a shamanic god.[68] Yi went on to trace "original" male shamans (*nammu*) in ancient records to show that such men flourished in Korea's golden past.[69] These men were synonymously called sorcerers (*paksu*) and flower boys (*hwarang*). Yi found evidence of ancient practices where "attractive sons from among the noble people were selected and dolled up with cosmetics and adornments. Called flower boys, all the people of the country revered and served them."[70] These beautifully masculine shamans were considered venerable elders (*chonjang*) at the top of the Silla dynastic (57 BCE–935 CE) social hierarchy.[71] Yi discovered numerous occasions between the eleventh century and the fourteenth century when shaman men (*mugyŏk*) were invited to the royal court to conduct "rain prayers," a practice that reveals a copacetic relationship between shaman men and the state.

Like Ch'oe, his co-author, Yi Nŭng-hwa proceeded to document the transgender nation's historical decline. He juxtaposed positive assessments of venerable elders and flower boys with what he claimed were more recent feminine forms of shamans. The bulk of Yi's findings on female shamans derived from the last dynastic period to show shamanism's increasing disfavor by the Chosŏn state. A Ministry of Justice record from 1482, for example, presented a legal initiative to "increase punishment" against those people known as "feminine flower boys" and "female shamans." In his estimate, the mounting criticism of "shaman work" during the Chosŏn Dynasty stemmed from flower boys "turning girly," female shamans running amok, and increasing factionalism in the Chosŏn government. Abundant court records showed that kings, queens, and royal families solicited female shamans for rituals and entertainment while the literati attempted to restrict their entry.

Yi identified a time when male shamans were becoming emasculated and argued that this event was the moment that marked when and how the nation began its decline. He asked his readers to consider a historical basis for the derogatory term *hwarangnyŏ* (female flower boys), emphasizing that "the common custom these days to call the male shamans flower boys holds a different meaning from what the term originally meant."[72] He then said that flower boys were not always "one and the same" with female shamans; the term indicated a historical practice of flower boys colluding with female shamans. Their recent transgender activity was a historical metonym of the masculine Korean nation reduced to a submissive Japanese colony. In a document from 1471, Yi described how King Sŏngjong's officials suspected flower boys of engaging in illicit behavior similar to that of female shamans. Court records from

February 1503 reported that people in Ch'ungch'ŏng, Chŏlla, and Kyŏngsang provinces recruited a particular type of male shaman (*rangjung*) to conduct ancestor rituals for their families. Provincial governors struggled to eradicate these types of practices but had little success. It was even rumored that male shamans were disguising themselves as women to come and go among noble homes.

Echoing Ch'oe's continental focus, Yi attached Korea closely to its continental neighbor, China. The flower boy feminization thus functioned as a critique of Chinese diffusionism.[73] Yi implied that the Chosŏn Dynasty sealed its fate by blindly mimicking Chinese antiquarianism instead of diverging from it to move toward modernization.[74] He transcribed a Chŏlla provincial record from 1513 that discussed boys mingling with shamans to illustrate this historical retrogression:

> There are stories about men and women lustfully intermingling and acting lewdly in all sorts of ways, making people that hear about it afraid as they slap themselves laughing in pleasure. Once in a while, a young man who has yet to develop a beard will change into women's clothes and put on makeup and come and go from people's houses in the dark of night. The [young men] sit among the female shamans in the shrine chambers and then seize the opportunity to trick someone's wife or daughter. However, this evidence is kept secret and is difficult to expose.[75]

This document shows that officials speculated about what was going on in women's quarters, a space they could not access. If cross-dressing flower boys did have this kind of access, one can ask many questions about sixteenth-century Korea, such as, "Was the real threat for this petty official men *passing* as women in the interest of other men?" and "Were attractive boys dressed as women because this aesthetically pleased their spiritual community?" This document does more than feed our imaginations of neo-Confucian impropriety; it makes real the possibility that homosocial, gender-bending practices existed "on the ground" for hundreds of years leading up to Yi's time. More than that, these stories of gender transgression were ways for Yi to ask his readers to retrace their steps away from their emasculated colonized present and to imagine historically a time of national strength and manly beginnings.

Ch'oe Nam-sŏn and Yi Nŭng-hwa's sentimental renditions of a masculine ancient past presented a glimmer of hope that the nation could be resuscitated. In contrast, their negative assessments of shamanism in its contemporary form was a part of a general hysteria among colonial intellectuals that Korean society was overly feminized; it produced a logic of gender-based social degeneration and resulted in the nation's succumbing to its foreign ruler. Hyaeweol Choi notes about New Women during the colonial period, "They offended or threatened the rigidly constrained sense of Korean nationalism and patriarchal hierarchy."[76] Gender- and sex-non-normative women converged with shamanism as Ch'oe and Yi wrestled to determine who should be considered positive and negative or conventional and transgressive members of society. Ch'oe's Siberian survey and Yi's Chosŏn history projects made Korean shamans into "conspicuous indigenes," revealing the slippery slope between forming indigenous solidarity and colonial exoticization.

These writers imagined and yearned for a "whole" nation. While silently mourning colonization, Ch'oe and Yi used the opportunity of cultural politics to debut memorials to their nation. In this sense, they occupied a colonial hybrid space in which modernity is contingent on premodernity's (even nonmodernity's) very existence. Their longing for a precolonial spiritual community looked to a past that questioned present conditions and offered hope for alternative futures.[77] Approaching resistance from this angle, I propose a nuanced understanding of colonialism by questioning assertions that, for example, the Japanese prohibited shamanism or that shamanism was their "Orientalist invention."[78] As problematic as Ch'oe and Yi's treatment of their subjects may be to us today, I want to allow space for colonized agency by showing how these writers paved the path for Korean shamanism studies. They offered a formula for decolonization by weaving Siberian male-to-female transgendering shamanic customs into a new collective of continental spiritual comradeship, prying the peninsula free from Japan's continental grip by personifying a history that was ethnically, sexually, and culturally un-Japanese. These colonized intellectuals were compelled to produce reactionary projects, using culture to question the politics of assimilation, whether they were current Japanese policies or former Chinese forms.

Colonial Drag

As I have suggested, shamanism was used for colonialist and nationalist purposes. Here, I suggest a third purpose: ritualists reproduced shamanic tropes to manipulate and problematize the empire *and* the nation. While nationalist newspapers were working to keep the embers of the March 1 Movement alive, they were also finding traces of assimilation and imperial devotion. These organizations were not only met with colonial "approval." The *East Asia Daily* also claimed that Koreans and Japanese alike were participating in all levels of the guild's administration. In fact, the Japanese were the ones orchestrating these organizations.[79] The paper was picking up on the fact that Japanese residents in Seoul were drawn to the guild's activities to the extent that even Japanese companies and government workers gave it donations and packed its auditoriums.

By acting out their Shintōness through such imperialist venerations, these ritual experts could simultaneously interact with indigenous and foreign ghosts, scrutinize the social constructions of state-driven patriarchy, and manipulate cultural-spiritual hegemony itself. Guild members went to the main Shintō shrine, Korea Shrine, to venerate Emperor Meiji, a new foreign deity.[80] The newspapers reported on ritual fakery and *mudang* (the most common name used to refer to female shamans) disguising themselves as Shintō devotees, abusing these new policies, and duping colonial authorities. Sungsinin "thievery," "criminality," and "social evils" showed the *East Asia Daily* that "there [were] no authoritative controls."[81] The paper urged the Ministry of Police Affairs to seriously reassess its sanctions. Because the colonial government was not providing adequate administrative oversight, the newspapers took it upon themselves to begin tracking mudang registering at Shintō shrines and monitoring those involved in Shintō worship.

I flip this nationalist accusation of "fakery" on its head by calling what Korean ritualists were doing "colonial drag," which I consider a radical form of resistance.[82] To access new forms of ritual power, Korean ritualists needed to acknowledge the most powerful political figures of their time, such as Amaterasu Ōmikami and Emperor Meiji, two deities that represented the official ideology of a historically unbroken line of the Japanese imperial monarchy.[83] When the newspapers reported that mudang were continuing to "build a good relationship with the Japanese empire," this accusation posed the dangerous possibility that female shamans were acting, pretending, and faking their devotion.[84] Such practices of cultural assimilationism reveal a type of colonial subjecthood in which tourists might have witnessed an odd show, act, or performance. For the ritual community, however, the patronizing of Japanese spirits was not merely a way to embrace the colonizers. It was also an essential syncretic practice in shamanic ritual pluralism.[85] These ritual specialists were expert at recognizing the deities of their contemporary environment and encouraging local participation.[86] Paying homage to an imperial spiritual cosmology was more than ambivalent mimicry (a difference that is almost the same but not quite); these young female performers could have been "dragging" their colonizers, relishing the obvious fact that what they were doing was "not quite" Japanese or Korean, male or female, and pushing the envelope of *gendered*-ethnic identities to fulfill their community's needs and desires.[87] Just as Muñoz considers the politics of drag performers to "strategize survival and imagine assertions of self in a cultural sphere that is structured to deny visibility to such bodies" and Judith Butler argues that drag subverts "the distinction between inner and outer psychic space," I see Sungsinin's Shintō patronage and avant-garde experimentation as dragging statist, patriarchal ritualism for the guild's own cultural survival.[88]

Their flexible and inventive nature put shamans in an uneasy position between spiritual pragmatism and political opportunism, fueling negative views of shamanism in the 1920s. Painting Shintō-style shamanic worship as a kind of parody reveals the participatory nature of cultural policies in which people could both join and subvert the very expression of imperial affinity. These criticisms showed that colonial identity could be "dragged" and that colonial policies could be manipulated through parodic imitation and repetition, meaning and value subversion, and heteronormative performance in an effort to destabilize truths about one's own ethno-spiritual identity.[89] Nationalist concerns about mudang skirted around the fact that Sungsinin members were masters of ritual play, driven by an acute awareness of their ethnically and politically diverse audience, acting out expectations of the obedient subject and giving colonialists what they came for.[90] While colonialists may have delighted in what they saw as crude imitations of themselves, nationalists railed against the depictions as inauthentic and attempted to shut these ritualists down, addressing universal primordialism as a means for self-preservation. Sungsinin demonstrated shamans' greatest strength to trespass political barriers to embrace politically powerful religions and syncretize them in ritual commemoration.[91]

Sungsinin Chohap did more than conduct religious and cultural events. It engaged in the most modern projects, such as cultural education, professional licensure, and nonprofit fundraising and philanthropy. It acquired licenses to develop local offices, solicited private donors and members, collected dues, and conducted community work. Although guild members were sometimes accused of accumulating, laundering, and bullying for money, they also offered their services and resources in times of need.[92] When Seoul was hit by flooding and other natural disasters that left many homeless, Sungsinin put together fundraising drives for clothes donation, first aid, and other emergency relief.[93] On these occasions, the media praised the guild for its social contributions and for setting a good example for other organizations.

Unlike freelance mudang who most commonly provided services that promised to heal their clients and their families, Sungsinin strategically strayed from private home- and neighborhood-based rituals. (Private rituals usually involved some form of curative service that violated colonial medical laws.[94]) Instead, the guild prioritized large public performances to recognize important spiritual birthdays, shamanic anniversaries, auspicious days, sacred holidays, and the like.[95] They pushed the boundaries of their shamanic communities by conducting masked dance performances, avant-garde theater (mixing shamanic elements with Western theater elements), and more traditional forms of public rituals (kut). Sungsinin's events promised excitement, laughter, and a lot of noise. The audiences were equally lively, socioeconomically varied, and ethnically mixed. To the dismay of Korean elites, these events were incredibly popular and well supported in the 1920s.[96]

While they were sometimes cast in a positive light, Sungsinin's ritual specialists were more often chastised because they broke gender rules, presenting radically dissident ways of being.[97] Nationalists treated them as female anomalies as a way to steer society toward heterosexist norms. The ritual specialists were often young women but not just that: they had to transcend their cisgender donning of the hats and swords of Korean masculinity, flaunting personas such as flower boy warriors, Confucian sages, and even the Tan'gun Ruler and perform ritualized drag in their performances. Meanwhile, their male ritual attendants and spouses were characterized on the other side of the gender binary, as effeminate and impotent.[98] Often, ritual specialists did not enter into human marriage because they were married and tied to their guardian spirits. These women claimed to be bound to service their spiritual partners, a spiritual consummation that could determine the course of their material lives. Whether or not they stayed single, divorced, had sex (with members of the same or the opposite sex), or gave birth were decisions that had to be weighed against the will of their anthropomorphic spirits.[99] If guardian spirits did not want their spiritual hosts to engage in human marriages, the female ritualists did not see this lifestyle as their liberation from men but, rather, their burden to be bound to their difficult spirits. If they married, they did so with practitioners of other marginalized religions.[100] In turn, the print media disregarded these spiritual relationships and suspected shamans and their associates of sexual proclivities or improprieties.[101]

The media obsession with shamans overlapped with the colonial "woman problem," as both subjects were affecting the strength of the population.[102] Korean nationalists were primarily interested in "their" women bearing healthy children, and they believed that shamans hindered this national goal. Ironically, most ritual services aimed to support heteronormative expectations of family and reproduction. For instance, shamans were sometimes considered good matchmakers, or they gave referrals for people to find reputable matchmakers. Mothers sought out shamans to find suitable opposite-sex marriage partners for their children. To sever these networks, the *East Asia Daily* published an article in 1934 that hoped to "exterminate shamans and sorcerers" and "gather all fortune-tellers and matchmakers!" The article grouped people who told fortunes through ancestral tablets with those who told fortunes on marriages.[103] The *Chosŏn Chung'ang Ilbo* (Korea Central Daily) cautioned readers to be on the lookout for shamanic marriages. It told the story of a man and woman who were "engaged and on the eighth day of the tenth month in the lunar calendar at the bride's house . . . the wedding ceremony was conducted without incident. But then, around 9:00 PM the fact that the bridegroom was the son of a shaman was revealed, which greatly startled the bride's family and caused a huge disturbance. At that point, the bridegroom ran away."[104] The article implored readers to be vigilant of shaman offspring attempting to pursue "normal" lives, assuming that its readers already knew that such children allegedly inherited "abnormal" traits from their shaman mothers. The *East Asia Daily* believed that the "nation's health" was at risk because the police were not doing their job to recognize shamans as "unlawful" women.[105] The *East Asia Daily* also noted that "it is a fact that more women than men believe in" shamans.[106] But shaman clientele, and even the men associated with shamans, were characterized as "violent," "insane," "suicidal," and "murder[ous]." The *East Asia Daily* claimed that such abnormalities were either the cause or the effect of superstition. While newspapers fought to promote modern networks for marriage, they just as strongly believed in negative eugenics and birth control for shamans and their associates, who were labeled unhealthy stock.[107]

The shamanism issue collided with the woman question over the public campaign for "girls' education." The Korean media's steadfast position was that unqualified people such as female shamans acted as experts on "women's work," and this was a formula for social chaos. This new area of girls' education was mostly limited to two topics—home care and childcare—while organizations such as Sungsinin Chohap were training and licensing young women to practice professions outside the home. The *East Asia Daily* recorded an increase in well-paid shamans servicing "high homes and government officials" in the southwestern part of the peninsula: "Mudang, chŏmjaengi, sangjaengi, sajujaengi, chakmyŏngjaengi, etc., work by begging money out of the pockets of ignorant people. If we add these 1,489 men and 1,541 women in South Chŏlla Province together, the sum of 3,030 can be said to be big trouble."[108]

Through this type of work, women could become independently wealthy. The article suggested that these women had an "evil influence over the general public."[109] To resolve this problem, it suggested that young men's groups were best suited to research and advise the public on ways to eliminate this "new culture" generated by the Sungsinin Chohap.[110]

Conclusion

When negative depictions of shamans in the colonial media proliferated, why did shamans not write in their own defense? Until 1920, shamanic ritual specialists often organized informally, and even secretly, under constant threat of locally initiated criminalization.[111] Irrespective of which regime was in power, ritualists labored to enact permanent structural change while they expressed the importance of local, everyday struggles of resistance.[112] Social demand for shamans was high: when it was impossible to ask the patriarchs of empire, nation, or families to acknowledge human injustices, shamanic ritual became the only method of redress.[113] In fact, privileging performance over script may have caused a "worldmaking power of disidentification."[114]

The lack of self-authorship did not necessarily limit the shaman community. Its members were not silent, empty vessels, encoded into existence by others; as their organizing efforts show, they were active, public-social agents engaged in intimate economies, commodifying their spiritual activity as value-producing forms of exchange in the early twentieth century. Their refusal to engage in textual self-authorship may, in fact, have allowed them more room to create, mimic, mock, and shape-shift their political, gender, and spiritual identities while keeping police officers, technocrats, ethnographers, and patriarchal nationalists at bay. With their outlaw sensibilities, Sungsinin Chohap paraded through the front door of cultural policies during the 1920s, invigorating indigenous spiritual resistance.[115]

A final point on this colonial moment is one through which I intersect with other authors in this book in relation to straight time. The rhetoric of modernization promised a path of eventual national maturation. This colonialist linearity can be seen as a form of straight time.[116] In this sense, I would call ritual specialists' and cultural nationalists' asynchrony with modernity and refusal of progressivist history a queer phenomenon. The numerous ways in which indigenous rituals were performed and written shows capitalism's desynchronizing effects in concrete situations.[117] The media subjugated, marginalized, disavowed, and made illegitimate the experiences of indigenous ritual agents through a hegemonic development scheme. Just as ritual specialists could produce an alternative understanding of the past through a rearrangement of communal pleasure, historians of shamanism reframed popular historical consciousness in ways opposite to what Liu sees as "chrononormative organization of human bodies toward maximum productivity."[118] The adoptive spiritual community socialized its surrogate families and interethnic origins through elaborate rituals and ancient texts, often mirroring the most basic unit of traditionally patriarchal social organization, but sometimes straying from it, establishing a temporal asynchrony with modernity and a queer colonial time.

Notes

1   "Sowi sungsin kyohoe chohap sŏllip cha Kim Tae-ik," *Chosŏn Ilbo*, July 2, 1920, 3. Kim Tae-gon found otherwise that Kim Chae-hyŏn formed this group: Kim Tae-gon, *Han'guk musok yŏn'gu* (Seoul: Chipmundang, 1981), 456–57. Murayama Chijun also believed that Kim Chae-hyŏn founded the guild but dates its establishment to June 1, 1920. He argued that the 1920s was a "golden age" for shamans and their guild: Murayama Chijun, *Chōsen minzoku no kenkyū* (Seoul: Chōsen Sōtokufu, 1938).

2   *Hwarang* was listed among associates: *Tong'a Ilbo*, May 22, 1924, 3; *Chosŏn Ilbo*, July 5, 1938.

3   *Tong'a Ilbo*, March 24, 1923, 3; March 5, 1932, 3.

4   *Tong'a Ilbo* stated that the organization "practice[d] drums, folk instruments and woodwinds to the extent of devil worship in an established theatre and raised the curtain on unmentionable 'erotic pageant' performances; first wives go with husbands, many second wives go dressed in all types of attire": *Tong'a Ilbo*, March 5, 1932, 3.

5   *Tong'a Ilbo*, March 24, 1923, 3.

6   *Tong'a Ilbo*, February 11, 1922, 3; March 24, 1923, 3.

7   José Esteban Muñoz, *Cruising Utopia: The Then and There of Queer Futurity* (New York: New York University Press, 2009). Because such a conversation stems from my analytical imagination of the past, any misrepresentation of Muñoz or Liu's theories are my errors alone.

8   Yi Yong-bŏm, "Musok e taehan kŭndae Han'guk sahoe ŭi pujŏngjŏk sigak e taehan koch'al," *Han'guk Musokhak* 9 (February 2005): 151–79.

9   Petrus Liu, *Queer Marxism in Two Chinas* (Durham, NC: Duke University Press, 2015), 7, 9, 15.

10   Laurel Kendall, "Of Gods and Men: Performance, Possession, and Flirtation in Korean Shaman Ritual," *Cahiers d'Extrême-Asie* 6 (1991–92): 45–63.

11   For a good example of the argument toward broad-reaching heterosexism, see Gayle Rubin, "Thinking Sex: Notes for a Radical Theory of the Politics of Sexuality," in *Pleasure and Danger: Exploring Female Sexuality*, ed. Carol S. Vance (Boston: Routledge and Kegan Paul, 1984), 143–78. Laurel Kendall, by contrast, argues that gender and sexual fluidity are part and parcel of shamanic communities.

12   These primary source documents are held in the National Archives of South Korea: http://www.archives.go.kr. Takaya Kawase details this in his work on religion and academic movements in the colonial era. Taehoon Kim further elaborates that the 1906 policy was meant to regulate Japanese missionaries in Korea and that the subsequent policy applied more directly to Korean colonial subjects on the Korean peninsula. Taehoon Kim, "The Place of 'Religion' in Colonial Korea around 1910: The Imperial History of 'Religion,'" *Journal of Korean Religions* 1, no. 2 (2011): 28–30.

13   *Kisaeng* were commonly associated with brothels and prostitution and has derogatorily meant "whores." For more on how *kisaeng* were understood during the colonial period, see Yi Chae-hŏn, *Yi Nŭnghwa wa kŭndae pulgyohak* (Seoul: Chisik Sanŏpsa, 2007), 18.

14   Hŭng-yun Cho argues that the Japanese were unsuccessful at eliminating *mudang* activities from Korea because they were so pervasive. Instead, they worked at controlling and regulating them: Cho Hŭng-yun, *Mu wa minjok munhwa* (Seoul: Minjok Munhwasa, 2003), 212–13. See also Kim, *Han'guk musok yŏn'gu*, 45–57.

15   Until 1920, only 107 such shrines existed on the peninsula. Over the next ten years, 297 more shrines were unveiled: Michio Nakajima, "Shintō Deities That Crossed the Sea," *Japanese Journal of Religious Studies* 37, no. 1 (2010): 26, 29.

16   *Tong'a Ilbo*, October 3, 1929, 2.

17   *Tong'a Ilbo*, July 13, 1923, 3; May 22, 1924, 3.

18   As early as June of 1910, the *Taehan Maeil Sinbo* reported that a "Japanese man by the name of Kokkumushi formed a Sinri Religion and female shamans contributed five hwan each to him." This man disappeared with the money and the shamans were working with a southern regional police department to recover their money. *Taehan Maeil Sinbo*, June 26, 1910: 1.

19   *Tong'a Ilbo*, November 21, 1921, 1.

20   *Tong'a Ilbo*, May 22, 1924, 3.

21   *Tong'a Ilbo*, October 3, 1929, 2.

22   *Tong'a Ilbo*, October 3, 1929, 2–3.

23   Gi-wook Shin, *Ethnic Nationalism in Korea: Genealogy, Politics, and Legacy* (Stanford, CA: Stanford University Press, 2006), 44. For more on colonial religion policies, see Ch'oe Sŏk-yŏng, *Ilcheha musongnon kwa singminji kwŏllyŏk* (Seoul: Sŏgyŏng Munhwasa, 1999); Chang Pyŏng-gil, "Chosŏn ch'ongdokpu chonggyo

chŏngch'aek," in *Han'guk chonggyo wa chonggyohak* (Seoul: Ch'ŏngnyŏnsa, 2003), 217–33.

24 Kōji Ōsawa, "Kokusai bukkyō kyōkai to 'Toa bukkyō.'" Paper presented at the 19th World Congress of the International Association for the History of Religions, Tokyo, March 28, 2005, 66–78.

25 Chu Yŏng-ha, "Chosŏn ŭi chesa wa sahoe kyohwaron," in *Cheguk Ilbon i kŭrin Chosŏn minsok*, ed. Chu Yŏng-ha, Im Kyŏng-t'aek, and Nam Kŭn-u (Sŏngnam: Han'gukhak Chungang Yŏungang Yŏn'guwŏn, 2006), 162.

26 Buddhist historians have argued that no other East Asian religious order collaborated more with Japanese imperial policies than did Buddhists (all Mahayana sects, including Southeast Asian Theraveda sects in the late 1930s): Kawase Takaya, "Jōdo-Shinshu no Chōsen fukyō: Bunmeika no shimei?" Paper presented at the 19th World Congress of the International Association for the History of Religions, Tokyo, March 28, 2005, 35.

27 Indigenous theism broadly termed *sin'gyo*.

28 Most religious journals conveniently positioned themselves in opposition to these silent shamans (often using superstition, or *misin*, in their binary arguments), revealing their own unstable distance from those indigenous practices. The monthly *Our House* reiterated a common enlightenment notion that "it is difficult to judge superstition as religion." It then asked, "What is superstition? . . . [I]t can be said to be an unreasonable faith . . . from one religion to another, all have superstition": Kim Chong-man, *Urijip* 8 (Fall 1932): 12.

29 Chun-sŏk (Mishinhae), "Solution to superstition," Ch'ŏndokyohŏewolbo 7 (February 1911): 22. This monthly bulletin was one of a number of journals that periodically associated with the colonial-era Tonghak movement: See Sin Il-ch'ŏl, *Tonghak sasang ŭi ihae* (Seoul: Sahoe Pip'yŏngsinsŏ, 1995), 169–84. See also Kwangshik Kim, "Buddhist Perspectives on Anti-religious Movements in the 1930s," *The Review of Korean Studies* 3, no. 1 (July 2000): 58.

30 Kwang-sik Kim, "Panjonggyo undong e taehan kwanch'al," *Kaebyŏk*, November 1925, 2. *Kyŏnghyang Chapji* was a Catholic magazine that published regular reports by the Roman Catholic Church and engaged in stories of irrational shamans.

31 Michael Robinson argues that "finessed" rule was a method for deeper and broader surveillance during the cultural rule period: Michael Robinson, "Broadcasting, Cultural Hegemony, and Colonial Modernity in Korea, 1924–1945," in *Colonial Modernity in Korea*, ed. Gi-Wook Shin and Michael Robinson (Cambridge, MA: Harvard University Press, 1999), 52–69.

32 *Tong'a Ilbo* argued that a Japanese expatriate, Komine Kensaku, working under the Korean alias Kim Chae-hyon, was the founder of Sungsinin Chohap. *Tong'a Ilbo*, May 30, 1920. See also note 1.

33 Todd Henry finds that indigenous deities were gradually incorporated into Seoul Shrine and its grand festival in 1929 and that Korean participation was not compulsory before the 1930s. "Even after the administrative reordering of Keijō and its

parish organization, Seoul Shrine's ethnocentric leadership continued to undercut the Government-General's officially stated goal of spiritual assimilation": Todd A. Henry, *Assimilating Seoul: Japanese Rule and the Politics of Public Space in Colonial Korea, 1910–1945* (Berkeley: University of California Press, 2014), 66.

34 For more on colonial religious assimilation, see Ryu Sŏng-min, "Ilje kangjŏmgi ŭi Han'guk chonggyo minjokjuŭi," in *Han Il kŭnhyŏndae wa chonggyo munhwa,* ed. Ryu Pyŏng-dŏk and the Korea-Japan Religion Research Forum (Seoul: Ch'ŏngnyŏnsa, 2001), 171–76.

35 Kim Tae-gon, "Regional Characteristics of Korean Shamanism," in *Shamanism: The Spirit World of Korea,* ed. Yu Chai-shin and R. Guisso, trans. Yi Yu-jin (Berkeley: Asian Humanities, 1988), 119.

36 For more on ancient religious melding of Korean shamanism and Mahayana Buddhism, see Hyun-key Kim Hogarth, "Rationality, Practicality and Modernity: Buddhism, Shamanism and Christianity in Contemporary Korean Society," *Transactions of the Royal Asiatic Society, Korea Branch* 73 (1998): 41–54.

37 For more on Korean shamanism sharing Taoistic characteristics, see Yu Chai-shin, "Korean Taoism and Shamanism," in Yu and Guisso, *Shamanism,* 98–118.

38 Shaman regulations were enforced by the Chosŏn state from the seventeenth century onward. But shaman semiofficial alliances were formed as early as the eighteenth century and continued to evolve through the twentieth century: Im Hak-sŏng, "Chosŏn hugi hojŏk charyo rŭl t'onghae pon Kyŏngsangdo mudang ŭi 'muŏp sesŭp yangt'ae: 17–19 segi Tansŏnghyŏn ŭi sarye punsŏk," *Han'guk Musokhak* 9 (February 2005): 47–75.

39 Seoul's Tongmyo (Eastern Shrine) is a good example of this. The legendary Chinese Commander Guan Yu (162–219), recognized as a war hero from the civil war that collapsed China's Eastern Han Dynasty, became a popular Taoist deity during the Ming. Guan Yu shrines were erected in Chosŏn to symbolize Korea's appreciation of the Middle Kingdom. In late Chosŏn, these shrines fell into disfavor, but Korean shamans have embraced the deity, turning him into an entrepreneur guardian spirit who continues to draw an annual celebration among street peddlers in Seoul today. I thank Jun Y. K. Kim of the Royal Asiatic Society Korea Branch for conducting this tour on April 13, 2016.

40 For more on historical tax incentives, see Kyung Moon Hwang, *Beyond Birth: Social Status in the Emergence of Modern Korea* (Cambridge, MA: Harvard University Asia Center, 2004). On the physical boundaries for shaman activity, see Boudewijn Walraven, "Interpretations and Reinterpretations of Popular Religion in the Last Decades of the Chosŏn Dynasty," in *Korean Shamanism: Revivals, Survivals, and Change,* ed. Keith Howard (Seoul: Royal Asiatic Society, Korea Branch, 1998), 55–72.

41 Sŏ Yang-ja, "Chosŏn sidae ŭi musok," *Kyŏnghyang Chapji* 1386, September 1983, 46–49.

42 The terms "shamanism studies" and *musokhak* emerged under colonialism.

43 Isabella Bishop noted that shaman and sorcerer "guilds . . . are the Trades Unions of Korea, and the Government has imposed registration on another class": Isa-

bella Bird Bishop, *Korea and Her Neighbours: A Narrative of Travel, with an Account of the Recent Vicissitudes and Present Position of the Country*, repr. ed. (Seoul: Yonsei University Press, [1898] 1970), 402.

44 Various chapters such as the Chehwa Church, Sinri Church, Sŏnghwa Church, and Yŏngsin Organization emerged throughout the 1920s: Kim, *Han'guk musok yŏn'gu*, 456–57.

45 Although state Shintō policy was unique to 1930s colonial rule, unregulated Shintō was a minor practice in Korea for nearly three hundred years. The first Japanese Shintō shrine, the Kindo Shrine, was established in 1678 (the fourth year of Sukjong) in Pusan, Korea. The most popular Shintō sect in Korea was known as the Tenri Church. The Tenri denomination of Shintō gained the first substantial number of Korean converts in 1893 and it had grown to nearly eighty thousand members by the end of the colonial period: Duk-whang Kim, *A History of Religions in Korea* (Seoul: Daeji Monhwa-sa, 1988), 431–34.

46 Commission dates for Ch'oe Nam-sŏn were from 1928 to 1936 and for Yi Nŭng-hwa from 1922 to 1938. This project was criticized for shortening Korean history to begin with the Three Kingdoms period (57 BCE–668 CE) and for glossing over events that led to colonialism, such as the Sino-Japanese War of 1894–95.

47 Roger Janelli, "The Origins of Korean Folklore Scholarship," *Journal of American Folklore* 99 (1986): 24–49.

48 Muñoz, *Cruising Utopia*, 31.

49 Hyung Il Pai, *Constructing Korean "Origins": A Critical Review of Archaeology, Historiography, and Racial Myth in Korean State-Formation Theories*, Harvard East Asian Monographs Series (Cambridge, MA: Harvard Asia Center, 2000), 8–9.

50 Chizuko Allen finds Ch'oe's religious writings a strong testament to his antico-lonial efforts: see Chizuko T. Allen, "Ch'oe Namsŏn at the Height of Japanese Imperialism," *Sungkyun Journal of East Asian Studies* 5, no. 1 (2005): 27–49. Kim Seong-Nae further argues that shamanism research developed as "intellectual nationalist self-consciousness" under colonialism: Kim Seong-Nae, "Han'guk ŭi syamŏnijŭm kaenyŏm hyŏngsŏng kwa chŏn'gae," *Han'guk Syamŏnijŭm Hakhŏe* (2003): 87–88. Also see her "Ilje sidae musok tamron ŭi hyŏngsŏng kwa kundaejŏk chaehyon," in *Chonggyowa singminji Kŭndae*, ed. Yun Hae-dong and Isomae Junicho (Seoul: Chaekgwa Hamkke), 347–89. (I use Kim Seong-Nae's preferred romanization of her name.)

51 For more on Korea's precolonial continental scholarship, see Andre Schmid, "Rediscovering Manchuria: Sin Ch'aeho and the Politics of Territorial History in Korea," *Journal of Asian Studies* 56, no. 1 (February 1997): 26–46.

52 For starters, he introduces the transliterated word "shaamanijŭm" to present a new "shamanism" framework to understand Korea's global history.

53 Siobhan Somerville expressed how George Chauncey discussed paradigms of sexuality that shifted according to changing ideologies of gender in the late nineteenth century: Siobhan Somerville, "Scientific Racism and the Invention of the Homosexual Body," in *The Gender Sexuality Reader: Culture, History, Political*

Economy, ed. Roger N. Lancaster and Micaela di Leonardo (New York: Routledge, 1997), 37.

54 In the years following his committee tenure, Ch'oe was deterred from nationalist projects but he continued to advance the language reform movement, publishing widely on Korean literature, history, and culture.

55 For more on this shared origin theory and Japanese assimilationism, see Ch'oe Sŏk-yŏng, *Ilche ŭi tonghwa ideollogi ŭi ch'angch'ul* (Seoul: Sŏgyŏng Munhwasa, 1997).

56 An entire issue of *Enlightenment Bulletin* (*Kyemyŏng Sibo*) was dedicated to shamanism studies as his contribution to Korea's ancient literature. The issue was broken into two sections. Ch'oe wrote the first section to provide a broad overview of global indigenous practices. The most notable characteristic of his essay "Records on Shamanism" (*Sarman'gyo ch'aki*) was its attempt to field shamanism research comprehensively: Ch'oe Nam-sŏn, "Sarmŏn kyoch'aki," *Kyemyŏng Sibo*, vol. 19, 1927, 3–51.

57 Ch'oe, "Sarmŏn kyoch'aki," 1–3. He explored the historical origins behind the homonym *syaamŏn*, outlining possible meanings behind its various transliterations, its original practices, and the gender differences among practitioners. Each practitioner was described according to epistemology, sacred articles, types of ceremonies, and social status within a shamanism hierarchy.

58 Ch'oe, "Sarmŏn kyoch'aki," 3. Edward Tylor believed that cultural survival was a phenomenon of modernity as a "survival and a revival of savage thought, which the general tendency of civilization and science has been to discard" and that "spiritualism was a 'survival' that should not find believers among the middle- and upper-classes, only among the lower." See Birgit Meyer and Peter Pels, eds., *Magic and Modernity: Interfaces of Revelation and Concealment* (Stanford, CA: Stanford University Press, 2003), 256–57.

59 While the term "transgender" is a direct translation of the primary text, I believe that gender is a social construction that arises from what medical specialists consider biological sex, but that gender operates at individual, social, institutional, and historical levels. What people see of a person's sex or gender (what Tauches refers to as "secondary sex characteristics") act as important symbols of gender attribution: Kimberly Tauches, "Transgendering: Challenging the 'Normal,'" in *Handbook of the New Sexuality Studies*, ed. Steven Seidman, Nancy Fischer, and Chet Meeks (New York: Taylor and Francis, 2007), 186–92.

60 "Transgender" is typically used as an umbrella term to describe people whose gender does not match the sex category they are assigned at birth. My research suggests that the term "transgender" is anachronistic to colonial Korea. However, my sources use terms such as "change of sex" and "sex change" to explain a history and society of "homosexualism." They apply early ethnographic models and taxonomies of "rites of passage" as "traditional" institutions that determined people's identities and social roles. Ch'oe considers gender and sexuality based on environmental determinism.

61 Ch'oe mentions *ch'eryangsŏng*, implying the changing of sex leads to sexual intercourse between cisgender men. Ch'oe, "Sarmŏn kyoch'aki," 3.

62 Ch'oe uses the term "change of sex" (*sŏng ŭi pyŏngyŏng*) to imply that gender reassignment was done in some mysterious shamanic ceremonial initiation. Ch'oe, "Sarmŏn kyoch'aki," 3.

63 Kristen Schilt and Laurel Westbrook attempt to decenter heteronormativity by replacing the concept of "non-normative" with "cis" as the etymological antonym of "trans": Kristen Schilt and Laurel Westbrook, "Doing Gender, Doing Heteronormativity: " 'Gender Normals,' " Transgender People, and the Social Maintenance of Heterosexuality," *Gender and Society* 23, no. 4 (August 2009): 440–64. Instead of calling these people "male-to-female shamans" or by the original ethnographic term "soft men," I credit their spiritual guardians and communities for their successful transitions. For lack of a better term, I refer to them as "trans-spiritualists."

64 "Change" in this case is permanent and could be considered "trans." Ch'oe, "Sarmŏn kyoch'aki," 3.

65 Armchair researchers such as Ch'oe tended to reject trans-spiritualists as women, discounting their successful transitions and their contributions to the cisgender societies that their spiritual communities embraced.

66 For more on his Buddhism publications, see Jongmyung Kim, "Yi Nunghwa, Buddhism, and the Modernization of Korea: A Critical Review," in *Makers of Modern Korean Buddhism*, ed. Jin Y. Park (Albany: State University of New York Press, 2010), 91–106.

67 Yi was more than twenty years Ch'oe's senior and lived most of his life under a deteriorating Chosŏn Dynasty. He may have been more politically conservative than his co-author, but with extensive years under Confucian schooling, he was arguably the best equipped to preserve Korea's ancient textual history, which he did throughout his life. For a general overview of Yi Nŭng-hwa's life, see Yi Nŭng-hwa, *Chosŏn haeŏ hwasa*, repr. ed., ed. Yi Chaegon (Seoul: Paengnok, [1927] 1992), 3–4.

68 Much has been written on the Tan'gun research during the colonial era. For a most interesting study on Tan'gun as an indigenous trope in "shamanism discourse" during the Japanese colonial era, see Kim Seong-Nae, "Ilje sidae musok tamron ŭi hyŏngsŏng kwa kŭndaejŏk chaehyŏn," in *Chonggyo wa singminji kŭndae*, ed. Yun Hae-dong and Isomae Junichi (Seoul: Ch'aek kwa Hamkkae, 2013), 347–89.

Yi states, "It has been said that Hwan-ŭwa, the God of Heaven, and Tan'gun Ruler were spirits that came down from the heavens and they were humans with divinity. In the olden days, shamans received the people's respect because they made sacrifices to the heavens and worshipped the spirits. Accordingly, the titles of Silla Kings reflected this and in Koguryŏ, their titles became those of master shamans." For this passage, he does not make references to sources to document the Tan'gun Ruler (*Tan'gun Wanggŏm*) legends. This may have originated from textual sources, but this is not cited in his work: Yi Nŭng-hwa, "Chosŏn musokko," *Kyemyŏng Sibo*, vol. 19, 1927, 10.

69　Yi was among several Korean scholars inspired by recent archeological dis-coveries of Unified Silla Dynasty (668–935 CE) artifacts that erupted a new subfield of "Tan'gun studies." Yi's contemporaries Sin Ch'ae-ho and Ch'oe Nam-sŏn wrote most prolifically on Tan'gun studies, but it should be noted that scholars have discussed the Tan'gun origin story for hundreds of years. For instance, Yi Ik, the famous reform scholar from the seventeenth century, ex-plored the sacred geography of Paektu Mountain and surrounding environs as the birthplace of Tan'gun: Yi Ik, *Sŏngho sasŏl*, trans. Ch'oe Sŏk-ki, 2d repr. ed. (Seoul: Han'gilsa, 2002), 54–59. A new religion surrounding Tan'gun (known as Tan'gungyo and Taejonggyo) was created in 1909. For more on this religion, see Cho Hŭng-yun, *Han'guk chonggyo munhwaron* (Seoul: Hyŏndae Sinsŏ, 2002), 200–221.

70　Yi Nŭng-hwa, "Chosŏn musokko," *Kyemyŏng Sibo*, vol. 19, 1927, 10.

71　*Ch'ach'aung* meant "venerable elders." For this, Yi studied the *Records of the Three Kingdoms* (*Samguk sagi*).

72　Yi Nŭng-hwa, "Chosŏn musokko," *Kyemyŏng Sibo*, vol. 19, 1927, 10.

73　Yi's shamanism research borrowed from a number of studies on *hwarang* that had already been published by the time of his treatise in 1927, including in his own writings on *Chibong yusŏl*, in Chŏng Yak-yŏng's *Aŏn kakpi*, and in Yi Kyu-kyŏng's *Mugyŏk pyŏnjungsŏl*, showing that this was a popular topic throughout the 1920s, as well: Yi Su-kwang, *Chibong yusŏl*, ed. Nam Man-sŏng (Seoul: Ŭ Se Munhwasa, 1994).

74　Kim, "Yi Nunghwa, Buddhism, and the Modernization of Korea," 2010.

75　The year 1513 CE was the eighth of Chungjong's reign: Yi Nŭng-hwa, "Chosŏn musokko," 17. Yi uses this and another court record from 1503 to introduce two categories of male shamans he variously phoneticizes as *rangjung*. He notes that they are sometimes also referred to as *hwarang*.

76　Hyaeweol Choi, *New Women in Colonial Korea: A Sourcebook* (New York: Rout-ledge, 2013), 13.

77　Muñoz, *Cruising Utopia*, 34.

78　Do-Hyun Han, "Shamanism, Superstition, and the Colonial Government," *Review of Korean Studies* 3, no. 1 (2000): 36. For a more nuanced treatment of colonialist rhetoric and strategies pertaining to shamans, see Ch'oe Sŏk-yŏng, *Ilcheha musongnon kwa singminji kwŏllyŏk* (Seoul: Sŏgyŏng Munhwasa, 1999).

79　*Tong'a Ilbo*, March 24, 1923, 3. *Tong'a Ilbo* also reported that Sungsinin Chohap held eight thousand "shamans who belong to associations" and claimed that they were "controlled by the Japanese." This argument that Japanese settlers were importing shamanism into Korea is not a new one. Nearly two decades earlier, in the dawn of the colonial era, the *Taehan Maeil Sinbo* often made similar charges. For the remainder of this section, I leave the term *mudang* untranslated to specify the type and present them within an array of ritual specialists (at the end of this section) as mentioned in these newspapers.

80 The dailies heavily targeted Sungsinin for its voluntary displays of devotion at this shrine. Amaterasu Ōmikami was the most prevalent enshrined deity, followed by Emperor Meiji and Kunitama no Ōmikami: Nakajima, "Shintō Deities That Crossed the Sea," 34. For the most thorough treatment of Shintō assimilationism, see Todd A. Henry, "Spiritual Assimilation: Namsan's Shintō Shrines and Their Festival Celebrations," in Henry, *Assimilating Seoul*, 62–91.

81 *Tong'a Ilbo*, October 3, 1929, 2.

82 As defined by Judith [Jack] Halberstam, a "Drag King is a performer who makes masculinity into his or her act (yes, there can be male Drag Kings). The Drag King may make costume into the whole of her performance, or s/he may lip synch or play air guitar or tell crude jokes about 'girlies' and 'homos'": Judith [Jack] Halberstam and Del LaGrace Volcano, *The Drag King Book* (London: Serpent's Tail, 1999), 36.

83 These two were the most commonly worshipped Shintō deities throughout the Japanese colonies.

84 *Tong'a Ilbo*, October 3, 1929, 2. See also Cho Hŭng-yun, *Mu wa minjok munhwa*, 212.

85 Michael Peletz discusses "ritual transvestism" in Southeast Asia in much the same way that I do here, as methods for women's autonomy, social control, ritual transvestism, gender transgression and transgender, and so on: see Michael Peletz, *Gender Pluralism: Southeast Asia since Early Modern Times* (New York: Routledge, 2009).

86 Post-1945 rituals sometimes invoked spirits such as that of General Douglas MacArthur in ceremonies that directly challenged the U.S. Army Military Government in Korea. In a similar vein, during the postwar years of the 1970s, the Korean Anti-Communist Worshipping Association was organized to appeal to the South Korean Cold War regime: Kim, "Regional Characteristics of Korean Shamanism," 119.

87 Homi Bhabha, "Of Mimicry and Man: The Ambivalence of Colonial Discourse," in *The Location of Culture* (New York: Routledge), 121–31.

88 Muñoz, *Cruising Utopia*, 55; Judith Butler, *Gender Trouble: Feminism and the Subversion of Identity* (New York: Routledge, 1990), 174. Snjezana Zoric has made a similar argument of *dodangje*, a Confucian state ancestor ritual that Korean shamans incorporated into their ritual performances when it was officially banned during the colonial period: Snjezana Zoric, "The Magic of Performance in Korean Shamanic Ritual—*Gut*," in *The Ritual Year 10: Magic in Rituals and Rituals in Magic*, ed. Tatiana Minniyakhmetova and Kamila Velkoborska (Tartu, Estonia: Innsbruck, 2015), 374–75.

89 Butler's model of gender performance and Bhaba's concepts of colonial hybridity and mimicry help me understand Korean shamans in Shintō drag as a form of colonial resistance: Butler, *Gender Trouble*; Homi Bhabha, "Remembering Fanon: Self, Psyche and the Colonial Condition," in *Colonial Discourse and Post-colonial Theory: A Reader*, ed. Patrick Williams and Laura Chrisman (New York: Columbia University Press, 1994), 112–24.

90   Halberstam's point that "excessive masculinity turns into a parody or exposure of the norm" helps me see these colonized communities experimenting with colonizer fantasies for their own self-empowerment: Judith [Jack] Halberstam, *Female Masculinity* (Durham, NC: Duke University Press, 1998), 3–4.

91   For examples of other types of syncretism, see Yu, "Korean Taoism and Shamanism."

92   An example of the prior is *Tong'a Ilbo,* December 16, 1927, 5.

93   Cho Hŭng-yun, *Mu wa minjok munhwa,* 212–13, 225.

94   Murayama Chijun's office oversaw the enforcement of public hygiene laws that monitored unsanctioned medical practices such as shamanic ritual for healing. "According to the colonial police, shamans violated the medical law": Han, "Shamanism, Superstition, and the Colonial Government," 42.

95   It is unclear whether they secretly performed private ceremonies, which may have been in violation of local ordinances.

96   *Tong'a Ilbo,* March 24, 1923, 3.

97   A good example of shamans' social trials for not conforming to heteronormative society is in Laurel Kendall, *The Life and Hard Times of a Korean Shaman: Of Tales and the Telling of Tales* (Honolulu: University of Hawai'i Press, 1988).

98   Travel writers such as Bishop made age-old comments about effeminized men who married or associated with shamans as types to "live in idleness on the earnings of his wife": Bishop, *Korea and Her Neighbours,* 423, 425.

99   The *Chosŏn Chung'ang Ilbo* (Korea Central Daily) was "dumbfounded" by a marriage "scandal" between a Buddhist monk and a female shaman. It warned "everywhere eyes are on the look-out for similar kinds of head monks," April 19, 1935, 7.

100 It claimed, "In Taedongkunbam, a Buddhist man by the pseudonym Yun Sŏk-han, the head monk of Tut'a temple, took a female *mudang,* Chŏng Nyŏ-hwa, as his wife": *Chungang Ilbo,* April 19, 1935, 7.

101 Whenever female shamans were involved with male spiritualists, journalists reveled in lambasting women's spiritual sexual perversion by attaching unfeminine and unvirtuous traits to these ritual specialists. Anne McClintock refers to writings on the sexualization of colonial subjects as "pornotropics": Anne McClintock, *Imperial Leather: Race, Gender, and Sexuality in the Colonial Contest* (New York: Routledge, 1995), 22.

102 On the "woman question," see Choi, *New Women in Colonial Korea.* See also Yun Nan-ji, "Musok kwa yŏsŏng e kwanhan Ilyŏn'gu (master's thesis, Ehwa Womans University, Seoul, 1978).

103 *Tong'a Ilbo,* March 3, 1934, 6.

104 *Chosŏn Chung'ang Ilbo,* November 27, 1934.

105 It also claimed that the chief of police in North Chŏlla Province was in cahoots with shamans: *Tong'a Ilbo,* May 17, 1921, 3. For another example, see November 21, 1921, 1.

106 Kim, Chong-man, *Urijip* 8 (Fall 1932): 12.

107 In the 1920s, Korean newspapers increasingly discussed women's reproductive roles in relation to the colonial population. On the "motherhood discourse," see

Chŏn Mi-gyŏng, "1920 30 yŏndae 'mosŏng tamnon' e kwanhan yŏn'gu: 'Sinyŏsŏng' e nat'anan ŏmŏni kyoyugŭl chungsim ŭro," *Han'guk Kajŏng kwa Kyoyuk Hakhoeji* 17, no. 2 (June 2005): 95–112. On women and colonial labor, see Chŏng Chin-sŏng, "Singminji chabonjuŭihwa kwajŏng esŏ ui yŏsŏng nodong ŭi pyŏnmo," *Han'guk Yŏan'guk* 4 (1988): 49–100.

108 Primary sources referenced in the order mentioned are *Tong'a Ilbo*, June 26, 1929, 2; October 3, 1929, 2; April 9, 1922, 3; and March 5, 1932, 3.

109 *Tong'a Ilbo* (Kwangju Branch), November 11, 1933, 3.

110 *Tong'a Ilbo*, July 13, 1923, 3.

111 For more on laws created explicitly to oppress shamanism, see Martina Deuchler, *The Confucian Transformation of Korea: A Study of Society and Ideology*, Yenching Institute Monograph Series (Cambridge, MA: Harvard University Press, 1992), 260.

112 For more on shamanism as a part of colonial collaborationist politics, see Kang Yŏng-si, *Ilje sigi kŭndaejŏk ilsang kwa singminji munhwa* (Seoul: Ehwa Women's University Press, 2008), 161.

113 Much of Kim Seong-Nae's work illustrates this point. She has worked with shaman communities on redress and reparations from the 1948 Cheju Massacre.

114 Muñoz argues that performance is a ritual of transformation and that these transformations may induce political reformulation: José Esteban Muñoz, *Disidentifications: Queers of Color and the Performance of Politics* (Minneapolis: University of Minnesota Press, 1999), x, xiv, 13.

115 In 1928, a year after *Treatise on Korean Shamanism* was published, Ch'oe Nam-sŏn and Yi Nŭng-hwa were appointed to the Committee on the Investigation of Korean Antiquities. A few years later, Sungsinin Chohap dissolved as quickly and mysteriously as it had emerged: Kim Tae-gon, "Han'guk musok yon'gusa sŏsul pangsik e taehayŏ," *Pigyo Minsok Hakhoe* 1, no. 12 (1995): 455–58.

116 In his gorgeous book *Cruising Utopia: The Then and There of Queer Futurity*, Muñoz argues that, "to live inside straight time and ask for, desire, and imagine another time and place is to represent and perform a desire that is both utopian and queer." I would stress that while *mudang* grapple in the business of the past, their peculiar temporality is queer time—a creative return to the past that historicizes through a dialectical injunction, one that offers potentiality, promise, ecstasy, and a utopian horizon: Muñoz, *Cruising Utopia*, 26–28.

117 Liu, *Queer Marxism in Two Chinas*, 120.

118 Liu, *Queer Marxism in Two Chinas*, 123.

Works Cited

NEWSPAPERS AND MAGAZINES

Chosŏn Ilbo
Chosŏn Chung'ang Ilbo
Kaebyŏk

Kyemyŏng Sibo
Kyŏnghyang Chapji
Taehan Maeil Sinbo
Tong'a Ilbo
Urijip

KOREAN- AND JAPANESE-LANGUAGE SOURCES

Chang Pyŏng-gil. "Chosŏn ch'ongdokpu chonggyo chŏngch'aek." In *Han'guk chonggyo wa chonggyohak*, 217–33. Seoul: Ch'ŏngnyŏnsa, 2003.

Cho Hŭng-yun. *Han'guk chonggyo munhwaron*. Seoul: Hyŏndae Sinsŏ, 2002.

Cho Hŭng-yun. *Mu wa minjok munhwa*. Seoul: Minjok Munhwasa, 2003.

Ch'oe Sŏk-yŏng. *Ilcheha musongnon kwa singminji kwŏllyŏk*. Seoul: Sŏgyŏng Munhwasa, 1999.

Ch'oe Sŏk-yŏng. *Ilche ŭi tonghwa ideollogi ŭi ch'angch'ul*. Seoul: Sŏgyŏng Munhwasa, 1997.

Chŏn Mi-gyŏng. "1920 30 yŏndae 'mosŏng tamnon' e kwanhan yŏn'gu: 'sinyŏsŏng' e nat'anan ŏmŏni kyoyugŭl chungsim ŭro." *Han'guk Kajŏng kwa Kyoyuk Hakhoeji* 17, no. 2 (June 2005): 95–112.

Chŏng Chin-sŏng. "Singminji chabonjuŭi wa kwajŏng esŏ ŭi yŏsŏng nodong ŭi pyŏnmo." *Han'guk Yŏsŏnghak* 4 (1988): 49–100.

Chu Yŏng-ha. "Chosŏn ŭi chesa wa sahoe kyohwaron." In *Cheguk Ilbon i kŭrin Chosŏn minsok*, ed. Chu Yŏng-ha, Im Kyŏng-t'aek, and Nam Kŭn-u, 157–198. Sŏngnam: Han'gukhak Chungang Yŏn'guwŏn, 2006.

Im Hak-sŏng. "Chosŏn hugi hojŏk charyo rŭl t'onghae pon Kyŏngsangdo mudang ŭi 'muŏp sesŭp yangt'ae: 17–19 segi Tansŏnghyŏn ŭi sarye punsŏk." *Han'guk Musokhak* 9 (February 2005): 47–75.

Kang Yŏng-si. *Ilje sigi kŭndaejŏk ilsang kwa singminji munhwa*. Seoul: Ehwa Women's University Press, 2008.

Kim Seong-Nae. "Han'guk ŭi syamŏnijŭm kaenyŏm hyŏngsŏng kwa chŏn'gae." *Han'guk Syamŏnijŭm Hakhŏe* (2003): 85–124.

Kim Seong-Nae. "Ilje sidae musok tamron ŭi hyŏngsŏng kwa kŭndaejŏk chaehyŏn." In *Chonggyo wa singminji kŭndae*, ed. Yun Hae-dong and Isomae Junichi, 347–389. Seoul: Ch'aek kwa Hamkkae, 2013.

Kim Tae-gon. *Han'guk musok yŏn'gu*. Seoul: Chipmundang, 1981.

Kim Tae-gon. "Han'guk musok yŏn'gusa sŏsul pangsik e taehayŏ." *Pigyo Minsok Hakhoe* 12 (1995): 455–58.

Murayama Chijun. *Chōsen minzoku no kenkyū*. Seoul: Chōsen Sōtokufu, 1938.

Ōsawa, Kōji. "Kokusai bukkyō kyōkai to 'Toa bukkyō.'" Paper presented at the 19th World Congress of the International Association for the History of Religions, Tokyo, March 28, 2005, 66–78.

Ryu Sŏng-min. "Ilje kangjŏmgi ŭi Han'guk chonggyo minjokjuŭi." In *Han Il kŭnhyŏndae wa chonggyo munhwa*, eds. Ryu Pyŏng-dŏk and the Korea-Japan Religion Research Forum, 171–89. Seoul: Ch'ŏngnyŏnsa, 2001.

Sin Il-ch'ŏl. *Tonghak sasang ŭi ihae*. Seoul: Sahoe Pip'yŏngsinsŏ, 1995.

Takaya, Kawase. "Jōdo-Shinshu no Chōsen fukyō: Bunmeika no shimei?" Paper presented at the 19th World Congress of the International Association for the History of Religions, Tokyo, March 28, 2005.

Yi Chae-hŏn. *Yi Nŭnghwa wa kŭndae pulgyohak*. Seoul: Chisik Sanŏpsa, 2007.

Yi Ik. *Sŏngho sasŏl*, trans. Ch'oe Sŏk-ki, 2d repr. ed. Seoul: Han'gilsa, 2002.

Yi Nŭng-hwa. *Chosŏn hageŏ hwasa*, repr. ed., ed. Yi Chaegon. Seoul: Paengnok, [1927] 1992.

Yi Su-kwang. *Chibong yusŏl*, 2 vols., ed. Nam Man-sŏng. Seoul: Ŭlyu Munhwasa, 1994.

Yi Yong-bŏm. "Musok e taehan kŭndae Han'guk sahoe ŭi pujŏngjŏk sigak e taehan koch'al." *Han'guk Musokhak* 9 (February 2005): 151–79.

Yun Nan-ji. "Musok kwa yŏsŏng e kwanhan Ilyŏn'gu." Master's thesis, Ehwa Womans University, Seoul, 1978.

ENGLISH-LANGUAGE SOURCES

Allen, Chizuko. "Ch'oe Namsŏn at the Height of Japanese Imperialism." *Sungkyun Journal of East Asian Studies* 5, no. 1 (2005): 27–49.

Bhabha, Homi. "Of Mimicry and Man: The Ambivalence of Colonial Discourse." In *The Location of Culture*, 121–31. New York: Routledge, 2004.

Bhabha, Homi. "Remembering Fanon: Self, Psyche and the Colonial Condition." In *Colonial Discourse and Post-colonial Theory: A Reader*, ed. Patrick Williams and Laura Chrisman, 112–24. New York: Columbia University Press, 1994.

Bishop, Isabella Bird. *Korea and Her Neighbours: A Narrative of Travel, with an Account of the Recent Vicissitudes and Present Position of the Country*, repr. ed. Seoul: Yonsei University Press, [1898] 1970.

Butler, Judith. *Gender Trouble: Feminism and the Subversion of Identity*. New York: Routledge, 1990.

Choi, Hyaeweol. *New Women in Colonial Korea: A Sourcebook*. New York: Routledge, 2013.

Deuchler, Martina. *The Confucian Transformation of Korea: A Study of Society and Ideology*. Yenching Institute Monograph Series. Cambridge, MA: Harvard University Press, 1992.

Halberstam, Judith [Jack], and Del LaGrace Volcano. *The Drag King Book*. London: Serpent's Tail, 1999.

Halberstam, Judith [Jack], *Female Masculinity*. Durham, NC: Duke University Press, 1998.

Han, Do-Hyun. "Shamanism, Superstition, and the Colonial Government." *Review of Korean Studies* 3, no. 1 (July 2000): 34–54.

Henry, Todd A. *Assimilating Seoul: Japanese Rule and the Politics of Public Space in Colonial Korea, 1910–1945*. Berkeley: University of California Press, 2014.

Hwang, Kyung Moon. *Beyond Birth: Social Status in the Emergence of Modern Korea*. Cambridge, MA: Harvard University Asia Center, 2004.

Janelli, Roger. "The Origins of Korean Folklore Scholarship." *Journal of American Folklore* 99 (1986): 24–49.

Kendall, Laurel. *The Life and Hard Times of a Korean Shaman: Of Tales and the Telling of Tales*. Honolulu: University of Hawai'i Press, 1988.

Kendall, Laurel. "Of Gods and Men: Performance, Possession, and Flirtation in Korean Shaman Ritual." *Cahiers d'Extrême-Asie* 6 (1991–92): 45–63.

Kim, Duk-whang. *A History of Religions in Korea*. Seoul: Daeji Monhwa-sa, 1988.

Kim, Jongmyung. "Yi Nunghwa, Buddhism, and the Modernization of Korea: A Critical Review." In *Makers of Modern Korean Buddhism*, ed. Jin Y. Park, 91–106. Albany: State University of New York Press, 2010.

Kim, Kwangshik. "Buddhist Perspectives on Anti-religious Movements in the 1930s." *The Review of Korean Studies* 3, no. 1 (July 2000): 58.

Kim Tae-gon. "Regional Characteristics of Korean Shamanism." In *Shamanism: The Spirit World of Korea*, ed. Chai-shin Yu and R. Guisso, trans. Yi Yu-jin, 119–30. Berkeley, CA: Asian Humanities, 1988.

Kim Hogarth, Hyun-key. "Rationality, Practicality and Modernity: Buddhism, Shamanism and Christianity in Contemporary Korean Society." *Transactions of the Royal Asiatic Society, Korea Branch* 73 (1998): 41–54.

Liu, Petrus. *Queer Marxism in Two Chinas*. Durham, NC: Duke University Press, 2015.

McClintock, Anne. *Imperial Leather: Race, Gender, and Sexuality in the Colonial Contest*. New York: Routledge, 1995.

Meyer, Birgit, and Peter Pels, eds. *Magic and Modernity: Interfaces of Revelation and Concealment*. Stanford, CA: Stanford University Press, 2003.

Muñoz, José Esteban. *Cruising Utopia: The Then and There of Queer Futurity*. New York: New York University Press, 2009.

Muñoz, José Esteban. *Disidentifications: Queers of Color and the Performance of Politics*. Minneapolis: University of Minnesota Press, 1999.

Nakajima, Michio. "Shintō Deities That Crossed the Sea." *Japanese Journal of Religious Studies* 37, no. 1 (2010): 21–46.

Pai, Hyung Il. *Constructing Korean "Origins": A Critical Review of Archaeology, Historiography, and Racial Myth in Korean State-Formation Theories*. Harvard East Asian Monographs Series. Cambridge, MA: Harvard University Asia Center, 2000.

Peletz, Michael. *Gender Pluralism: Southeast Asia since Early Modern Times*. New York: Routledge, 2009.

Robinson, Michael. "Broadcasting, Cultural Hegemony, and Colonial Modernity in Korea, 1924–1945." In *Colonial Modernity in Korea*, ed. Gi-Wook Shin and Michael Robinson, 52–69. Cambridge, MA: Harvard University Press, 1999.

Rubin, Gayle. "Thinking Sex: Notes for a Radical Theory of the Politics of Sexuality." In *Pleasure and Danger: Exploring Female Sexuality*, ed. Carol S. Vance, 143–78. Boston: Routledge and Kegan Paul, 1984.

Schilt, Kristen, and Laurel Westbrook. "Doing Gender, Doing Heteronormativity: "'Gender Normals,'" Transgender People, and the Social Maintenance of Heterosexuality." *Gender and Society* 23, no. 4 (August 2009): 440–64.

Schmid, Andre. "Rediscovering Manchuria: Sin Ch'aeho and the Politics of Territorial History in Korea." *Journal of Asian Studies* 56, no. 1 (February 1997): 26–46.

Shin, Gi-wook. *Ethnic Nationalism in Korea: Genealogy, Politics, and Legacy.* Stanford, CA: Stanford University Press, 2006.

Somerville, Siobhan. "Scientific Racism and the Invention of the Homosexual Body." In *The Gender Sexuality Reader: Culture, History, Political Economy,* ed. Roger N. Lancaster and Micaela di Leonardo, 37–52. New York: Routledge, 1997.

Tauches, Kimberly. "Transgendering: Challenging the 'Normal.'" In *Handbook of the New Sexuality Studies,* ed. Steven Seidman, Nancy Fischer, and Chet Meeks, 186–92. New York: Taylor and Francis, 2007.

Walraven, Boudewijn. "Interpretations and Reinterpretations of Popular Religion in the Last Decades of the Chosŏn Dynasty." In *Korean Shamanism: Revivals, Survivals, and Change,* ed. Keith Howard, 55–72. Seoul: Royal Asiatic Society, Korea Branch, 1998.

Yoo, T. Jun. *The Politics of Gender in Colonial Korea: Education, Labor, and Health, 1910–1945.* Berkeley: University of California Press, 2008.

Yu Chai-shin. "Korean Taoism and Shamanism." In *Shamanism: The Spirit World of Korea,* ed. Chai-shin Yu and R. Guisso, 98–118. Berkeley, CA: Asian Humanities Press, 1988.

Zoric, Snjezana. "The Magic of Performance in Korean Shamanic Ritual—*Gut.*" In *The Ritual Year 10: Magic in Rituals and Rituals in Magic,* ed. Tatiana Minniyakhmetova and Kamila Velkoborska, 367–75. Tartu, Estonia: Innsbruck, 2015.

Chapter Two

TELLING QUEER TIME IN A STRAIGHT EMPIRE

YI SANG'S "WINGS" (1936)

John Whittier Treat

> The here and now is a prison house.
> —José Esteban Muñoz, *Cruising Utopia*

> The only thing that bothered me was the slowness of time.
> —Yi Sang, "Wings"

Hegel still convinces us that time, bundled as History, moves inexorably forward. But we also know that some of us linger behind, stalled in its eddies, while others race ahead thinking they can outrun it. Most of us struggle to stay aware of just whatever the clock or calendar may insist on in our quotidian routines. But everyone does these things: we inhabit multiple, overlapping, and contesting times, those mandated at work and those we manage to steal as leisure. Some are near-hegemonic: the stages of life we are told will happen to us inexorably; more collectively, the times to which our nation, people, ethnicity, or tribe are consigned by the rule of a global legislation of modernity, development, productivity. Yet at other times we decamp from the imperfective discipline of enforced time to resist or even sabotage—from being purposefully late for a meeting to lying about our true age, betting on an uncertain future, even waging armed struggle against "advanced" nations seeking to impose their timelines for social and economic progress on us.

And then there is queer time. In this essay, I address two things not ordinarily mapped in tandem—colonial time and queer time—because in scholarly discourse their historical conjuncture is fragile: the nineteenth century was already onto the coerced reorganization of everyday life under colonization, but it was only in the twentieth century that we began to think of the lives of queer people as analogous, under varying regimes of compulsory heteronormativity, to that of Asian and African peoples under European domination—or, as is my example in this essay, Koreans under the Japanese. Queer time, or QT, should be seen as "subaltern" in this context and an ambivalent challenge to the imposed normativities of many sorts. I argue that QT has something to teach us about colonial time, and vice versa: that queer time is no spectral effect of colonial modernity but, in the case of Korea, was there from the start.

The chronological sequence of the nineteenth and twentieth centuries neatly sandwiches the life and career of Yi Sang (1910–37), Korea's most celebrated and castigated modernist writer. Yi sits historically where we might locate a nexus of the colonial with, or versus, the queer. His entire brief life (his career as a writer lasted all of eight years) he played with scandalous names, including his own.[1] Born one week after the annexation and raised in the heart of traditional Seoul (renamed Keijō by the Japanese), he was given the perfectly proper name Kim Hae-kyŏng at birth but chose a pen name whose puns, some ribald, are still debated. Most accounts suggest that this eventual literary modernist par excellence aspired to be an artist at first but would train as an engineer and architect, and chose his name because Japanese coworkers in the architecture section of the Japanese Government-General hailed him, in the colonial language they shared, as "Yi-*san*" or "Mr. Yi." But that is not correct, since we know that he was already calling himself Yi Sang while still a student at the elite Kyŏngsŏng [Keijō] Advanced Industrial College, the only Korean among the dozen-plus students in the architecture department. More preposterously, one person has suggested that *Yi* 李 is Japanese *sumomo* (plum tree), and *Sang* 箱 is rightly written *kan* 棺 (coffin), invoking the image of falling petals alighting atop his resting place in a morbid Romantic image quite unlike any he deployed in any of his avant-garde poetry. Still others would read "Yi Sang" as 理想 (ideal)—again, hardly an association consistent with his life or his writings. Recently, his name has been read as 已喪 "already dead."[2] We are left with "Yi Sang" as a homonym for the common Korean adjectival verb *isang* 異常, often translated as "abnormal" or "odd." Yi's first published poem was in fact entitled "Ijō [*isang* in Korean] na kagyaku hannō" (An

Abnormal Reverse Reaction, 1931). But for reasons explored later, I render all *yisang*s as "queer."

Via Yi and his signature short story, "Nalgae" (Wings [1936]), I approach the dialectical workings of colonial and queer times. With apologies, I begin with this lengthy quote as my demonstration of just how Yi occupied both:

> Written squarely in the middle of a blackboard more than forty feet long were the flesh-colored numerals "69." It was a sign with an odd name for a café, not your typical "Bellflowers" or "Carry Me Home." A customer who had entered with his head bowed sat down in a chair and was perplexed even more.
>
> The chair was extremely low. He was nearly sitting on the floor. Having fallen back into it with a thud, the customer now noticed the interior was dark and gloomy, not like other cafés.
>
> When he looked around, he saw the café was not decorated with as much as a vase of flowers. All there was a single oil painting hanging on a wall, a portrait of a man with a beard shaped like the scabbard of a spear.
>
> While thinking this was a strange café indeed, the customer remembered the sign "69" he had seen when he entered. He realized that the inscrutability of the café began with its very name.
>
> "69? *Yukku*?" the customer mumbled with his head cocked, as if now he understood.
>
> "That's it! *Yukkuri*. It's Japanese for 'come in and relax.'"
>
> A man sitting near the counter heard the customer and gave him a wry look. He had a beard that resembled that of the man in the painting—he must be the owner of this café. Thinking his expression might be a bit rude, he changed it to a slight smile.
>
> Why a smile? Because the gentle customer who had come up with a cryptic explanation for "69" was *tongmunsŏdap*—way off base. Proposing Japanese *yukkuri* for the mystery was not going to solve the problem. Interpreting it as "blowing the bamboo flute and fishing for abalone" might make one think of a graceful drinking party under moonlight, but memories of lines from Li Po's poetry would be of no use here.
>
> So, just what foolish equation could explain "69"? Equations are equations, and this one is *yin* plus *yang*. The round parts of those Arabic numerals were the heads of a man and a woman, and the long parts the lower halves of their bodies. In other words, it was an offensive pictograph of the *yin-yang* equation utterly turned upside down.

Moreover, such an insolent, impertinent pictograph was brazenly painted in flesh colors on the black board. Gentle customers would, to a man, only think of it as Japanese *yukkuri*—"Make yourself at home." Yes, that's just what you common people would make of it, thought the owner with a scabbard-like beard, as he let loose a small grin on his face.[3]

This extended quote is from Im Chong-guk (1929–89), whose most important work, *Ch'inil Munhangnon* (Pro-Japanese Literature [1966]), exempts Yi Sang, the bearded man, from condemnation as a collaborationist because Yi died too soon to be put to the test his longer-lived contemporaries endured during the later years of total war. But nationalists already regarded his dedicated affinities with Japanese writers such as Yokomitsu Riichi and Anzai Fuyue with suspicion. If not *ch'inil* (pro-Japanese) in any overtly political sense—his name does not appear among the 3,090 names in South Korea's notoriously inclusive *Ch'inil Immyŏng Sajŏn* (Dictionary of Japanese Collaborators [2009])— he was widely regarded during his lifetime as wayward and even heretical in his repudiation of Korean literary tradition and his substitute embrace of an apolitical modernism. Under the tutelage of the pioneering poet Chŏng Chi-yong, he participated in the opening of Korean poetry to new ideas already familiar in the West and, less so, in Japan. He quit his government job in 1933 and began his second career, not as successful, as a café proprietor. He rose to prominence in 1934 as a member of the Kuinhoe (Circle of Nine) group of writers, among whom he was prominent for his experiments with Dada and surrealism, as well as mathematics. (Albert Einstein is cited as an influence on Yi's concrete poetry.) In the fall of 1936, Yi's rising fame was ironically cut short when he, recently married, left his family to travel alone to Tokyo, telling no one of his plans. That winter, the authorities in Tokyo arrested him for being an unruly Korean (*futei senjin*). He was held in a Nishi-Kanda jail on the additional suspicion of having committed thought crimes (*shisō-han*). A month later, when his chronic tuberculosis worsened, he was transferred with the help of friends to the Tokyo Imperial University Hospital. He died on April 17 of that year. The Korean consensus maintains Yi Sang's imprisonment caused his health to collapse. As the young scholar Ch'oe Chin-sŏk has recently put it, "In Tokyo, Yi was a futei senjin before he was a literary modernist."[4] Legend has it that he died sniffing a lemon, a reference to the Japanese modernist Kajii Motojirō, who himself died of tuberculosis a few years after writing his famous story "Lemon" (Remon [1925]) about a fellow consumptive who places one on a bookstore shelf and fantasizes that it explodes.

The legend makes a good story, if an overdramatic one. Yi meant to wreak havoc himself. The words "offensive," "impertinent," and "insolent" in Im Chong-guk's quote about him were not meant ironically. During his lifetime, Yi was already attacked as ludicrously narcissistic. The portrait on the walls of Café 69 might have been the actual self-portrait that Yi, who once wanted to be a painter, submitted to the 1931 Senten juried art exhibition. At the time, the national aspirations of the Korean people were largely assumed to be literature's paramount concern under the weight of Japanese occupation. His long poem *Ogamdo* (Crow's Eye View [1934]) was so unconventional it made some readers doubt his sanity.[5] Others merely demanded a halt to its publication after only halfway through its intended thirty installments.[6] It is still debated whether Yi was a prodigy or just mentally ill.[7]

With the help of a hostess (*kisaeng*) whom he met at a hot spring while convalescing (one of the few times he ever left Seoul), Yi would run a number of ill-fated cafés (including one called Chebi in Korean, or Tsubame in Japanese; literally, "swallow," but also slang for a young gigolo) in both Korean Insadong and Japanese Honmachi, neighborhoods north and south of the dividing line of the Ch'ŏnggye Stream. When his health started to fail, he abandoned his day job as an architect and dedicated himself to writing poetry, short stories, and essays. He became Korea's homegrown Bohemian dandy, with long hair and a beard; he was as fond of bowties as any East Asian "modern boy," and his life was criticized, including after liberation, as libertine and corrupt. There were rumors that he used narcotics; attended orgies; and engaged in bigamy and, possibly, bisexuality. One American writer called him Korea's "darker conscience, a drug addicted, tubercular *poète maudit*."[8] Closer to home in Korea, the critic Kim U-chang said that all of the "degenerative processes of Korean society" could be seen in Yi Sang's "atomic individualism of alienation and anomie" and even called him an artist with "no social constituency." Kim writes, "In Yi Sang, alienation of the artist in colonial society is brought to a quintessential expression,"[9] thereby rendering Yi a spurious by-product of baneful Japanese influences, someone who retreated from words into inorganic numbers (69?) and technical symbols and vocabulary (equations?) in his concrete poetry and elsewhere.[10] Referring to Yi as "half-caste," Kim concludes that, "like Yi Sang's coffee-house, his stories, . . . express contradictions of the acculturated colonial man suspended between the abstract freedom of a man released from feudal obligations and the ultimate constraint of colonialism that fosters this freedom and at the same time renders it meaningless."[11]

But eventually Yi would be credited with greater agency by critics and even resurrected as preternatural proof of modern Korean literature's ability to produce a daring bête noire only two decades after Ch'oe Nam-sŏn initiated the project of a modern Korean poetry. Since 1977, there has even been a prestigious literary prize named after him. For a long time, the question was asked whether Yi was "premature" for Korea, but the answer today seems to be no.[12] Chris Hanscom is not mocking Yi when he says his "unkempt hair and white shoes . . . befitt[ed] young artists desiring the elusive modern."[13] It also is a key part of Yi's present rehabilitation that his "queerness"—white shoes, really?— is grounds no longer for criticism but for celebration. Combing the modern East Asian canon for signs of queerness is a popular academic sport nowadays.[14] When evidence is found, it propels China, Korea, and Japan into the post-heteronormative world with the newly coined cultural capital of sexual perversity. Yi Sang easily presents himself as such a candidate and has, as a result, become something of a poster boy for Korea's modern literary precocity, if in the implicit comparative context of Japan and the West.

Almost twenty years ago, Walter Lew gave us this newly valorized Yi Sang in his important and wide-ranging essay "Jean Cocteau in the Looking Glass: A Homotextual Reading of Yi Sang's Mirrors Poems." Lew begins by noting that the wide range of literary influences on Yi—"ranging from Li Po, Jean Arthur . . . and Maxim Gorki to Kōda Rohan . . . and fellow poet Chŏng Chi-yong," just to start—"(dis)appears throughout Yi Sang's work."[15] He uncannily anticipates what (dis)appears in criticism of that same work: the homoerotic. Lew chooses to focus, originally, on Yi's crafty "collaboration" with Jean Cocteau, just the kind of literary collaboration Wayne Koestenbaum described as having "the lovely aura of contraband":[16]

Reading Yi Sang in relation to Cocteau helps disengage heterosexualist assumptions that have crippled studies devoted to an author who wrote that, no matter how exhausted, he should "stand forth bravely and even if alone become something special far beyond male vs. female." . . . [W]hen . . . the object of affection was another man, Yi Sang needed to resort to poetic puzzles and innovative encodings grafted almost imperceptibly from the characters, scenes and symbols in homoerotically shaded works by such authors as Cocteau, Wilde, and Robert Lewis Stevenson.[17]

Lew is not interested in "outing" a homosexual Yi Sang, but he is cognizant of the lacunae of any mention of the homoerotic in the copious criticism of his work and that of other Korean writers. It could have been, Lew says, Yi's well-known devotion to Cocteau that was "the most 'homosexual' relation in Yi Sang's life." The two men never met in person (they just missed each other in Tokyo), but Lew persuasively argues that Yi was acquainted with Cocteau's work via the Japanese translations that circulated in Korea. Lew's gaze is not focused on Yi the author as much as it is on critics before Lew who, despite what is "so temptingly implied in previous studies," now wonders whether "their authors have already long shared the secret that apparently cannot be published."[18] What Lew discloses is not Yi's problematic sexuality but, rather, literary history's studied nondisclosure of the "homotextual."

There are plenty of ways to mine Yi Sang's poetry for traces of the queer. Here is one example: in "Poem No. 2" of *Crow's Eye View*, Yi writes,

> when my father dozes off beside me i become my father and also i become my father's father and even so while my father like my father why do i repeatedly my father's father's. . . . when I become a father why must i lopingly leap over my father and why am i that which while finally playing all at once my and my father's and father's father's and my father's father's father's roles must live?[19]

Lew interprets this passage as expressing "anxiety about departing from the uniform successions of patriarchal descent."[20] Fair enough, but beyond that I can offer a specifically queer mechanism as work, as well: the stutter-like repetition of "father" recalls Lauren Berlant's insight in her book *Cruel Optimism* (in an expression of utopianism to which I return at the end of this essay) that "repetition, heavily marked as a process of reading and rereading, has a reparative effect on the subject of an unwieldy sexuality. The queer tendency of this method is to put one's attachments back into play and pleasure, into knowledge, into words. It is to admit they matter."[21] Like the passionate reiteration of a lover's name during sexual intercourse, the anaphora in Yi's poem homoeroticizes what Lew would call the Oedipal, rendering the "struggle" as incest with the father instead of the mother. But that is not the road Lew, writing long before Berlant, chose to follow. Lew instead focuses on the frequency of mirror imagery—often the major motif—in Yi's work, especially, but not exclusively, in the poetry. The voice in the poem or story approaches his image in the mirror, aware that it is himself, but is frustrated in his attempt to enter into or even just converse with the image: "The narrator finds it difficult to survive without his reflection in view, [but] the mirror that transmits the reflection is also a wall that prevents the two from shaking each other's hands."[22] Lew has an agenda here, and it is an Oedipal one of his own. Previous scholarship (e.g., by Kim Yun-sik, Yi Ŏ-ryŏng, and Im Chong-guk, the critics to whom Lew filially dedicates his essay) reads this "split self" in one of three rote ways: psychoanalytically, as the narrator works out his Oedipal struggle; anticolonial ("nationalist or Korean self vs. colonized self"); or the ideal versus the mundane in "the very fact of self-consciousness."[23] What this scholarship does *not* imagine, Lew writes, is

> two other traces of alterity and doubling in Yi Sang's work: 1) its intensely sub-merged desire for or adoration of other male figures, and 2) its intertextual re-flection of works by other authors and artists that make striking use of mirror symbolism. In the present article, these two traces are integrated in an analysis of the mirror poems' "homotextuality," elaborated as a desired, textual male Other (or tain) *behind* the glass of Yi Sang's mirrors, cleverly disguised as a Self-contained "I in the mirror."[24]

What scandalizes Lew is not Yi Sang but the "absence throughout Korean lit-erary history scholarship in general of discussions of male gayness," including of how the mirror poems, despite their debt to a writer as fey as Cocteau, "are drained of their homoerotic suggestiveness, . . . hiding a male object of desire whose true name cannot be uttered"—even the case of Poem No. 9 in *Crow's Eye View*, where Yi's line, "In my bowels I feel the weighty barrel of the gun and its slippery mouth against my tightly shut lips," is reduced after Korean critics' pained peregrinations to "a conceit of solitary heterosexual onanism."[25]

It seems unfair to chide Korean critics too harshly for this lapse. It is surely more a reading of Lew's moment and our own than it is of previous genera-tions. It has not been that long since Melville, Forester, and Sōseki have been "queer," either. This is a new project for critics. And who knows what as yet un-named "paradigms" we are not seeing in Yi Sang's work as we read him today. But Lew's essay is surely a step forward, if by that we mean he has expanded the contexts in which we are free to read Yi without shame or embarrassment, for the writer or ourselves. Still, in my estimation, Lew continues to commit, as did earlier scholars, to a certain congruency of identity between Yi and his texts when he thematizes "forbidden love or unattainable gay desire" in them as the poetically masked and critically unmentionable elephant in the room "because of the social taboo on public gay relations."[26] Yi was known for being autobiographical in his work, but that is not the overlap that matters: it is the location of homoerotic or queer desire in the enunciated *subject* (in Yi—that is, the first-person familiar pronoun *na* [I], which is often taken to be the writer himself) in the verse or prose.

Like Lew, I am not focused on Yi Sang's "debauched" (Lew's word) sexuality, or on Yi Sang the human being at all, whatever his orientation.[27] What I want to do is approach the queer in the signifier "Yi Sang," specifically the short story "Wings," as a monologue said to be the first literary work in Korea to use stream-of-consciousness narration. "Wings" has been the subject of many cogent readings in the West, as well as in Korea, such as the historian Henry Em's ideological take on it some years ago. Em describes the difficult language of the story (actually, it is one of Yi's easier works to read) as symptomatic of the "writer under colonial rule," but those symptoms echo those of the closeted homosexual. Yi's is "the language of a dismembered discourse incapable of communicating openly, venturing out from its hiding places to express, only half coherently, ideas and urges it must keep repressed," Em writes. "I suggest that 'Wings' can be read as an allegory of how an entire generation of intellectuals sought to survive in a colonial setting by becoming entirely private, shielding themselves with self-deceptions until even that became impossible."[28]

I return to what is simultaneously "queer" and "anticolonial" in Yi's signature story to suggest that many self-nominated queers are recognizably "postcolonial" themselves, but first I want to interrogate two critical concepts of relatively recent vintage but useful applicability. These concepts—those of straight time and queer time—have the advantage of provisionally releasing us from the inevitably psychological regime of "desire" (and its inevitable home in the putative biographeme of an anthropologized subject) to migrate elsewhere—to the movement of people, "queer," "straight," or otherwise, through time organized in often incommensurable chronotropes, including the "deviant" or "perverted."

I date the parlance of "straight time" and "queer time," conjoined because homosexuals inhabit both, to Judith [Jack] Halberstam's *In a Queer Time and Place: Transgender Bodies, Subcultural Lives* (2005). Unhelpful in learning anything outside Western cultures, Halberstam nonetheless gives us something with which to work, beginning with the commonplace observation that "queerness of time and space develop, in part, in opposition to the institutions of family, heterosexuality, and reproduction."[29] No argument here: gay people often lead lives, certainly in their spare time, with small regard for the schedules of the majority. "On time" for us can mean no more than an hour or two late, as anyone who has scheduled a brunch for gay men can attest. But more seriously, QT (pun intended) also refers to the truncated life spans my generation of gay men in the United States came to half expect. Years ago, having to take your AZT at precisely timed intervals struck many as particularly irksome. Wristwatch alarms would go off in movie theaters and restaurants at inopportune "times." You could not skip any of your pills; it was one of the traumas of living by straight time in our gay lives. Somehow being "on time" has always reeked of the Law of the Father and his rules. "In acclimatizing to the discourses and demands of new treatment regimens, gay men with HIV experienced a significant shift in their experience of temporality," writes Kane Race. "We have all had to rearrange our daily living schedules to fit the drugs in at the right time and dosage," he quotes Michael Flynn as saying. "Going out to dinner, meeting friends for a drink, staying away from home or partying all night long now have to be carefully planned like a military operation."[30] In other words, our gay *compliance* with those regimens is as compulsory as any Korean colonial subject's *obedience* might once have been, and both disrupt the normal hours of the day and night.

Everything that clocks and calendars tell us is already straight time, if not quite how Halberstam means it. What is the "queer" in "queer time," exactly? For nonreproductive queer people, there is no "our children's lives" or our "grandchildren's lives," expressions that are reserved for straight time. But the point lies elsewhere. Queer time is more than a simple failure to picture time beyond our immediate selves, and it often expresses itself as a positive aesthetic. There is modernism, for example. Baudelaire was involved with "the transient, the fleeting, the contingent," and so is the "queer."[31] And so was Yi Sang, for whom Modernism and Baudelaire were so important. "I sauntered aimlessly here and there," Yi writes through his narrator in "Wings," "not knowing why I was doing this."[32] My point is that all sorts of us live in QT. Drug addicts (Yi Sang was rumored to have been one) do, for instance, because they exist in "rapid bursts" of time that are perceived as "immature and even dangerous."[33] But QT is also a hopeful, liberating place to be. "Queer time for me," writes Halberstam,

> is the dark nightclub, the perverse turn away from the narrative coherence of adolescence—early childhood—marriage—reproduction—childrearing—retirement—death, the embrace of late childhood in place of early adulthood or immaturity in a place of responsibility. It is a theory of queerness as a way of being in the world and a critique of the careful social scripts that usher even the most queer among us through major markers of individual development and into normativity.[34]

Halberstam goes further, quite nearly alighting on *utopia*, which I would argue is always the subtext of our discussion of QT. "One of my central assertions has been that queer temporality disrupts the normative narratives of time that form the base of nearly every definition of the human in almost all of our modes of understanding."[35] That includes the conventionally "heterosexual" and "homosexual." Halberstam asks us to detach queerness from sexual identity. This is one of the reasons that the term "queer" is of quite limited applicability, but let us put that aside for the moment. Halberstam prefers we understand it as not a way of having *sex*, but as having a way of *life*, which must be more unnerving to some. This is how Yi Sang, if he was not queer *then*, certainly is *now*—remembering that, in Korean straight time, he is annually awarded as a literary prize.

Halberstam quotes the gay poet Mark Doty: "All my life I've believed with a future which constantly diminishes but never vanishes."[36] But it was left to the late José Esteban Muñoz, in *Cruising Utopia: The Then and There of Queer Futurity*, to take up queer time and provocatively toss it into the ongoing controversy about gay people and the prospect of a future, debated most by the psychoanalytical team of Lee Edelman (in his influential *No Future: Queer Theory and the Death Drive* [2004]) and Leo Bersani (in his even more influential *Homos* [1996]). They theorized what Muñoz dismisses as "the so-called thesis of antirelativity," with which people more sanguine about our futures, such as Berlant and Muñoz, take issue.[37] All we get from Edelman and company are those "little deaths" that come with our sexual climaxes, and that is not much, Muñoz figures.

> Political hope fails queers because, like signification, it was not originally made for us. It resonates only on the level of reproductive futurity. Instead, Edelman recommends that queers give up hope and embrace a certain negation endemic to our abjection within the symbolic. What we get in exchange . . . is a certain *jouissance*. . . . Edelman's psychoanalytic optic reveals that the social is inoperable for the always already shattered queer subject.[38]

Muñoz believed we can do better than this. His queer future is not Doty's "vanishing" one. It looms large and ever present as an aura. It is an "ideality" we have yet to reach and may never. But we feel it "as the warm illumination of a horizon imbued with potentiality," as we must, since our "here and now is a prison house," and "the future is queerness's domain."[39] "Queerness," as Muñoz defined it, "is a longing that propels us onward, . . . that thing that lets us feel this world is not enough, that indeed something is missing." This is how many of us milling around in queer time already imagine, if not always experience, the world. Following Ernst Bloch, Muñoz writes, "In our everyday life abstract utopias are akin to banal optimism. . . . Concrete utopias are the realm of educated hope."[40] And under conditions of compulsory heterosexuality, queers are nothing if not schooled.

Edelman and others have insisted that because gay people do not reproduce unassisted, we lack the enabling possibility of a future time, which is the province of the child. We know what he means, surely every time an SUV double stroller forces us off the sidewalk in our gay neighborhoods, to use Muñoz's example. But some queers, if not Edelman, have come up with a solution, which is to have "families" after all. Elsewhere, I have argued that there is no concept of "same-sex marriage" without an implicit child, even if it is apparitional: "What makes all marriage heterosexualist and materialist is the *imaginary* of the child, whether he or she is really there or not. Heterosexualist because that is what reproduction is (until we clone, and perhaps still then), and materialist because that is what *production* is. . . . The child, then, is *always* the object of desire, whatever one does in bed."[41] Yi Sang had plenty of opportunity to do so, but he did not make any babies to our knowledge. Yes, he was married (multiple and overlapping times), but he could hardly be said to have inhabited straight time. What Muñoz would immediately call out as queer would be the ways Yi wrote, over and over again, about Seoul and Tokyo (never Korea and Japan) as his "apparitional" utopias: poems about a Seoul with tall buildings that hardly existed,[42] essays about a Tokyo that disappointed him as soon as he got there. Taken to the site of Japan's most renowned modern theater, the Tsukiji Little Theater, Yi thought it looked like "a badly designed coffee shop," a low-camp comment if there ever was one.[43] "If straight time tells us that there is no future but the here and now of our everyday life," reasons Muñoz, then "queerness is utopian, and there is something queer about the utopian."[44] Muñoz borrows Theodor Adorno's definition of utopia as "the determined negation of that which merely is."[45] We should keep that in mind as we read these excerpts from Yi's essay "Tokyo" (Tong'gyŏng [1936]):

> I had imagined that the **Marunouchi Building**—better known as **Marubiru**—would be at least four times bigger than this "Marubiru," something impressive. If I went to **Broadway** in New York, I might feel the same disappointment—anyway, my first impression of Tokyo was: "This city reeks of **gasoline**!"
>
> The Ginza is just a book of vanity. If you don't walk around here, you apparently lose your right to vote. When women buy new shoes, they have to come here and tread the Ginza's sidewalks before boarding a car.

The Ginza in the daytime is more than a little ugly because it is the skeleton for the Ginza at night. The twisted, poker-like iron that forms the frame of the winding **neon sign** saying **Salon Spring** is disheveled like the **permanent wave** of a bar girl who has been up all night.[46]

Yi's utopian hopes once invested in Tokyo are, upon arrival, immediately deferred: first to New York, and then to somewhere beyond that. "I've made it to Tokyo finally. What a disappointment," Yi wrote in 1936 in a letter from Japan. "Tokyo is a waste of a place."[47] Midway through "Tokyo," notes John Frankl, "[Yi] recites the names of all those who had bragged about having been to Tokyo . . . while casually relieving himself in an underground toilet in Kyōbashi."[48]

Yi, no more than any of us, is required to detail what our utopia would be; all we need, to return to Adorno, is to make a "determined negation of that which merely is." When Yi visits the Ginza during the wrong time (straight time?) of day and is hardly seduced by its women, that is enough to tell us what Yi dreams of is *not these things* in his here and now but something on Muñoz's "horizon imbued with potentiality." Certainly, it is reasonable to read this essay as the inevitable encounter of the colonized intellectual with the colonizers' metropole, and it has been many times.[49] But at this juncture, I want to try to connect queer time with "colonial" time and place each in a symmetrical, if not necessarily equidistant, relationship with the prospect of a queer/postcolonial utopia, my own, admittedly utopian move in the midst of what, for occupied Korea, were hardly ripe conditions for either sexual or national sovereignty.

I have assistance. Muñoz wrote that he understood "queerness as being filled with the intention to be lost." Soon thereafter, he said, "Freedmen escaping slavery got lost too, and this is a salient reverberation between queerness and racialization."[50] Yi Sang springs to mind, but not just Yi Sang the modernist, the Baudelairean flâneur "intending to be lost" whom Yi's friend and fellow author Pak T'ae-won described so well in his own work. The flâneur is not a man of the crowd, Walter Benjamin told us. "He is already out of place."[51] Yi might have wandered a Seoul he imagined to be Paris (or Tokyo), but Yi Sang the futei senjin was *really* lost in the phenomenal Japanese heartland, hardly able to recognize the famous landmarks of modernity he had pictured as so much grander. He was racialized, too, as a Korean "already out of place" in the center of the Japanese empire—and therefore, I suggest, queer: wandering Tokyo during the day the way other men might cruise the piers at night, risking arrest for being in the wrong place at just the right time.

Fredric Jameson's essay "Modernism and Imperialism" is of use to us here and will only momentarily distract us from the question of queer time, if not its relationship to the colonial. Jameson contends that imperialist novels do not have to be about empires per se, and seldom are. It is the *form* of the novel that conforms to imperialism, not necessarily its broadcast theme. And that form, in his examples of it, is not only modernist but also intensely political. "The structure of imperialism," he writes, "makes its mark on the inner forms and structures of that mutation in literary and artistic language to which the term modernism is loosely applied."[52] We may find that this is pertinent to Korean literature.

Jameson's model is James Joyce's *Ulysses* and the peripatetic appointments and encounters of Leopold Bloom over the course of a single day in Dublin in 1904, at the time a city under English rule. Like Seoul, the Irish looked east to what Dublin was not but what some wished it might be: London. In Jameson's retelling, the most canonical modernist novel of our time restages British imperialism, but via the peculiar quotidian wanderings of the half-Jewish Leopold Bloom, himself indifferent to the question of Irish nationalism in a city rife with it. Jameson sees the novel's ideological work as impossible to comprehend without exposing to view the imperial architecture that keeps the roof up:

> [I]n *Ulysses* space does not have to be made symbolic in order to achieve closure and meaning: its closure is objective, endowed by the colonial situation itself. . . . In Joyce, the encounter is at one with Dublin itself, whose compact size anachronistically permits the new archaic life of the older city-state. It is therefore unnecessary to generate an aesthetic form of closure distinct from the city, which in First World modernism must be imposed by the violence of form upon this last at compensation.[53]

I take Jameson to mean that the "modernism" of *Ulysses* was already guaranteed by its provincial Dublin setting; that it assumed its aesthetic form, its "closure," by virtue of its quasi-peripheral spatial position within British imperialism. I make a similar claim for Yi Sang's "Wings," set in provincial Seoul, a city Yi may have regarded as no more than a "quiet farming village."[54] I also argue that *time* is a structural vector that makes this story *queer*, just as space renders it modernist, and just as literary history has elected it one of the greatest logs of Korean duress under Japanese rule.

I turn to Yi Sang's "Wings" to link the queer with empire and propose an accord of postcolonial and queer readings of the story. Accurately if tersely summarized as the first-person account of "the mental life of an alienated intellectual who confines himself to his dark room except for frantic night time walks around the center of Seoul," "Wings" easily invites the expected analysis as the narrative of (1) the antiheroic "superfluous man" familiar in modern literature; and (2) the dispossessed colonial man at home nowhere whom we encounter in writers from Frantz Fanon and William Conrad to V. S. Naipaul and Chinua Achebe.[55] These readings are all loosely "existential" in that they take the plight of the protagonist as a protracted, unsuccessful attempt to wrest authentic Being from the social fetters that bind him. But that is too little and too much with which to credit the story, one I do not take to be philosophical or abstract in the least.

"Wings" begins with a first-person narrator (*na*) addressing us in the narrative present (*-o*). Some sections of the story switch to the narrative past (*-śda*), but it is a mistake to make too much of that other than to suggest that the narrator at times moves epistemically closer to the reader (the non-past aspect) and sometimes steps back (the past). In either instance, the narrator never cedes his point of view; the story is strictly confined to his own, claustrophobic consciousness, although irony frequently undermines any reader's trust in his perceptions and judgment. There is no dialogue in the story, only reported memories, impressions, and speculation. As Em notes, it is no more than a "silent soliloquy."[56]

Na, twenty-six, tells us he is happy (*yuk'wae*), but we immediately wonder why. His mind is a "white sheet of paper," the life he lives with a woman (*yŏin*)—possibly his wife (*anae*)—is "alienated from the strategies of love." Na imagines he has a future: "I again plan a life with a woman," but that future will never arrive.[57] They have neither children nor jobs. The two share a divided room in a tenement (House No. 33) that is home to eighteen other families, all of whom lead lives consistent with his "woman's" probable profession, prostitution. The hours everyone keeps are the opposite of how "normal" people might live:

> There is no sun, for they look away from the sun. They block the sun's way into the rooms under the pretext of airing their stained bedding quilts on the wash line under the eaves.
>
> They take naps in the dusky rooms. Don't they sleep at night? I do not know. I never know because I sleep both day and night. In the daytime, House No. 33 of eighteen families is very quiet.
>
> It is quiet only in the daytime. At dusk, they take their bedding quilts in. With the lights on, the eighteen rooms are brighter than they had been in the

daytime. The sound of opening and closing the sliding doors continues to the late hours. They become busy. (9)

Na loves his woman, but, to demonstrate it, he removes himself from her daily life, which, while hardly governed by industrial capitalism's time-keeping regime (though that of her clients might be), is still highly rationalized and scheduled. Na's own daily life, undistracted by work, is distinguished only by its tedium, a keyword in more than a few of Yi's other works; the narrator here is "bored to the bones by its ordinary events" (8). Naps, a willful suspension of time, take up much of his day. This is already a withdrawal from the vigorous tempo of the colonial city, a retreat into something his sloth enables: a life dedicated to the private space of his own thoughts stalled in time. "Everything was all right as long as I was allowed to loaf day after day. That I could idle in the room fitting like a well-tailored suit to my body and soul was a convenient and comfortable situation to be in, an ideal atmosphere far apart from the worldly speculations of happiness or unhappiness. I like that environment" (11). That Na does not work for wages raises the question of whether queer time is only available to those outside the requirements of capitalist colonial time, the product of leisure time unequally distributed on the basis of class. (Working-class gay men do not ordinarily have two-hour brunches in the middle of their workweek.) But Na's daily life cannot properly be called "leisure," because it is in no way earned entertainment, or a respite from mandated service: he unhappily labors in his alienated and abject lethargy.

Still, Na's womb-like isolation in his "absolute shelter" is not free of his woman's work-related interruptions. In fact, they obey their own set schedule. At home during the day he may cower on his side of their room's divide, idle and clueless. He can go days without eating; weeks without shaving. But at night, when men visit his woman and leave money (Why do they do that, he wonders?), he must leave to wander the streets until he thinks it is prudent to return. He prays "for time to flee like a shot arrow" (27), but it does not. He cruises the city in loitering-time deemed "wasteful" but, if one is a gay man looking for sex, "strategically opportunistic."[58] "I sneaked out of my room," says Na, "while my wife was out" (21), as if he were, in today's parlance, on the DL (down-low).

At the same, Na is grateful for what his woman does for him, including the meals she brings him like clockwork to eat alone on his side of the room, and for the spending money she leaves at the head of his bed. He is the adult dependent of a woman in the workforce, a fact over which he remains in denial.

"Does she have a job?" he asks himself more than once (16). He tries to provoke her one day by dumping her silver coins into the latrine, but to no avail. She simply replaces the money, though he can think of no way to spend it. He neither earns nor purchases; he is wholly purposeless and thinks of himself as "a lump like a pillow" (15). Their "relationship," writes Em, "is one that is structured around a strict segmentation of time and space. The daytime is for childlike play and the evening for adult business."[59] Another way to look at it might be: Na will never witness or acknowledge to himself the primal, heterosexual scene of the commissioned "adult business" on the other side of his thin curtain because it does not occur in his inverted time.

One night, Na does not return to the room quite late enough, and he interrupts the woman entertaining a male guest. Later, he apologizes, but the next morning she is nowhere to be found. Her comings and goings seem nearly random. He goes out himself that night, determined to stay away long enough to avoid the embarrassment he caused the previous evening. By this point in "Wings," normal (straight) time is completely vacated. His woman may wash her face at exactly eleven every morning, but for Na there is only "dark" and "light." People are away when they should be at home, and they are asleep when they should be awake, and vice versa. Na is worried that he will not know the hour and mistakenly return home too soon, so he makes a point of checking the tall clock tower outside the central train station (figure 2.1), which, he reasons, is obliged to be exact: "The clock there kept more accurate time than any other clocks" (30–31). "After I made sure by the big clock at Gyeongseong [Kyŏngsŏng in Korean; Keijō in Japanese] Station that it was after midnight, I headed for home" (28).

The clock tower was one of the most notorious structures built by the Japanese in Seoul. Like the clocks installed throughout modern empires, the imposition of twenty-four-hour punctuality enabled the regulation of productive time and disciplining of a subject population being organized for work in colonial modernity. The clock in general, according to Elizabeth Grosz, "imposes rather than extracts a unity and wholeness through homogenization and reduction."[60] The station's clock tower thus represents the epitome of colonial time, which I also call straight time. Na needs the clock to tell when a new day starts so that he can go home and try to resume a "normal" schedule. But home time—queer time—is unpredictable. Na can never be sure when his woman will be working at entertaining. Nor can he be sure what his woman/ wife is actually doing with her guests. Na's mental and bodily health suffer under the mounting stress and fatigue.

Figure 2.1 Clock tower on Seoul train station.

The next night, the woman encourages Na to stay out even later than usual. This time, he takes refuge at a café within the train station proper:

> What I liked about the place was that the clock there kept more accurate time than any other clocks anywhere. So I did not have to face any misfortune of returning home too early, mistaken by a stupid clock. I sat with nothingness in a booth and sipped a cup of hot coffee. Amid their busy hours, the passengers seemed to enjoy a cup of coffee with relish. They would gaze at a wall as if in deep thought, sipping the coffee in a hurry, and then they would leave. It was sad. But I truly loved that sadness about that place, something I cherished more than the depressing atmosphere of other street-side tea rooms. The occasional shrill screaming of the train hoots sounded more familiar and intimate to me than Mozart. (30–31)

Ruled over by the most punctual of clocks, passengers have their modern drink in a modern café, only to rush off when a modern steam whistle announces their modern trains' departures. Na, the only customer in the café without a "modern" task to perform, finds it sad yet appealing. He lives in both their straight time and his own queer time. Is it a coincidence that, in the West, large railway stations appear in the late nineteenth-century cityscape at the same time as does the modern phenomenon of the homosexual? As the sociologist Henning Bech has observed, they both *"concentrate the city. . . . All the elements are there, compacted and condensed within a delimited space: the crowd, the constant flux of new people, the mutual strangeness and indifference."*[61] But Seoul's train station, with its arrivals and departures, schedules colonial time as precisely as it organizes transit's geographical space. Neither is of concern to Na. Traveling nowhere and with hours to kill, he can sip his coffee slowly and contemplate—cruise—his utopia.

Still, he returns home too soon and again interrupts his woman in her half of their quarters. He wakes the next day with a fever and consequently pays a price: the medicine his wife feeds him each day may be sleeping pills, keeping Na sedated in bed for a month and thus further taking him outside normal time: "Did she want me to die gradually?" (36). As usual, Na is unsure. Rather than confront her, he roams the city for hours, eventually finding himself on the top of the Mitsukoshi department store (like the station and its clock tower an icon of Japanese modernity; the only proper names in all of "Wings" are those for the train station and this store). There he recollects the "twenty-six years" of his life (38). The crowds he sees on the street below remind him of the goldfish confined in the fishbowl for sale in the rooftop's garden store. He reflects that he and his woman are similarly trapped in their own, alienated relationship: "We were like a lame couple, destined not to harmonize with each other's gait. I did not need to summon any logic to justify her behavior or mine. There was no need for any defense. We would stumble on and on, truth and misunderstanding on their own separate ways. Was that not the usual way?" (39).

His thoughts are interrupted when a loud siren announcing noon fills the air. "It was a glorious noon, people vigorously whirling around amid the commotion of glass, steel, marble, money and ink"—all the trappings of colonial Seoul's, and the global modern's, straight time. The action of Yi's story ends here, with Na imagining wings he once had but are now only the "deleted phantasms of hope and ambition" (39). The reader is left to imagine whether the hero leaps off the roof of the Mitsukoshi to his death or not, although the momentum of the story leads many critics to assume he does and, moreover, that his jump symbolizes Yi's desire to leave Seoul for the promised land (*shintenchi*) of Tokyo.[62] That unsettled question—no work of modernist Korean literature has a conclusion as debated as this one[63]—does not interest me as much as does the intrusion of that loud siren into Na's melancholy musing. It is like a summons issued to him to return to straight/colonial time and leave his queer time behind, but rather than do so, he makes the most dramatic of exits. The last lines of "Wings" read as if verse:

I stopped my pace and wanted to shout.
Wings, spread out again!
Fly. Fly. Fly. Let me fly once more.
Let me fly just once more. (40)

Poetry perhaps, but read prosaically by critics. "Wings" is the title of the story, and someone surely needed to "fly," be it off a building or on Yi Sang's ferry ride to Japan. But with no evidence other than the fact Yi (like his fellow modernists) was an avid cineaste, I wonder whether he saw Paramount's silent film *Wings*, released under the title *Tsubasa* in Japan and Korea, where it made the film journal *Kinema Junpō*'s ten-best list for 1927.[64] Starring Clara Bow—who epitomized the "modern girl" for her East Asia fans—it is the story of a love triangle (two military men and one woman) set during World War I. Noted in film history not only for its innovative cinematography and its Academy Award for Best Picture, it contains the brief cameo of a lesbian couple in a Paris nightclub and is the first film ever to feature one man kissing another on the lips. It is hard to imagine that Yi Sang missed this picture. It was as scandalous—queer?—for the time, as his writings would be soon enough.

Yi Sang, like his fictional character in "Wings" and the cinematic airman in *Wings*, died young. Nineteen thirty-seven was not a "happy" year for Koreans, but worse would follow. In her study *When the Future Disappears*, Janet Poole begins with the line that the "question of time lies at the heart" of her book. She argues that the last decade of the Japanese occupation, including the years of "total war" that Yi never experienced, "was fueled by the sense of a disappearing future and the struggle to imagine a transformed present."[65] This reminds me of the debate among American queer theorists, among them Edelman and Muñoz, about futurity and the prospect of gay lives within it. Edelman insists that such things (children, political power, a sense of life beyond ourselves) are not for us, and Muñoz counters that we have to rework our understanding of "utopia" to ensure that we can lay claim to *different* things, queer things, for ourselves: "Queerness is utopian, and there is something queer about the utopian."[66]

It is tempting to read "Wings" as an allegory of all Koreans under colonialism, as Em and others have. And why not? But there are contexts other than the nationalist-historical at work, too. "Modern Korean literary history criticism," notes John Frankl, "is often a totalizing account as all experience on the peninsula as 'Korean,' and in which there is little or no room for individual experiences and proclivities." I hesitate to endorse the view that "Wings" is allegory, because it makes the narrator *all* Koreans. I prefer to regard the narrator as singularly *queer*—surely what, with Frankl, we can circumspectly call a "proclivity":

> Korean writers under Japanese colonial rule are often judged not on their works' artistic merits but on their purported national consciousness or resistance— however cryptic—to foreign governance. When works are not overtly unconcerned with the Korean ethnonation's predicament under foreign domination and oppression, their crypto-nationalist allegorical meanings are liberally excavated by critics. When no such readings are possible, the writers are excoriated for their lack of national consciousness. Yi Sang is stuck squarely in the middle of this binary.[67]

Allegory has to be allegory of something, and that something ordinarily unfolds in straight time. May I propose a compromise that allows us an anticolonial and queer reading all at once? And not one in which one is "collective" and the other "individual," but one in which events unfold in multiple frames? This returns us to the fulcrum of time, *their* time and/versus *our* time—time that is structural (heterosexual, imperial) and subjective (queer, colonial). Where an anticolonial reading would tend to render the narrator's story tragic, though brave, I see in it something positive *and* brave, in the spirit of Muñoz's recasting of death drive–ridden melodrama as our prospective gay farce.

Earlier in this essay, when I mentioned Berlant's seemingly oxymoronic "cruel optimism," I promised a return to utopianism in my conclusion. By that I meant a "happy ending" with no guarantee it would be conventionally "happy" at all: only simply *not this*. Utopia might lie in that "negation" of everything here and now, even in the nihilistic taking of one's own life by leaping off a building. For the first time, after all, Na may be making a resolute decision. We cannot pretend to know whether what follows his decision is, in the end, better than what he was facing as an alternative. And if it is not, then there will be another utopia to imagine in the queer times to come, but "not yet," as Muñoz would append.

"Chrononormativity," an idea formed in the wake of that of hetero- and homonormativity, is a concept one might think has universal currency.[68] But Halberstam uses the idea to say that "*in Western cultures*, we chart the emergence of the adult from the dangerous and unruly period of adolescence as a desired process of maturation . . . and pathologize modes of living that show little or no respect for longevity."[69] The problem with Halberstam's "we" aside, there is no reason to accept the qualification "in Western cultures" as anything other than a conceit for an unfamiliarity with any others. I would propose that Yi Sang's "Wings," read with attention to the particular history of colonial Korea in the 1930s, demonstrates much the same point. Just as Yi's story repudiates the "reproductive futurism" (Edelman's term) of both heterosexuality and nationalism, Halberstam's invocation of a stretched-out "adolescence" is Na's attenuated, childlike dependence on his woman; it is moreover the immaturity that, ascribed to Korea, served as a rationale for Japanese imperialism. The contribution, also an amendment, that "Wings" conceivably makes to queer theory is to see QT as something hardly definable solely against hetero-chrononormativity, but something produced through the queer encounter with other chrononormativities, including the modern colonial. To Tom Boellstorff's definition of straight time as "shaped by linked discourses of heteronormativity, capitalism, modernity, and [the linear, millenarian framework of] apocalypse," we will add the discourse of colonialism, and to queer time its refusal.[70] The point of this cannot be to decide that Yi Sang's "Koreanness" is a subset of queerness on account of some uncanny, shared morphology. That would only affirm the universality of the West against the particularity of everywhere else. In my view, it also masks the historical fact that our talk of queerness is the *result* of the historical experience that produced modernity, the nation-state, capitalism, the industrial revolution, and colonial expansion—and, with them, the homosexual, too.

"It is worth trying to counterfeit yourself," Yi Sang writes in "Wings." "Your creation would be sublime and conspicuous among the ordinary things you have never seen" (8). Could anything be more queer? Do queer people not have to believe this to endure in places and times straight people design for themselves without us in mind? But it is also what Fanon said in as many words about living in French Martinique and Achebe said about his Nigeria under the heel of the British. When Yi finally made it to Tokyo and found the city thoroughly "counterfeit," he was reacting not as a queer person but as a subject of its East Asian empire. But, then again, what queer person would not want the object of his desires to disenchant him, over and over again, because the future must be endlessly deferred, never now and always "not yet"? In recent years, queer theory has made much of failure as a way of being in the world. "Failing," writes Halberstam in a book dedicated to the topic, "is something queers do and always have done exceptionally well."[71] New York, Yi Sang wrote near the end of his life, would surely disappoint him just as much as Tokyo.[72] But he would be very much at home there.

Notes

1 Sano, "Kankoku modanizumu no isō," 31.
2 Sone, "The Mirror Motif," 201.
3 Im, "Yi Sang," 49–50.
4 Ch'oe, "Kindai o dassuru," 44.
5 Kawamura, "Yi Sang no Keijō," 5.
6 Yi, "Yi Sang no shi," 128.
7 Saegusa, "Yi Sang no modanizumu," 117.
8 Stephens, *The Dramaturgy of Style*, 197.
9 Kim, "The Situation of the Writers under Japanese Colonialism," 7–8.
10 Henry Em points out, Yi uses the number 18 elsewhere as a homonym for Korean slang *sippal* ("fuck"): Em, "Yi Sang's *Wings* Read as an Anti-Colonial Allegory," 111. See also Yi, "Nalgae," 344–45, n7.
11 Kim, "The Situation of the Writers under Japanese Colonialism," 9.
12 Chō, *Chōsen—kotoba—ningen*, 338.
13 Hanscom, "Modernism, Hysteria, and the Colonial Double Bind," 620.
14 For more on anachronistically "queer" readings of Korean fiction, see Treat, "Introduction to Yi Kwang-su's 'Maybe Love.'"
15 Lew, "Jean Cocteau in the Looking Glass," 119.
16 Koestenbaum, *Double Talk*, 8.
17 Lew, "Jean Cocteau in the Looking Glass," 120.
18 Lew, "Jean Cocteau in the Looking Glass," 121.
19 Yi Sang, "Crow's-Eye View," 80.
20 Lew, "Jean Cocteau in the Looking Glass," 122.
21 Berlant, *Cruel Optimism*, 123.
22 Lew, "John Cocteau in the Looking Glass," 122.
23 Lew, "Jean Cocteau in the Looking Glass," 124.
24 Lew, "Jean Cocteau in the Looking Glass," 125.
25 Lew, "Jean Cocteau in the Looking Glass," 130–32, 136.
26 Lew, "Jean Cocteau in the Looking Glass," 140.
27 Lew, untitled essay, 72.
28 Em, "Yi Sang's *Wings* Read as an Anti-Colonial Allegory," 105–6.
29 Halberstam, *In a Queer Time and Place*, 1.
30 Race, *Pleasure Consuming Medicine*, 32, 113.
31 Race, *Pleasure Consuming Medicine*, 2.
32 Yi, "The Wings," 21.
33 Race, *Pleasure Consuming Medicine*, 4–5.
34 Halberstam, in Dinshaw et al., "Theorizing Queer Temporalities," 182.

35   Halberstam, in Dinshaw et al., "Theorizing Queer Temporalities," 152.

36   Halberstam, in Dinshaw et al., "Theorizing Queer Temporalities," 2.

37   Muñoz, *Cruising Utopia*, 11.

38   Muñoz, *Cruising Utopia*, 91.

39   Muñoz, *Cruising Utopia*, 1.

40   Muñoz, *Cruising Utopia*, 3.

41   Treat, "Returning to Altman," 276–77.

42   Kawamura, "Yi Sang no Keijō," 11.

43   Sano, "Kankoku modanizumu no isō," 92.

44   Muñoz, *Cruising Utopia*, 22, 26.

45   Muñoz, *Cruising Utopia*, 64.

46   Yi, "Tokyo," 96, 98.

47   Chō, *Chōsen—kotoba—ningen*, 339; Choi, "Seoul, Tokyo, New York," 133.

48   Frankl, "Distance as Anti-Nostalgia," 43.

49   See, e.g., Kim, "Sŏul kwa Tong'gyŏng sai."

50   Muñoz, *Cruising Utopia*, 72–73.

51   Benjamin, "Some Motifs in Baudelaire," 174.

52   Jameson, "Modernism and Imperialism," 44.

53   Jameson, "Modernism and Imperialism," 91.

54   Chō, *Chōsen—kotoba—ningen*, 339.

55   Poole, *When the Future Disappears*, 44; Kim, "The Situation of the Writers under Japanese Colonialism," 9.

56   Em, "Yi Sang's *Wings* Read as an Anti-Colonial Allegory," 106.

57   Yi, "The Wings," 7. Hereafter, page numbers from this work are cited in parentheses in the text.

58   See Nguyen Tan Hoang, in Dinshaw et al., "Theorizing Queer Temporalities," esp. 192.

59   Em, "Yi Sang's *Wings* Read as an Anti-Colonial Allegory," 108.

60   Grosz, "Thinking the New," 18.

61   Bech, *When Men Meet*, 158–59.

62   Ch'oe, "Kindai o dassuru," 33.

63   Jung, *Nikkan kindai bungaku no kōsa to danzetsu*, 68.

64   For the complete list, see http://www.kinenote.com/main/award/kinejun/y1928 .aspx. I thank Aaron Gerow for this reference.

65   Poole, *When the Future Disappears*, 1.

66   Muñoz, *Cruising Utopia*, 1.

67   Frankl, "Distance as Anti-Nostalgia," 40.

68   Elizabeth Freeman defines chrononormativity as "the use of time to organize individual human bodies toward maximum productivity": Freeman, *Time Binds*, 3.

69   Halberstam, *In a Queer Time and Place*, 4, emphasis added.

70   Boellstorff, "When Marriage Fails," 228.

71   Halberstam, *The Art of Queer Failure*, 3.

72   Yi, "Tokyo," 96.

Works Cited

KOREAN- AND JAPANESE-LANGUAGE SOURCES

Chō Shōkichi. *Chōsen—kotoba—ningen*. Tokyo: Kawade Shobō, 1989.

Ch'oe Chin-sŏk [Chie Jinsoku]. "Kindai o dassuru: Ri Seki 'kentai' ron." *Shakai Bungaku*, no. 42 (2015): 32–47.

Im Chong-guk. "Yi Sang—Yo o sakasa ni ikita hito." *Koria Hyōron* 29, no. 294 (December 1986): 49–58.

Jung Baeksoo [Chŏng Paek-su]. *Nikkan kindai bungaku no kōsa to danzetsu—nikō tairitsu ni kōshite*. Tokyo: Akashi Shoten, 2013.

Kawamura Minato. "Yi Sang no Keijō—1930 nendai no 'bungei toshi' Seoul." *Chōsenshi Kenkyūkai Ronbunshū*, no. 30 (October 1992): 5–23.

Kim Yun-sik. "Sŏul kwa Tong'gyŏng sai." In *Yi Sang yŏn'gu*, 143–72. Seoul: Munhak Sasangsa, 1987.

Saegusa Toshikatsu. "Yi Sang no modanizumu—Sono seiritsu to genkai." *Chōsen Gakuhō*, no. 140 (July 1991): 131–78.

Sano Masato. "Kankoku modanizumu no isō—Yi Sang no shi to Anzai Fuyue o megutte." *Shōwa Bungaku Kenkyū*, no. 25 (1992): 31–43.

Yi Bok-suk. "Yi Sang no shi ni okeru moderniti—sono danzetsusei ni tsuite." *Hikaku Bungaku Kenkyū*, no. 52 (October 1987): 128–39.

Yi Sang. "Nalgae." In *Yi Sang munhak chŏnjip—Sosŏl*, ed. Kim Yun-sik, 318–47. Seoul: Munhak Sasangsa, 1991.

ENGLISH-LANGUAGE SOURCES

Bech, Henning. *When Men Meet: Homosexuality and Modernity*, trans. Teresa Mesquit and Tim Davies. Chicago: University of Chicago Press, 1997.

Benjamin, Walter. 1968. "Some Motifs in Baudelaire," trans. Harry Zohn. In *Illuminations*, ed. Hannah Arendt, 157–202. New York: Harcourt, Brace and World, 1968.

Berlant, Lauren. *Cruel Optimism*. Durham, NC: Duke University Press, 2011.

Boellstorff, Tom. "When Marriage Fails: Queer Coincidences in Straight Time." GLQ 12, nos. 2–3 (2007): 227–48.

Choi Won-sik. "Seoul, Tokyo, New York: Modern Korean Literature Seen through Yi Sang's 'Lost Flowers,'" trans. Janet Poole. *Korea Journal* 39, no. 4 (Winter 1999): 118–43.

Dinshaw, Carolyn, Lee Edelman, Roderick A. Ferguson, Carla Freecero, Elizabeth Freeman, Judoth Halberstam, Annamarie Jagose, Christopher Nealon and Nguyen Tan Hoang. "Theorizing Queer Temporalities: A Roundtable Discussion." GLQ 13, nos. 2–3 (2007): 177–95.

Em, Henry. "Yi Sang's Wings Read as an Anti-colonial Allegory." In *Muæ: A Journal of Transcultural Production*, ed. Walter K. Lew, 104–11. New York: Kaya Production, 1996.

Frankl, John M. "Distance as Anti-Nostalgia: Memory, Identity, and Rural Korea in Yi Sang's 'Ennui.'" *Journal of Korean Studies* 17, no. 1 (2012): 39–68.

Freeman, Elizabeth. *Time Binds: Queer Temporalities, Queer Histories.* Durham, NC: Duke University Press, 2010.

Grosz, Elizabeth. "Thinking the New: Of Futures Yet Unthought." In *Becomings: Explorations in Time, Memory, and Futures,* ed. Elisabeth Grosz, 15–28. Ithaca, NY: Cornell University Press, 1999.

Halberstam, Judith [Jack]. *The Art of Queer Failure.* Durham, NC: Duke University Press, 2011.

Halberstam, Judith [Jack]. *In a Queer Time and Place: Transgender Bodies, Subcultural Lives.* New York: New York University Press, 2005.

Hanscom, Christopher P. "Modernism, Hysteria, and the Colonial Double Bind: Pak T'aewon's One Day in the Life of the Author, Mr. Kubo." *Positions* 21, no. 3 (Summer 2013): 607–36.

Jameson, Fredric. "Modernism and Imperialism." In *Nationalism, Colonialism, and Literature,* ed. Terry Eagleton, Fredric Jameson, and Edward W. Said, 43–66. Minneapolis: University of Minnesota Press, 1990.

Kim, Uchang [Kim U-chang]. "The Situation of the Writers under Japanese Colonialism." *Korean Journal* 16, no. 5 (May 1976): 4–15.

Koestenbaum, Wayne. *Double Talk: The Erotics of Male Collaboration.* New York: Routledge, 1989.

Lew, Walter K. "Jean Cocteau in the Looking Glass: A Homotextual Reading of Yi Sang's Mirror Poems." In *Muæ: A Journal of Transcultural Production,* ed. Walter K. Lew, 118–47. New York: Kaya Production, 1996.

Lew, Walter K. Untitled essay. In *Muæ: A Journal of Transcultural Production,* ed. Walter K. Lew, 71–73. New York: Kaya Production, 1996.

Muñoz, José Esteban. *Cruising Utopia: The Then and There of Queer Futurity.* New York: New York University Press, 2009.

Poole, Janet. *When the Future Disappears: The Modernist Imagination in Late Colonial Korea.* New York: Columbia University Press, 2014.

Race, Kane. *Pleasure Consuming Medicine: The Queer Politics of Drugs.* Durham, NC: Duke University Press, 2009.

Sone, Seunghee [Sone Sŭng-hi]. "The Mirror Motif in the Crow's Eye View (Ogamdo) Poems." *Seoul Journal of Korean Studies* 29, no. 1 (June 2016): 193–217.

Stephens, Michael. *The Dramaturgy of Style: Voice in Short Fiction.* Carbondale: Southern Illinois University Press, 1986.

Treat, John Whittier. "Introduction to Yi Kwang-su's 'Maybe Love' (Ai ka, 1909)." *Azalea* 4 (2011): 315–27.

Treat, John Whittier. "Returning to Altman: Same-Sex Marriage and the Apparitional Child." In *After Homosexual: The Legacies of Gay Liberation,* ed. Carolyn D'Cruz and Mark Pendleton, 265–81. Perth, WA: University of Western Australia Press, 2013.

Yi Sang. "Crow's-Eye View," trans. Walter K. Lew. In *Muæ: A Journal of Transcultural Production*, ed. Walter K. Lew, 80. New York: Kaya Production, 1996.

Yi, Sang. "Tokyo," trans. Michael D. Shin. In *Muæ: A Journal of Transcultural Production*, ed. Walter K. Lew, 96–101. New York: Kaya Production, 1996.

Yi, Sang. "The Wings," trans. Ahn Jung-hyo. In *The Wings*, 7–40. Seoul: Jimoondang, 2001.

Chapter Three

PROBLEMATIZING LOVE

THE INTIMATE EVENT AND
SAME-SEX LOVE IN COLONIAL KOREA

Pei Jean Chen

I n the face of various social and political transformations, the leading intellectuals of East Asia addressed the problem of modernity in relation to Confucianism in the late nineteenth and early twentieth centuries.[1] This resulted
in the revolution of the social system and political formation, the liberation
of individuals from traditional kinship relations, and advocacy of modern
education and civilization. When "love" emerged as a social phenomenon
in twentieth-century East Asia, it coincided with the discourses of "civilization," "modernization," and "nation building."[2] It soon became naturalized as a
transparent, universal value and emerged as a dominant narrative that defined
people's social relationships. Thus, to examine the construction of modern
love is to further reveal the dominant ideology that created and divided different social subalterns.

Korea also experienced drastic changes from a traditional social system
to a modern colonial one during the late nineteenth century. The reform of
marriage (free marriage) and new forms of intimate relationships (free love)
played an important role in the development of modern society and literary
production. Between 1910 and the 1930s, debates on free marriage and free
love in Korea centered on social reforms and the civilizing project.[3] While

the experience of love was an important moment to rediscover oneself in the process of modernization via colonial power, the colonized were caught up between the demands of individual autonomy and social constraints that structured the binary division of colonial power. Anthropologist Elizabeth Povinelli terms this situation "intimate events" in her study of settler colonies in the United States and Australia. She elucidates how "intimate events" might have functioned in a colonial situation by tracing how conceptions of love are produced at the intersection of individual freedom and social bondage.[4] Applying this understanding to colonial Korea, the dual forces from the individual and the social result in an emancipation-oppression mechanism that operated in the name of love, one that underscores the pervasive yet largely unacknowledged infusion of colonialism into Korean culture.

To better understand this historical situation, I examine public debates and literary representations about love as intimate events produced during transformative moments of the early twentieth century. More important, I discuss how the notion of same-sex love operates within colonial conceptions of romantic love. I also unveil the internal contradictions of and challenges to the institutionalization of love in advancing "civilization"—that is, in the name of equality, liberation, and progressiveness.

The Institutionalization of Modern Love

When examining the emergence of the modern concept of love, it is important to emphasize the transnational and translational features of this cultural phenomenon. It is also important to revisit the different phases of love discourses. First, the emergence of modern love in colonial Korea, which paralleled the development of the "new novel" (sin sosŏl), was built on the idea of free marriage (chayu kyŏrn) in the enlightenment period (1876–1910). This was a time when Japanese imperial power expanded and started to invade Asia. It aroused Koreans' sense of patriotism and led to various social reforms during the late nineteenth century and into the new century. As the cultural and literary scholar Kwŏn Podŭrae argues, "Throughout the 1900s, love became a public value under the influence of Christianity and patriotism, as Christianity preached the ethics of love, and devotion and passion for the state were strongly encouraged in the formation of the nation-state."[5] During this period, "love" had little to do with sexual or romantic desires.[6] According to Kwŏn, the English word "love" can be translated as yŏnae or sarang in Korean; the significant difference between the two is that:

the [translated] word *yŏnae* only connotes the love between man and woman. The love of God, humans, parents, or friends is not *yŏnae*. . . . The word *sarang* . . . is widely known, coming from the Korean word *sarang hada*, and has a deep-rooted meaning of "to think of" or "to feel." . . . After the importation of Christianity, the idea that *sarang* meant the love of God became widespread. In the 1900s, the word was also used in the field of national discourse. . . . *Sarang* first became legitimized in the backdrop of God and Nation.[7]

Kwŏn thus distinguishes *yŏnae* from *sarang* to focus on the development of the term *yŏnae* and its connection to romantic love.

Furthermore, after the occupation of Korea by Japan in 1910 and the failure of the March 1 Independence Movement of 1919, a passion for educational and cultural reform emerged in public media and coincided with various discussions on *yŏnae*. During this phase, *yŏnae* gained popularity and gradually formed its core meaning of romantic love, but it was already embedded in the ideology of nation building. It thus possessed a paradoxical structure of being liberating and repressive at the same time. In their research, Chŏng Hye-yŏng and Yu Chong-yul argue that "virginity" played a dominant role in the discourse of love in which "spiritual love" replaced carnal desire. They explore literary writings by leading intellectuals and novelists whose works illustrate how carnal relationships between men and women led to tragedy and condemned them having lost their virtue, thereby securing the spiritual form of the relationship.[8] Influenced by European scholarship and Japanese translations of Western works, these intellectuals and writers devoted a considerable amount of writing to the reformation of marriage and the advocacy of free love. For example, East Asian societies at that time shared highly influential ideas about love from such figures as the Swedish feminist Ellen Key (1849–1926) and her work *Love and Marriage*, whose English edition was published in 1911. This important text for early twentieth-century feminist movements in Japan and the West was the basis for many social critics' ideas on love, marriage, and motherhood.[9]

Observed from a considerable number of public critiques on women's liberation written by male intellectuals, women were treated in a paradoxical manner. While promoting women's social rights, education, and free will, leading intellectuals disqualified women from pursuing self-autonomy and thus reproduced the patriarchal subjugation of women. In this way, they advocated love while criticizing New Women. For example, the Korean writer and literary critic Kim Tong-in's "Kim Yŏn-sil chŏn" (The Story of Kim Yŏn-sil

[1939]) is believed to have been written based on the famous New Woman Kim Myŏng-sun.[10] In it, he criticizes the New Woman by stating that "the love (yŏnae) she comprehends is nothing but 'intercourse.' Literature is love, and love cannot be separated from intercourse. . . . She learned this idea of love from Ellen Key and Kuriyagawa Hakuson.[11] . . . Kim Yŏn-sil, who was born in Korea, does not know what yŏnae means."[12] What Kim suggested here is that New Women blindly pursued the fashion of love but were incapable of understanding the civilizing and spiritual soul of it. This kind of critique, however, is at odds with the "free" nature of love that these intellectuals promoted for their people.

Throughout the period when Confucianism was criticized and nations built, discourses on modern love vacillated between the ideological tendency of cultivating women as new national subjects and reinforcing traditional and regulative ideas about them. Even though arguments on love in this period dealt directly with universalized sexual desire, women were usually doubly characterized as old and new in media critiques or literary works (i.e., kisaeng and New Woman, traditional mother and rebellious daughter), and they usually failed in the realm of the modern family (for being too ignorant or ending up taking their lives through suicide). The promotion of "wise mother, good wife" during the colonial era shows how women's given gender role and subordinated position were never redeemed by the liberation of love or sex.[13] One might then ask: Who is qualified to pursue modern love, and what is wrong with love when it is associated with sexual intercourse? To be more specific, what is the relation between love and sex in the discourses of modern love? To answer these questions, it is helpful to revisit the historical construction of modern love and sex in Japan, Korea's colonizer.

The cultural and literary critic Saeki Junko has analyzed the important role of "love" in Japan's enlightenment and its influence on modern literature since the Meiji period (1868–1912).[14] According to Saeki, the Victorian concept of love, which emerged in the Meiji period and was translated in hiragana as rabu and as the Chinese character ai, came to replace iro, which existed outside marriage as a form of sexual desire/act in the Edo period (1600–1868). Furthermore, ai, which is often used in conjunction with ren to create the compound term renai, refers to romantic love and accentuates a spiritual relationship rather than carnal desire. For Japanese writers after 1885, the modern form of "love" was a vital element and was used to radically transform the relationships between the men and women by promoting a spiritual form of love and repressing carnal desires/sexual acts in their writings. Writers at that time, including Tsubouchi Shōyō (1859–1935), Ozaki Kōyō (1868–1903), and Mori Ōgai (1862–1922), subscribed to the separation of the soul and flesh or body and celebrated pure and ideal love, as opposed to *iro*, a relationship that involved physical contact or desire. In this way, the separation of love and sex (or of spirit and flesh) helped generate the emergence of "modern sex." As Kōjin Karatani elucidates, "modern sex" should be considered a "new" form of sex, with its existence produced through repression.[15]

The Japanese experience of modern love greatly influenced the development of love in colonial Korea, as the two countries shared a transnational mode of translation. According to Kwŏn, the term *yŏnae* was used in 1910 in Ch'oe Nam-sŏn's partial translation of Victor Hugo's *Les Misérables* (1862). There, the term *yŏnaedang* (lit., love gang, or romance chaser) appears to describe the character who "loves flowers, plays the flute, and writes vulgar songs. He has compassion for people, feels sad for women, smiles at children, and bears strong hatred against the revolutionaries' beheading of noblemen."[16] It should be noted that Ch'oe's Korean translation, published in the literary magazine *Sonyŏn* (Youth [1908–11]), which he helped found, derived from a Japanese translation, not the French original. The term *yŏnaedang* was thus adopted from a Japanese creation. A similar situation can be found in other literary translations. The term *yŏnae* first appeared in connection to romantic love in the serial novel *Ssangongnu* (Tears of the Twin Jade). This novel was published in the *Maeil Sinbo* (Daily News) in 1912–13 with the catchphrase, "I would teach you that the *yŏnae* of young men and women is an extremely sacred thing." A sentence similar to "*yŏnae* is a sacred thing" is also found in *Changanmong* (Long and Regrettable Dream [1913]), which Ch'oe also penned and serialized in the same newspaper. It should be noted that these two novels were all published under the name Cho Chung-hwan and are adaptations of the Japanese novels *Ono ga Tsumi* (One's Own Sin [1899–1900]), by Kikuchi Yuho, and *Konjiki Yasha* (The Golden Demon [1897–1902]), by Ozaki Kōyō. *The Golden Demon* is a translation of the English novelist Bertha M. Clay's *Weaker Than a Woman* (1878).[17]

To some extent, these translations inherited the spiritual notion of love from Meiji culture. But the result of the circulation of these translated novels and of *yŏnae*, the term for romantic love, means that they are multilayered and multitextual. For example, the perceptions of *Long and Regrettable Dream* were represented in the following advertisement for the publication notice of the serial novel:

A New Novel (Sin Sosŏl), Changanmong

– It is not a usual novel.

– It portrays human nature and social conditions.

– How can anyone not cry while reading this?[18]

The advertisement introduces Cho Chung-hwan's translation as "A New Novel."[19] The underlying ideology of the new novel, especially as a method to "enlighten" Korean people, influenced Cho's intention to translate *The Golden Demon*, as well as his hope of offering the spiritual food to young people.[20] Scholarship on Cho Chung-hwan's translation of *The Golden Demon* has illustrated the differences between the original Japanese and the Korean translation and established the popularity of both novels in colonial Korea.[21] What I want to highlight here is that Cho's translation of Japanese popular novels embodies the intersection of modern love, translation activities, and the practice of the new novel in a local context. And more important, the localization of a foreign text can be achieved only when both the spiritual (desire to be modern) and the material (equipped with modern technologies) are ready to serve the modernization of a nation. Both the translation/adaption and the original influenced the local literary and social contexts of colonial Korea. Specific evidence of this phenomenon can be seen in the creation of Yi Kwang-su's *Chaesaeng* (Rebirth [1924–25]), which illustrates how "love" obtains its exchange value through transcultural communication and the growth of capitalism.[22]

Furthermore, when Japanese writers developed the modern concept of love in Japanese literature, they could not avoid tracing the connotations of each character in the Japanese language.[23] However, this linguistic negotiation was absent in the translations of love in colonial Korea. The problem of translation revolves around the unquestioned equivalence between different languages and concepts. In other words, colonial intellectuals borrowed the Japanese *renai* and adopted the term *yŏnae* to translate the equivalent concept from Japanese and Western sources without negotiating; this argument can be applied to other new concepts as well.[24] I argue that this convenience of unswerving adoption of the modern Japanese invention of love, which was mediated by the shared linguistic source of Chinese characters, led to the naturalization of this concept as a transparent and universal value. In the case of colonial Korea, the full embrace of "love" without social or linguistic negotiations signifies the colonial ambivalence that the colonized desired to be modern even as they failed to be so—that is, they sought to overcome colonial reality but were, in fact, incapable of action. To some extent, the shared experience of love functions in bridging the gap between different classes and genders in Korean society and Korea's relations with imperial powers.

Accordingly, the concept of love remained more aspirational than real in colonial Korea.[25] Regardless of ideological or sexual differences, most scenarios of modern love constructed at that time agreed that the experience of love was based on an individual's own choice.[26] However, "choice," as Kath Weston argues in her queer reading of kinship, "is an individualistic and, if you will, bourgeois notion that focuses on the subjective power of an 'I' to formulate relationships to people and things, untrammelled by worldly constraints."[27] Weston implies, then, that to privilege "choice" as the core of kinship is to privilege those with the fewest bodily differences and local attachments that would preclude the full exercise of this autonomy. An investigation of social and literary discourses on romantic love thus reveals a modern formation of love-sex that manifests an emancipation-oppression mechanism wherein Koreans invariably experienced the ambivalence of a modernity largely reinforced by colonial power.

This argument is supported by the social phenomenon of same-sex love. In the next section, I illustrate how same-sex love exposes the paradox and dilemma of the civilization process and is of vital importance in its exceptional status of securing normatively intimate and social relationships. As Povinelli elucidates, we (might) all have freedom to participate in the intimate event, "unless you happen to be, or are considered to be, a woman, a homosexual, not white." This shows "the imaginary of the intimate event is always disrupted and secured by the logic of exception."[28] This phenomenon can be seen in how colonial society allowed certain groups, such as schoolgirls, to engage in same-sex love to keep young people away from heterosexual intercourse and thereby celebrated spiritual civilization. At the same time, same-sex love was medicalized, with sex education aiming to promote reproductive relationships.

Representations and Temporalities of Same-Sex Love

The Japanese terminology for same-sex love first appeared as a Japanese-coined Chinese character (*wasei kango*), *dōseiai*, in the 1920s.[29] In many ways, the formation and transformation of the Japanese term *dōseiai* had an influence on the Korean concept of *tongsŏng'ae*. Modern knowledge was imported from Japanese and European sexology to Korea after the annexation. Examples such as Richard von Krafft-Ebing's *Psychopathia Sexualis* (1886), which was translated into Japanese in 1913, and Sakaki Yasusaburō's (1870–1929)

Seiyoku kenkyū to seishin bunsekigaku (Studies of Sexual Desire and Psychoanalysis [1919]) introduced same-sex love as sexual perversion to East Asian societies. After 1910, the Korean word compounds for same-sex love, including *tongsŏng'ae, tongsŏng yŏnae*, and *tongsŏnggan ŭi sarang*, replaced premodern terms, such as "male colors" (*namsaek*). These terms coexisted in the translations of foreign works and were used to reference same-sex love and homoeroticism.[30] However, from the second half of the 1920s to the 1930s, the term *tongsŏng'ae* began to predominate, especially in reference to same-sex love between women. It should be noted that the emergence of the term *tongsŏng'ae* at this time does is not tantamount to the existence of homosexual subjects or a lesbian identity as we know them today. But the emergence of the term does indicate the power of *naming*. In this sense, to trace the temporality, language difference, and referents of terminologies is to locate sociohistorical specificity, as well as the diachronicity and the synchronicity, of these modern concepts.

These conceptual points can be observed from the following examples from colonial Korea. When it first emerged during the 1910s, same-sex love was quickly pathologized and medicalized. As the Korean doctor Chŏng Sŏk-tae once stated, "'Sexual desire' is basically between different sexes and does not exist between the same sex. When it happens between the same sex, everyone would identify it as a disease. It is called 'sexual desire between the same sex,' or, in other words, 'same-sex love.'"[31] In his essay on sexual desire, Chŏng normalized sexual desire between heterosexuals and medicalized its same-sex counterpart. These views were common among medical experts and other intellectuals during this period. Kim Yun-kyŏng, for example, likened same-sex behavior to perverted sexuality such as rape, bigamy, and kinky abuse that resulted in sexual disease and homicide.[32] Such medical narratives denied autonomy or agency to those who were deemed ill or "perverted" subjects. These medical narratives were complicit with various social institutions, such as pedagogy, family/marriage, and medical science, to name a few, all of which aimed to normalize "sex" as "a natural sexual desire between men and women." Clearly, the aim of these discourses was to exclude diverse sexual forms from idealized practices of reproductive heterosexuality. Along with masturbation and sexually transmitted diseases such as syphilis, same-sex love was viewed as a sexual behavior that did not lead to reproduction and was thus of little use to empire building and military power.

Paradoxically, however, there was one part of colonial societies where same-sex love was permitted: the spiritual love between schoolgirls. This viewpoint of "female-exclusive same-sex love" can be seen in statements such as, "When talking about tongsŏng'ae, I think it is more imaginable and reasonable to think of women, though the strange and even pathological phenomenon can also be found between men. . . . Today, I think the general impression is that tongsŏng'ae is an exclusive possession of women."[33] The writer Yi Sŏk-un produced this statement from his reflection on double suicide between women that took place in colonial Korea.[34] His use of terms such as *sŏngyok* (sexual desire), *pyŏngjŏk* (pathological), and *sŏng ŭi toch'ak* (sexual perversion) shows his knowledge of sexology. Therefore, his discussion of tongsŏng'ae under conditions of modernity aimed to pathologize and categorize it as an unconventional form of normative love. Yi later introduced same-sex culture in the second part of the essay, in which he discussed the terms *namsaek* and *oip-chaengi* (womanizer), which were sexual practices men used to secure their power and fame during the Chosŏn Dynasty (1392–1910).[35] His tracing of a modern tongsŏng'ae through the premodern namsaek resonates with Saeki Junko's observation of the Japanese *iro* to *ai*, which also represented a clear rupture between spiritual and carnal practices.

Later, the writer and reformer Kim Yŏ-je (1895–1968) wrote a long essay in which he discussed same-sex love cultures in various countries (including America, Egypt, England, France, Germany, and Italy), focusing on the specific cultural context of each society. With a broad understanding of the subject, Kim calls the public's attention toward same-sex love by explaining that "it is not just a psychological or medical issue, but also an educational and social one."[36] Interestingly, Kim differs from Yi's interest in exploring the cultural history of namsaek and tongsŏng'ae and instead states, "Considering that we still can see that the words *namsaek* and *tongsŏng yŏn'ae* exist in our society, we can presume the malady of this unsolved problem."[37] He continues, "Although it is a fact that tongsŏng yŏn'ae is an expression of human nature, for the full development of both male and female sexes and the balance of sexual life, antisocial instincts such as tongsŏng yŏn'ae need to be controlled and converted, no matter what. We have to keep working hard on this."[38] What both Yi and Kim suggested in their lengthy essays is that the phenomenon of tongsŏng'ae should be regulated to secure a healthy society. The tragedy (suicide and crime) and perversion (deviant desire and immorality) associated with tongsŏng'ae suggest that same-sex love was, for them, exceptional to normative love and social order.

Terms such as *namsaek* and *tongsŏng'ae* embody specific cultural references to colonial Korea and the modernization of its language and individual subjects during this period. This cultural specificity requires special consideration. As discussed in the previous section, the transformation of sexual desire from carnal to spiritual, the civilizing ideology, and the practices of translation and literary production all influenced the discourse and construction of the concept of love and are all thus indispensable for understanding the discourse of same-sex love. As we observed from the terms *namsaek* and *tongsŏng'ae*, there was also an explicit gender difference in the development of same-sex intimacy between men and that between women.

In the following section, I argue that male-male intimacy in the 1910s and female same-sex love during the 1920s and 1930s were all strongly spiritualized to avoid the mentioning of sexual acts; however, male writers often depicted erotic scenes in the representation of female-female intimacy. The gender difference shows that the female sex and body were of great significance to the regulative mechanism of love. Furthermore, depictions of male and female same-sex love in popular media and literary representations appeared as "incomplete projects." I thus propose to read same-sex love not merely as a failed version of love and modernization but, rather, as a counterdiscourse that opposed the totalization of different forms of life. To this end, I conclude by suggesting that same-sex love be viewed as an important site to explore alternative possibilities for "queer modes of life" in Korean history.[39]

Male Same-Sex Love as Civilizing Spirit: Sympathy

Before representations of female same-sex love came to preoccupy the mass media in the 1930s, male same-sex love appeared in the literary writings of colonized intellectuals during the 1910s.[40] As scholars have demonstrated, these discourses of love were underwritten by two political impulses. The first arose out of critiques of traditional social relationships, especially the Confucian social order. Marriage and family were thus targeted for reform in the liberation of modern individuals. The second was to cultivate the individual for the civilization project by enhancing spiritual love while diminishing physical desire. However, as I show in the following discussion, "love" between the male protagonists had little to do with sexual desire; it was, instead, focused on spiritual caring or sympathy (*tongjŏng*), with love always remaining an incomplete project.

In his short novel *Tongjŏng ŭi nu* (Tears of Sympathy [1920]), for example, the writer and art critic Paek Ak states:

In the relationship of B and I, there is an attraction of love; we spiritually comfort each other. Even when we cannot see each other for just one day, the thought of seeing the other becomes stronger, and the mind is confused. I just feel sorry about B's situation and express my sympathy, and B feels my sympathy and love. He accepts them, and his love toward me naturally grows. . . . But from a third person's point of view, our relationship would be called same-sex love (*tongsŏng'ae*).[41]

Among literary works depicting "love" between men, Paek's is the only one that mentions the term *tongsŏng'ae*, which he equates to the broad idea of sympathetic love. As Yi Chŏng-suk argues, "For the difficulty of the nation, the emotional solidarity that enables 'sympathy' is necessary, and it is stabilized and realized by the relationship of 'same-sex love' in the form of 'friendship.'"[42] Yi makes this argument by examining several literary works by Paek Ak, Yi Kwang-su, and others. She uses these works to highlight sympathy as a rhetorical device for the fulfilment of enlightenment, and that impulse coincides with same-sex love in discovering the national spirit.

As Kim Hyŏn-ju argues, this effort to promote the national spirit was not just aimed at the creation of new subjects, such as the individual and the nation; it sought to produce a new view of culture and literature and a revolt against colonial power.[43] The politics of sympathy in modern Korean literature certainly resonated with the idea of spiritual civilization in the 1910s. Yi Kwang-su once expressed his thoughts on the subject, writing:

What is called sympathy signifies that my body and mind are concerned with the position and situation of others, as well as those persons' thought and behavior. In fact, among the noble qualities of human beings, it is the most noble. Sympathy is in direct proportion to the development of spirit (which is the development of humanity). . . . The higher the development of spirit, the individual or nation will have deep thoughts of sympathy, or the contrary.[44]

This emphasis on sympathy, as Sŏ Yŏng-ch'ae argues, shows that "Yi Kwang-su tried to connect his protagonists' inner struggles with the passion of enlightenment to save Korean people in need and who were hungry."[45] Most of the characters in the literary works produced around this time were young men who suffered unhappy childhoods, and that trauma turned into sorrow and loneliness.[46] The remedy was thus usually expressed through companionship, friendship, or love. Literary critic Kim Yun-sik comments on the features in Yi Kwang-su's works as "the consciousness of an orphan" and "the symptom of being hungry for love," which he equates to the shared experience of young people in Yi's generation.

However, I emphasize that the catastrophic nature of same-sex love depicted by Yi Kwang-su highlights the incomplete project of enlightened civilization and nation building. During the 1910s, Yi Kwang-su produced several short pieces of fiction that dealt with same-sex love.[47] His intertextual short novels *Ai ka* (Maybe Love [1909]) and *Yun Kwang-ho* (Yun Kwang-ho [1917]), are evidence of this incomplete project of love. Scholarship on these two novels has focused on their colonial complexity through a close reading of racial dimensions and the ambivalence of colonial intellectuals.[48] This scholarship highlights how racial differences between Koreans and Japanese brought about an imbalanced flow of desire.[49] According to these analyses, Korean youth embraced and, at the same time, resisted colonial desire, which was thus a mixed feeling of being civilized while also being colonized. In the two novels, the Korean protagonists Mun-gil and Kwang-ho's love for and surrender to the colonizers, Misao and P, resonate with Frantz Fanon's notion of the mentality of the "man of color to become a white man" and with what Ashis Nandy terms the "intimate enemy," both of which are forms of self-colonization.[50]

Nonetheless, the colonial ambivalence manifest in these works is obscured by their same-sex thematics. The reception of *Yun Kwang-ho* shows that people at that time disapproved of same-sex love, which resulted in suicide. Yi Kwang-su's contemporary Pak Yŏng-hŭi clearly identified the story as lost love from a man (*namsaek ŭi silyŏn*), not a woman. Even as he compared this desire to the sadness of a lost love, Park described this "unpleasant atmosphere of *namsaek*" as even stranger.[51] Yi himself also clarified this point, saying that although "*Yun Kwang-ho* is based on a true story," he avoids revealing his identity to protect the person's reputation.[52] These comments show that same-sex love was well recognized by readers, as it had already gained notoriety during the late 1910s. Notwithstanding the negative connotation of same-sex love in these comments, the terms *tongjŏng* (sympathy) and *aejŏng* (affection) appear several times in *Yun Kwang-ho*, much as *ai* was repeatedly used in *Maybe Love* when the Korean protagonist struggled with his innermost feelings toward a Japanese man in a monologue of self-doubt. The Korean protagonist's practice of *jŏng* (a wider scope of emotions and love) in accusing his Japanese counterpart of being *mujŏng* (heartlessness) and causing *silyŏn* (lost love) represents self-reflection and empowerment. As John Treat nicely puts it, it is "an introspective change in the protagonist's character, and with it the manufacture of a modern, interiorized self."[53] In both novels, the catastrophic nature of love and the suicidal tendencies of the protagonists symptomize the desperate state of mind of colonial intellectuals while generating reflection on the projects of colonization and modernization. Literary writings on male same-sex love thus show that the process of constructing sexual/power relations is not just related to the order between male/female, heterosexual/homosexual, but should also include colonizer/colonialized and nation-building/political subversion.

Female Same-Sex Love and Queer Modes of Life

Contrary to the purely spiritual way in which male writers wrote about male-male relationships in the literature discussed earlier, the depiction of female same-sex relationships by male writers was closely related to eroticism, thus revealing a gender hierarchy in their conception of same-sex love. For example, in Yi Kwang-su's *Mujŏng* (Heartless [1917]), Wŏl-hwa, a famous kisaeng, became the female protagonist of Yŏng-ch'ae's mentor when Yŏng-ch'ae's mentor had to sell herself to save her family. The two became intimate:

> Once, when Wŏl-hwa and Yŏng-ch'ae came back from a party late at night and had slept together in the same bed, Yŏng-ch'ae put her arms around Wŏl-hwa in her sleep, and kissed her on the mouth. She laughed to herself, "So you have awakened as well," she thought. "Sadness and suffering lie ahead of you." She woke Yŏng-ch'ae. "Yŏng-ch'ae, you just put your arms around me and kissed me on the mouth." Yŏng-ch'ae buried her face in Wŏl-hwa's breasts, as though [she] were ashamed, and bit her white breasts. "I did it because it was you," she said.[54]

Yi Kwang-su thus employs female-female eroticism to replace Yŏng-ch'ae's sexual desire toward men.[55]

A similar depiction can be found in Yi Hyo-sŏk's *Kaesalgu* (Wild Apricots [1937]), in which two women of different social classes engaging in female homoeroticism: "She had fallen for the Seoul woman in the same way that Chae-su had. She felt fortunate to have been born a woman so that she could wait on such a beauty who all of the village's men desired. . . . Sometimes, when she prepared a bath for the Seoul woman, and while scrubbing her white back, Chŏm-sun was overwhelmed by the desire to hold that beautiful body against hers."[56] Male writers took the middle ground in replacing carnal desire between men and women, which was erased in modern literature, and love with female same-sex eroticism. Also, when they associated female subjects with eroticism, they disqualified women in the pursuit of modern love; thus, women failed in the project of civilization and nation building. This tendency is similar to Kim Tong-in's depiction of New Women that I discussed earlier. Despite that, many more representations of female same-sex love placed emphasis on the spiritual relationship.

In representations by women, female intellectuals emphasized the lofty sentiment of sympathy and veiled the possibility of sexual desire. The article "Yŏryu myŏngsa ŭi tongsŏngyŏn'ae gi" (Stories of Same-Sex Love of Female Celebrities), published in the magazine *Pyŏlgŏn'gon* (Another World) in 1930, featured four New Women: Hwang Sin-dŏk, a journalist; Hŏ Yŏng-suk, a gynecologist and Yi Kwang-su's wife; Yi Tŏk-yo, a Christian activist; and an anonymous fourth woman.[57] These New Women were interviewed about their experience of "same-sex love" in their high school years, with the text organized as a first-person narrative of each interviewee. In their narratives, same-sex love was a shared experience and trend during the women's schooldays, and it emerged from sympathy and caring for one another. Hwang Sin-dŏk wrote:

> There should be no one who has not experienced same-sex love during a girl's school days. I myself experienced it many times. When recalling it, many interesting things come to mind. I was very close to a friend from T'aech'ŏn when studying in Sungŭi Girls School. The friend was an orphan and lived in poverty. It might have been the sympathy toward her situation in the beginning, but then the seedling of loving emotions grew. . . . This was my very first experience of same-sex love. Although I was very close to many other friends thereafter, I never experienced this kind of pure love.[58]

Hŏ Yŏng-suk wrote:

> I had many experiences of same-sex love when studying at Chinmyŏng School when I was approximately fourteen or fifteen years old, as many others did. When I was studying at Paehwa Girls School, I had many interesting experiences with the wife of a current professor at Central General High School named Kim Kyŏng-hŭi. . . . Since she lived in the dormitory and I was at home, we could only meet once a week in the church. I waited and waited until the day came; we were so happy and had lots of things to talk about with each other when we met. . . . One more person was a senior named Pae Yŏng-sun at Chinmyŏng School. She was very adorable to me. . . . One day when I heard the *ŏnni* (older sister) whom I deeply loved was in love with another person, I became so angry that I seized the *ŏnni*, cried out loud, and said to her that if she refused to break up with the other person, I would die. Anyway,

I was extremely jealous. Also, when the *ŏnni* got married, I was so heartbroken that I wailed bitterly.[59]

Several points are repeated in Hwang's and Ho's narratives: the popularity of same-sex love at girls' schools,[60] the purity of that love, and scenes of girls' dormitories and churches. These points illustrate what I argued previously— namely, that the Western/Christian concept of love impacted the discourse of love in early twentieth-century East Asia and that it set spiritual love apart from physical desire or sexual behavior as a symbol of civilization.

A conspicuous repression of physical desire or sexual behavior can be observed in Yu's narrative. Yu's story is similar insofar as it mentions the life experiences at girls' schools, scenes of the dormitory, and the mixed emotions of love and sympathy. However, Yu revealed a detail from her past experience that disgusted her:

> The way she likes me, compared to my love toward her, is somehow more scary. It is not about P's face or body or her love for me. To me, it is just about her hand. In the night or daytime, when I looked at her hand, I suffered from fatigue because it looks so scary and creepy; I could not bear it. In the night, before we sleep together, her hand came to me; it just made me feel like a big snake attacking me, and thus very creepy and scary. Even now when thinking about her, the hand comes to my mind first. The hand and foot [of one person] are so ugly that there was no love between couples. . . . Oh my, her hand![61]

Even though she did not expose her full name, Yu wrote the longest account and recounted more negative thoughts than the others. The problematic "hand" raises the question of the repression of physical desire. At the end of Yu's narrative, she states that the hand she experienced was scarier than a "devil's hand" in a movie. One can easily connect the hand with the sexual behavior between two women, revealing how Yu made the experience something evil and disavowed it.

New Women's practice of same-sex love was often located in Christian schools and churches.[62] New Women intellectuals in colonial Korea played an extremely complex social role. They embodied the hope that knowledge can bring individuals (and even the nation) toward civilization. For them, the experience of love was one way to release individuals from traditional social relations and lead them toward the project of modernization. However, colonial modernity also limited the New Woman, who, as a new modern subject and cultural construction, became a site for the display of knowledge-power. The text quoted earlier shows both the construction (the determined experience of love) and the destruction (the experience is gone for good) of the self. One should ask: Why is that pure love never experienced again?

In addition to similar elements in their narratives, the experiences of same-sex love all started and ended during a certain period of the girls' high school days. In contrast to the sustainable, reproductive relationships of heterosexuality, the relatively short period of spiritual same-sex love relationship functions as a "backward glance," as Fran Martin has discovered in contemporary Chinese representations.[63] Female same-sex relations in a woman's youth are thus represented as both cherished (mostly celebrating its pure emotion) and forcibly given up (to become qualified as an adult citizen). Accordingly, while this narrative encodes critical queer agency, its proliferation also reflects the social prohibition of adult lesbianism. Returning to the article mentioned earlier, Ho remembered her failure to maintain or argue for the relationship with the ŏnni when she got married, and Ho had nothing to do but think about death while she herself married Yi Kwang-su. In the same manner, Hwang had advocated love between husband and wife in a different interview published earlier. Most same-sex love practitioners thus "gave up" pure love and moved on to the next stage of their lives. One might ask: What if they wanted to keep the relationship and fight against mainstream expectations? The answer is not a positive one, at least in terms of what public records tell us.

What we can find are tragic examples, such as the double suicide committed by Hong Ok-im and Kim Yong-ju in 1930:

> At 4:45 PM on April 8, [1930], there were two young females who committed suicide by jumping in front of a high-speed train at Yŏngdŭngp'o Station. One of the victims was Hong Ok-im, a twenty-one-year-old student at Kyŏngsŏng Iwha School; her father is Doctor Hong. The other was Kim Yong-ju, a senior student at Tongdŏk Girls Senior High School (who is married to the elder son of a wealthy family; her father is Kim Tong-jin, who runs a bookstore). The reason for their suicide is not yet clear.[64]

As the media often reported on the phenomenon of double suicides (chŏngsa) at that time, their deaths became a sensation and sparked contentious debates.[65] A search of databases and archives brings up the Japanese term dōsei shinju and the Korean term tongsŏng'ae chŏngsa, both of which mean "same-sex [love] double suicide." These terms began to circulate in the public media in the 1920s. In addition, double suicide was the key incident that brought female same-sex love to public attention. Almost all of the reported incidents of same-sex couples were female pairs, in contrast to Yi Kwang-su's depiction of solo suicides by male figures. The high visibility of female same-sex (love) double suicide reveals society's interest in women, who were targeted as the site for colonial society to develop regulative ideas.

Accordingly, the critiques of female same-sex love and double suicide centered on "women questions" and the regulation of modern female subjects. Generally speaking, reports on female same-sex double suicide incidents featured a diverse range of modern female subjects. Even nonsexual romantic friendships between women could elicit the allegedly unnatural act of mutual self-destruction. The titles of related articles tended to highlight their professions, such as "Double Suicide of Two Barmaids" and "Female Workers of Same-Sex Love."[66] Barmaid (*chakbu*) and female worker (*yŏjikkong*) were neologisms that represented the advent of these female professions at that time. The cause of female same-sex double suicide discussed in the public media concentrated on "marriage issues": women either wanted to escape from marriages or were unhappy in their marriages (e.g., because of an age gap with their husbands or quarrels with family members). In the case of the double suicide mentioned earlier, the two educated young women were from middle-class backgrounds: the doctor's daughter was still single, while the other woman, the daughter of an intellectual, was married to a soldier in the air force.

The incident occurred in 1931, and widespread media coverage produced much discussion and writing related to issues of suicide. Media circles later defined it as a "same-sex love double suicide." They identified the cause of the tragedy as the pessimism of one of the women and the unhappy marriage of the other. Nonetheless, critics drew attention less to the personal situations and private lives of the young women themselves than to the incident's negative influence on teenagers and the larger society. Criticism of, compassion for, and condemnation of the incident converged on the following points: (1) the decline of filial piety and righteousness due to individualism; (2) solutions that families and schools can take to prevent this kind of tragedy; (3) critiques of arranged marriages; (4) methods for preventing mental illness; and (5) warnings not to overlook the problem of same-sex love and chastity. Yun Ch'i-ho, a Korean social reformer, presented yet another cause, suggesting that the tragedy was caused by "pessimism" and that "the excessively sentimental novels of Japanese writers—in which the heroines are never happy unless they kill or commit suicide—are doing much harm to educated Korean girls."[67]

Although these critiques connected the incident to social institutions, they failed to grasp the core of the issue. As with the cases of schoolgirl romances, the inconvenient truth of these social issues is nothing other than the "impossible futurity" of same-sex love. This is the opposite of what Lee Edelman terms "reproductive futurism," by which he means a political notion about the future. By contrast, queerness "should and must redefine such notions as 'civil order' through a rupturing of our foundational faith in the reproduction of futurity."[68] The impossible future reflected in double suicides and same-sex love shows the limits of free love itself. This freedom is conditional and restricted to spiritual romance, whereas "true" love leads to a reproductive relationship.

The lived experiences of these colonial women—their narratives of same-sex desire as struggle, depression, and death—offer me the possibility to consider resistance not only through women's nostalgia for their youth and their refusal to grow up, but also through the tragedies that are repeated in virtually every story. This excessive dysphoria should not be considered passivity, or an internal prohibition, but should instead be understood as resistance through the repetition of subaltern voices. As Jennifer Robertson has suggested, "Lesbian double suicides and attempted suicides were predicated on—and both used and criticized as a trope for—a revolt against the normalizing functions of 'tradition' (*qua* the 'Good Wife, Wise Mother') as sanctioned by the civil code."[69] Hence, the underlying logic of discourses on love, especially its regulative ideas about women, is further problematized through the investigation of female same-sex love and suicide. Finally, these lived experiences in the past teach us that if modern love in colonial Korea was typically framed in terms of a dominant imagination of monogamous, heterosexual, and reproductive relationships, same-sex love and double suicide created alternative practices with which to think about that oppressive history. These subaltern voices speak to and inter-reference each other while challenging and revising dominant pasts and enabling an alternative alliance of queer modes of life.

Conclusion: Toward the Decolonization of Love

In the middle of 2012, a musical performance titled *K'ongch'ilp'al Saesamnyuk* (lit., gossiping for trifles) debuted in Seoul; it used as its theme the female same-sex double suicide that, as discussed earlier, took place in Seoul in the 1930s. According to an interview with the writer and the composer, the musical was inspired by the "verdant and pure love" they found in the incident. The work does not aim to make any social statement; instead, it presents a story "just about love."[70] Yet, the definition of love in today's dictionary still suggests that intimate relationships should be exclusively between members of the opposite sex and that the future of that love is ultimately marriage.[71] Although enlightening civilization and national ideology are not directly imposed on the meaning of love here, the tendencies of compulsory heterosexuality, marriage as the ultimate goal, and the targeting of women as objects for regulation are inherited from notions of love that developed during the colonial era.

In this chapter, I have pointed out how colonialism and nationalism were interconnected in complex ways and how they helped shape the development of modern sexuality and love in occupied Korea. As demonstrated earlier, the discourse of love as an intimate event shaped ideas about the modern self, gender differences, and literary modernity, while one's "liberation" simultaneously create conditions for oppression. This return to love restages questions concerning the trajectories of civilization and modernity, which closely relate to histories of coloniality. I have argued that the discourses of free love and sexology contributed to the emergence of modern (national/sexual) subjects under the specific historical context of colonial Korea. In so doing, I problematized the notion of modern love to shed light on the false consciousness of love being equal and free. Although love is often perceived as universal and applicable to all members of society and even to all human beings, other forms of love (i.e., same-sex love) are disavowed. To be more specific, the paradox here is that the universality of love must always be maintained and secured by the logic of "exception." After all, although these "others" embody the contradictions of modernization, they are of great importance to the mainstream ideology of colonialism and nation building. To put it differently, "others" are not an obstacle to the realization of modernization or nation building but are necessary for these projects.

Symbolic others are not prerequisites to maintain the homogeneity of a society or nation but to ensure the alliance between dominant powers. For example, those who have venereal disease, have had an abortion, have engaged in prostitution, have committed (love/double) suicide, or were involved in other kinds of "perverted" sexualities (including same-sex love) are disqualified in the practice of modern love wherein colonialism, patriarchy, capitalism, and heterosexuality are already in alliance to secure reproductive relationships, gender divisions, markets, and military force to build the empire/nation.[72] In so doing, these "others," although they existed before "modern love" emerged, were generated from the discourses of love, and thus became a normative standard. In the process, these subjects were named, summoned, and divided for the new social system or social relations (and the various power mechanisms behind them) in which regulatory techniques are even more delicate and comprehensive. Nonetheless, the examples of same-sex love and love suicides during colonial times and the recollection of the colonial incident in the contemporary musical performance represents the very being of sexual subalterns that enables a direct critique of the false equality of love. Once subalterns overcome the division by their own power alliance, they will be able to revise this oppressive history.

Notes

1   In Japan, for example, Fukuzawa Yukichi (1835–1901) defended the new education against criticisms of surviving Confucians and offered his thoughts on social relations and morality. In Korea, Yi Kwang-su (1892–1950) severely criticized the rigidity of the Confucian moral code and Korea's "reliance" on Chinese culture as barriers preventing Korea from "progressing." He stated that "literature in the past, whether prose or poetry, remained strictly within the boundaries of Confucian morality." In his famous novel *A Madman's Diary*, Lu Xun (1881–1936) condemned the oppressive nature of Chinese Confucian culture as a "man-eating" society where the strong devour the weak. The madman's reading of ancient texts to discover evidence of cannibalism is a parody of traditional Confucian scholarship: Fukuzawa Yukichi, "Tokuiku Ikan," *Fukuzawa Yukichi Zenshû* 5 (1959): 349–64; Yi Kwang-su, "What Is Literature?" trans. Rhee Jooyeon, *Azalea* 4 (2011): 293–313; Lu Xun, "Kuangren Riji," *Xin Qingnian*, May 1, 1918.

2   For the scholarship on this topic, see Mark J. McLelland and Vera C. Mackie, eds., *Routledge Handbook of Sexuality Studies in East Asia* (New York: Routledge, 2015); Michiko Suzuki, *Becoming Modern Women: Love and Female Identity in Prewar Japanese Literature and Culture* (Stanford, CA: Stanford University Press, 2009); Sabine Frühstück, *Colonizing Sex: Sexology and Social Control in Modern Japan* (Berkeley: University of California Press, 2003); Kwŏn Podŭrae, *Yŏnae ŭi sidae: 1920 nyŏndae ch'oban ŭi munhwa wa yuhaeng* (Seoul: Hyŏnsil Munhwa Yŏn'gu, 2003); Sŏ Chi-yŏng, *Yŏksa e sarang ŭl mutta: Han'guk munhwa wa sarang ŭi kyebohak* (Seoul: Isup, 2011); Kō Ikujo, *Kindai Taiwan joseishi: Nihon no shokumin tōchi to "shinjosei" no tanjō* (Tokyo: Keisō Shobō, 2001); Haiyan Lee, *Revolution of the Heart: A Genealogy of Love in China, 1900–1950* (Stanford, CA: Stanford University Press, 2007).

3   Prior to the emergence of discourses on free marriage and free love, marriage issues, including early marriage and the remarriage of widows, were legally

reformed under the Kabo Reforms in 1894, and thus changed traditional social relationships.

4 According to her conception, the intimate event is a hierarchical pyramid of governance in which the relationship between the colonizer and the colonized as well as between different genders and social classes is recalibrated through discourses of love that blur relational lines. Connecting this social hierarchy to practices of colonial governance and modernization is a deeply personalized project of achieving normatively acceptable relations over oneself and others: see Elizabeth Povinelli, *The Empire of Love: Toward a Theory of Intimacy, Genealogy, and Carnality* (Durham, NC: Duke University Press, 2006), 3–4.

5 Kwŏn, *Yŏnae ŭi sidae*, 204.

6 Kwŏn, *Yŏnae ŭi sidae*, 218. Kwŏn makes this argument by examining eminent new novels written in the 1900s, such as Yi In-jik's *Tears of Blood* (*Hyŏl ŭi nu* [1906]), in which the protagonist, Ong-nyŏn, is in a marriage that is neither a traditional arrangement nor free and romantic.

7 Kwŏn, *Yŏnae ŭi sidae*, 15–16.

8 Chŏng Hye-yŏng and Yu Chong-yul, "Kŭndae ŭi sŏngnip kwa 'yŏnae' ŭi palgyŏn: 1920 nyŏndae nat'anan 'ch'ŏnyŏsŏng' sŏngnip kwajŏngŭl chungshim ŭro," *Han'guk Yŏndae Munhangn Yŏn'gu* 18 (December 2005): 227–51.

9 According to Michiko Suzuki's research, the two central aspects of modern love ideology as articulated in the work of Ellen Key can be delineated as follows. First, love is integral to female selfhood, a process of self-development ultimately leading to one's true identity. In her view, both the individual and the human race can become whole and attain completion through love. Second, love is both a spiritual and a sexual experience that completes the individual. Key's point is that true love, rather than following a hierarchical framework in which spiritual or platonic love is superior to sexual love, must combine both elements. This idea of love became an ideal that helped to define and shape sex/gender difference and equality. Although men were understood to experience love first through sexual desires and women were perceived to feel spiritual love before awakening to sexual love, both men and women had to experience spiritual and sexual love in order to progress and attain a modern self: see Suzuki, *Becoming Modern Women*, 13–14.

10 Sŏ, *Yŏksa e sarang ŭl mutta*, 229.

11 Kuriyagawa Hakuson (1880–1923) was a Japanese writer and literary critic, whose *Modern Views on Love* (Kindai no ren aikan, 1922) was widely circulated and translated in East Asia.

12 Kim Tong-in, "Kim Yŏn-sil chŏn," 33–34.

13 See Hyaeweol Choi, "Wise Mother, Good Wife: A Transcultural Discursive Construct in Modern Korea," *Journal of Korean Studies* 14, no. 1 (2009): 1–34.

14 For more on state technologies of love in the regulation of marriage, kinship, and reproductive health, see Sonia Ryang, *Love in Modern Japan: Its Estrangement from Self, Sex and Society* (London: Routledge, 2006).

15   Kōjin Karatani, *Origins of Modern Japanese Literature* (Durham, NC: Duke University Press, 1993), 79.

16   Requoted from Kwŏn, *Yŏnae ŭi sidae*, 192.

17   Bertha M. Clay was born Charlotte Mary Brame (1836–84).

18   *Maeil Sinbo*, May 9, 1913, 3.

19   The emergence of the new novel or new fiction (*sin sosŏl*) was grounded in the enlightenment era and gained its momentum through the growing distribution and circulation of newspapers. Scholarship such as *Han'guk sinsosŏl chŏnjip* (The Complete Collection of Korean New Novels [1968]) defines 1900–17, the time from the first appearance of Yi In-jik's novel to Yi Kwang-su's *Mujŏng*, as the era of the new novel.

20   Cho Chung-hwan himself wrote an essay to express his thoughts on the translation of both Japanese novels: *One's Own Sin* and *The Golden Demon*. To set the novels in Korea, he changed the background setting and the names of the characters to fit the colonial context: see Cho Chung-hwan, "Pŏnyŏkhoego, *Changanmong* kwa *Ssangongnu*," *Samch'ŏlli*, September 1, 1934, 234.

21   For a detailed discussion on Cho's translation/adaptation, see Pak Chin-yŏng, "Ilchae Cho Chung-hwan kwa pŏnan sosŏl ŭi sidae," *Minjong Chunhaksa Yŏn'gu* 26 (2004): 199–230.

22   Yi Kwang-su's *Chaesaeng* (Rebirth) was serialized in 218 installments in *Tong'a Ilbo* from November 9, 1924, to September 28, 1925. My discussion here is based on the original publication. The notable relationships among *The Golden Demon*, *Long and Regrettable Dream*, and *Rebirth* are illustrated in Sŏ Yŏng-ch'ae, "Chagi hŭisaeng ŭi kujo: Yi Kwang-su ŭi *Chaesaeng* kwa Ojak'i Koyo ŭi *Kŭmsaegyach'a*," *Minjok Munhwa Yŏn'gu* 58 (2013): 207–42. Yi's contemporary Kim Tong-in also pointed out that *Chaesaeng* was heavily influenced by *The Golden Demon*: see Kim Tong-in, "Ch'unwŏn yŏn'gu 7," *Samch'ŏlli*, July 1, 1935, 263–64.

23   According to Saeki Junko and Yanabu Akira, in Edo literature, the nature of love was expressed with different words like *iro* (eros), *koi* (attraction/passion), and *jŏ* (sentiment/emotion). But when sexual relationships were described, *iro* was most commonly used. In the late Meiji period, the words *ai* and *renai* began to replace *iro* in literature when referring to romance between lovers that went beyond the sexual. When the purely spiritual aspect of the relationship was emphasized, the English term *rabu* (love) was used in katakana: see Saeki Junko, "*Iro*" to "*ai*" no *hikaku bunkashi* (Tokyo: Iwanami Shoten, 1998), 7–31; Yanabu Akira, *Ai* (Tokyo: Sanseido, 2001).

24   These new concepts include "freedom," "equality," "revolution," and "civilization," to name a few.

25   Kim Ki-jin commented on the speculative nature of the famous English statement "love is best." As he writes, "Though there are some guys who have the leisure to say 'love is best,' saying that *yŏnae* is a kind of emotional game and product of the bourgeoisie is a prejudice against life. Though it might be right to say this in

some situations, it does not give the full picture. To humans who live in the ruins of the mind or in the pathetic majority, there are so many people hungry for love. If [*sarang*] has a certain condition and ideal, it is close to 'perfection.' If so, eventually '*sarang*' is nothing but a means of living. People who say *rŏbu isŭ pesŭtŭ* (love is best) are crazy. There is the *sarang* of fantasy. And a *sarang* as real as the ideal kind of *sarang* exists, too. There, the distance between fantasy and ideal is far": Kim Ki-jin, "Maŭm ŭi p'ehŏ, kyŏure sŏsŏ," *Kaebyŏk*, December 1, 1923, 132.

26 Suh Ji-young [Sŏ Chi-yŏng], "Collision of Modern Desires: Nationalism and Female Sexuality in Colonial Korea," *Review of Korean Studies* 5, no. 2 (2002): 111–32.

27 Kath Weston, *Families We Choose: Lesbians, Gays, Kinship* (New York: Columbia University Press, 1991), 110.

28 Povinelli, *The Empire of Love*, 191–93.

29 According to the Japanese sociologist Furukawa Makoto, it is not easy to determine when the compound *dōseiai* was used for the first time, but it likely appeared around 1922 in a sexological text. Moreover, before *dōseiai* was established as the mainstream term for same-sex love or desire, compounds like "dōsei no ai," "dōsei no ren," and "dōsei renai" appeared in public media during the 1910s. It should be noted that these compounds replaced existing terms like *nanshoku* (male colors) and mainly referred to male-male eroticism in the 1910s. Later, it came to cover all love between the same sex. Then, gradually, during the 1930s, it came to specify female-female relationships and sex and love: See Furukawa Makoto, "Dōsei 'ai' kō," *Imago* 6, no. 12 (1995): 201–7; Furukawa Makoto, "Sexuaritii no henyō: Kindai Nihon no dōseiai o meguru mittsu no kōdo," *Nichibei Josei Jaanaru* 17 (1994): 29–55; Gregory M. Pflugfelder, *Cartographies of Desire: Male-Male Sexuality in Japanese Discourse, 1600–1950* (Berkeley: University of California Press, 1999).

30 See Sin Ji-yŏn, "1920–30 nyŏndae tongsŏng (yŏn)ae kwallyŏn kisa ŭi susajŏk maengnak," *Minjok Munhwa Yŏn'gu* 45 (2006): 265–92.

31 Chŏng Sŏk-tae, "Sŏngyok ŭi saengni wa simni," *Pyŏlgŏn'gon*, February 1, 1929, 64.

32 Kim Yun-kyŏng, "Sŏngkyoyuk ŭi chuch'ang," *Tonggwang*, March 5, 1927, 27.

33 See Yi Sŏk-un, "Tongsŏng'ae mandam," 2, *Tong'a Ilbo*, March, 17, 1932.

34 The same-sex double suicide Yi referred to in the article was committed by Hong Ok-im and Kim Yong-ju in April 1931. I discuss this incident later.

35 The original content says, "It is said that the flourishing of *tongsŏng'ae* reached its zenith in the Chosŏn period. It was known as *namsaek* and, in that period, it served as a weapon and form of capital in the pursuit of success, like the practice of corrupt officials' scheming to offer up their beloved wives to their superiors in exchange for bureaucratic advancement. Among the civil and military *yangban*, it was, of course, common practice, but even if one had no ability, by submitting to the thrall of *namsaek* one could easily obtain a coveted official appointment and so-called worldly success and fame. With respect to all this, I have no documents and cannot provide any concrete examples, but *namsaek* in the Chosŏn period was probably more or less on par with the 'male sexuality' that played such a great role in the culture of ancient Greece. In the Chosŏn period, the term *o-ip-changi*

referred not to men who chased after women but in fact to men who chased after men. We cannot help but be surprised that the term is said to have referred to men who engaged in such activity. In the future, after thorough study, I would like to write more about the interesting *tongsŏng'ae* among men in this period": quoted in JaHyun Kim Haboush, ed., *Epistolary Korea: Letters from the Communicative Space of the Chosŏn, 1392–1910* (New York: Columbia University Press, 2009), 243–44. It should be noted that the term *o-ip-changi* is transliterated from 오입창이 and was used by Yi Sŏk-un in the original script. Today, it is usually referred to as 오입쟁이.

36 Like many other intellectuals, Kim tends to mobilize various modern social institutions to address the issue by stating that "simply condemning *tongsŏng yŏn'ae* as a dirty custom or darkness of the fin de siècle is our attitude. But, I think trying to study the subject with scientific ways and treat it with a fair attitude is necessary. Parents, needless to say, and educators, religions, scholars of law, intellectuals and writers should understand the issue better": see Kim Yŏ-je, "Tongsŏng yŏn'ae," *Chogwang*, March 1, 1937, 288–94.

37 Kim, "Tongsŏng yŏn'ae," 294.

38 Kim, "Tongsŏng yŏn'ae," 294.

39 Judith [Jack] Halberstam, *In a Queer Time and Place: Transgender Bodies, Subcultural Lives* (New York: New York University Press, 2005).

40 I thank Gabriel Sylvian for his introduction and suggestion of several texts related to male-male same-sex love that are discussed in this section.

41 Paek Ak, "Tongjŏng ŭi nu 1," *Hakjigwang*, January 26, 1920, 179.

42 Yi Chŏng-suk, "1910–20 nyŏndae ŭi 'tongsŏngae' mot'ip'ŭ sosŏl yŏn'gu," *Hansŏng'ŏi Munhak* 26 (2007): 371.

43 Kim Hyŏn-ju, "Munhak yesul kyoyuk kwa tongjŏng," *Sanghŏ Hakbo* 11 (2004): 167–94.

44 Yi Kwang-su, "Tongjŏng," *Ch'ŏngch'un*, December 1, 1914, 57–58.

45 Sŏ Yŏng-ch'ae, *Sarang ŭi munbŏp: Yi Kwang-su, Yŏm Sang-sŏp, Yi-Sang* (Seoul: Minumsa, 2004), 167.

46 Hatano Setsuko, *Yi Kwang-su, "Mujō" no kenkyū: Kankoku keimō bungaku no hikari to kage* (Tokyo: Hakuteisha, 2008), 303.

47 These works include Yi Kwang-su, "Ai ka," *Shirogane Gakuhō*, December 1, 1909; "Sonyŏn ŭi piae," *Ch'ŏngch'un*, June 16, 1917; Yi Kwang-su, "Ŏrinbŏsege," *Ch'ŏngch'un*, July 26, September 16, and November 16, 1917; Yi Kwang-su, "Panghwang," *Ch'ŏngch'un*, March 16, 1918; Yi Kwang-su, "Yun Kwang-ho," *Ch'ŏngch'un*, April 16, 1918; Yi Kwang-su, "H Kun ege," *Ch'angjo*, July 25, 1920. See Yi, "1910–20 nyŏndae ŭi 'tongsŏngae' mot'ip'ŭ sosŏl yŏn'gu," 366. Some of them are recognized by the literary critic Kim Tong-in as featuring same-sex love: See Kim, "Ch'unwŏn yŏn'gu 2," 146–49.

48 See the discussions in Kwŏn, *Yŏnae ŭi sidae*, 6; John Whittier Treat, "Introduction to Yi Gwang-su's 'Maybe Love' (Ai ka, 1909)," *Azalea* 4 (2011): 318; Yi, "1910–20 nyŏndae ŭi 'tongsŏngae' mo'ip'ŭ sosŏl yŏn'gu," 374. Yim Ŭn-hŭi, "T'alchu hanŭn sŏng, han'guk hyŏndae sosŏl," *Han'guk Munhak Iron Kwa Pip'yŏng* 47 (2010): 237.

49   The beauty of the appearance and voice of Misao and P causes Mun-gil and Kwang-ho's inferiority. The background of these short pieces is a school in Tokyo. Misao in *Ai Ka* is clearly identified as Japanese, while P in *Yun Kwang-ho* is not racially identified. I follow Yi Sŏng-hŭi's observation to identify P as possibly Japanese due to his physical superiority over Yun Kwang-ho here: see Yi Sŏng-hŭi, "Yi Kwang-su ch'ogi tanp'yŏn nat'anan 'tongsŏngae' koch'al," *Kwanak ŏmunn Yŏn'gu* 30 (2005): 267–89. However, one might argue that the other pair, Kim Chun-wŏn, and a young Japanese man, are presented as an opposite example in the fiction: Chun-wŏn was a "beautiful boy" (*bishōnen*), with whom the young Japanese man crazily fell in love. In both cases, beauty in appearance wins over talents, while the former is inherent and the latter is acquired. I tend to read this as a racial symbol.

50   "By loving me [a white woman] proves that I am worthy of white love. I am loved like a white man. I am a white man": see Frantz Fanon, *The Wretched of the Earth* (New York: Grove, 1968), 63. See Ashis Nandy, *The Intimate Enemy: Loss and Recovery of Self Under Colonialism* (Delhi: Oxford University Press, 1983).

51   See Pak Yŏng-hŭi, "Munhaksang ŭro pon Yi Kwang-su," *Kaebyŏk*, January 1, 1925, 86.

52   See Yi Kwang-su, "Nae sosŏlgwa model," *Samch'ŏlli*, May 1, 1930, 64.

53   Treat, "Introduction to Yi Gwang-su's 'Maybe Love,'" 320.

54   Quoted in Ann Sung-hi Lee, *Yi Kwang-su and Modern Korean Literature: Mujong* (Ithaca, NY: Cornell East Asia Program, 2005), 148. For more discussion on the depiction of same-sex relationships in Yi Kwang-su's writings, see Han Sŭng-ok, "Tongsŏngaejŏk kwanjŏm esŏ pon mujŏng," *Hyŏndae Sosŏl Yŏn'gu* 20 (2003): 7–29. For other depictions on schoolgirls' same-sex love during colonial times, see Ko Bŏm, "Yŏja ŭi ilsaeng," *Pyŏlgŏn'gon*, February 1, 1933; Yi Kwang-su, "Aeyok ŭi p'ian," *Chosŏn Ilbo*, May 1–December 21, 1936.

55   Right before the depiction of same-sex eroticism between the two women, one can find the following description: "Yŏng-ch'ae had also begun to feel a longing for the male sex. Her face grew hot when she faced a strange man, and when she lay down alone at night, she wished that there was someone who would hold her": see Lee, *Yi Kwang-su and Modern Korean Literature*, 148.

56   Yi Hyo-sŏk, *Wild Apricots* (Seoul: Literature Translation Institute of Korea, 2014), 11.

57   In the article, readers can tell the first and last characters of the fourth interviewee from the text only as "Yu o-jun"; the middle character of the name is veiled: see "Yŏryu myŏngsa ŭi tongsŏngyŏnae gi," *Pyŏlgŏn'gon*, November 1, 1930, 121.

58   "Yŏryu myŏngsa ŭi tongsŏngyŏn'ae gi," 120.

59   "Yŏryu myŏngsa ŭi tongsŏng yŏnae gi," 121. The term *ŏnni* literally means older sister in Korean as used among both girls and women; it often signifies an intimate relationship between two females.

60   The schools mentioned here are missionary schools established between 1903 and 1906 and which were the pioneers of modern education for women. The same-sex

love culture in girls' schools is common knowledge: see "Yŏhaksaeng sŭk'ech'i" [Sketch], *Yŏsŏng*, July 1, 1937. For example, an article observes, "Love, this thing is mainly between schoolgirls, also the students in the dormitory. In their relationships, the one who tends to be masculine would be called *cchkakp'ae* (partner or companion) in this kind of love. To speak of it with a fashion term would be what is called *tongsŏng'ae*." The author listed several schools' names to show its popularity: see "Yosae ŭi Chosŏn sinyŏja," *Sinyŏsŏng*, November 1, 1923.

61 "Yŏryu myŏngsa ŭi tongsŏngyŏnae gi," 122.

62 For more on same-sex love among New Women, see Sŏ, *Yŏksa e sarang ŭl mutta*, 213–22.

63 See Fran Martin, *Backward Glances: Contemporary Chinese Cultures and the Female Homoerotic Imaginary* (Durham, NC: Duke University Press, 2010).

64 Extract from "Ch'ŏngch'un tu yŏsŏng ŭi ch'ŏldo chasal sakkŏn kwa kŭ pip'an," *Sinyŏsŏng*, May 1, 1931.

65 When I searched on the keyword *chŏngsa* in the *Tong'a Ilbo*, nearly ten thousand news items emerged from the colonial period. For more on the phenomenon in colonial Korea, see Kwŏn, *Yŏnae ŭi sidae*, 185–93; Sŏ, *Yŏksa e sarang ŭl mutta*, 251–66. A shared experience among East Asian societies, much scholarship has been written on same-sex love and its subjects, especially love suicide in Japan: see Suzuki, *Becoming Modern Women*; Jennifer Robertson, "Dying to Tell: Sexuality and Suicide in Imperial Japan," in *Queer Diasporas*, ed. Cindy Patton and Benigno Sánchez-Eppler (Durham, NC: Duke University Press, 2000), 38–70; Jennifer Robertson, *Takarazuka: Sexual Politics and Popular Culture in Modern Japan* (Berkeley: University of California Press, 1998). See also Pflugfelder, *Cartographies of Desire*.

66 See "Chakbu tu myŏng ŭi chŏngsa," *Sidae Ilbo*, May 6, 1924; "Tongsŏngae ŭi yŏjikkong," *Tong'a Ilbo*, August 28, 1937.

67 Yun's opinion was shared by other public critiques, such as "Chŏngjo kyŏngsi ŭi sosŏl chŏngsa tongsŏng'ae ŭi yech'an ŭn pulga," *Tong'a Ilbo*, September 14, 1938.

68 Lee Edelman, *No Future: Queer Theory and the Death Drive* (Durham, NC: Duke University Press, 2004), 16–17.

69 Robertson, "Dying to Tell," 65.

70 For details of the interview, see Kim Tae-hyŏng, "Se yŏja ga mal hanŭn 1930 nyŏndae 'Chinjja chayu' yŏnaesa, myujik'ŏl k'ongch'ilp'al saesamnyuk," *The Hankyoreh*, July 3, 2012, http://www.hani.co.kr/arti/culture/music/540762.html.

71 For example, the definition of *yŏnae* is "man and woman who long for or love each other," and the usages suggested by the dictionary are "She married a diligent student after three years of dating" and "We got married after six years of dating." The dictionary referred to here is the *Korean Standard Dictionary*, issued by the National Institute of the Korean Language, http://stdweb2.korean.go.kr/main.jsp. Data used in this chapter were collected on April 13, 2017.

72 These subjects were listed in Kim, "Sŏngkyoyuk ŭi chuch'ang." I discuss this essay in the previous section.

Works Cited

NEWSPAPERS AND MAGAZINES

Ch'angjo
Ch'ŏngch'un
Chogwang
Chosŏn Ilbo
Hakjigwang
The Hankyoreh
Kaebyŏk
Maeil Sinbo
Pyŏlgŏn'gon
Samch'ŏlli
Shirogane Gakuhō
Sidae Ilbo
Sinyŏsŏng
Tong'a Ilbo
Tonggwang
Xin Qingnian
Yŏsŏng

JAPANESE-LANGUAGE SOURCES

Fukuzawa Yukichi. "Tokuiku Ikan." *Fukuzawa Yukichi Zenshû* 5 (1959): 349–64.
Furukawa Makoto. "Dōsei 'ai' kō." *Imago* 6, no. 12 (1995): 201–7.
Furukawa Makoto. "Sexuaritii no henyō: Kindai nihon no dōseiai o meguru mittsu no kōdo." *Nichibei Josei Jaanaru* 17 (1994): 29–55.
Hatano Setsuko. *Yi Kwang-su, "Mujō" no kenkyū: Kankoku keimō bungaku no hikari to kage*. Tokyo: Hakuteisha, 2008.
Kō Ikujo. *Kindai Taiwan joseishi: Nihon no shokumin tōchi to "shinjosei" no tanjō*. Tokyo: Keisō Shobō, 2001.
Saeki Junko. *"Iro" to "ai" no hikaku bunkashi*. Tokyo: Iwanami Shoten, 1998.
Yanabu Akira. *Ai*. Tokyo: Sanseido, 2001.

KOREAN-LANGUAGE SOURCES

Chŏng Hye-yŏng, and Yu Chong-yul. "Kŭndae ŭi sŏngnip kwa 'yŏnae' ŭi palgyŏn: 1920 nyŏndae munhake nat'anan 'ch'ŏnyŏsŏng' sŏngnip kwajŏngŭl chungshim ŭro." *Han'guk Yŏndae Munhangn Yŏn'gu* 18 (December 2005): 227–51.
Han Sŭng-ok, "Tongsŏngaejŏk kwanjŏm esŏ pon mujŏng." *Hyŏndae Sosŏl Yŏn'gu* 20 (2003): 7–29.
Kim Hyŏn-ju. "Munhak yesul kyoyuk kwa tongjŏng." *Sanghŏ Hakbo* 11 (2004): 167–94.

Kwŏn Podŭrae. *Yŏnae ŭi sidae: 1920 nyŏndae ch'oban ŭi munhwa wa yuhaeng.* Seoul: Hyŏnsil Munhwa Yŏn'gu, 2003.

Pak Chin-yŏng. "Ilchae Cho Chung-hwan kwa pŏnan sosŏl ŭi sidae." *Minjong Chunhaksa Yŏn'gu* 26 (2004): 199–230.

Sin Ji-yŏn. "1920–30 nyŏndae tongsŏng(yŏn)ae kwallyŏn kisa ŭi susajŏk maengnak." *Minjok Munhwa Yŏn'gu* 45 (2006): 265–92.

Sŏ Chi-yŏng [Suh Ji-young]. *Yŏksa e sarang ŭl mutta: Han'guk munhwa wa sarang ŭi kyebohak.* Seoul: Isup, 2011.

Sŏ Yŏng-ch'ae. "Chagihŭisaeng ŭi kujo: Yi Kwang-su ŭi chaesaeng kwa ojak'i koyo ŭi kŭmsaegyach'a." *Minjok Munhwa Yŏn'gu* 58 (2013): 207–42.

Sŏ Yŏng-ch'ae. *Sarang ŭi munbŏp: Yi Kwang-su, Yŏm Sang-sŏp, Yi-Sang.* Seoul: Minumsa, 2004.

Yi Chŏng-suk. "1910–20 nyŏndae ŭi 'tongsŏngae' mot'ip'ŭ sosŏl yŏn'gu." *Hansŏng'ŏ Munhak* 26 (2007): 359–78.

Yi Sŏng-hŭi. "Yi Kwang-su ch'ogi tanp'yŏn nat'anan 'tongsŏngae' koch'al." *Kwanag ŏmun Yŏn'gu* 30 (2005): 267–89.

Yim Ŭn-hŭi. "T'alchu hanŭn sŏng, han'guk hyŏndae sosŏl." *Han'guk Munhak Iron kwa Pip'yŏng* 47 (2010): 231–57.

ENGLISH-LANGUAGE SOURCES

Choi, Hyaeweol. "Wise Mother, Good Wife: A Transcultural Discursive Construct in Modern Korea." *Journal of Korean Studies* 14, no. 1 (2009): 1–34.

Edelman, Lee. *No Future: Queer Theory and the Death Drive.* Durham, NC: Duke University Press, 2004.

Fanon, Frantz. *The Wretched of the Earth.* New York: Grove, 1968.

Frühstück, Sabine. *Colonizing Sex: Sexology and Social Control in Modern Japan.* Berkeley: University of California Press, 2003.

Halberstam, Judith [Jack]. *In a Queer Time and Place: Transgender Bodies, Subcultural Lives.* New York: New York University Press, 2005.

Karatani, Kōjin. *Origins of Modern Japanese Literature,* trans. Brett de Bary. Durham, NC: Duke University Press, 1993.

Kim Haboush, JaHyun, ed. *Epistolary Korea: Letters from the Communicative Space of the Chosŏn, 1392–1910.* New York: Columbia University Press, 2009.

Lee, Ann Sung-hi. *Yi Kwang-su and Modern Korean Literature: Mujong.* Ithaca, NY: Cornell East Asia Program, 2005.

Lee, Haiyan. *Revolution of the Heart: A Genealogy of Love in China, 1900–1950.* Stanford, CA: Stanford University Press, 2007.

Martin, Fran. *Backward Glances: Contemporary Chinese Cultures and the Female Homoerotic Imaginary.* Durham, NC: Duke University Press, 2010.

McLelland, Mark J., and Vera C. Mackie, eds. *Routledge Handbook of Sexuality Studies in East Asia.* New York: Routledge, 2015.

Nandy, Ashis. *The Intimate Enemy: Loss and Recovery of Self under Colonialism*. Delhi: Oxford University Press, 1983.

Pflugfelder, Gregory. *Cartographies of Desire: Male-Male Sexuality in Japanese Discourse, 1600–1950*. Berkeley: University of California Press, 1999.

Povinelli, Elizabeth. *The Empire of Love: Toward a Theory of Intimacy, Genealogy, and Carnality*. Durham, NC: Duke University Press, 2006.

Robertson, Jennifer. "Dying to Tell: Sexuality and Suicide in Imperial Japan." In *Queer Diasporas*, ed. Cindy Patton and Benigno Sánchez-Eppler, 38–70. Durham, NC: Duke University Press, 2000.

Robertson, Jennifer. *Takarazuka: Sexual Politics and Popular Culture in Modern Japan*. Berkeley: University of California Press, 1998.

Ryang, Sonia. *Love in Modern Japan: Its Estrangement from Self, Sex and Society*. London: Routledge, 2006.

Suh Ji-young [Sŏ Chi-yŏng]. "Collision of Modern Desires: Nationalism and Female Sexuality in Colonial Korea." *Review of Korean Studies* 5, no. 2 (2002): 111–32.

Suzuki, Michiko. *Becoming Modern Women: Love and Female Identity in Prewar Japanese Literature and Culture*. Stanford, CA: Stanford University Press, 2009.

Treat, John Whittier. "Introduction to Yi Gwang-su's 'Maybe Love' (Ai ka, 1909)." *Azalea* 4 (2011): 315–27.

Yi Hyo-sŏk. *Kaesalgu* [Wild Apricots], trans. Steven D. Capener. Seoul: Literature Translation Institute of Korea, 2014.

Yi Kwang-su. "What Is Literature?" trans. Rhee Jooyeon. *Azalea* 4 (2011): 293–313.

Weston, Kath. *Families We Choose: Lesbians, Gays, Kinship*. New York: Columbia University Press, 1991.

Chapter Four

FEMININITY UNDER THE WARTIME SYSTEM AND THE SYMPTOMACITY OF FEMALE SAME-SEX LOVE

Shin-ae Ha

TRANSLATED BY KYUNGHEE EO

Same-Sex Love: Remembering Girls' Schools and the Peculiar Custom of "Sisters"

Pak T'ae-wŏn's "Minyŏdo" (Portrait of a Beauty [1939]), serialized in the literary magazine *Chogwang* (Morning Light), takes its readers "some fifteen, sixteen years back," urging them to remember certain rather peculiar cultural practices that took place in the inner quarters of girls' schools.[1] The novella begins with a subsection titled "P'ungsok" (Customs), in which Pak provides a detailed description of "matchmaking tours." Guided by professional matchmakers, well-to-do ladies in elaborate, pomade-styled hairdos roamed the hallways of girls' schools in the hopes of spotting "good wife material" for their sons.[2] The second (and perhaps more interesting) custom he describes is the practice of same-sex love between girl students, commonly referred to by girls as *ssisŭt'a* (sister) relationships.[3] Judging from Pak's literary sketches of these two very disparate customs, girls' schools in 1920s colonial Korea were a place full of contradictions and ambivalence, a space in which two distinct temporalities collided. This space was vulnerable to the intrusion of a premodern gaze as represented by the would-be mothers-in-law who were free to "wander around its corridors and thrust their heads inside classroom windows" without any admonition from the faculty.[4] At the same time, it was also a space in which the modern concept of sisterhood was born, a new form of intimacy that enabled girls to swear they would "never marry, and instead love each other eternally."[5]

Preexisting scholarship on same-sex love between girls in the colonial period, however, emphasizes that the phenomenon was contained within the parameters of schools and dismissed by its contemporaries as a transient phase along the longer arc of female maturation. The common argument is that the ephemerality of these relationships makes them qualitatively different from homosexuality in the contemporary sense, which is more of a fixed sexual orientation and identity category.[6] In such studies, same-sex love amounts to little more than a fashionable trend within schoolgirl culture in the 1920s, the proof of which was that, after graduation, most female students who had partaken in such relationships eventually married men and had children. Published in the 1930 November issue of the magazine Pyŏlgŏn'gon (Another World), an article titled "Yŏryu myŏngsa ŭi tongsŏngyŏn'ae gi" (Stories of Same-Sex Love of Female Celebrities) more or less corroborates such an interpretation. The article is a collection of short memoirs by female socialites of the time, such as Hwang Sin-dŏk, Hŏ Yŏng-suk, and Yi Tŏ-gyo. It begins with Hwang Sin-dŏk's claim that "there were only a handful of women who had not experienced same-sex love at least once during their student years," which illustrates just how widespread the practice of same-sex love was among girls at the time.[7] Hŏ Yŏng-suk, moreover, reminisces about how her emotions for "my beloved Miss Kim" were "far more passionate than any romance between men and women could ever be."[8] Nevertheless, all of the contributors had already transitioned into the role of wife and mother long before the article was published. It comes as no surprise, then, that female same-sex love in this period was often condoned as a transient emotion that would "easily and rapidly dissipate."[9] Regarded either as a vicarious pleasure for girls to indulge in while "resisting the temptation to get romantically involved with boys" or an opportunity to develop their "emotional sensibilities" before meeting potential male partners, same-sex love between girls was deemed a "relationship that is virtually harmless."[10] Despite its remarkable prevalence, therefore, very few considered female same-sex love a consciously gendered social practice that could threaten heterosexual social norms. It was assumed that same-sex-loving girls would also eventually become subsumed under the gaze of a matchmaker, peering imperiously through the window of their schools.

Although same-sex love remained safely within the boundaries of sexual normativity in those times, much is lost when contemporary scholars remaining uncritically faithful to such historical perceptions, limit the phenomenon to a form of adolescent experimentation or a mere practice run for heterosexual romance. In other words, the unique qualities of the relationship remain woefully invisible when it is treated simply as a rite of passage for "sexually ignorant" girl students who were forbidden to have heterosexual sex until marriage.[11] The famous Yŏngdŭngp'o train suicide of the early 1930s is one historical event that deserves to be reevaluated in this regard. An article published in 1931 in *Another World* illustrates how deeply troubled and fascinated the public was by the double suicide of Kim Yong-ju and Hong O-gim. This was perhaps more so because Kim and Hong were "well-educated young women from highly reputable families" who fit comfortably within the category of New Women. Both recent graduates from the prestigious Tongdŏk Girls' School, the two women were "quite intimate" during their schoolgirl years but were not necessarily known as same-sex lovers. After graduation, however, Kim was married off against her will into the family of "Sim Chŏng-t'aek, the famous Tongmak millionaire," while Hong, who was famous for having "started the fad of same-sex love at the school" and boasted a "long chain of same-sex lovers," fell into a bout of depression after not only being betrayed by her male lovers but also witnessing her own father's extramarital affairs. The article suggests that these events were what enticed the two young women to "rapidly develop into passionate lovers." Whether confined within a "tyrannically premodern" marriage or anguished by "unfaithful" men who roam the "red light districts," the only "mild consolation" available to these women was each other.[12] Kim and Hong's relationship, then, appears to be less of a practice run for heterosexual marriage than a reaction against or an escape from the patriarchal social order that they were forced into through heterosexual dating and marriage.

Through same-sex relationships, moreover, young women were able to maintain ties to modern cultures and lifestyles that they had been exposed to within the institutional space of girls' schools. Kim and Hong, for instance, are pointedly remembered as having spent their days together wandering around parks, movie theaters, or other urban spaces that they had frequented during their student years.[13] Meanwhile, journalistic descriptions of their suicide betray a keen interest in certain details of their death scene: the image of a fast-approaching train and their Western-style skirts billowing behind them as they jumped.[14] This goes to show that the very way the two women staged their own deaths was a statement of their strong self-identification with modernity. Same-sex relationships such as Kim and Hong's thus reveal the female desire to remain within the space of the "modern," outside the patriarchal social order. Through the romantic bonds and communities that they developed with one another, women managed to reaffirm their identities as modern individuals. In sum, same-sex love in the case of Kim and Hong was not in any sense a gratuitous and transitional phase for sexually ignorant adolescent girls; it was, rather, a serious relationship that two women consciously and deliberately chose to develop between themselves.

To return to Pak T'ae-wŏn's "Portrait of a Beauty," one discovers in the story a relationship of same-sex love that serves a similar liberatory function to that of Kim and Hong. At first, the female protagonist, Nam Po-bae, is resistant to the idea of same-sex love and dismisses the romantic advances of an elder girl student, Chŏng Kyŏng-su. Amused by how "even her name sounds masculine," Po-bae refuses to answer a love letter from Kyŏng-su, delivered in an "envelope patterned with flowers" and lovingly signed, "From your sister."[15] Meanwhile, Po-bae is troubled by the sudden return of her father, who had previously abandoned his wife and children. With a "countenance glistening with greed," he demands that Po-bae leave home to accompany him to Manchuria, with the ulterior motive of "selling over his daughter to traffickers."[16] Po-bae, who is sixteen, feels increasingly threatened not only by the intrusive gaze of the aforementioned matchmakers peering in through the classroom windows but, more appallingly, by her own father waiting at the school gate to "snatch her by the wrist" and drag her off to Manchurian traffickers.[17] In that moment of peril, Po-bae's thoughts drift back to Kyŏng-su, the older girl whom she had consistently ignored, and she finds herself seized by a sudden pang of "nostalgia" and "affection."[18] When she is forced to quit school for fear of being captured by her father, Po-bae ends up seeking refuge in a same-sex romance with Kyŏng-su. Through this relationship, Po-bae overcomes the despair of having had to leave school because of the looming threat of abduction. Even as she jumps at the mere sight of a "random man on the street, for fear of his being her father," Po-bae manages to recover a sense of freedom that she had experienced during her schoolgirl years.[19] What same-sex love holds for Po-bae is the allure of a new and sophisticated lifestyle, an alternative to the dismal future that her "repulsive and frightening" father has in store for her.

The flower-embossed love letter that Po-bae receives from her "sister" is an invitation not only to a same-sex relationship but, perhaps more important, also to modernity itself. In other words, it is not just any love, but *modern* love, that the two girls aspire to indulge in together. Even though she has already lost her status as a schoolgirl, Po-bae regains her membership in modern society by taking part in a romantic coupling with Kyŏng-su. And unlike heterosexual relationships that often entail the danger of either becoming ensnared in a feudal family structure or ending up as a married man's mistress, same-sex love functions as a platform in which the girls can jointly construct their identities and fulfill their desires as "modern women." Thus, the two women's oath never to marry must be decoded as an articulation of the female will to remain modern women forever. It can be said, then, that same-sex relationships of this period blossomed at the intersection between women's aspirations toward modernity and their desire to escape the mandates of a patriarchal social order. It is crucial, therefore, to acknowledge the multiple layers of desire hidden beneath the common belief that same-sex love between girls was a socially undisruptive practice run for heterosexual mating.

The tragedy of the Yŏngdŭngp'o train suicide incident and the tale of Nam Po-bae, however, beg the question: How sustainable were the liberatory spaces created through same-sex romance during the early 1930s? Or, to put it more bluntly, how long could girls such as Po-bae have remained safe from the ill intentions of their fathers? To answer this question, one must take a closer look at the changes that took place in public discussions of same-sex love. In an essay published in 1937 titled "Same-Sex Love," for example, the poet and educator Kim Yŏ-je claims that same-sex love is an "antisocial instinct" that must be "controlled and neutralized through proper treatment."[20] The antagonistic stance that Kim takes toward same-sex love in the essay is rather surprising, especially when one compares it with news articles from the 1920s that condoned same-sex love between girls as a harmless phenomenon. It also differs significantly from the lighthearted testimonies of female socialites who openly boasted in the early 1930s about their "gleaming track record of same-sex romance."[21] It is evident that by the late 1930s, public discourse surrounding same-sex love had already taken a radical departure from that of the years preceding it.

This abrupt discursive shift coincided with the onset of the total war era, a time in which all social resources were channeled into military efforts led by the divine emperor-patriarch. Women were subsumed under the ideology of motherhood, for their primary role in the war was to "produce a new generation of fighters for the nation."[22] In this new social order, same-sex love between women had no grounds for existence and soon became a target of social derision. Negative perceptions of same-sex love in relation to motherhood are exemplified by the following joke in Pak Yŏng-hŭi's serialized novel *Pallyŏ* (Companion): "Some same-sex couples even end up having full intercourse, . . . but at least they will not have to worry about birth control."[23] At a time when reproductive labor was considered a sacred duty for wartime women, it was only natural that same-sex love was shunned as an antisocial act. And since frugality and a command economy constituted the backbone of the wartime system, the common practice of exchanging flower-patterned envelopes and gold rings between sisters was considered a sinful indulgence originating from Western capitalism. It is not difficult to imagine what might have become of Kim Yong-ju and Hong O-gim had they survived their suicide attempt, or of Nam Po-bae had she been captured by her greedy father. They would have found themselves in a society where same-sex love was proclaimed hazardous and therefore subject to patriarchal control. Under the surveilling eyes of the imperial state, these women would have had very few options available to them other than being forced into the role of "military mothers." Indeed, this was a time in which the numerous sisters of the previous decades were called on to become *hyŏnmo yangch'ŏ* (wise mothers and good wives) of the empire. What meaning, then, did their experiences of modern girlhood and same-sex love have in such circumstances, and how were those experiences remembered or forgotten?

For women trapped in the imperial wartime system, collective memories of same-sex love became a symptom of their repression, signifying their desire for a modernity that had become off-limits to them. The same-sex love they had witnessed and personally experienced during their schoolgirl years became a "dreamy, romantic and exciting" memory that stood in stark contrast to the grim reality facing them.[24] In this regard, it is no coincidence that, just as colonial Korean femininity was becoming mobilized for the imperial war, Pak T'ae-wŏn wrote a novella about a female character who aspired to escape her menacing father by engaging in a relationship of same-sex love. It also explains why so many female authors who had to reckon with their newly imposed identity as imperial subjects chose to write about female characters whose old memories of sisterly solidarity led them to question their loyalty to the empire. In the next sections of this chapter, I examine representations of same-sex love in the literary work of female writers of the total war era to gain insight into the lives and interiority of women during this period. I also contemplate same-sex love as a literary trope of female resistance against the patriarchal social order of the wartime system.

The Way of the Empire: Memories of Narcissism

The imperial project was always already a gendered one insofar as women were singled out to fulfill the role of military mothers or "warriors on the home front." It is important to remember, moreover, that the transformation of colonial Korean women into female imperial subjects was predicated on their disavowal of a *modern* self-identity. After the outbreak of the Asia-Pacific War (1937–45), the empire propagated a binary logic between the East and the West, promoting the former as a "civilization of morality" that stood against the "materialism and greediness" of the latter.[25] The "seductive sheen" of Western modernity was treated as a threat whose "desirability could lead people toward voluntary enslavement" and must therefore be subject to regulation.[26] Women were considered especially prone to contamination and were chastised for their traitorous preference for foreign goods and lifestyles. At a rally hosted by the Korean Association of Wartime Patriots in 1942, for example, the writer Mo Yun-suk condemned Anglo-American civilization for its "hedonism and individualistic world-view" and outlined a litany of its "Satanic crimes."[27] Listing all of the temptations she had fought off throughout her lifetime as a woman, she bemoaned, "[The West is] the land of fragrances, the land of music, the land of movies, the land of youthfulness, the land of spirit, the land of money. . . . For how long have they seduced the good young men and women of the East? And how deeply have the women in our country yearned to have a taste of all they possess?"[28] Even as Mo takes a reprimanding stance, a feeling of nostalgic wistfulness toward modernity and all the "fragrances, music, movies, youthfulness, spirit and money" of which it consists resonate in her language. In other words, the very qualities of the West that Mo derides in her speech ends up summoning memories of consumption and pleasure that she and her audience presumably enjoyed in their youth.

Shuttered inside the parameters of the empire's command economy, women no longer enjoyed the modern goods and resources that had been available to them during the previous decades. Female aspirations for expensive Western dresses, hair perms, and heavy makeup were now considered "indulgent" and "disgraceful" proclivities that had to be "rooted out at once."[29] Women were also expected to give up their "penchant for wasting money on movie-going and loitering around the city streets" and instead invest "whatever extra wŏn they had on government bonds."[30] In her speech, Mo Yun-suk insisted that this not be considered a loss, since women would soon be given the opportunity to "realize their potential outside the home, thanks to the new world" that the war would create.[31] What she did not mention, however, is that this "new world" was one in which women would have to disown the female solidarity they had formed with one another as students and instead retreat into a patriarchal social order. Meanwhile, the self-sacrificial mothers of the ancient Confucian sage Mencius (372–289 BCE) and the Chosŏn Dynasty scholars Chŏng Mong-ju (1337–92) and Yi Yul-gok (1536–84) were summoned as ideal female figures whom women should aspire to emulate.[32] The grand task was for women to embody their newly appointed identities as "Asian women," meaning that they should bury their past aspirations for modernity and be content to dress themselves in humble *monpe* (baggy) pants as they marched down the virtuous way of the empire.[33]

As such, the construction of Korean women's identity as female "imperial subjects" not only required a *racial* transformation from Korean to Japanese, but also a *cultural* regression from a modern to traditional womanhood. This is because in the case of women, allegiance to the Japanese spirit meant that they had to perform the feminine ideal of being wise mothers and good wives. Unlike men, their imperial subjecthood hinged on a retreat from colonial modernity to a more traditional way of life. The "imperialization" of women under the wartime system was not simply a linear process of transforming Koreans into Japanese subjects; it was a much more complex and multilayered process in which Korean women had to forfeit their modern femininity to embody the traditional womanhood sanctioned by the state.[34] For this reason, the study of colonial identity formation under the wartime system requires careful attention to "culture" as another crucial variable.

In the case of women, we must consider that the transformation of one's cultural identity might have posed a bigger threat than the shift in one's racial or national identity. For women, imperialization entailed a complete restyling of gendered traits, habits, and lifestyles that they had cultivated throughout their lifetimes. As Ch'oe Yŏng-hŭi points out, the impact of imperialization on a colonial subject's sense of self varied widely depending on the subject's gender, age, and social status, especially in societies such as colonial Korea, where practices of gender segregation and social discrimination based on gender hierarchies remained strongly intact.[35] This observation leads us to ask: What might have been the bigger factor for a colonial female subject's resistance to the empire: her loyalty to the nation or her infatuation with modernity? It is important to note how, during the total war period, which was when the project of imperialization was enforced at a breakneck pace, women fought most fiercely against new "cultural" policies, especially the new dress code regulation that mandated that they wear monpe pants in public spaces.[36] Many colonial Korean women rejected the ordinary monpe and instead used Western fabric and high-heeled shoes to create a "fashionable (*haikara*) monpe look with a touch of Western chic."[37] In this case, women rebelled against the empire's call out of allegiance not to their ethnic identity but, rather, to their cultural identity as *modern* women.

Looking at women's literary writing of the period, we see how this problem of cultural identity caused narrative fissures that cannot be explained away with a monolithic focus on the nation-empire binary. In Korean women's writing in the 1942–44 period, for example, which was when the war effort was at its peak, a host of female characters curiously emerged who looked back wistfully to their schoolgirl years. Why, at this point in history when they had already long settled into their roles as military mothers and warriors on the home front, did women suddenly idealize their girlhood as a type of paradise lost? And why were these women writers, who otherwise faithfully reproduced the war propaganda fed to them by the imperial state, suddenly beholden to phantom images of their girlhood sisters? These questions lead us back to the intimate relationship between girls' schools and modernity: educational institutions were the main means through which girls in colonial Korea became integrated into modern public spaces and discourses.[38] Women's memories of their schoolgirl years, then, are equivalent to their memories of the "modern" and signify a latent desire to recover their modern selfhood. Because modern femininity as a specific mode of conduct was now prohibited by the imperial state, women had gradually come to deny their past gendered identities as "erroneous ways" or "deviant thoughts" of their youthful years.[39] The ghost of the sister who returned to haunt women's writing about the total war period, however, points to women's attachment to their long-lost modern selves and their guilt for having had to deny this crucial aspect of their identity.

The return of this repressed self can be understood as a type of symptom that reveals how colonial Korean women were still subconsciously attached to the modern femininity that they had performed in their younger years, despite having long been exposed to imperialist discourses of womanhood. Chang Tŏk-jo's "Haengno" (The Journey [1944]) is a short story that shows precisely how this inner contradiction surfaced in the thoughts and behavior of women, even those who had already publicly pledged to walk the "way of the empire." Written in Japanese, the story was published in *Short Stories from the Peninsula*, an anthology that featured the work of colonial Korean writers with strong propagandist undertones. At a surface level, "The Journey" appears to be a celebratory tale of the transformation of colonial women into military mothers of the empire. It begins with an unnamed female protagonist who boards a southbound train with her son to visit her parents in Taegu. The ostensible purpose of the trip is to nurse her bedridden father back to health, but the train ride from Seoul to the southern countryside exhibits another symbolic meaning as well. Early in the story, the narrator remarks how the destination of this train might as well be considered the metropole rather than Pusan, since the train connects directly to a ferry line from Pusan to Shimonoseki. The protagonist's trip south, then, can also be understood as a metaphor of her inner journey toward the space of the empire. Once they arrive at their destination, the protagonist and her son are welcomed by "imperial flags rippling like waves and military songs echoing vibrantly across the sky," and will thereby metaphorically be reborn as loyal mother and soldier to the empire.[40] The journey that they take in this story, therefore, not only signifies the physical train ride itself but also a process of their identity transformation into imperial subjects.

As the protagonist begins this internal process of imperialization, she is initially struck by an emotion that is, curiously, a type of girlish melancholy. Her train is nearly empty of passengers due to the grim atmosphere of war. As she sits gazing listlessly out the window, she spots an old woman slowly spreading out rice hulls in the sun. Struck by the contrast between the high speed of the train she is riding and the old woman's static demeanor, the protagonist recalls a host of private memories that also remain frozen outside the whirlwind of present-day warfare. The memories are none other than those of her schoolgirl years, memories of "field trips to the ancient capitals of Kyŏngju and Puyŏ" and "the name of a friend whose face she can no longer remember." As she sits with these "forgotten memories of her maiden years," she feels "her heart fill with fondness and longing."[41] What is the meaning of this melancholy that seizes her at the cusp of her embrace of imperial subjecthood? Why does she heave a "heavy sigh" as "a woman who has already sped through her thirties and is now at the onset of her forties," peering back into her past?[42] Even as she is aboard a train that is chugging toward the metropole at high speed, it is evident that this woman from colonial Korea holds a peculiarly strong attachment to the past, perhaps because, as a woman nearing forty, her schoolgirl years were the only period in her life during which she fully dwelled in the space of the modern. The text indicates that, for the previous couple of decades, the protagonist has had to exist as either "mother to Yŏng-ok and Yŏng-ch'ŏl" or as "Mr. Han's wife" and will, moreover, soon be initiated into the sacred role of military mother once she enters the space of the empire.[43] So as she heaves that heavy sigh, she struggles to remind herself of the Korean proverb, "The body may age, but the soul stays forever young," but to no avail.[44] She is already fully aware of the fact that once she completes the internal process of imperialization, there will no longer be a chance for her to recover the modern self she was in her maiden days. The girlish melancholy that marks her journey into the empire can be understood as a type of wistfulness or grief for this lost self.

Interestingly, the desire for modernity that defined the protagonist's girlhood manifests itself through feelings of adoration that she had held toward one of her classmates, Yun Ae-ra. "Famous among classmates for her beauty, musical talent and eloquence," Ae-ra had become "a celebrity writer after graduating from a college in the metropole"—and thus, for the protagonist, an object of identification, as well as the very embodiment of modern femininity that the protagonist aspired to emulate.[45] As a "fierce advocate for women's rights" with "liberal views on marriage," the girl was once the representative of her peers, who were eager to embrace more modern conceptions of womanhood.[46] For the protagonist, Ae-ra was thus a role model whose very life trajectory perfected modern discourses of womanhood. Even after she had long been conventionally married and integrated into the patriarchal social order, the protagonist's memories of Ae-ra had repeatedly incited within her a desire to recover her past modern self. Interestingly, ten or so years earlier, the two women had experienced a chance encounter inside the same southbound train. The protagonist remembers how elegant her sister looked "in a short bob cut," holding in her "fair and soft arms" a lovechild whom "she planned to return to its natural father."[47] Arguing for women's rights of self-preservation, Ae-ra had emphasized to the protagonist that "we women must put our own lives first, no matter what the sacrifice may be." This had made the protagonist's face turn pale from embarrassment for her own parochial belief that "a mother should never relinquish her role as the child's primary caregiver, no matter what the circumstances may be."[48]

But almost as if to answer to the protagonist's nostalgic mood, Ae-ra walks into her train car precisely when she was lost in her memories of girlhood and asks, "Excuse me, but aren't you Sun-dŏk? Kim Sun-dŏk?"[49] The protagonist's given name, Sun-dŏk, which no one had called her since her girlhood, is revealed for the first time in the story, perhaps allowing the female protagonist one last encounter with a long-forgotten self before it vanishes forever. But in the ten years since they had last met, Ae-ra had shockingly transformed into a "Buddhist nun with a cleanly shaved head." Wearing "a traditional black tunic (turumagi), straw sandals (chip'sin), and a pair of deep green glasses," Ae-ra displays a humble demeanor that no longer had anything to do with the modern femininity she had so fashionably embodied in the past.[50] Recounting her past to Sun-dŏk, Ae-ra laments how she "had been betrayed by [her] lover, and shunned by society" and at one point had even "thrown herself on railway tracks to die."[51] Ae-ra's confession takes us back to the harrowing image of Kim Yong-ju and Hong O-gim's suicide, for whom death was a final resort against the oppressive patriarchal order. The fact that Ae-ra's rebellion against patriarchal society had ended in complete social ostracization and a life that hovers "somewhere between the living and the dead" must have undoubtedly been a harsh reality check for colonial Korean women readers who were reluctant to wholeheartedly submit to the empire.[52] The text seems to suggest that the only conclusion left for Sun-dŏk is to embrace her duties as a military mother and become a good role model for her prodigal friend.

There must, however, be a deeper analysis of the two women's reunion on the train and what the writer may have intended to portray through this scene. After hearing about Ae-ra's past, Sun-dŏk encourages her friend to "break out of her old shell and embrace" her womanly duty to "raise good children."[53] Because of this element, the story seems to follow the conventions of the "penitent woman" narrative, thereby justifying previous critiques of "The Journey" as a story by a female collaborator who "internalized the imperialistic ideologies of Japan."[54] Nevertheless, I argue that the relationship between the two women must be treated as a narrative layer distinct from any propagandist intention of the text. If the text had singularly intended to present a propagandist message, why does Sun-dŏk respond to the empire's interpellation with a strange girlish melancholy instead of steadfast enthusiasm? One must not forget that within the enclosed space of a girl's school, Sun-dŏk and Ae-ra had once shared intense attachments and dreams for a better future. What might Sun-dŏk really have felt when she reencountered this important figure from her past, who had once been the ideal of femininity that she so deeply wished to embody?

To answer these questions, one must pay more attention to the narrative of same-sex love and modern femininity that lies beneath the story's more prominent propagandist message. Even though they had not met in a decade, the two women obviously do not perceive each other as military mothers and failed citizens. Rather, each sees in the other the image of a sister she had dearly loved during her girlhood. In other words, Ae-ra calls out to Sun-dŏk using her given name because she instantly recognizes in the middle-aged woman "remnants of her girlish features."[55] Likewise, despite her past idol's decrepit appearance as a Buddhist nun, Sun-dŏk gazes into Ae-ra's "eyes flashing behind her deep green glasses" and finds herself thinking that "they are still quite beautiful."[56] The social logic of the empire thus falls into the background as the two women jointly summon their girlhood memories.

The relationship between the two female characters, moreover, ends up creating various narrative fissures in the patriotic message of the text. Toward the end of their reunion, for example, a repentant Ae-ra proclaims that she will renounce the "individualistic, liberal and Anglo-American thoughts" that led her to "pursue only her selfish desires."[57] Instead, she will "live a new life for the nation" by being loyal to her "womanly duties . . . on the home front."[58] During this impassioned speech, Sun-dŏk suddenly interrupts her beloved friend and asks, "Then will you leave the monastery and return to secular life?"[59] This deeper interrogation into Ae-ra's private life as a woman seems rather out of place, as it is irrelevant to the ideological function of her repentant speech. Ae-ra dismisses this question, answering, "Yes. But that is not what is important here."[60] Whether she will return to a secular lifestyle is beside the point, at least within the propagandist context of the story. Having decided to "turn away from all frivolities of life and yearn only for the truth," Ae-ra firmly concludes that "as long as one's heart is in the right place, the body will naturally follow."[61] What is important within the logic of the empire is whether her heart is rightly focused on patriotism, regardless of whether she chooses a religious or secular lifestyle.

The primary interest for Sun-dŏk, however, is whether Ae-ra's body will regain the modern femininity that Sun-dŏk once so fervently desired to emulate but now must relinquish. It is apparent that the abject appearance of present-day Ae-ra arouses in Sun-dŏk a fear that, once she fully embraces military motherhood, she will also end up losing whatever remnants of modern femininity that she had been clinging to over the years. Although Sun-dŏk asks Ae-ra whether she will return to a secular life, the question is, in a way, directed to herself as well. If Sun-dŏk now forfeits her modern feminine identity for the sake of imperial motherhood, will she still be able to "renounce the cloth" and recover her old self one day? If, like the proverb about the eternally youthful soul at the beginning of the story, she manages to keep her heart in a girl-like state, will she be able to find her way back to her past self someday? What becomes evident at this point is Sun-dŏk's reluctance to lose her self-identity and her desire to remain within the space of the modern. Her reunion with Ae-ra makes evident that modernity is still much more appealing than any vague imperialist ideals for women on the home front.

Nevertheless, the train will soon arrive at Taegu station, where "imperial flags ripple like waves, and military songs echo vibrantly across the sky."[62] Here Sun-dŏk will get off the train and accept her role as a military mother who sends "her silent blessings from afar" to her soon-to-be-drafted son.[63] Knowing this, Sun-dŏk sheds "hot tears" as she encourages her friend (and perhaps herself) to "keep on with life."[64] But is the way of this "life" to be imperial or modern? Meanwhile, Ae-ra remains seated on the train, which is still making its figurative journey toward the empire. Clutched in her hand is a letter of endearment from her son, whom she had abandoned as an infant. Left behind on the train are Sun-dŏk's hesitance, nostalgia, and memories of a hidden self that can be accessed only with an affectionate calling of her given name. Along with the girlish melancholy that Sun-dŏk had felt in the earlier pages of the story, the surfacing of these emotions shows how the singular narrative of imperialist propaganda is bound to be intruded on by the complexities of life and human desire.

"The Journey," therefore, is as much a product of the female desire for modernity as it is a record of imperialist discourse, a fluctuating space in which propaganda and modern desires intersect. The figure of the sister constantly threatens the seemingly unshakable imperialist narrative. In spite of the mass propagation of imperialist ideology during the war, it exposes how women were still quite resistant to new gender roles that the empire imposed on them. It also urges us to question facile critiques of female writers of the wartime period who allegedly "sympathized with the call for mass mobilization" to attain "social prestige" or "female liberation" within the imperial order.[65] On the contrary, the text reveals that more than anyone else, women themselves were already acutely aware of what the empire was demanding they give up. Self-identification as an imperial subject required an annihilation of the modern self, which meant that imperialization was closer to the *repression* of the female subject than to her *liberation*. What lies underneath the seemingly impenetrable language of propaganda is colonial women's anxiety for their future and a concomitant nostalgia for the past. It is perhaps only natural, then, that we see the figure of the sister emerge from the past, constantly delaying and disturbing the process of imperialization that colonial Korean women are expected to undergo.

Woman as Symptom of Woman: The Injured Female Body and the Return of the Repressed

I begin this section by returning briefly to Pak T'ae-wŏn's "Portrait of a Beauty." What might have happened to Nam Po-bae, who was struggling to escape from her menacing father and an oppressive, patriarchal system? In my reading of "The Journey," women's memories of same-sex love were symptomatic of their attachment to a modern femininity and grief for its impending loss. In the case of Sun-dŏk, nostalgia for her schoolgirl years was the last thing that held her back from passing into the realm of the empire. For women who had already undergone the process of imperialization and settled into their roles as military mothers, however, their desire to reconnect with a modern self was much more severely repressed, though perhaps never completely rooted out. In this section, I examine another short story in which this repressed female desire for modernity emerges in a more covert, symptomatic form. While "The Journey" deals with the internal process of imperialization through the spatial metaphor of the train, Ch'oe Chŏng-hŭi's "Yŏmyŏng" (Daybreak [1942]) presents a colonial female character who has already accepted her place within the imperial order as a militant mother.

Compared with "The Journey," the world depicted in Ch'oe's story is one in which colonial subjects are under much higher pressure to labor visibly for the imperial cause. Unlike Sun-dŏk, who stands perpetually at the threshold of imperialization, the female protagonist in "Daybreak" is introduced as someone who is already quite accustomed to the surveilling eye of the empire. She does not vocalize any sort of attachment to her past life ways or express dissatisfaction with her current ones. While same-sex love in this story is also connected to a desire for modern femininity and the urge to escape from the patriarchal imperial order, it is repressed to the extent that it surfaces not in the form of conscious emotional responses (such as Sun-dŏk's girlish melancholy or wistful sighs) but through the coded language of various nonverbal signs.

Curiously enough, "Daybreak" also begins with the sudden return of a sister from the past. It is the night of New Years' Eve in the sixteenth year of the Shōwa period (1941), and the female protagonist, Ŭn-yŏng, is heading home from the busy streets of Chongno. Just as she is about to board a streetcar, she sees someone reaching out and grabbing her hand. Ŭn-yŏng is deeply affected by this unexpected encounter with He-bong, an old friend from her schoolgirl years. "Gazing into the face of" her captor, Ch'oe writes, the protagonist finds herself wondering "whether she is in a dream."[66] Once she realizes that it is indeed He-bong, Ŭn-yŏng joyously clutches her hand "with even greater force than that of her friend."[67] Though the two women had not seen each other in a decade, as schoolgirls they had once been close enough for everyone to think they were a same-sex couple. The narrator describes how, on graduation day, they "locked each other in their arms and wept for hours in an obscure corner of their classroom . . . for, without each other, they thought they would simply die."[68] But Ŭn-yŏng's happiness at reuniting with He-bong, whom "she had once loved more than anyone else in the world," quickly dissipates after hearing He-bong's comment: "Your face has lost all its glow! Only your lips retain some traces of your former prettiness."[69] Ŭn-yŏng instantly recoils at this remark, which she finds to be "the most depressing thing she has heard in years."[70] Compared with Sun-dŏk in "The Journey," whose reunion with her long-lost sister had stirred up feelings of tender nostalgia, Ŭn-yŏng ends up feeling a strange wariness and gloom. Ŭn-yŏng's appearance has changed not only because of aging but also because her identity has shifted from schoolgirl to imperial female subject, which is why she cannot help but feel hypersensitive to He-bong's comment about her looks.

As someone who knew Ŭn-yŏng before her integration into the imperial order, He-bong becomes a potential threat who can expose her past and disrupt her current ways of life. Ŭn-yŏng's fear of exposure is by no means mere paranoia; the story makes it clear that the surveilling eyes of the imperial state have indeed infiltrated even the most intimate quarters of her life. Her home is in Hwanggŭmjŏng, the central area of colonial Seoul, and is therefore under the tight grip of wartime discipline. Her own children pose an even bigger threat as fledgling imperial subjects who, in Ŭn-yŏng's eyes, "are as devoted as anyone can ever be."[71] Like prison guards, they discipline their mother by monitoring her every move and "reprimanding her for the smallest shortcomings."[72] At a movie theater, for example, they ask her why she "will not cheer and display her happiness" while watching news footage of imperial soldiers' hurrahs.[73] During the Lunar New Year holiday, moreover, she fears that her children may scold her for being wasteful with her cooking while "soldiers on the front are shivering in the cold with no rice cakes to eat."[74] When she complains about the cold weather, they declare she is spoiled and ungrateful compared with the "soldiers' real struggles on the war front" and announce that, in the future, they will enforce "a penalty of one *chŏn*" every time she complains about the cold.[75] Ŭn-yŏng has nowhere to escape from the patriarchal social order, not even in the safety of her own home, due to the surveillance of her children, who are on the way to becoming offspring of the empire. The only option left for her is to fully accept her identity as a female imperial subject, "cleanse" herself of all useless "feelings," and "try her best to keep up with" her patriotic children.[76] The narrator describes her internal struggles to "make herself as clean a slate as her children" and how she is struggling to meet her children's demands to walk the "way of light."[77] This preoccupation with self-refashioning is most likely why Ŭn-yŏng had not felt motivated to reconnect with any of her old classmates prior to her reunion with He-bong.[78] The wariness and resistance she shows against revealing her past or her true feelings, then, can be understood as a kind of survival tactic under imperial rule.

But why is Ŭn-yŏng so blue, especially at a point in her life when it seems that she has finally achieved self-coherence, purged herself of all feelings from her past, and successfully met the expectations of her children? And if the imperialization of women is something the text intends to promote to its readers, why does it describe her as a forlorn woman whose face has lost its glow instead of giving her the beaming countenance of a female imperial subject? After her remark about Ŭn-yŏng's changed appearance, He-bong insists they have much to catch up on and ushers her friend into a nearby café. The reader may safely assume that He-bong is bound to pry underneath Ŭn-yŏng's new façade as imperial subject and examine the kinds of damage and distortion that have been done to her old identity. And as someone who still remembers Ŭn-yŏng's past, He-bong will naturally strive to recuperate the glimmer of prettiness she has detected in Ŭn-yŏng's lips.

The two women's conversation at the café thus consists of a complex layer of subtexts in which unspoken signs between old lovers are woven into the explicit propagandist message of the story. At a surface level, the scene is a simple contrast between an ideal female character who has already settled into her role as a military mother and an "unenlightened woman" who "has not yet found the righteous path."[79] In this type of reading, both "Daybreak" and "The Journey" are essentially educational narratives of an enlightened pioneer and a repentant follower. For example, when He-bong takes a skeptical stance toward Pan-Asian ideology, Ŭn-yŏng reminds her of the "blood and spirit of the East" that courses through her Asian body and stresses that she must therefore withdraw her loyalty to the "Western educators who had nurtured her."[80] And along with her one billion Asian brothers and sisters, Ŭn-yŏng enjoins, He-bong must "roll up [her] sleeves" and join the imperial cause. She says, "Armed with their Bibles and opium, Westerners have invaded all corners of the East. . . . [Y]ou must wake yourself from their sorcery and magic spells, and realize the way in which they have cheated and exploited you."[81] Through this passionate speech, which is as good as any Pan-Asian propaganda gets, Ŭn-yŏng reconfirms her own transformation into the Asian woman the empire has demanded she become.

But despite the unequivocal nature of Ŭn-yŏng's ideological language, there is something about her character that makes her seem rather unstable and at risk: in her attempt to condemn the empire's enemies, Ŭn-yŏng ends up canceling out her own past. In other words, Ŭn-yŏng's own days as a young student also come under fire, for she was also brought up by Western educators and enchanted by the sorcery and magic spells of Western modernity. It is only through a complete alienation of the self from her own girlhood desires for modernity that Ŭn-yŏng can safely perform her role as an imperial subject without contradiction. Ironically, however, the very stage for this performance is the modern space of a "brightly lit café in which the news of the imperial army's victory is blaring out from the radio."[82] Against this backdrop, Ŭn-yŏng's forlorn face is itself a cypher that holds various contradictory meanings: it is at once a battle scar of the injury inflicted on her past identity, proof of her ideological conversion to imperialism, and the cause of her current state of depression.

With "eyes full of compassion," He-bong still manages to discover traces of Ŭn-yŏng's former prettiness that lie beneath these complex layers and thereafter attempts to communicate with Ŭn-yŏng outside the linguistic parameters of imperialist ideology.[83] When Ŭn-yŏng argues that it is her duty to "lead wayward women toward the righteous path . . . even if it means dragging them along by force," He-bong questions where exactly this "righteous path" leads.[84] Even if Pan-Asian prosperity "is the obvious goal that awaits us," she points out, "don't we have a moral obligation to remember the love and kindness we received" from our Western educators?[85] She then pleads with an "earnest face" that, although she knows what she must do for the greater good for the empire, "I cannot help but be held back by my long-held habits and lifestyles."[86] With a "wistful countenance," moreover, He-bong reminds her friend of the Western principal at their girls' school as well as their English teacher, Mrs. Wŏn, and argues that "not all Western people are bad."[87] Here, He-bong's role as antagonistic interlocutor is twofold: first, she exposes logical errors of the West-versus-East dichotomy within Pan-Asian discourse; and second, she attempts to revive Ŭn-yŏng's memories of the self prior to imperialization. Had they not been the prime beneficiaries of modernity as students? Had they not enthusiastically interpellated each other as objects of modern love and together indulged in the modern lifestyle of wandering around parks and movie theaters? Through these implicit questions, He-bong reminds Ŭn-yŏng of a desire for modernity that she was forced to sacrifice for the fictional ideal of a Pan-Asian empire.

He-bong attempts to conjure within Ŭn-yŏng feelings of nostalgia toward their shared schoolgirl years, a "Western-style world" that has now receded into the past. Unsurprisingly, the memories of modernity that He-bong presents to Ŭn-yŏng feel much more *natsukashii* (endearing) than the future of Pan-Asia that Ŭn-yŏng offers.[88] Ŭn-yŏng suddenly feels "her head being clouded over" by "dreamy, romantic and exciting" memories of her girlhood, and a desire to "revert" back to modernity emerges.[89] Hastily reminding herself that "she must not openly speak of her feelings in front of He-bong," Ŭn-yŏng struggles to recollect herself by silently vowing "not to think of anything, and try [her] best to forget everything" related to her past.[90] Through these painstaking efforts at self-indoctrination, Ŭn-yŏng barely manages to keep her identity intact as an imperial woman. Unlike in "The Journey," the world depicted in "Daybreak" is one in which the tight leash of the patriarchal social order prohibits female subjects such as Ŭn-yŏng from displaying even a slight moment of hesitation, let alone express any type of nostalgia or grief toward her past identity. At a time when women feel compelled to forget everything and transform themselves into clean slates, the nostalgia that He-bong conjures is "nothing more than cheap sentimentalism" that must be "rooted out from one's head at once."[91] The only legitimate option available to women was to become militant mothers whose "sole purpose in life is to make their children happy."[92] In this way, women's memories of the past are treated as something unspeakable, almost as if to persuade them into believing that their girlhood never existed.

While this eradication of modern femininity leads to the creation of a peculiar void within the symbolic order of the empire, modern femininity ends up asserting its presence through this very void. In other words, the gloomy faces of imperial women such as Ŭn-yŏng's are symptomatic of the empire's inability to grant them full subjecthood. As psychoanalytic theory reminds us, "What was foreclosed from the Symbolic returns in the Real of the symptom," and this symptom arises "where the circuit of . . . symbolic communication was broken" in the form of a "stain which cannot be included in the . . . social bond network."[93] When the circuit of modern femininity formed by women's same-sex relationships is broken and replaced with a new Pan-Asian world order, a stain appears on the injured bodies of colonized women, though they themselves may not even be aware of what it is they have lost. This stain, or the deprivation of femininity from women's bodies, not only exposes the sham of imperial subjecthood, but also becomes the cause of their depression. Even within a propagandist text such as "Daybreak," the figure of the fallen sister reemerges as a narrative stain, threatening to collapse the logical coherence of the imperial worldview. The symptom, moreover, is "a kind of prolongation of the [broken circuit] by other means" and a "coded, cyphered" message that "is addressed to the big Other."[94] Ŭn-yŏng's glowless face, then, is the symptom that attests to the painful elimination of her femininity, exposing hidden feelings of grief and anguish after having been subsumed under the patriarchal order. But more than that, it is presented to the reader as a nonverbal code loaded with covert meanings: first, it shows how underneath her façade as a loyal imperial woman, Ŭn-yŏng is still attached to the female solidarity she experienced in a same-sex relationship; and second, it warns its readers of the fact that the path toward imperial womanhood begins with a violent erasure of one's past.

What, then, are we to make of the character of He-bong, who exists in the story as the primary witness of Ŭn-yŏng's symptoms? As the conversation at the café nears its end, Ŭn-yŏng "leans into the table so far that her face almost touches He-bong's" and vehemently asks her friend, "Do you understand now, He-bong?"[95] The story ends with He-bong's obedient answer: "I understand. I understand it better coming from you."[96] But what might Ŭn-yŏng's old lover really have been thinking as she "quietly gazed at Ŭn-yŏng's tight face," looking "neither impressed nor annoyed" by Ŭn-yŏng's didactic speech?[97] What we might guess is that He-bong, who is remembered by Ŭn-yŏng as having been a "remarkably intelligent" girl, sees something beyond the propagandist message that Ŭn-yŏng struggles to deliver.[98] It is none other than Ŭn-yŏng's sad and lackluster face that sends a warning message that unknowingly contradicts the empire's orders—namely, the fact that the only way to survive as an imperial subject is through the complete erasure of one's past identity.

"Daybreak" must therefore be read as an ambivalent text that offers two parallel subtexts that end up canceling each other out. Although the overall theme of the story is explicitly propagandist, the image of the injured female body (face) is coded with desires/signifiers that contradict the imperialist intentions of the text. The homogeneity of empire's official voice is broken by the image of a (forbidden) collusion with a sister. Bodily signs and facial expressions, moreover, function as nonverbal signs delivering a message that opposes the propagandist language of the empire. Despite the didactic format of her speech, the ultimate message that Ŭn-yŏng conveys to her "unenlightened" old lover is not to transform herself into an imperial woman but, rather, to escape while she can from the call of the empire.

The ambivalent nature of the character of Ŭn-yŏng in "Daybreak" is reflective of the inner conflict that women in colonial Korea experienced during the war. It reveals how imperialization was never a fully attainable goal for women. Even those like Ŭn-yŏng who seemed already to have completed the process of identity transformation often found themselves transported back to the starting line, hesitating and reluctant to proceed. Stuck at the crossroads between their past identities and present obligations, women secretly nursed an urge to flee the patriarchal order, waiting to be triggered by something as trifling as an encounter with a sister on the street. Unleashed through this encounter are memories of a past self that had once openly desired and embodied modern femininity. Despite the intensification of the imperial social order under the wartime system, these memories leave behind indelible stains on the faces of imperial women who were pledging their loyalty to the empire. The memories make unexpected returns in the form of symptoms, suddenly grabbing women's hands on the busy streets of Chongno, urging them to "renounce the cloth." "Daybreak" attests to the power of such memories, as they held the potential to threaten the very foundations of the imperial social order. Sustained only through a temporary and ultimately futile suppression of such unstable factors, the promise of imperial subjecthood to colonial women was, therefore, always bound to be broken.

The Way of the Empire and the Coded Unconscious

Previous scholarship on wartime women writers has mostly examined their work in relation to the categories of the nation and empire. The writings of Chang Tŏk-jo and Ch'oe Chŏng-hŭi, for example, have often been treated simply as a means to illustrate "the extent to which women of the colonial period had internalized" Japan's imperialist ideologies.[99] However, readings that focus solely on the categories of the nation and empire tend to ignore other crucial factors, such as gender, culture, customs, lifestyles, and "the way in which these factors intersect with one another."[100] The result has been linear, teleological readings that are grounded in a simple dichotomy between collaboration and resistance. In this essay, I have used culture as an alternative framework that can allow us to move beyond the question of pro-Japanese collaboration and the nation-versus-empire binary and, instead, access the hidden layers of meaning within women's writing of the period. As a type of culture, trend, and custom that were constitutive of modern Korean women's identities, I consider same-sex love a keyword that can help us read into their interiority. Such an alternative reading reveals the crisis of cultural conversion that confronted women of colonial Korea and how conflicted they felt as they prepared their transformation into the role of traditional Asian women that the empire demanded of them.[101]

Women's imperialization during the wartime era is often thought to have been motivated by a desire to achieve female liberation, either through the elevation of their social status or increased participation in the public sphere. Indeed, Mo Yun-suk provides a good example of how some female intellectuals seem to have considered the war an opportunity for colonial Korean women to advance their social standing. In her famous speech, she beseeched women to "become faithful wives and daughters-in-law of the nation, even if it means turning away from your real families-in-law."[102] Many scholars have criticized Mo Yun-suk and her female contemporaries for "perceiving women's liberation as a simplistic power struggle between women and men" and for becoming a "mere pawn in the larger scheme of imperialist gender politics" by "promoting women's rights in isolation and without a deeper consideration of its complex relationships with sexuality, ethnicity and class."[103] I argue, however, that it is precisely these types of readings that fail to grasp the complexities of women's identity reconstructions under the imperial wartime system. Imperialization was not a monolinear process of transforming colonial Korean women into imperial subjects; it also included the process of *cultural* conversion in which women were forced to trade in their modern femininity for a traditional womanhood sanctioned by the state. This multilayered process of wartime identity formation is precisely what exposes the limits of a nation-versus-empire binary approach and calls for a textual analysis that considers cultural identity as a third factor. Such an analysis illustrates the fact that the modern femininity, as well as the national identity, of colonial Korean women was excluded in the process of imperialization. It also reveals how the liberation of women that colonial female subjects allegedly pursued through their identity transformation was, in fact, much closer to female *repression*. That imperial women would gladly and willingly have accepted imperial subjecthood for the sake of self-interest is thus rather unlikely.

Just like the "modern boys" of colonial Korea who struggled to maintain their dandy lifestyles during the war, women remained attached to modern femininity, even if they might already have succumbed to the call of empire. The life and writings of Kim Hwal-lan, the first Korean principal of Iwha Yŏjŏn (Ewha Women's Professional School) and a common example of a female collaborator of the period, offers a good case in point. When U.S.-Japanese relations soured in the spring of 1939, Alice Appenzeller was forced to leave colonial Korea after being dismissed from her post as the sixth principal of Ewha. Even though she was well aware of Pan-Asianism's anti-Western stance as well as the fact that the "imperial government was looking at the situation with a hawk's eye," a resolute Kim paid her respects to Appenzeller, "who so lovingly planted the seeds of life for her Korean daughters," by accompanying Appenzeller all the way to the port of Inch'ŏn.[104] In her autobiographical writings, Kim looks back on how the anti-Western/antimodern policies of the total war period affected education in colonial Korea. It is interesting to see how she uses the expression "sorrowful punishment" to describe the school's banning of English as an "enemy language" and the Ministry of Education's open condemnation of Ewha for having been "an enclave of American missionaries."[105] These episodes reveal how even a well-known female imperial subject such as Kim Hwal-lan still held deep attachments to Western modernity.[106] They also illustrate the internal conflicts women experienced because of the empire's ban on modern customs, lifestyles, and identities. A study of the wartime system must therefore take into consideration multiple social factors, such as religion, custom, and culture, rather than focus solely on the standoff between nation and empire. In turn, womanhood under the wartime system must not be understood as a static product of imperialism but, rather, as an unstable, heterogeneous, and fluctuating identity that is formed at the intersection of imperialism, coloniality, and culture.

This essay has demonstrated how the wartime imperialization policies posed as big a threat to colonial Korean women's modern identity as it did to their national identity. It has also illustrated how collective memories of modern femininity and female solidarity made an unexpected return within state-sanctioned propagandist narratives through the figure of sisters, which functioned as a potential source of female resistance against the empire. Memories of schoolgirl same-sex love in women's writing sheds light on how not only ethnic nationalism but also women's desires for modern femininity held the potential to mobilize colonial Koreans against imperialization policies. Either by clinging to the skirts of women hesitating at the threshold of imperialization or urging them to return to their previous modern selves, these memories emerge from propagandist narratives in symptomatic form, driving female characters to either fight or take flight from the patriarchal order of the empire.

Although propagandist texts were designed to present visions of a Pan-Asian *future*, what we find in the stories of schoolgirl same-sex love couched within these texts are desires for a modern identity that can be attained only through a return to the *past*. It was not the state-sanctioned ideal of "Asia" but that of the "modern" that still captivated the hearts of colonial Korean women. Stories of same-sex love led to the unexpected conclusion that modernity (rather than nation, empire, or war) is an apt keyword through which we might tap into the true interiority of wartime military mothers. In other words, while the importance of sociopolitical events launched in the name of the nation or empire must not be underestimated, any comprehensive study of femininity under the wartime system must begin with a clear understanding of the centrality of modern cultures in women's lives. What we ultimately see in the characters in "The Journey" and "Daybreak," therefore, are women's desires to reconnect with such modern cultures and to recuperate female solidarities formed through their experience of same-sex love, which constituted a crucial aspect of women's gendered identity under the wartime system.

Notes

This chapter was originally published in Korean as Ha Sin-ae [Shin-ae Ha], "Chŏnsi ch'ejeha ŭi yŏsŏngsŏng kwa chinghu rosŏ ŭi tongsŏng'ae," *Pangyo Ŏmun Yŏn'gu*, no. 32 (2012): 389–424.

1   Pak, "Minyŏdo," 261.
2   Pak, "Minyŏdo," 261.
3   Pak, "Minyŏdo," 264. Here Pak describes other neologisms attached to the practice, such as "beloved big sister" (*sarang ŏnni*) and "beloved little sister" (*sarang tongsaeng*).
4   Pak, "Minyŏdo," 261.
5   Pak, "Minyŏdo," 313.
6   Chŏn, *Kyŏngsŏng chasal k'üllŏp*, 197.
7   "Yŏryu myŏngsa ŭi tongsŏng yŏnaegi," *Pyŏlgŏn'gon*, November 1930, 120.
8   "Yŏryu myŏngsa ŭi tongsŏng yŏnaegi," 120.
9   Hyŏn Ru-yŏng, "Yŏhaksaeng kwa tongsŏng yŏnae munje," *Sin Yŏsŏng*, December 1924, 22–25.
10 So Ch'un, "Yottae ŭi Chosŏn sinyŏja," *Sin Yŏsŏng*, November 1923, 58.
11 Hyŏn, "Yŏhaksaeng kwa tongsŏng yŏnae munje," 22–25.
12 Pok Myŏn-a, "Kŭ yŏjadŭl ŭn oe ch'ŏldo chasal ŭl hayŏnna? Hong Kim yang yŏja, Yŏngdŭngp'o ch'ŏldo chasal sakkŏn humun," *Pyŏlgŏn'gon*, May 1931, 18.

13 "Ch'ŏllo ŭi isŭl toen iryun ŭi mulmangch'o 5," *Chosŏn Ilbo*, April 17, 1931.

14 "Hongsu wa nokhan ŭl sirŭn ch'unp'ung! Ch'ŏngch'un yang yŏsŏng ch'ŏldo chŏngsa," *Tong'a Ilbo*, April 10, 1931.

15 Pak, "Minyŏdo," 265, 272.

16 Pak, "Minyŏdo," 286, 292.

17 Pak, "Minyŏdo," 293.

18 Pak, "Minyŏdo," 302–3.

19 Pak, "Minyŏdo," 303.

20 Kim Yŏ-je, "Tongsŏng yŏnae," *Chogwang*, March 1937, 286–94.

21 "Yŏryu myŏngsa ŭi tongsŏng yŏnaegi," 120.

22 Kim, *Yŏsŏng ŭi kŭndae, kŭndae ŭi yŏsŏng*, 57.

23 Pak Yŏng-hŭi, "Pallyŏ," *Samch'ŏlli Munhak*, April 1938, 51. This novel was left un-finished after the publication of its second installment in the magazine *Samch'ŏlli Munhak*.

24 Ch'oe Chŏng-hŭi, "Yŏmyŏng," *Yadam*, May 1942, 81.

25 Chosŏn Imjŏn Pogukdan (Association of Wartime Patriots in Chosŏn), "Pando chidoch'ŭng puin ŭi kyŏljŏn poguk ŭi taesajahu!" *Taedong'a*, March 1942, 94.

26 Chosŏn Imjŏn Pogukdan, "Pando chidoch'ŭng puin ŭi kyŏljŏn poguk ŭi taesajahu!" 94.

27 Chosŏn Imjŏn Pogukdan, "Pando chidoch'ŭng puin ŭi kyŏljŏn poguk ŭi taesa-jahu!" 114.

28 Chosŏn Imjŏn Pogukdan, "Pando chidoch'ŭng puin ŭi kyŏljŏn poguk ŭi taesajahu!" 113.

29 Chosŏn Imjŏn Pogukdan, "Pando chidoch'ŭng puin ŭi kyŏljŏn poguk ŭi taesa-jahu!" 103, 110. After the National Total Mobilization Law was passed in 1938, the Korean branch of the National Spiritual Mobilization Federation introduced the Regulations on Citizens' Standards of Life during States of Emergency, legislation that actually included certain dress codes for women, such as a ban on women's "hair perms as well as other extravagant beauty products and clothing": An, "Ilche mal chŏnsi ch'ejegi yŏsŏng e taehan pokjang t'ongje," 6.

30 Chosŏn Imjŏn Pogukdan, "Pando chidoch'ŭng puin ŭi kyŏljŏn poguk ŭi taesajahu!" 99.

31 Chosŏn Imjŏn Pogukdan, "Pando chidoch'ŭng puin ŭi kyŏljŏn poguk ŭi taesa-jahu!" 112.

32 See Hŏ, Yŏng-sun, "Yŏsŏng kwa mosŏng'ae," *Yŏsŏng*, September 1938, 36–39; Song, *Sin Saimdang*.

33 The successful installment of the new (wartime) system was considered to depend upon the full eradication of female vanity from society; conversely, whatever lifestyles and behaviors that went against the war effort were often condemned as manifestations of female vanity. There already exists a strong misogynistic element in the term "vanity" itself, as it was a wholesale denounce-ment of liberal and individualistic modern female identity in general: Kwŏn, *Yŏksajŏk p'asijŭm*, 200.

34 Kwŏn, *Yŏksajŏk p'asijŭm*, 164.

35 Ch'oe, "Ch'inil munhak ŭi tto tarŭn ch'ŭngwi," 393–94. It is also important to remember that colonial Koreans may very well have not based their sense of self-identity solely on nationality: Shin and Robinson, "Introduction," 15.

36 The "Monpe Enforcement Campaign," which began in August 1944, prohibited women who were not wearing *monpe* pants from boarding buses/streetcars and entering municipal buildings/public assembly halls: An, "Ilche mal chŏnsi ch'ejegi yŏsŏng e taehan pokjang t'ongje," 11–12.

37 An, "Ilche mal chŏnsi ch'ejegi yŏsŏng e taehan pokjang t'ongje," 26. Transcription from a 1945 oral interview with Nam Chŏnghŭi, a student at Kyŏngsŏng Women's Professional School.

38 It was through girls' schools that young women were given a chance to move beyond the courtyards, kitchens, and dens of their homes and develop a sense of their modern identity. It was also within the space of these schools that girls came to familiarize themselves with "Western" lifestyles, resources, and values: Mun, "Konggan ŭi chaebaech'i wa singminji kŭndae ch'ehŏm," 276–78.

39 Chang, "Haengno," 100.

40 Chang, "Haengno," 103.

41 Chang, "Haengno," 92.

42 Chang, "Haengno," 92.

43 Chang, "Haengno," 93.

44 Chang, "Haengno," 92.

45 Chang, "Haengno," 94.

46 Chang, "Haengno," 94.

47 Chang, "Haengno," 95.

48 Chang, "Haengno," 96.

49 Chang, "Haengno," 93.

50 Chang, "Haengno," 93.

51 Chang, "Haengno," 97.

52 Chang, "Haengno," 97.

53 Chang, "Haengno," 99–100.

54 Chang and Kim, "Yŏsŏng chakka sosŏl esŏ pon naesŏn ilch'e changch'i," 186–87.

55 Chang, "Haengno," 94.

56 Chang, "Haengno," 93.

57 Chang, "Haengno," 100.

58 Chang, "Haengno," 101.

59 Chang, "Haengno," 101.

60 Chang, "Haengno," 101.

61 Chang, "Haengno," 101.

62 Chang, "Haengno," 103.

63 Chang, "Haengno," 104.

64 Chang, "Haengno," 104.

65 Yi, "Yŏsŏng haebang ŭi kidae wa chŏnjaeng tongwŏn ŭi nolli," 265; Yi, "Singminji esŏŭi yŏsŏng kwa minjok ŭi munje," 80.

66 Ch'oe, "Yŏmyŏng," 76.
67 Ch'oe, "Yŏmyŏng," 76.
68 Ch'oe, "Yŏmyŏng," 77.
69 Ch'oe, "Yŏmyŏng," 76–77.
70 Ch'oe, "Yŏmyŏng," 76.
71 Ch'oe, "Yŏmyŏng," 82.
72 Ch'oe, "Yŏmyŏng," 81.
73 Ch'oe, "Yŏmyŏng," 82.
74 Ch'oe, "Yŏmyŏng," 83.
75 Ch'oe, "Yŏmyŏng," 84.
76 Ch'oe, "Yŏmyŏng," 81–82.
77 Ch'oe, "Yŏmyŏng," 82.
78 Ch'oe, "Yŏmyŏng," 76.
79 Ch'oe, "Yŏmyŏng," 79.
80 Ch'oe, "Yŏmyŏng," 80.
81 Ch'oe, "Yŏmyŏng," 80.
82 Ch'oe, "Yŏmyŏng," 78.
83 Ch'oe, "Yŏmyŏng," 77.
84 Ch'oe, "Yŏmyŏng," 79.
85 Ch'oe, "Yŏmyŏng," 79.
86 Ch'oe, "Yŏmyŏng," 80–81.
87 Ch'oe, "Yŏmyŏng," 81.
88 Ch'oe, "Yŏmyŏng," 81.
89 Ch'oe, "Yŏmyŏng," 81.
90 Ch'oe, "Yŏmyŏng," 81.
91 Ch'oe, "Yŏmyŏng," 81.
92 Ch'oe, "Yŏmyŏng," 82.
93 Žižek, *The Sublime Object of Ideology*, 79, 82.
94 Žižek, *The Sublime Object of Ideology*, 79.
95 Ch'oe, "Yŏmyŏng," 82.
96 Ch'oe, "Yŏmyŏng," 82.
97 Ch'oe, "Yŏmyŏng," 79–81.
98 Ch'oe, "Yŏmyŏng," 79.
99 Sim, *Han'guk munhak kwa seksyuŏllit'i*, 253.
100 Kim, "'Pŏmju usŏnsŏng' ŭi munje wa Ch'oe Chŏng-hŭi ŭi singminji sigi sosŏl,"
     225.
101 A textual analysis that foregrounds same-sex love and modern women's culture
     may appear to be rather peripheral compared to ones that focus on nationhood,
     imperialism, or politics. However, "the view that culture is an effervescence, a de-
     rivative of movements in social and political structures," shuts down more mean-
     ingful conversations about culture as an analytical tool. Rather than to see culture
     as something that "cannot account for things, at least not important things . . .
     [but] can only be accounted for," it is crucial to "recognize that culture was being

formed and fought over and that history was being made in the process": Wells, "The Price of Legitimacy," 196.

102 Chosŏn Imjŏn Pogukdan, "Pando chidoch'ŭng puin ŭi kyŏljŏn poguk ŭi taesa-jahu!" 114.

103 Yi, "Yŏsŏng haebang ŭi kidae wa chŏnjaeng tongwŏn ŭi nolli," 268; Yi, "Singminji esŏ ŭi yŏsŏng kwa minjok ŭi munje," 80.

104 Kim, Hwal-lan paksa somyo, 72.

105 Kim, Kŭ pit sok ŭi chagŭn saengmyŏng, 161–63, also quoted in Yim, "Singminji yŏsŏng kwa minjok/kukka sangsang," 63–66.

106 Kim Hwal-lan, along with many of her female contemporaries, treats Western modernity as interchangeable with Christianity.

Works Cited

NEWSPAPERS AND MAGAZINES

Chogwang
Chosŏn Ilbo
Pyŏlgŏn'gon
Samch'ŏlli Munhak
Sin Yŏsŏng
Taedong'a
Tong'a Ilbo
Yadam
Yŏsŏng

KOREAN-LANGUAGE SOURCES

An T'ae-yun. "Ilche mal chŏnsi ch'ejegi yŏsŏng e taehan pokjang t'ongje: Momppe kangje wa yŏsŏngsŏng yuji ŭi chŏllyak." *Sahoe wa Yŏksa* 74 (2007): 5–33.

Chang Mi-kyŏng and Kim Sun-chŏn. "Yŏsŏng chakka sosŏl esŏ pon naesŏn ilch'e changch'i: Ch'oe Chŏng-hŭi 'Maboroshi no heishi' wa Chang Tŏk-jo 'Haengno' rŭl chungsim ŭro." *Ilbonŏ Kyoyuk*, no. 51 (2010): 183–95.

Chang Tŏk-jo. "Haengno," trans. No Sang-nae. In *Pando chakka tanp'yŏnjip*, ed. Chosŏntosŏch'ulpanchusikhoesa, 89–104. Seoul: Cheienssi, 2008.

Ch'oe Kyŏng-hŭi [Choi Kyoung-hee]. "Ch'inil munhak ŭi tto tarŭn ch'ŭngwi: Chendŏ wa 'Yagukch'o.'" In *Haebang chŏnhusa ŭi chaeinsik*, vol. 1, ed. Lee Yŏnghun, 387–433. Seoul: Ch'aeksesang, 2006.

Chŏn Pong-gwan. *Kyŏngsŏng chasal k'ŭllŏp*. Paju: Sallim Ch'ulp'ansa, 2008.

Kim Hwal-lan. *Kŭ pit sok ŭi chagŭn saengmyŏng*. Seoul: Iwha Yŏdae Ch'ulp'anbu, 1965.

Kim Hwal-lan paksa somyo. Seoul: Iwha Yŏdae Ch'ulp'anbu, 1959.

Kim Kyŏng-il. *Yŏsŏng ŭi kŭndae, kŭndae ŭi yŏsŏng*. Seoul: P'urŭnyŏksa, 2004.

Kim Pok-sun. "'Pŏmju usŏnsŏng' ŭi munje wa Ch'oe Chŏng-hŭi ŭi singminji sigi sosŏl." In *Ilche malgi ŭi midiŏ wa munhwa chŏngch'i*, ed. Sanghŏhakgoe, 253–94. Seoul: Kip'ŭnsaem, 2008.

Kwŏn Myŏng-a. *Yŏksajŏk p'asijŭm*. Seoul: Ch'aeksesang, 2005.

Mun Yŏng-hŭi. "Konggan ŭi chaebaech'i wa singminji kŭndae ch'ehŏm." In *Han'guk ŭi singminji kŭndae wa yŏsŏng konggan*, ed. T'ae Hye-suk, 163–88. Seoul: Yŏiyŏn, 2004.

Pak T'ae-wŏn. "Minyŏdo." In *Han'guk kŭndae tanp'yŏn sosŏl taegye*, vol. 9, ed. T'aehaksa, 261–319. Paju: T'aehaksa, 1988.

Sim Chin-gyŏng. *Han'guk munhak kwa seksyuŏllit'i*. Seoul: Somyŏng Ch'ulp'an, 2006.

Song Yŏng. *Sin Saimdang*. Seoul: Tongyangkŭkchang, 1945. (Reprinted as "Sin Saimdang." In *Haebang chŏn kongyŏn hŭigokjip*, vol. 2, ed. Lee Jae-myŏng, 289–358. Seoul: P'yŏngminsa, 2004.)

Yi Sang-kyŏng. "Singminji esŏ ŭi yŏsŏng kwa minjok ŭi munje." *Silch'ŏn Munhak* 69 (February 2003): 54–82.

Yi Sŏn-ok. "Yŏsŏng haebang ŭi kidae wa chŏnjaeng tongwŏn ŭi nolli." In *Ch'inil munhak ŭi naejŏk nolli*, ed. Park Yun-jŏng, 239–72. Seoul: Yŏngnak, 2003.

Yim U-gyŏng. "Singminji yŏsŏng kwa minjok/kukka sangsang." In *Han'guk ŭi singminji kŭndae wa yŏsŏng konggan*, ed. T'ae Hye-suk, 41–77. Seoul: Yŏiyŏn, 2004.

ENGLISH-LANGUAGE SOURCES

Shin, Gi-Wook, and Michael Robinson. "Introduction." In *Colonial Modernity in Korea*, ed. Gi-Wook Shin and Michael Robinson, 1–20. Cambridge, MA: Harvard University Press, 1999.

Wells, Kenneth M. "The Price of Legitimacy: Women and the Kŭnuhoe Movement, 1927–1931." In *Colonial Modernity in Korea*, ed. Gi-Wook Shin and Michael Robinson, 191–220. Cambridge, MA: Harvard University Press, 1999.

Žižek, Slavoj. *The Sublime Object of Ideology*. London: Verso, 2008.

Chapter Five

A FEMALE-DRESSED MAN SINGS A NATIONAL EPIC

THE FILM *MALE KISAENG* AND THE POLITICS OF GENDER AND SEXUALITY IN 1960S SOUTH KOREA

Chung-kang Kim

A tall man with a muscular body loves knitting, needlework, and doing laundry. Provoking the abhorrence of his company president due to his effeminacy, he is fired. Working in a *kisaeng* house in female masquerade to make ends meet, he eventually becomes its most popular entertainer. Still beset with guilt over his "immoral" lifestyle, he abandons his newfound profession to marry his girlfriend and begins a proper life as a cosmetics salesman.

This is the storyline of the comedy film *Namja kisaeng* (Male Kisaeng), produced as part of a boom in the genre of what I call "gender comedy films" in late 1960s South Korea. The film title attracts audiences' immediate attention to the *kisaeng* figure—a female entertainer in premodern Korea who served men—and to *kisaeng*'s link to a man, stimulating their curiosity. Despite these films' technical flaws and stock plot elements (typically focusing on poor and rural men and women who overcome the adversities of modern urban life to find love and a family), the audiences loved them. *Male Kisaeng*'s director, Sim U-sŏp, who directed more than thirty films between 1968 and 1970, was particularly prolific in this genre. Many of his films went on to set box office records, particularly *Namja singmo* (Male Maid), which brought in more than 120,000 people in its first two weeks of screening in Seoul and saved the famous but financially struggling Shin Film from bankruptcy.[1] These comedy films often exposed audiences to queer motifs, such as cross-dressing, gender-role reversal, and homosexuality, and they displayed diverse sexual themes of male sexual impotence and sadomasochism.[2] Although it is hard to call these films "queer" insofar as they don't consciously question an essentialist notion of identity politics, they challenge the normalcy of gender and sexual categories and practices.[3] One can tell that this form of South Korean popular culture was brimming with what Judith Butler has called "gender trouble."[4]

What is more particular about the production of these films is that they were made during the dictatorial regime of President Park Chung Hee (1961–79). Park's regime has been described as "developmental" in the sense that it set economic prosperity as the most significant national agenda, implementing various economic, educational, and legal policies that were meant to expedite export-led development. Although the political and economic aspects of this regime, along with Park's seemingly omnipotent rule and the counterinsurgent social and political movements to his economic policies have been thoroughly investigated,[5] we know far less about the social interactions and cultural dynamics of this regime. In fact, it is only recently that historians and other scholars have begun to pay attention to how the "technology of government" not only operates from the top down but also permeated the capillaries of people's everyday lives during this regime.[6] Feminist scholarship has been particularly productive in this regard, employing the lens of gender and sexuality to explore the ways in which public policies interacted with private life to consolidate the male-centered regime of Park's militarized developmentalism. They have demonstrated that normative structures supporting this regime were premised on family-oriented definitions of gender and sexual identities that constructed the male as the "pillar of industry" and the female as the "homemaker."[7]

But the mode of feminist analysis that focuses on this separation of male and female roles has had the unintended side effect of reinforcing a heteronormative gender binary, and it does not adequately explore the multiplicity of marginalized sexualities during the Park regime. Also, it contributes to a focus on the omnipotence of this regime and its system. These analyses tend to concentrate on state-sponsored violence, such as the national promotion of prostitution near American military bases and sex tourism for Japanese visitors, without paying enough attention to the marginalized voices of historical actors who worked in those industries.[8] To provide more balance to the history of gender and sexual norms during this era, this chapter explores how the ideological recuperation and cultural appropriation of diverse queer representations in the comedy films of the late 1960s provide evidence for the multiple "state effects" of this developmental regime and the extent to which it relied on assumptions about the biological essentialism of sex to establish its gendered capitalist order.[9]

I draw inspiration from Michel Foucault's discussion of how the governmentality of modern European states crucially relied on the control of sexuality and how the proliferation of discourses of sexuality worked to constitute a regime of truth around sex as a mode of biopolitics.[10] As in the Cold War United States, where discourse targeting homosexuality as a national threat was common, controlling sex was fundamental to the disciplining and normalization of people's bodies and lives in Cold War South Korea.[11] People of non-normative or perverse sexualities were rhetorically demonized as either a serious threat to the goals of anticommunism or an inferior cultural influence that might contaminate healthy national morality and culture.[12]

I view B-grade gender comedy films as one of the few existing cultural windows through which to discuss the gender and sexual politics of the Park Chung Hee regime. This gender and sexuality politics firmly buttressed the heteropatriarchal and capitalistic developmental system of the Park regime, yet its expression deviates from such ideology at the same time. Paying attention to the large number of gender comedy films that contained "queer" or gender-dissonant elements in the 1960s, I ask how an ideology of national development based on sexual normalcy historically intruded into society and culture through this visual medium. Government regulation of sex through specific production codes, censorship, and subsidization of "good quality" (*yangjil*) films functioned as state apparatuses to control gender and sexuality politics during the Park Chung Hee regime of the 1960s. I also argue that gender comedy films produced in late 1960s South Korea were complex cultural texts that revealed a liminal space between the heteronormative codes of mainstream national culture and the potentially transgressive codes of a marginalized sexual subculture. Resisting the impulse to see popular films as simply a manifestation of the state's top-down ideological force, as many cultural historians have tended to do, I view them as a dialectical site of cultural struggle between hegemonic and antihegemonic power.[13] While the idealized image of family based on normative gender roles helped to regulate sexuality by functioning as a disciplinary and self-regulatory power, it always met both contestation and resistance. Queer representations in gender comedy films are but one example of this contestation.

Cinema as Part of the Ideological State Apparatus

Between 1950 and 1953, the Korean War brought massive physical destruction, the intensification of an ideological struggle between the now politically divided North Korea and South Korea, and irreparable psychological damage to the Korean people. The country's first president, Syngman Rhee (1948–60), relied on colonial bureaucracy and Cold War politics to exercise his authoritarian control, and anticommunism prevailed as the ultimate form of ideological power. Initially, this technique of using film as a means of achieving ideological aims was developed by the Japanese colonial government during the Asia-Pacific War and continued in postcolonial South Korea. After liberation, Korean-language films could attract much larger audiences; thus, the government could disseminate state propaganda more efficiently.

In terms of regulating gender and sexual morality, the Ministry of Culture and Education first announced limitations on the free expression of sexual themes in public performances in 1957. It prohibited the depiction of "sexual vulgarity" such as "incest," "immoral intercourse," "rape, sexual passion, sexual urges and perversion," and "the normalization of prostitution," as well as "violent and lewd kissing, hugging, and other suggestive postures."[14] For the first time in Korean history, the state thus set out to define the nature of a "proper" sexual relationship between men and women.

These criteria actually had the temporary effect of blocking the growing production of popular films that had displayed gender inversion in postwar South Korean society. Before the new production codes came into effect, sexually powerful women were often depicted in Korean films. For example, *Chayu puin* (Madame Freedom [1956]), a melodrama that told the story of a middle-class housewife's affair, provoked controversy among intellectuals because of its alleged contravening of sexual morality. Other films described the luxurious lives of prostitutes serving American GIs (*yanggongju*), depicting these women as symbols of a purportedly threatened gender order. This sex inversion was largely due to the war experience when many women had to work outside of the home to make ends meet.[15]

After Park Chung Hee's military coup in 1961, the state became even more active in regulating film through the promulgation of laws and censorship codes. After seizing power, the Park government consolidated private film companies into an industry and standardized film production. Under the 1962 Yŏnghwabŏp (Film Law) and its 1963 revision, the government forced more than sixty film companies to merge into six, with the goal of replicating the Hollywood studio system. Each company had to produce fifteen or more films per year to be economically viable.[16] As various cultural historians have argued, the films of this period tended to display highly ideological themes and motives and thus lacked artistic quality.[17] State-controlled film production was also responsible for propagating idealized images of the nation that normalized conventional gender and sexual roles.[18] By controlling the content of feature films, the government sought to impose a normative vision of sexuality that made the family a metonym for the nation. The government began to produce so-called culture films (*munhwa yŏnghwa*), such as family-planning films (*kajok kyehoek yŏnghwa*) that encouraged Koreans to reduce family size, while others promoted a new model of the modern nuclear family.[19] Meanwhile, the depiction of "sex" in feature films and performances was strictly regulated.

Most films made in the early 1960s mimicked the narratives, styles, and techniques of classic Hollywood films and focused on the theme of an emerging urban middle class. A distinctive motif of many films from the early 1960s was how a happy home could overcome the crisis of patriarchal authority that had been destroyed by the Korean War. Films such as *Romaensŭ ppappa* (Romance Papa [1960]) and *Samdŭng kwajang* (A Petty Middle Manager [1960]) depicted the mutual love and support of family members as central plot devices and generally ended on the happily optimistic note of the family conquering all.[20] The depiction of the everyday struggles of middle-class patriarchs and the emerging lifestyles of the younger generation were particularly popular themes. They were visualized as evidence of the growing centrality of family-based morality in the nation.

Nonetheless, given the inevitable gap between these idealized images of happy middle-class life and the everyday struggles of people who were almost entirely responsible for the costs of their own social reproduction during this period,[21] the actual impact of such ideological depictions is uncertain. The happy images of family life in state-sponsored films and other forms of media in the early 1960s presented a stark contrast with the abject poverty of the vast majority of South Koreans after the Korean War.[22] Even if they were not propaganda, strictly speaking, these films still played an instrumental role in disseminating idealized images of wholesome familial and national subjects.

They also reflected the concerns of those desperate to escape the poverty of the post–Korean War era.[23]

Burgeoning Sexual Subcultures and the Production of Gender Comedy Films

It was not until the late 1960s that the theme of patriarchal and family crisis would reappear in Korean popular cinema. Public approval of these new films was exemplified in the unprecedented popularity of the melodrama *Miwŏdo tasi hanbŏn* (Bitter, but Once More [1969]), which drew on one of the most popular themes of the period by depicting an extramarital affair between a married man and an innocent country girl. Unlike the focus on the nuclear family in earlier filmic allusions to the crisis of patriarchy, new films relied on themes of the troubled middle-class family, extramarital affairs, male sexual impotence, and representations of queerness. Among B-grade movies, the gender comedy was the fastest genre growing in the second half of the 1960s.[24] Seemingly removed from the ideological manipulation of idealized depictions of the family of the early 1960s, transgressive gender comedy films enjoyed their heyday between 1968 and 1971.

Before analyzing this emerging genre, it is important to understand the historical and economic conditions that helped to produce this thematic shift toward the production of gender comedy films. According to the film historian Yi Yŏng-il, the first gender comedy, *Yŏja ka tŏ choa* (I Prefer Being a Woman [1965]), attracted almost thirty thousand viewers in Seoul. But the peak of the popularity of these gender comedies did not arrive until the late 1960s with the production of *Male Maid.* The success of *Male Maid* introduced new comic themes into the film industry and sparked a series of sequels and copycats, including *Namja miyongsa* (Male Hairdresser [1968]), *Male Kisaeng, T'ŭkdŭng pisŏ* (Top Secretary [1969]), and *Namja singmo II* (Male Maid II [1970]). Although Sim U-sŏp had been working as a film director since the late 1950s, he only became famous with the popularity of these films in the late 1960s. His quick turnover time and sparing use of film (the most significant part of the production cost) made him particularly popular with production companies. When I interviewed him in 2004, he told me that it took him only a week to make a film.[25] Sim's enormous commercial success led other film directors to complain that he was pressuring them to make films with ever lower budgets and shorter production schedules.[26]

Gender comedy films were popular due not only to the dexterous hands of their directors but also to the transformation of film-viewing culture made possible by the rapid increase of the urban population in Seoul in the late 1960s. Although the Park government had promised economic development for the entire nation after seizing power in 1961, the unevenness of national development by the late 1960s, especially between the urban center and the countryside, had produced increasing social unrest. Demographic pressure exacerbated the situation. From 1968 to 1970, Seoul's population grew by more than 15 percent as young adults fled agricultural areas.[27] Far exceeding government projections, the population of the city jumped from 2.4 million in 1960 to 5.8 million in 1970.[28] High inflation and unemployment also became problems in urban areas, leading to the creation of large slums. Young adults without families were numerous among the three million people (one-third of Seoul's population) who lived in dilapidated housing projects known as *pŏlt'ong* (beehives).[29] To accommodate the needs of this impoverished population and ease the housing crisis, experts called for the development of suburbs. By the 1970s, 10 to 15 percent of Seoul's population had been transplanted to the suburbs. Urban neighborhoods such as Chongmyo, a red-light district, lost up to 55 percent of their population to twelve new suburban centers circling the old city center.[30]

The demand for entertainment grew in tandem with this burgeoning urban population. Film production went up from approximately one hundred films a year in 1960 to approximately two hundred between 1968 and 1971.[31] The size of cinema-going audiences also increased dramatically, from approximately 58 million in 1961 to more than 171 million in 1968; there was a 20 percent increase between 1962 and 1966, with growth peaking in the early years of the 1970s. Much of this growth was confined to the cheap theaters located in the suburbs. For example, in 1970, seven million of the eighty-five million visits to cinemas were to second-run theaters, which used both low admission prices and easy accessibility to attract audiences.[32] While first-run theaters retained their prestige, second-run theaters began to exploit their commercial strength by demanding greater flexibility in booking new films.[33] All of this meant that, in the late 1960s, urban and suburban audiences in South Korea had far more opportunity to see newly released films than they ever had before.[34]

The producers of gender comedy films took advantage of these new moviegoing possibilities to boost their profits. After the success of *Male Maid*, Sim went on to make *Male Kisaeng* for Shin Film and *Male Hairdresser* for Yŏnhap Productions.[35] Although neither film attracted as many people as *Male Maid*, which was released in the first-run Kukje Theater, both managed to be commercially successful because of their low production costs and the

Figure 5.1 Newspaper advertisement for *Male Kisaeng* in *Kyŏnghyang Sinmun*, December 30, 1968.

cheap theater rental fees of the day. *Male Kisaeng*, for instance, was distributed to five second-run theaters just before New Year's Day (figure 5.1). The film's advertising blurb, "Watch a famous film in your neighborhood," makes it clear that the distributor was targeting the so-called second-runners of Yŏngdŭngp'o (Seoul Theater), Yongsan (Yongsan Theater), Myŏngdong (Korea Theater), Chongno (Tongdaemun Theater), and Ch'ŏngnyangni (Tongil Theater). In addition to highlighting the convenience of not having to travel to a first-run theater in the city, distributors emphasized their low admission cost (90 wŏn, compared with 130 wŏn at a first-run theater).[36]

The emphasis on the low cost of gender comedy films as a chief selling point contributed to critics' tendency to regard them as lowbrow "cheap films" suitable only for common people in second-run theaters. By 1968, articles in tabloid weekly magazines such as *Weekly Han'guk, Sunday Seoul, Weekly Chosŏn, Weekly Chung'ang,* and *Weekly Woman* provided film reviews and analyses to appeal to the tastes of popular culture.[37] Beginning publication in 1964, these magazines featured many pages of celebrity gossip, sex stories, and sensual photographs that did not often appear in major newspapers and magazines, thus helping to ensure that gender comedy films and B movies in general became fixtures of urban subculture.[38] What we might therefore call lowbrow popular culture was not entirely the product of economic stratification but was at least partly formed out of the initiative of a new subculture exercising its powers of consumption.[39]

Gender Trouble in *Male Kisaeng*

The films made for this newly emerging moviegoing culture catered to the tastes of second-run theater audiences and the lives of people who had recently moved to Seoul.[40] For example, *Male Kisaeng,* the archetype for these films, tells the story of a man from a rural area who, unable to find job in Seoul, turns to male-to-female masquerade to make ends meet. Instead of featuring urban development and middle-class imagery, gender comedy films seemed to revel in the atmosphere of panic about the breakdown of family in the late 1960s. It was particularly common to portray the gritty reality of lower-class women's lives—a feature of urban life that was rarely represented in the grand narratives and political rhetoric of the Park regime. As the film titles suggest, the protagonists of these films were often men from the countryside, yet these films also reflected the lives of lower-class women who lacked an educational background or marketable skills to achieve a comfortable middle-class existence.[41] Despite their contributions to the economy, they were generally viewed as a threat to the nation's family-based social and economic system.[42] In gender comedy films, these working-class women in the service industry were depicted simultaneously as the source of most "gender trouble" and the entertaining subject of a voyeuristic gaze.

Male Kisaeng also provides a compelling description of the complicated situation between South Korea's national development and the troubled family in this period. With its recently urbanized audience in mind, the film begins with a scene of the rural protagonist, Ku T'ae-ho, first entering Seoul.[43] *Male*

Kisaeng was the third in Sim's film series; viewers had already followed Ku in *Male Maid* and *Male Hairdresser*. As in the previous two films, the camera in *Male Kisaeng*, which adopts Ku's point of view, pans across mannequins in clothing stores, urban theaters and cultural centers, and modern townhouses. The film thus portrays the confusion of a country bumpkin adrift in a new and complex urban setting. Two contrasting spaces become central to the plot: the family home and the kisaeng house. In contrast to the Park regime's projection of an idealized patriarchal family, the family portrayed in *Male Kisaeng* is one in which the wife wears the pants. The housewife, played by To Kŭm-bong, an actress known for her wild and sexy image, keeps her husband, Hŏ, the overachieving president of Tongsin Cashmere, under tight surveillance; she squanders his money and even physically assaults him. The patriarchal father figure is thus transformed into a henpecked husband and an object of derision. Meanwhile, Hŏ's former employee, Ku, has failed to make a living as a male housemaid and hairdresser after losing his job at Tongsin Cashmere. Both men flee to the kisaeng house, one as a patron and the other as an employee. Ku overcomes his moral reservations and begins masquerading as a female kisaeng. Whether as a refuge from a wild wife or the last resort in the face of economic necessity, the kisaeng house is the site of sexual promiscuity and one that quickly leads to gender trouble.

The most troubled space of *Male Kisaeng* is the kisaeng house itself, where both male protagonists, Ku and Hŏ, nimbly cross gender and sexual boundaries. When a kisaeng mocks Ku for his masculine appearance, he responds by trying to win over his co-workers with a fictional justification for his career choice: "Who wants to be a kisaeng? Like others, I just wanted to be a good housewife. But that was not to be. Instead, I fell in love with a college student. Our relationship developed until his parents, disapproving of my lower-class background, quickly put an end to our relationship." Having told his story in a manner typical of popular melodramas, soap operas, and weepies, the women's genres of popular culture, he starts to cry, compelling the other kisaeng women to cry along with him and accept him into their female community. This scene likely elicited much laughter from the audience, who would have reveled in Ku's ability to masterfully exploit melodramatic genres. But when Ku starts trying to befriend the other kisaeng as fellow women, the film's queer subtext becomes clear. Having been accepted as a woman by the other kisaeng, Ku starts to date one of them, Chŏng-mi. Since Chŏng-mi is the only one who knows that he is a man, his close relationship with her appears as lesbian desire, a misperception that Ku does nothing to dispel.

He even goes as far as to say, "Yes! We are involved in a same-sex love affair [*tongsŏng yŏnae*]!"[44]

Ku's oscillation between male and female personas further complicates the picture of his sexuality, an effect that was heightened by Ku Pong-sŏ's star character. Famous for his masculine and handsome but funny persona, the actor Ku could provoke laughter with a simple effeminate gesture.[45] Even when he was in full drag with heavy makeup and a long wig, the audience was never confused about Ku's male gender. The minor gender dissonance of the film's plot is thus never allowed to develop into full-blown gender subversion.

In contrast to Ku, the character of Hŏ, the company president and henpecked husband, is depicted as possessing a strong and hidden homosexual desire. Hŏ, who had initially fired Ku because of his discomfort with Ku's effeminacy, ends up falling in love with him, not recognizing him as Ku in his new disguise as a woman. Despite his stated hatred of the "womanly man," Hŏ is attracted to a manly woman who, he says, reminds him of his first love in a kisaeng house. In Hŏ's case, therefore, the kisaeng house becomes a refuge from his fixed gender and sexual identity as a heterosexual man.

Hŏ's queerness emerges at the beginning of the film when he asks the bar madam whether she has a "new face." An employee who had been playing the guitar briefly disappears and returns disguised as a woman. This (wo)man with full makeup and wig wears a red bikini covered by a see-through black veil. Watching with lustful eyes as this presumably female body starts to dance to exotic music, Hŏ reveals the dubiousness of his heterosexuality. The gender-bending effect is heightened, and Hŏ's queer desire for a male-to-female body is reinforced when the dancer removes his/her veil to reveal the heavily made-up face and body of the man who had just disappeared.

In depicting the repeated efforts of Hŏ to seduce Ku, the film intensifies the transgressive pleasures of an ambiguous queer sexuality. For instance, in one hotel room sequence, Hŏ gropes Ku's body and asks him to spend the night. Because the audience knows that Ku is a man masquerading as a female, this scene confronts us with the spectacle of two men about to have sex. However, the sexual tension quickly dissipates when Ku wilily eludes Hŏ's grip. Although framed in terms of Hŏ's antics to win Ku's love, a certain pleasurable tension of homoerotic possibility remains.

Even after the two characters return to their gender-normative selves at the end of the film, they are not depicted as entirely straight. In the final scene, Ku, now working as a cosmetics salesman, confesses to Hŏ that he was the woman to whom Hŏ was attracted. Angered by Ku's revelation, Hŏ yells at

Ku. But when Ku starts to cry and explains that it was economic necessity that drove him to a life as a male kisaeng, Hŏ forgives him. After offering to take Ku back as an employee, Hŏ kisses him impulsively, a scene that is captured in a provocative close-up. The ostensible recuperation of the two characters into gender-normative selves is instantly rendered fragile, and viewers come to realize that their queer selves cannot be easily "straightened out." The film thus oscillates between acts of subversion and recuperation, producing the overall effect of an unstable mix of gender trouble.

These examples of queer pleasures provide evidence for the subversive potential of gender comedies. As Butler has argued, gender parodies are potentially subversive of dominant notions of gender and sexuality.[46] This observation may be particularly true in the context of politically repressive regimes. Indeed, the Park regime's strenuous efforts to normalize gender divisions and the heteronormative family established the firm rhetorical boundaries that the film *Male Kisaeng* could exploit through parody. As Marjorie Garber argues, acts of drag/transvestism and same-sex desire, and homosexuality, can transgress strictly biological definitions of sex and create a certain *jouissance*.[47] Ku's drag and the same-sex desire of Hŏ subvert the conservative norms of gender and family while providing intense pleasure to the audience.

State Effect: Censorship and the Discourse of High and Low Culture

B-grade movies thus constituted a subversive space under the authoritarian and gender-normative regime of Park Chung Hee. This space of sexual freedom shrank, however, when the government instituted its repressive censorship of sexual expression. As discourses about troubled sexualities proliferated, state power penetrated into everyday modes of conduct, and the normative sexual culture of South Korea fragmented into categories of high/proper/healthy and low/improper/depraved sexuality.[48] The South Korean government regarded 1960s subculture—that is, anything associated with drugs, hippies, gangsterism, prostitutes, and the non-normative gender/sexual elements in gender comedy films—as low culture and sought to purge it from the nation.

Following President Park's announcement of a "purification movement" to stem the rising tide of lowbrow popular culture during the late 1960s, various popular dramas and radio programs immediately became targets of government censorship.[49] Representations of gangsterism, prostitution, and drugs in popular culture also became recategorized as "unhealthy national culture" (*nara wa sahoe e ak'yŏnghyang ŭl mich'inŭn hŏdahan pijŏngsangjŏk hyŏnsang*).[50] In its Detailed Enforcement Plan for the Purification of Decadent Culture, the government specified acts and entities that were regarded as lying outside the perimeters of a moral visual culture, including the visualization of "the half or fully naked body of a woman," "pornography," and "homosexuality." Depicting such things in film was thought to disrupt the country's "moral order and customs."[51] In rejecting this vulgar culture as a manifestation of perverted Western influences, the government adopted a strongly nationalistic tone. The journalist Cho P'ung-yŏn wrote that "sex morality in the West and our sex morality cannot be the same."[52] Sexual scenes of a "man's tongue being inserted into a woman's mouth" or "a woman's toes being sucked by a man" were mercilessly deleted by government censors as part of this new moral environment,[53] and the directors and producers of films such as *Ch'unmong* (Spring Dreams [1967]), *Pyŏk sok ŭi yŏja* (Woman in the Wall [1969]), *Naesi* (A Eunuch [1968]), and *Nŏ ŭi irŭm ŭn yŏja* (Your Name Is Woman [1969]) became subject to arrest and inspired moral controversies, all because of overt sexual expressions or deviant sex in their films, which were often called vulgar films (*ŭmhwa*).[54]

The film director Yu Hyŏn-mok was even charged for making vulgar films due to the indecent exposure of a naked female body for six minutes in *Spring Dreams*. Appeals by the film's director and producer were subsequently denied, and a 30,000 wŏn ($300) fine was imposed.[55] In the ruling, the judge stated that the film contained "morally disgusting scenes" that corrupted "healthy and normal persons."[56] The context for such rulings is evident in statements of the director of the Bureau of Public Information, Hong Ch'ŏn, who insisted in 1966 that films should be "bright" (*pakko*) and "constructive" (*kŏnsŏljŏgin*) because the nation was still technically at war with North Korea. In such an environment, explicit scenes of sex or nudity were seen as subversive acts undermining South Korea's anticommunist spirit.[57]

These repressive measures provoked protests among both intellectuals and the filmmaking community, although the contestations were stratified by class. Many so-called A-grade filmmakers and journalists were less focused on resisting government censorship than they were on demanding fair and transparent standards.[58] They complained that B-grade movies enjoyed a "free pass" from government censors while A-grade films were mercilessly censored. For instance, *Odae pokdŏkbang* (Grandfather's Real Estate Agency [1968]) managed to pass government censors despite its lowbrow sexual content.[59] Newspapers such as *Chosŏn Ilbo* argued that this B movie, which "raised the eyebrows of ordinary people," should be censored. Many filmmakers complained, "Isn't it ridiculous that B movies with vulgar titles such as *Female Room* (*Yŏja ŭi pang*) or *Male Kisaeng* should not be censored while more 'innocent' films like *Dark Clouds* (*Mŏkkurŭm*) and *Wife's Sister* (*Ch'ŏje*) are?"[60] Public criticism of the Bureau of Public Information responsible for these censorship standards intensified with the increasing amount of non-normative sexual representation in B movies. In a 1970 review of Korean films, cultural critic Yun Ik-sam criticized gender comedy films for displaying "a disproportionate number of female gangsters" and "female-masquerading men." He complained, "These films poison the minds of good citizens and turn them into 'drug addicts.'"[61] The metaphor of drugs highlighted the supposed unhealthy but seductive qualities of these illicit gender transgressions.

The ultimate effect of such censorship was to draw a clear boundary between high and low cultures. While intellectuals and A-grade filmmakers believed that protecting freedom of expression was important even in a nominal democratic society such as Park Chung Hee's military dictatorship, they were unwilling to support this freedom of expression for lowbrow culture, which they considered beyond the pale of proper civility. So strong was this moral boundary making between these two cultures that the actor Ku Pong-sŏ, a fixture of the *Male* series of films, admitted to me that he did not want them included in his filmography. He regretted taking roles in B movies because the films were never positively received by the film critics, and he was accordingly never regarded as a good actor.[62]

Despite these attitudes toward B movies, it is clear that their directors and producers also had to accommodate themselves to the government's surveillance system. For example, when the film *Male Kisaeng* was first submitted to the Department of Culture and Public Information, its officials asked for the insertion of "and" between the words, "male" and "kisaeng," because the title "Male Kisaeng" was unacceptable. To a censorship committee composed mostly of men, the idea of a man going to a kisaeng house sounded acceptable, but not the idea of a male kisaeng. As a result, *Male Kisaeng* was released under the original title *Namja wa kisaeng* (Man and Kisaeng) in 1969 (figure 5.2).[63]

Such acts of accommodation and compromise within B movies were also visible in the practices of *taesak* and *hwasak*—that is, the deletion of dialogue and the deletion of entire scenes. Together, they constituted the notorious "double" censorship of films at the levels of both the scenario and the finished product. Given that films such as *Male Kisaeng* were heavily subjected to taesak and hwasak, it is difficult to conclude that B movies emerged entirely

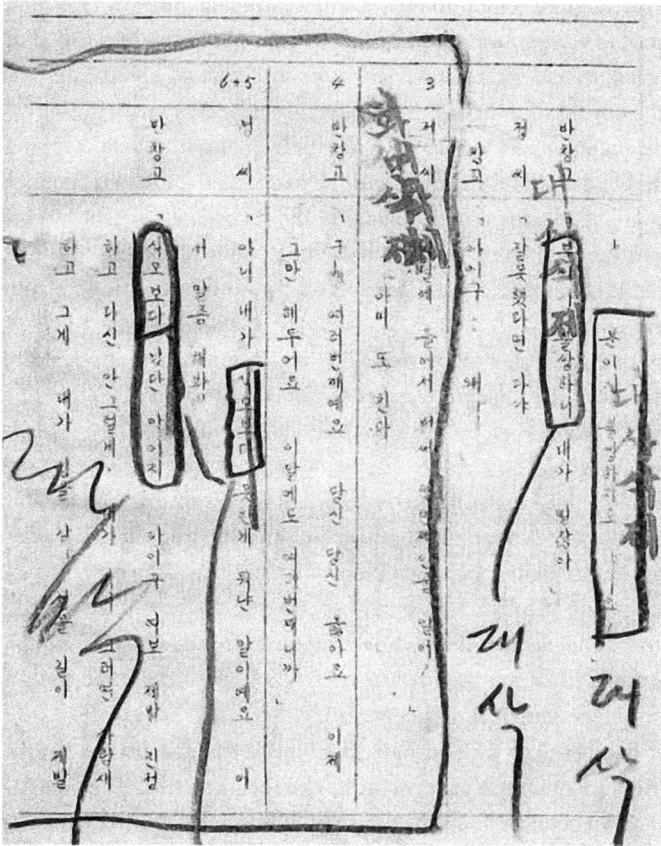

Figure 5.2 Censored script for *Male Kisaeng*. Courtesy of the Korean Film Archive.

unscathed from censorship, as many contemporary critics seemed to believe. Nevertheless, Sim U-sŏp and Ku Pong-sŏ both believe that the films in the *Male* series were rarely subjected to heavy censorship. The term "heavy" is key because the director used various tactics and strategies to avoid the most oppressive acts of censorship, although he could not avoid them altogether.

Incongruous Moments in B Movies

The presumption that censorship was always and absolutely repressive is belied by the fact that filmmakers developed various techniques to avoid it.[64] As Thomas Doherty has argued for Hollywood, in its attempt to regulate, state censorship can inadvertently help to create a new language for film.[65] Similar filmmaking practices were routinely performed by Korean film directors. For example, to suggest sexual intercourse, directors either used a close-up of a man's back or the sound of a moaning woman. To suggest fellatio, the director of *Spring Dreams* showed a woman in a dentist's chair with saliva dripping from her mouth. Despite the film's mounting sexual tension, created through ever more frequent close-ups of the female body, its sexual content is ultimately disavowed when all is revealed in the end to be nothing but a dream in the film. Such film techniques managed to portray sex in ways hidden from the surface of the script.

In addition to the use of allegory to deal with sensitive sexual matters, more overt strategies to fool the censors were common. For instance, the prolific film director of the 1960s, Kim Su-yong, deliberately added sexually explicit scenes that he knew would be censored as a smokescreen for the ones he actually wanted to keep. Yu Hyŏn-mok also took advantage of the controversy generated by government censorship to boost audience turnout for *A Eunuch*, which depicted homosexuality between court ladies in the Chosŏn Dynasty (1392–1910). As a result, the film managed to succeed at the box office despite the critics' protestations against its lowbrow content. These tactics, although not always successful, illustrate the myriad ways in which film directors navigated the censorship system during this period.[66]

Another way for directors of B movies to navigate the censorship system was by superficially meeting the government's quality standards. The government had combined its censorship policies in the 1960s with efforts to impose the concept of "good" cinema. Good films were defined as those supporting the national policies of anticommunism, for instance, and they were expected to include various public messages even though they were not propaganda per se. This necessity led directors to comment that if they wanted to avoid government censorship, they just needed to make "erotic films with anticommunist themes."[67] Nonetheless, including direct anticommunist messages was difficult for directors who made films such as melodramas, historical dramas (often set in premodern Korea), and thrillers with a more structured causative narrative and with more suspense. In contrast, B-movie action films and comedies could incorporate such moments because their stories were less plausible. For instance, one of the popular themes of action films was catching North Korean spies and becoming a millionaire overnight. These films often included an incongruous moment when a character disrupted the "fourth wall" of the filmic diegesis to preach the glories of the nation. These transformations of the medium of film into a didactic national epic earned these films the reputation of being lowbrow quality films by the film critics, although they were precisely the same features that made the government assess the film as "good."

An example of these dynamics of incongruity appear in *Male Kisaeng*. When a male customer asks Ku to sing and dance, he mounts the stage and breaks into a song with the following message: "How foolish you husbands are! Do you really have that much money? If not, drink a glass of ice water and cleanse your stomachs. Then go home and take care of your families while you think about what you can do for the nation!" Ku is addressing two different audiences: the bar regulars in the film's diegesis and the film's audience in the theater. There are innumerable other examples of such forms of dual address. In *Male Hairdresser*, Ku again preaches to female customers about the value of national cosmetics products and thus explicitly promotes the government's "Movement to Support National Production." While treated as comic, such jarring moments of incongruence, which might have been motivated by the desire to avoid censorship, also ended up reinforcing the national development plan.

Inserting such incongruous moments into a film text inevitably involved a gendered dimension. At the end of *Male Kisaeng*, Ku tells the wives of the husbands who frequented the kisaeng house how to perform their roles: "In order to serve your husband properly, the first thing to keep in mind is 'service.' So is the second thing as well as the third." In this scene, Ku's male-to-female persona becomes an opportunity for him to preach to the women about how to perform the femininity that he is only mimicking. The moral voice of Ku asking for both the fathers to return to their homes and the housewives to properly perform their motherly/wifely roles thus served to bolster the state's goal of national development. Although the narrative structure of the film centers on the breakdown of the family as well as gender norms and sexuality, the film ultimately concludes that it is still important to keep the family system intact and insists that only a healthy family can provide the basis for national development. Further compromising the subversive nature of Ku's male-to-female performance in *Male Kisaeng* is the fact that, once he reverts to his own male identity, he becomes extremely rational and self-controlled. In the final scene, for instance, Ku reflects on his experience in the kisaeng house and tells his girlfriend, "I realized that man should be faithful and sincere to his own family." In response, she says, "Why don't we try to live clean and healthy lives even though it is just the two of us?" Through such scenes of ideological reassertion, the film reifies the normative images of proper citizen and family.

In a personal interview in 2004, I asked Sim U-sŏp, the director of *Male Kisaeng*, to comment on the didactic moments in his films. Contradicting the assumptions of many scholars that these films were a simple reflection of the government's control over the filmmaking process, he replied that they reflected his own views of family.[68] His answer can be read as support for the nation's family-centered ideology, or it can be read as a reflection of his desire to elevate B movies to a higher status as social satire through a critique of the dark sexual underside of the Korean nation. But he could not provide an answer to why he put such excessive emphasis on the country's "dark side." When I asked him about the kind of films he wanted to make in the future, he replied that he wanted to make a film about the secretive sex lives of high school girls. Whether he wants to make such films to support sexual freedom for South Korean schoolgirls or to criticize them remains uncertain. In the case of gender comedy films, it is also uncertain what lessons the audience of B movies drew from such didactic messages. The intentions of film directors such as Sim notwithstanding, one thing is clear: such moments of incongruity managed to describe the marginalized sexual cultures that otherwise would have remained invisible.

Conclusion: Representations of the (In)visible

This chapter has explored how normative sexuality was constructed under the regulatory regime of the early Park Chung Hee era and how such normative images changed during the late 1960s in response to shifting audiences and economic circumstances. By analyzing the appearance of "queerness" in *Male Kisaeng*, this chapter has discussed the subversive nature of popular forms of entertainment as sites for the exploration of non-normative sexuality and gender variance. Although Park Chung Hee's authoritarian regime remains infamous for its oppressive control of gender and sexuality, the representations of queerness in gender comedies illustrate how the tastes of a new suburban audience were incorporated into the dominant national culture. To cater to these tastes while still staying ahead of the censors, the directors and producers of these films developed new filmic techniques of storytelling and representation. Gender comedy films often employed purposefully incongruous scenes, for instance, which paradoxically combined the narratives of national propaganda with representations of non-normative sexuality and thus served the goals of both entertainment and didactic messaging. As we have seen, under Park Chung Hee's rule, the convergence of emerging intellectual discourses on sex and the direct intervention of the state through censorship laws contributed to the stratification of national culture into high/normal/healthy and low/abnormal/depraved streams. Given these divisions, the use of incongruity in gender comedy films can also be viewed as a tactic of directors and producers of B movies to navigate the repressive censorship policies of a highly authoritarian society. Survival strategies and tactics made it possible for them to carve out a liminal space of non-normative sexual expression within the seemingly omnipotent heteronormative culture of South Korea's development regime.

The stratification of national culture into such a high-low binary was entangled with the cultural politics of representing marginal elements of South Korea's social life during this developmentalist period. In December 1969, for example, *Chosŏn Ilbo* published a documentary report about a transsexual man, Kim, who eerily mirrored the plot of the *Male* film series. According to this report, the man first discovered his sexuality while experimenting with other boys when he was twelve. After being kicked out of his family, Kim worked for several years as a male maid, male kisaeng, and male hairdresser.[69] The films in the *Male* series of the late 1960s thus were not only imaginative representations of the queer body; they also spoke directly to the lives of marginalized sexual subjects such as Kim, who had to resort to such practices of gender-bending and labor within the shadowy realm of a subcultural sexual economy to survive.

Even after the emergence of the gay and lesbian movement in South Korea in the 1990s, it is still difficult to find sexual minorities represented as anything but outsiders in mainstream culture. The B movie and its description in yellow journalism could thus be said to have provided a valuable window into the liminal space of queer sexuality, a space that conservative society continues to disavow.

Notes

This essay is a slightly revised version of an article originally published as Chung-kang Kim, "Nation, Subculture, and Queer Representation: The Film *Male Kisaeng* and the Politics of Gender and Sexuality in 1960s South Korea," *Journal of the History of Sexuality* 24, no. 3 (September 2015): 455–77. Copyright © 2015 by the University of Texas Press. All rights reserved.

1   Because South Korea operated under an indirect distribution system from the middle of the 1960s to the early 1990s, it is difficult to determine exact statistics on audience numbers. However, considering that the population of

Seoul was 2.5 million in the late 1960s, the film seems to have been a remarkable box office hit. It is often said that if the theatrical opening of a film (*kaebonggwan*) had an audience of 100,000, the production cost would be covered. For detailed studies of the old Korean film distribution system, see Kim Mi-hyŏn, ed., *Han'guk yŏnghwa paegŭpsa yŏn'gu* (Seoul: Korean Film Commission, 2003), 14–28.

2   There were many comedy films with queer motifs. The following films and scenarios are contained in the Korean Film Archive: Chang Il-ho, dir., *Ch'onggak kimch'i* (Taehan Yŏnhap Yŏnghwa, 1964), script; Im Kwŏn-t'aek, dir., *Namja nŭn anp'allyŏ* [Man Is Not for Sale] (Taewŏn Yŏnghwasa, 1963), script; Kim Ki-p'ung, dir., *Yŏja ka tŏ choa* [I Prefer Being a Woman] (Yŏnbang Yŏnghwasa, 1965), script; Kim Hwa-rang, dir., *Salsari mollatjji*? [Salsari, You Didn't Know?] (Asea Film, 1966), Korean Film Archive, D0159, DVD; Kim Ki-p'ung, dir., *Manjŏman popsida* [Let Me Just Touch] (Yŏnbang Yŏnghwasa, 1966), script; Sim U-sŏp, dir., *Namja singmo* [Male Maid] (Shin Film, 1968), Korean Film Archive, D0317, DVD; Sim U-sŏp, dir., *Namja miyongsa* [Male Hairdresser] (Yŏnhap Yŏnghwasa, 1968), Korean Film Archive, D0183, DVD; Sim U-sŏp, dir., *Namja kisaeng* [Male Kisaeng] (Shin Film, 1969), Korean Film Archive, DKD012965, VOD; Sim U-sŏp, dir., *Namja singmo II* [Male Maid II] (Saehan Film, 1970), VHS.

The diversity of subjects may have been related to a boom in movies with sexual themes at this time. See, e.g., Kim Su-yong, dir., *Chuch'ajang* [The Parking Lot] (Kŭkdong Film, 1969), scenario; Yi Hyŏng-p'yo, dir., *Nŏ ŭi irŭm ŭn yŏja* [Your Name Is Woman] (Asea Film, 1969), script; Kim Su-yong, dir., *Sibaljŏm* [The Beginning Point] (Yŏnbang Yŏnghwasa, 1969), VHS; Chu Tong-jin, dir., *Sarang hanŭn maria* [Lovely Maria] (Yŏnbang Yŏnghwasa, 1970), script; Ch'oe Kyŏng-ok, dir., *Ae wa sa* [Love and Death] (Anyang Yŏnghwa, 1970), script; Chu Tong-jin, dir., *Manim* [Madam] (Yŏnbang Yŏnghwasa, Sambu Production, 1970), VHS; Yi Hyŏng-p'yo, dir., *Pijŏn* [Queen's Palace] (T'aech'ang Hŭng'ŏp, 1970), script; Yi Hyŏng-p'yo, dir., *Pang ŭi purŭl kkŏjŭo* [Please Turn Off the Light] (T'aech'ang Hŭng'ŏp, 1970), scenario; Sin Pong-sŭng, dir., *Haebyŏn ŭi chŏngsa* [Sex at the Beach] (Tongyang Yŏnghwa Hŭng'ŏp, 1970), scenario; Hwang Hye-mi, dir., *Ch'ŏt kyŏnghŏm* [The First Experience] (Pohan San'ŏp, 1970), script; Yi Hyŏng-p'yo, *Purŭn ch'imsil* [Blue Bedroom] (Asea Film, 1970), scenario.

3   "Queer film" usually refers to films that were produced from the early 1990s in Western nations and contain a clear intention to problematize the essentialist approach of gender and sexuality: see Alexander Doty, "Queer Theory," in *The Oxford Guide to Film Studies*, ed. John Hill (Oxford: Oxford University Press, 1998), 148–51.

4   Criticizing the formulation of gender as a monolithic and singular construction, Judith Butler emphasizes that non-normative sexual practices challenge the stability of gender: Judith Butler, *Gender Trouble: Feminism and the Subversion of Identity* (New York: Routledge, 1999), 1–25.

5   This type of scholarship often focuses on state-led economic plans and hegemonic sociopolitical structures as the driving forces of the nation-state: see, e.g., Acad-

emy of Korean Studies, ed., *5.16 kwa Pak Chŏng-hŭi chŏngbu ŭi sŏllip* (Seongnam, South Korea: Academy of Korean Studies Press, 1999); Kang Man-gil, *Han'guk chabonjuŭi ŭi yŏksa* (Seoul: Yoksa Pip'yŏng, 2000); Eun Mee Kim, *Big Business, Strong State: Collusion and Conflict in South Korean Development, 1960–1990* (Albany: State University of New York Press, 1997). Others focus on the recalcitrant and dynamic counterhegemonic movement of *minjung* (the masses). For an excellent overview of the counterhegemonic *minjung* movement in South Korea, see Hagen Koo, ed., *Korean Workers: The Culture and Politics of Class Formation* (Ithaca, NY: Cornell University Press, 2001).

6   The concept of "technology of government" is outlined in Michel Foucault, *The Birth of Biopolitics* (New York: Palgrave Macmillan, 2008), 297. In a similar vein, there have been intensive debates over various technologies of Park Chung Hee's government. See, e.g., the account of the debate between Lim Jie-Hyun and Cho Heeyeon on this subject in Chang Mun-sŏk and Yi Sang-nok, eds., *Kŭndae ŭi kyŏnggye esŏ tokjae rŭl ikta* (Seoul: Kŭrinbi, 2006), 1–8; Kim Chun, "Pak Chŏng-hŭi sidae ŭi nodong: Ulsan Hyŏndae chosŏn nodongja rŭl chungsim ŭro," in Chang and Yi, *Kŭndae ŭi kyŏnggye esŏ tokjae rŭl ikta*, 257–92. For vivid anthropological accounts of progressive movement in 1980s South Korea, see Nancy Abelmann, *Echoes of the Past, Epics of Dissent: A South Korean Social Movement* (Berkeley: University of California Press, 1996); Namhee Lee, "Making Minjung Subjectivity: Crisis of Subjectivity and Rewriting History, 1960–1988" (PhD diss., University of Chicago, 2001).

7   See Cho Hae-joang, *Sŏng, kajok, kŭrigo munhwa: Illyuhakjŏk chŏpgŭn* (Seoul: Chimundang, 1997); Elaine H. Kim and Chungmoo Choi, eds., *Dangerous Women: Gender and Korean Nationalism* (New York: Routledge, 1998); Seungsook Moon, *Militarized Modernity and Gendered Citizenship in South Korea* (Durham, NC: Duke University Press, 2005); Hyun Mee Kim, "Work, Nation and Hypermasculinity: The 'Woman' Question in the Economic Miracle and Crisis in South Korea," *Inter-Asia Cultural Studies* 2, no. 1 (2001): 53–68.

8   Park Jeong-mi, "Paljŏn kwa seksŭ: Han'guk chŏngbu ŭi sŏngmaemae kwan'gwang chŏngch'aek, 1955–1988," *Han'guk Sahwoehak* 48, no. 25 (2014): 235–64.

9   Timothy Mitchell argues that governance operates within the system of social practice, "yet still creates the effect of an enduring structure": see Timothy Mitchell, "Society, Economy, and the State Effect," in *State/Culture: State-formation after the Cultural Turn*, ed. George Steinmetz (Ithaca, NY: Cornell University Press, 1999), 77–78.

10   Michel Foucault, *The History of Sexuality, Volume 1: An Introduction* (New York: Vintage, 1990), 3–13.

11   On American Cold War homophobic culture, see K. A. Cuordileone, "Politics in an Age of Anxiety: Cold War Political Culture and the Crisis in American Masculinity, 1949," *Journal of American History* 87, no. 2 (2000): 515–45; Robert J. Corber, *Cold War Femme: Lesbianism, National Identity, and Hollywood Cinema* (Durham, NC: Duke University Press, 2011); Robert J. Corber, *Homosexuality in Cold War*

America: Resistance and the Crisis of Masculinity (Durham, NC: Duke University Press, 1997).

12 In fact, it was not until the 1990s that a movement representing sexual minorities appeared in the South Korean public sphere, a development that continues to produce debates about valid sexual identities and the scapegoating of some groups.

13 On the role of film in conveying ideological messages, see Yi Yŏng-il, *Han'guk yŏnghwa chŏnsa* (Seoul: Sodo, 2004); Chu Yu-sin, ed., *Han'guk yŏnghwa wa kŭndaesŏng* (Seoul: Sodo, 2000); Chang Sŏk-yong, *Han'guk nyuweibŭ ŭi chinghu rŭl ch'ajasŏ* (Seoul: Hyŏndae Mihaksa, 2002); Eung-jun Min, ed., *Korean Film: History, Resistance, and Democratic Imagination* (Santa Barbara, CA: Praeger, 2003); Kim Si-mu, *Yesul yŏnghwa ongho* (Seoul: Hyŏndae Mihaksa, 2001). Stuart Hall emphasizes the double movement of popular culture, which is both "containment (of traditional conservative culture) and resistance": Stuart Hall, "Notes on Deconstructing 'the Popular,'" in *People's History and Socialist Theory*, ed. Raphael Samuel (London: Routledge and Kegan Paul, 1981), 227–28.

14 *Munkyo wŏlbo*, 32 (Seoul: Ministry of Culture and Education), April 1957.

15 Regarding the gender inversion that occurred after the Korean War, see Yi Im-ha, *Yŏsŏng, chŏnjaeng ŭl nŏmŏ irŏsŏda* (Seoul: Sŏhae Munjip, 2004). For a discussion of overt challenges to women's sexuality in Korean popular culture in the mid-1950s and its transition in the late 1950s and early 1960s, see Kwŏn Podŭre, ed., *Apres-ggŏl sasanggye rŭl ikta* (Seoul: Dongguk University Press, 2009).

16 For a general discussion of the film industry's formative years, as exemplified by Shin Film, see Steven Chung, *The Split Screen Korea: Shin Sang-ok and Post-war Cinema* (Minneapolis: University of Minnesota Press, 2014), 88–102.

17 Film cultures under authoritarian regimes, such as Nazi Germany, fascist Italy, and the Japanese empire, have received increasing attention in recent years. See, e.g., Steve Ricci, *Cinema and Fascism: Italian Film and Society, 1922–1943* (Oakland: University of California Press, 2008); Linda Schulte-Sasse, *Entertaining the Third Reich: Illusions of Wholeness in Nazi Cinema* (Durham, NC: Duke University Press, 1996); Michael Baskett, *The Attractive Empire: Transnational Film Culture in Imperial Japan* (Honolulu: University of Hawai'i Press, 2008).

18 Hae-joang Cho outlines the history of father-centered family ideology and its role in gendering the nation-state: see Hae-joang Cho, "You Are Trapped in an Imaginary Well: The Formation of Subjectivity in a Compressed Development," *Inter-Asia Cultural Studies* 1, no. 1 (2000): 62–64.

19 Pyŏn Chae-ran, "Taehan nyusŭ, munhwa yŏnghwa, kŭndaejŏk kihoek ŭrosŏ ŭi 'kajok kyehoek," *Yŏnghwa Yon'gu* 52 (2012): 207–35.

20 Sin Sang-ok, dir., *Romaensŭ ppappa* (Shin Film, 1960), Korean Film Archive 3293, DVD; Yi Pong-nae, dir., *Samdŭng kwajang* (Huban'gi Production, 1960), Korean Film Archive, 5582, DVD; Pak Sŏng-bok, dir., *Haebaragi kajok* [Sunflower Family] (Taesŏng Yŏnghwasa, 1961), Korean Film Archive, D0286, DVD; Yi Pong-nae, dir., *Maidongp'ung* [Talk to the Wind] (Huban'gi Production, 1961),

scenario; Pak Sŏng-bok, dir., *Insaeng kap'ŭlbyŏng* [Lives of A, B and C] (n.p., 1961), scenario; Yi Hyŏng-p'yo, dir., *Sŏul ŭi chibung mit* [Under the sky of Seoul] (Shin Film, 1961), Korean Film Archive, 7931, DVD; Sin Sang-ok, dir., *Romansŭ kŭrei* [Romance Grey] (Shin Film, 1963), Korean Film Archive, 8031, DVD; Kim Su-yong, dir., *Wŏlgŭp pongt'u* [The Pay Envelope] (Han'guk Yesul Yŏnghwasa, 1964), scenario.

21   Hwang Chŏng-mi, "Paljŏn kukka wa mosŏng: 1960–1970 nyŏndae 'punyŏ chŏngch'aek ŭl chungsim ŭro," in *Mosŏng ŭi tamron kwa hyŏnsil*, ed. Sim Yŏng-hŭi (P'aju, South Korea: Nanam, 1999), 103.

22   Although not many films reflected the lower class's situation, there were a few attempts to do so. *The Way of All Flesh* (Yukch'e ŭi kil, Cho Kŭng-ha, 1959), *House Maid* (Hanyŏ, Kim Ki-yŏng, 1960), and *Coach Man* (Mabu, Kang Tae-jin, 1960), for example, portrayed the themes of imperiled middle-class patriarchal masculinity, the collapse of middle-class families, and the struggle of lower-class men to adapt themselves to a rapidly urbanizing life.

23   No Chi-sŭng, "Yŏnghwa, chŏngch'i wa sidaesŏng ŭi chinghu: Tosi chung'gan kyech'ŭng ŭi yongmang kwa kajok," *Yŏksa Munje Yon'gu* 25 (2011): 169–76.

24   I use the term "B movie" to refer to the "lowbrow taste" (*chŏsok ch'wihyang*) film of the late 1960s. As in Hollywood, in contemporary Korea the term is used to refer to films with little artistic value and cheap production, such as those I discuss in this chapter. However, in the late 1960s there was no equivalent term that referred to these films. They were just called films of lowbrow taste (*chŏsok ch'wihyang*).

25   Sim U-sŏp, interview with the author, Seoul, September 4, 2004.

26   Yu Hyŏn-mok, "Chŏjil yŏnghwa chŏngbu ka ch'aegim chŏya," *Chosŏn Ilbo*, November 29, 1970.

27   The incomes of farmers, which were higher than those of urban workers in the early 1960s, were almost 40 percent lower by the end of the 1960s. In 1969, the family income of the countryside was 65.3 percent that of the urban laborer: Kim Su-haeng and Pak Sŭng-ho, *Pak Chŏng-hŭi ch'eje ŭi sŏngnip kwa chŏn'gae mit mollak* (Seoul: Seoul National University Press, 2007), 62.

28   Korean Statistical Information Service website, http://kosis.kr.

29   Kim and Pak, *Pak Chŏng-hŭi ch'eje ŭi sŏngnip kwa chŏngae mit mollak*, 73.

30   Seoul T'ŭkpyŏlsi, *Sŏul tosi kibon kyehweok chojŏng surip* (Seoul: Seoul-si, 1970), 199–200.

31   The number of film productions per year were 74 in 1958, 111 in 1959, 87 in 1960, 79 in 1961, 112 in 1962, 148 in 1963, 137 in 1964, 161 in 1965, 172 in 1966, 185 in 1967, 212 in 1968, 229 in 1969, and 231 in 1970. The number dropped sharply in the 1970s, to about 100: Korean Film Commission, *Han'guk yŏnghwa charyo p'yŏllam* (Seoul: Korean Film Commission, 1978), 156.

32   Korean Film Commission, *Han'guk yŏnghwa charyo p'yŏllam*, 52. There were almost one hundred theaters in South Korea in the late 1960s, with many of them located in these suburbs. Eight of these were "first runners" while the rest were so-called second, third, fourth, and fifth runners: see the testimony of Chin Hang-bŏm in Yi

Kil-sŏng, Yi Ho-gŏl, and Yi U-sŏk, *1970 nyŏndae Sŏul ŭi kŭkjang sanŏp mit kŭkjang munhwa yŏn'gu* (Seoul: Korean Film Commission, 2004), 153.

33   For example, in 1968 Yŏnhŭng Theater (Yŏngdŭngp'o region), Tongil Theater (Ch'ŏngryangni region), Taehan Theater (Chongno region), Sŏngnam Theater, and P'yŏnghwa Theater all bypassed the dominant distribution system to demand the screening of new releases from the Central Cinema Distributor, a joint venture of five suburban theaters: Yi et al., *1970 nyŏndae Sŏul ŭi kŭkjang sanŏp mit kŭkjang munhwa yŏn'gu*, 141–53.

34   Regarding the regional distribution of films, see Kim, *Han'guk yŏnghwa paegŭpsa yŏn'gu*, 20–22. The growing popularity of second-run suburban theaters meant that more people had access to this cultural art form. While many media experts predicted the demise of cinema with the rapid increase of television sets in people's homes, they also expected an increase in viewership for suburban second-run theaters that catered to lower class people who did not own their own television sets: "Kwan'gaek ŭi 20 p'ŏsent'ŭ sangsil, TV wihyŏp soge hŭndŭllinŭn panghwa," *Maeil Kyŏngje*, February 20, 1970.

35   "Sirizŭmul i chal pallyŏ," *Chosŏn Ilbo*, April 26, 1970.

36   On average, the regular theater entrance fee was 130 wŏn in 1968–69: Kim Tong-ho, "1960–70 nyŏndae ŭi paegŭp yut'ong kujo wa sangyŏnggwan," in *Han'guk yŏnghwa sangyŏnggwan ŭi pyŏnch'ŏn kwa paljŏn panghyang*, ed. Kim Tong-ho (Seoul: Munhwa Kwangwangbu, 2001), 24–42.

37   For more on these publications, see Henry in this volume.

38   The boom in urban lowbrow popular culture at this time needs further analysis. For one study, see Henry in this volume.

39   In his analysis of early twentieth-century audiences, Stuart Hall describes a new "popular class" that did not directly coincide with working- or lower-class status but was the product of the identity-forming effects of the consumption of popular culture: Hall, "Notes on Deconstructing 'the Popular,'" 229. The number of this "popular class" audience expanded in the 1970–80s, rejuvenating the declining South Korean film industry when the industry was often referred to as "having hit a low point." Molly Hyo Kim also discusses how such "realistic (or deviant)" descriptions of prohibited subjects, such as the stories of prostitutes, could play a great role in sustaining the South Korean film industry of the 1970s. She argues that, by producing "hostess films" that deal with the stories of people who migrated to the suburbs of Seoul, the South Korean film industry could sustain this long dark age in the 1970–80s. Although she mostly focused on textual analysis of these films, it is important to note the transformation of audiences in this time from middle class to this "popular class": see Molly Hyo Kim, "Genre Convention of South Korean Hostess Films (1974–1982): Prostitutes and the Discourse of Female Sacrificer," *Acta Koreana* 17, no. 1 (2014): 1–21.

40   In a similar context, Yu Sŏn-yŏng has examined 1970s Korean movies with sexual content and argues that this subculture created a certain cultural space for re-

sistance: Yu Sŏn-yŏng, "Tongwŏn ch'eje ŭi kwaminjokhwa pŭrojekt'ŭ wa seksŭ yŏnghwa," *Ŏllon kwa Sahwoe* 15, no. 2 (2007): 42–44.

41 Many of these women found work as housemaids, kisaengs, hairdressers, and prostitutes. Licensed prostitution was officially outlawed in 1948, but these women continued to provide sexual services with the government's tacit approval. Although being a housemaid was more respectable, it also often left the woman vulnerable to sexual approaches by male employers. The barber shop also became an iconic site of female prostitution: see Pak Chong-sŏng, *Han'guk ŭi maech'un* (Seoul: In'gan Sarang, 1994).

42 This depiction of lower-class female workers in film is an accurate portrayal of their place in society. Jeong-mi Park has analyzed the paradoxes of the state's system of controlling sex workers, describing it as a "toleration-regulation" system: see Jeong-mi Park, "Paradoxes of Gendering Strategy in Prostitution Policies: South Korea's 'Toleration-Regulation' Regime," *Women's Studies International Forum* 37 (2013): 73–84. Prostitutes who worked near U.S. military bases suffered even harsher regulation: see Bruce Cumings, "Silent but Deadly: Sexual Subordination in the U.S.-Korean Relationship," in *Let the Good Times Roll: Prostitution and the U.S. Military in Asia*, ed. Saundra P. Sturdevant and Brenda Stoltzfus (New York: New Press, 1993), 169–75. As I have argued elsewhere, these women were racialized and secluded from society: see Chung-kang Kim, "Skin-Deep? The Politics of Black Korean Identity in Post-1945 Korean Literature and Film," *Journal of Literature and Film* 15, no. 1 (2014): 5–41.

43 In the film, the last name of the actor is used for the character's name. For example, Ku is the last name of the actor Ku Pong-sŏ and Hŏ is the last name of the actor Hŏ Chang-kang. Both actors were stars at the time, and the scenario was written after the male protagonists were cast. But the female character's last name is not known either in the film or the scenario. Thus, in the plot summary, I use the last name for the male characters and the first name for the female character.

44 "Tongsŏng yŏn'ae" is both a medicalized term and a popularly used word in everyday life in South Korean.

45 Such negotiations of male-to-female masquerade could have been influenced by a director's own perception of gender normality. As the director Sim U-sŏp put it to me in our conversation, "I did not really like the idea of making Ku a totally womanly man." He therefore purposely created a masculine male-to-female masquerade: Sim U-sŏp, interview with the author, Seoul, December 10, 2013.

46 Butler, *Gender Trouble*, 146–47.

47 Marjorie Garber, *Vested Interests: Cross-Dressing and Cultural Anxiety* (New York: Routledge, 1992), 10–11.

48 My argument for Korea draws on more general insights from Foucault, *The History of Sexuality*, 23.

49 Debates about "vulgar" culture were common at the time. See, e.g., "Ta hamkke saeng'gakhae popsida: Ŭmnan ŭi han'gyenŭn?" *Kyŏnghyang Sinmun*, July 17, 1969; "Ŭmnan sŏhwa tansok munje," *Tong'a Ilbo*, July 17, 1969; "Chit'an pannŭn

ero chapchi ŭi kyuje wa chŏnghwa ŭi panghyang," *Tong'a Ilbo*, June 14, 1969; "T'woep'ye p'ungjo tansok e sŏnheang hal kŏt," *Tong'a Ilbo*, September 28, 1971.

50   "Hwan'gakche ŭi ssak put'ŏ jjallara," *Kyŏnghyang Sinmun*, February 25, 1971.

51   "T'oep'ye panghwa chŏnghwa pang'an maryŏn," *Maeil Kyŏngje*, October 2, 1971.

52   Cho P'ung-yŏn, "Yŏnghwa wa sŏng moral," *Korea Cinema*, March 1971.

53   Kim Su-yong, "'Kŏmyŏl,' igŏsi ŏpsŭmyŏn kŭkjang ŭn sahwoe ak ŭi sogul i toel kŏsin'ga?" *Chugan Han'guk*, vol. 82, no. 17, April 27, 1966, 24–25.

54   For the first time in the history of South Korea, Yu Hyŏn-mok, the director of the film *Spring Dreams*, was imprisoned for making a vulgar film (*ŭmhwa*) in 1969. See the detailed ruling summary in *Kyŏnghyang Sinmun*, July 17, 1969. Following this ruling, Sin Sang-ok, the director of *A Eunuch*, was investigated because his film described lesbianism. Yi Hyŏng-pyo, who made *Your Name Is Woman*, was also investigated by the prosecutor because the film included overtly sexual expression.

55   Thirty thousand wŏn would today be equivalent to ten million wŏn, or $10,000. See the consumer price index for Korea, accessed April 26, 2015, http://www .index.go.kr/potal/main/EachDtlPageDetail.do?idx_cd=1060.

56   "Yŏnghwa ch'unmong yujoe," *Kyŏnghyang Sinmun*, March 15, 1967.

57   The comment was made in a seminar on censorship held at Christian Academy, a religiously based nongovernmental organization based in Seoul. The discussions of the seminar were summarized in "Yŏnghwa kŏmyŏl ŭn p'ilyohan'ga?" *Kyŏnghyang Sinmun*, May 25, 1968.

58   For example, at the seminar described earlier, a constitutional scholar, Yi Hang-nyŏng, was the only one who seriously criticized that the standard of censorship published by the Bureau of Public Information was unlawful.

59   "Yŏnghwa kŏmyŏl ŭi munjejŏm," *Chosŏn Ilbo*, February 22, 1968.

60   "Kawijil in'ga nandojil in'ga? Yŏnghwa kŏmyŏl," *Chugan Han'guk*, vol. 193, June 2, 1968, 20.

61   Yun Ik-sam, "Han'guk yŏnghwa nŭn sayanggil e sŏtnŭn'ga?" *Arirang*, vol. 16, no. 9, September 1970, 194–97.

62   Ku Pong-sŏ, interview with the author, Seoul, September 2, 2004.

63   The word "and" between "male" and "kisaeng" is printed in a very small font, likely to hint at the original title (see figure 5.1).

64   Sŏ Kok-suk argues that many lowbrow comedy films came to internalize the rules and regulations of the film code, even though they were not seriously tampered with by the censors: Sŏ Kok-suk, "Han'guk yŏnghwa kŏmyŏl kwa k'omedi yŏnghwa," *Yŏnghwa Yŏn'gu* 36 (2008): 345–70.

65   Thomas Doherty argues that classical Hollywood films started to create "mental images" rather than direct descriptions of sex scenes after the Hays Code started to regulate "sex, immorality and insurrection" in early 1930s America: Thomas Doherty, *Pre-code Hollywood: Sex, Immorality, and Insurrection in American Cinema, 1930–1934* (New York: Columbia University Press, 1999), 2–3.

66   Kim, *Chugan han'guk*, 82.

67 Kim, *Chugan han'guk*, 82.
68 Yu Chi-na, "1960 nyŏndae han'guk k'omidi: Haeksim k'odŭ wa sahoejŏk ŭimi chakyong," *Yŏnghwa Yŏn'gu* 15 (2000): 283–306.
69 "Yŏjang 26 nyŏn ŭi chungnyŏn," *Chosŏn Ilbo*, December 7, 1969.

Works Cited

NEWSPAPERS AND MAGAZINES

Arirang
Chosŏn Ilbo
Chugan Han'guk
Korea Cinema
Kyŏnghyang Sinmun
Maeil Kyŏngje
Tong'a Ilbo

KOREAN-LANGUAGE SOURCES

Academy of Korean Studies, ed. *5.16 kwa Pak Chŏng-hŭi chŏngbu ŭi sŏllip*. Seongnam, South Korea: Academy of Korean Studies Press, 1999.
Chang Mun-sŏk and Yi Sang-nok, ed. *Kŭndae ŭi kyŏnggye esŏ tokjae rŭl ikta*. Seoul: Kŭrinbi, 2006.
Chang Sŏk-yong. *Han'guk nyuweibŭ ŭi chinghu rŭl ch'ajasŏ*. Seoul: Hyŏndae Mihaksa, 2002.
Cho Hae-joang. *Sŏng, kajok, kŭrigo munhwa: Illyuhakjŏk chŏpgŭn*. Seoul: Chimundang, 1997.
Chu Yu-sin, ed. *Han'guk yŏnghwa wa kŭndaesŏng*. Seoul: Sodo, 2000.
Hwang Chŏng-mi. "Paljŏn kukka wa mosŏng: 1960–1970 nyŏndae 'punyŏ chŏngch'aek' ŭl chungsim ŭro." In *Mosŏng ŭi tamnon kwa hyŏnsil*, ed. Sim Yŏng-hŭi, 82–104. P'aju, South Korea: Nanam, 1999.
Kang Man-gil. *Han'guk chabonjuŭi ŭi yŏksa*. Seoul: Yoksa Pip'yŏng, 2000.
Kim Chun. "Pak Chŏng-hŭi sidae ŭi nodong: Ulsan Hyŏndai chosŏn nodongja rŭl chungsim ŭro." In *Kŭndae ŭi kyŏnggye esŏ tokjae rŭl ikta*, ed. Chang Mun-sŏk and Yi Sang-nok, 257–92. Seoul: Kŭrinbi, 2006.
Kim Mi-hyŏn, ed. *Han'guk yŏnghwa paegŭpsa yŏn'gu*. Seoul: Korean Film Commission, 2003.
Kim Si-mu, *Yesul yŏnghwa ongho*. Seoul: Hyŏndae Mihaksa, 2001.
Kim Su-haeng and Pak Sŭng-ho. *Pak Chŏng-hŭi ch'eje ŭi sŏngnip kwa chŏn'gae mit mollak*. Seoul: Seoul National University Press, 2007.
Kim Tong-ho. "1960–70 nyŏndae ŭi paegŭp yut'ong kujo wa sangyŏnggwan." In *Han'guk yŏnghwa sangyŏnggwan ŭi pyŏnch'ŏn kwa paljŏn panghyang*, ed. Kim Tong-ho, 24–42. Seoul: Munhwa Kwangwangbu, 2001.

Korean Film Commission. *Han'guk yŏnghwa charyo p'yŏllam.* Seoul: Korean Film Commission, 1978.

Kwŏn Podŭre, ed. *Apres-ggŏl sasanggye rŭl ikta.* Seoul: Dongguk University Press, 2009.

No Chi-sŭng. "Yŏnghwa, chŏngch'i wa sidaesŏng ŭi chinghu: Tosi chung'gan kyech'ŭng ŭi yongmang kwa kajok." *Yŏksa Munje Yon'gu* 25 (2011): 169–76.

Pak Chong-sŏng. *Han'guk ŭi maech'un.* Seoul: In'gan Sarang, 1994.

Park Jeong-mi. "Paljŏn kwa seksŭ: Han'guk chŏngbu ŭi sŏngmaemae kwan'gwang chŏngch'aek, 1955–1988," *Han'guk Sahoehak* 48, no. 25 (2014): 235–64.

Pyŏn Chae-ran. "Taehan nyusŭ, munhwa yŏnghwa, kŭndaejŏk kihoek ŭrosŏ ŭi 'kajok kyehoek.'" *Yŏnghwa Yon'gu* 52 (2012): 207–35.

Seoul T'ŭkpyŏlsi. *Sŏul tosi kibon kyehweok chojŏng surip.* Seoul: Seoul-si, 1970.

Sŏ Kok-suk. "Han'guk yŏnghwa kŏmyŏl kwa k'omedi yŏnghwa." *Yŏnghwa Yŏn'gu* 36 (2008): 345–70.

Yi Im-ha. *Yŏsŏng, chŏnjaeng ŭl nŏmŏ irŏsŏda.* Seoul: Sŏhae Munjip, 2004.

Yi Kil-sŏng, Yi Ho-gŏl, and Yi U-sŏk. *1970 nyŏndae Sŏul ŭi kŭkjang sanŏp mit kŭkjang munhwa yŏn'gu.* Seoul: Korean Film Commission, 2004.

Yi Yŏng-il. *Han'guk yŏnghwa chŏnsa.* Seoul: Sodo, 2004.

Yu Chi-na. "1960 nyŏndae han'guk k'omidi: Haeksim k'odŭ wa sahoejŏk ŭimi cha-kyong." *Yŏnghwa Yŏn'gu* 15 (2000): 283–306.

Yu Sŏn-yŏng. "Tongwŏn ch'eje ŭi kwaminjokhwa pŭrojekt'ŭ wa seksŭ yŏnghwa." *Ŏllon kwa Sahwoe* 15, no. 2 (2007): 42–44.

ENGLISH-LANGUAGE SOURCES

Abelmann, Nancy. *Echoes of the Past, Epics of Dissent: A South Korean Social Movement.* Berkeley: University of California Press, 1996.

Baskett, Michael. *The Attractive Empire: Transnational Film Culture in Imperial Japan.* Honolulu: University of Hawai'i Press, 2008.

Butler, Judith. *Gender Trouble: Feminism and the Subversion of Identity.* New York: Routledge, 1999.

Cho, Hae-joang. "You are Trapped in an Imaginary Well: The Formation of Subjectivity in a Compressed Development." *Inter-Asia Cultural Studies* 1, no. 1 (2000): 62–64.

Chung, Steven. *The Split Screen Korea: Shin Sang-ok and Post-war Cinema.* Minneapolis: University of Minnesota Press, 2014.

Corber, Robert J. *Cold War Femme: Lesbianism, National Identity, and Hollywood Cinema.* Durham, NC: Duke University Press, 2011.

Corber, Robert J. *Homosexuality in Cold War America: Resistance and the Crisis of Masculinity.* Durham, NC: Duke University Press, 1997.

Cumings, Bruce. "Silent but Deadly: Sexual Subordination in the U.S.-Korean Relationship." In *Let the Good Times Roll: Prostitution and the U.S. Military in Asia,* ed. Saundra P. Sturdevant and Brenda Stoltzfus, 169–75. New York: New Press, 1993.

Cuordileone, K. A. "Politics in an Age of Anxiety: Cold War Political Culture and the Crisis in American Masculinity, 1949." *Journal of American History* 87, no. 2 (2000): 515–45.

Doherty, Thomas. *Pre-code Hollywood: Sex, Immorality, and Insurrection in American Cinema, 1930–1934*. New York: Columbia University Press, 1999.

Doty, Alexander. "Queer Theory." In *The Oxford Guide to Film Studies*, ed. John Hill, 148–51. Oxford: Oxford University Press, 1998.

Foucault, Michel. *The Birth of Biopolitics*. New York: Palgrave Macmillan, 2008.

Foucault, Michel. *The History of Sexuality, Volume 1: An Introduction*. New York: Vintage, 1990.

Garber, Marjorie. *Vested Interests: Cross-Dressing and Cultural Anxiety*. New York: Routledge, 1992.

Hall, Stuart. "Notes on Deconstructing 'The Popular.'" In *People's History and Socialist Theory*, ed. Raphael Samuel, 442–53. London: Routledge and Kegan Paul, 1981.

Kim, Chung-kang. "Nation, Subculture, and Queer Representation: The Film *Male Kisaeng* and the Politics of Gender and Sexuality in 1960s South Korea." *Journal of the History of Sexuality* 24, no. 3 (September 2015): 455–77.

Kim, Chung-kang. "Skin-Deep? The Politics of Black Korean Identity in Post-1945 Korean Literature and Film." *Journal of Literature and Film* 15, no. 1 (2014): 5–41.

Kim, Elaine H., and Chungmoo Choi, ed. *Dangerous Women: Gender and Korean Nationalism*. New York: Routledge, 1998.

Kim, Eun Mee. *Big Business, Strong State: Collusion and Conflict in South Korean Development, 1960–1990*. Albany: State University of New York Press, 1997.

Kim, Hyun Mee. "Work, Nation and Hypermasculinity: The 'Woman' Question in the Economic Miracle and Crisis in South Korea." *Inter-Asia Cultural Studies* 2, no. 1 (2001): 53–68.

Kim, Molly Hyo. "Genre Convention of South Korean Hostess Films (1974–1982): Prostitutes and the Discourse of Female Sacrificer." *Acta Koreana* 17, no. 1 (2014): 1–21.

Koo, Hagen, ed. *Korean Workers: The Culture and Politics of Class Formation*. Ithaca: NY: Cornell University Press, 2001.

Min, Eung-jun, ed. *Korean Film: History, Resistance, and Democratic Imagination*. Santa Barbara, CA: Praeger, 2003.

Mitchell, Timothy. "Society, Economy, and the State Effect." In *State/Culture: State-formation after the Cultural Turn*, ed. George Steinmetz, 76–97. Ithaca, NY: Cornell University Press, 1999.

Moon, Seungsook. *Militarized Modernity and Gendered Citizenship in South Korea*. Durham, NC: Duke University Press, 2005.

Namhee, Lee. "Making Minjung Subjectivity: Crisis of Subjectivity and Rewriting History, 1960–1988." PhD diss., University of Chicago, 2001.

Park, Jeong-mi. "Paradoxes of Gendering Strategy in Prostitution Policies: South Korea's 'Toleration-Regulation' Regime." *Women's Studies International Forum* 37 (2013): 73–84.

Ricci, Steve. *Cinema and Fascism: Italian Film and Society, 1922–1943.* Oakland: University of California Press, 2008.

Schulte-Sasse, Linda. *Entertaining the Third Reich: Illusions of Wholeness in Nazi Cinema.* Durham, NC: Duke University Press, 1996.

Chapter Six

QUEER LIVES AS CAUTIONARY TALES

FEMALE HOMOEROTICISM AND
THE HETEROPATRIARCHAL IMAGINATION
OF AUTHORITARIAN SOUTH KOREA

Todd A. Henry

> Only history, material conditions, and con-
> text can account for the specific content of
> gay kinship ideologies, their emergence at
> a particular point in time, and the variety of
> ways people have implemented those ide-
> ologies in their daily lives.
> —Kath Weston, *Families We Choose*

Since the turn of the century, South Korean filmmakers, visual artists, and other creators of alternative culture have worked to overturn derogatory and exploitative representations of sexual minorities, whose lives remain largely missing from historical accounts of their country's modernity.[1] Aligned to varying degrees with LGBTI activism, these intrepid self-expressions followed in the wake of more than four decades of military dictatorships and drew on the fruits of labor and antigovernment protests that ebbed and flowed across this tempestuous period.[2] Like many authoritarian regimes during the Cold War, South Korean leaders prioritized national defense and capital accumulation while subordinating the working classes, young women, and other vulnerable subpopulations to the officially sanctioned goals of their anticommunist nation. Despite such oppressive conditions, marginalized subjects, including those engaging in same-sex love and non-normative gender practices, managed to carve out laboring and living spaces through various forms of everyday resistance, cultural accommodation, and community building.

Pak Chae-ho's *Broken Branches* (1995), one of South Korea's first queer films, mirrors this tumultuous history of institutional violence and negotiated struggle.[3] This pathbreaking film traces the valiant story of Chŏng-min—a thirty-something man who falls in love with an older married man, Sŭng-gŏl. Although beholden to a wife and children, Sŭng-gŏl is won over by Chŏng-min, and the two men enter a romantic relationship. With Sŭng-gŏl by his side, Chŏng-min finally emancipates himself from the shackles of the Park Chung Hee regime (1961–79) and the equally oppressive dictates of his own patriarchal father. In the final scene, the couple visits Chŏng-min's mother to celebrate her seventieth birthday, an indication of her son's filial piety. But, in a dramatic departure from Confucian conventions which typically include a deep bow of respect, they serenade her with an amorous pop song, after which the two men boldly announce to the extended family that they are also married. Although the director portrays this secret as a campy joke that might soften their disclosure, Chŏng-min's mother proceeds to faint in response to their homosexual secret.

Broken Branches was one of the first gay films to suggest that same-sex intimacy could challenge the heteropatriarchal order of South Korea.[4] Subsequent works have also addressed the disruptive power of queer kinship ideologies, including those that existed in the past. These LGBTI artists/activists have thus positioned themselves as important historians of non-normative relations, which have not yet found their way into academic narratives of the contemporary period. For example, So Chun-mun's short film *Auld Lang Syne* (2007) tells the poignant tale of an unexpected reunion between two elderly men who dated during the late 1960s and early 1970s but were forced to separate under pressure to marry and reproduce.[5] For his part, Yi [Song] Hŭi-il—another well-known director and the creative genius behind *No Regret* (2006), *White Nights* (2012), and other popular films—conducted pioneering interviews with elderly men in the late 1990s, generating novel insights on the relationship between public space and gay sociality after the Korean War (1950–53).[6] However, perhaps because these stories appeared in *Buddy*, one of the country's first LGBTI magazines, they remain relatively unknown, even today. As a result, they have failed to reorient the assumptions and methods of most historical work on contemporary South Korea, which remains hetero-normative and empiricist in outlook.[7]

Meanwhile, several short films and documentaries on queer kinship practices have also revealed the silenced past of nonconforming women, foregrounding them as critical actors under authoritarian regimes of capital accumulation. In 2000, Kwŏn Chong-gwan directed one such film, *Uncle "Bar" at Barbershop*. Set during the explosive decade of the 1980s, this pathbreaking short features a woman who seeks to pass as a working-class barber by binding her breasts and dodging the misogynistic banter of male customers. Although the protagonist's female partner is excluded from the hypermasculine and heterosexist space of the barbershop, their queer relationship, evidenced by a heated argument about the difficulties of raising an adopted child, highlights the hetero-patriarchal pressures of South Korean development. More recently, Yi Yŏng's *Troublers* (2015), which has circulated in independent theaters, presents the unknown story of Yi Muk, a biological woman who, in large part, lived as a South Korean man during and after the Park Chung Hee period. Although none of Yi's romances with women lead to a long-lasting partnership, this individual's compelling story encourages moviegoers and progressive scholars to recognize the critical value of recounting such suppressed pasts. Pairing Yi's nonconforming life with rowdy scenes of fundamentalist Christian activism, *Troublers*, as the title suggests, forces us to think about the historical meaning of queer subjects amid increasingly vocal movements aimed at excluding sexual (and social other) minorities in South Korea today.

Given the ongoing marginalization of LGBTI subjects, queer kinship relations captured by filmmakers since the mid-1990s are remarkable manifestations of authoritarian subcultures that, as this chapter reveals, also regularly appeared in the print media and visual culture of the day.[8] Although exploited by newspapers and magazines for profit, non-normative forms of familial and communal intimacies, especially among women, can serve as critical lenses on the androcentric mechanisms that supported industrial capitalism under Cold War dictatorships. In what follows, I return to an archival form that, along-side film and radio, saturated the consumer market during the authoritarian era but remains relatively underused in historical accounts of contemporary South Korea. Launched by most newspaper companies during the mid- to late 1960s, weeklies (*chuganji*), which took their inspiration from similar Japanese publications and closely interacted with their Western counterparts, gained a popular following among men, boasting a combined annual circulation of more than one million copies by 1970. A far greater number of readers likely perused these commercial publications without cost at barbershops, coffee shops, train stations, military barracks, and other public places. Drawing on Christina Klein's study of Cold War Orientalism, I consider weeklies an inherently middlebrow genre, a plastic form perfectly situated to balance the serious facts of investigative journalism and the playful invention of fictional storytelling.[9] Although ignored by most scholars of Korea because of its rumorous content and salacious tone, a close reading of this popular source will show how male-dominated, heterosexist narratives about female homoeroticism served as cautionary tales in the production and maintenance of a capitalist patriarchy. By focusing on the political-economic underside of same-sex sexuality and gender variance in a Cold War setting, my analysis of the mass media and its national readership also aims to reorient a Western-centered queer studies that has tended to highlight atomized questions of subjectivity and consumption under (neo-)liberal regimes, especially in large cities. By contrast, I interrogate the lived realities of kinship strictures and economic inequalities under an illiberal regime of capital accumulation. Although filtered through the print media, I focus on the everyday struggles of queer women across the country who, by rejecting normative conventions of heteropatriarchy, sought to survive on the fringes of a mass culture intent on taming their life choices.[10]

Not unlike other "eccentric" topics addressed by weeklies, reports about female-female relationships contained a calculated balance of scandalous entertainment and sober moralizing. Together, they played an integral role in facilitating what Jie-Hyun Lim has innovatively called "mass dictatorship." According to this theory, the Park Chung Hee regime (and its successors) did not simply impose a set of draconian rules while citizens passively succumbed to these top-down edicts. Alongside various forms of coercion, the regime and its proxies also developed a system of persuasive power that relied on a nominally liberal politics but were instituted *for*, rather than controlled *by*, the citizenry. Under this Cold War system of "administrative democracy," Park also encouraged various forms of mass entertainment aimed at promoting what Lim calls the "disciplined uniformity" of anticommunism. Building on feminist critiques of this theory as overwhelmingly male-dominated and adding an avowedly queer analytic, I reorient mass dictatorship to examine how textual and visual representations of female homoeroticism facilitated popular participation in the creation and maintenance of a cultural common sense necessary to guide authoritarian development.[11] This common sense was, I insist, inherently androcentric and heteropatriarchal in both its expression and goals, an important point not fully recognized in most accounts of (South) Korean modernity.

Also an exploitative system, mass dictatorship demanded various corporeal sacrifices, particularly on the part of the proletarian and female masses.[12] Persistently hounded by resistance, authoritarian regimes could not operate effectively without providing at least some of its worker-citizens with psychic releases and compensatory pleasures. Consumed regularly by a wide range of male (and some female) readers, weeklies served these diversionary functions while also helping to produce a collective imaginary rooted in heteropatriarchal "traditions." Repeatedly normalized practices of kinship thus functioned as a default model of cultural purity against which sexual, gender, and racial deviations from "proper" life courses could be understood and, when possible, accommodated to its homogenizing logic. Weeklies thus expressed near constant concern that some citizens, including women who married women, were indeed "veering offtrack" (t'alsŏn), an ideological catchword of the authoritarian period. Ironically, however, morbid fascination with their social deviancy may have encouraged other "shadow-reading" women to pursue such stigmatized pleasures, especially given a relative lack of information available to queer subjects during this era.[13]

Whatever the case, newspaper weeklies, a new industry in need of constant profits, used a considerable amount of their media space to engage in what I call "capitalistic voyeurism." This entrepreneurial practice of mass entertainment encouraged fellow citizens, especially adult men, to privately—and, when read together, collectively—decry life practices that veered off track from national goals of economic production and biological reproduction. To this end, recurrent stories of weddings between women induced androcentric and homophobic laughter as gestures that, like B-grade films from the period, helped reassert readers' conformity to heteropatriarchal conventions. Even as they amused audiences, sensational accounts of female homoeroticism also expressed serious concern about "deviant" women who failed to perform expected duties as "wise mothers and good wives" (hyŏnmo yangch'ŏ) under Cold War capitalism. In contrast to the ethnographic richness of nonnormative subjectivities depicted in queer films since the 1990s, weeklies from the authoritarian period thus highlighted the alleged monstrosity of women partnering with one another and refusing to produce or raise children.

Although likely exaggerated for shock value, alarming accounts of gynocentric practices played an important role in controlling queer forms of kinship through various "epistemological interventions." These biopolitical strategies of knowledge production included superficially heteronormalizing the roles of partnered women as gender-normative "husbands" and "wives" rather than recognizing the subcultural terms *paji-ssi* (Ms. Pants) and *ch'ima-ssi* (Ms. Skirt). Aimed primarily at male audiences, the specter of such lesbian fantasies was, however, rhetorically curtailed by desexualizing same-sex relationships and framing them as platonic arrangements. Whatever the formula, weeklies actively disavowed female homoeroticism as personally deleterious and socially unsustainable. Through these cautionary tales, the mass media rewarded readers who, as normative citizens, already contributed to the (re) productive goals of their anticommunist nation. A multivalent instrument of social control, its "queersploitative" reporters, as I analyze them, also exhorted potentially nonconforming women to engage in heteropatriarchal practices needed to maintain social cohesion under a mass dictatorship of capitalist accumulation.

Social Criminality and Sexual Deviance in Early Post–Korean War Accounts

As research on gender history has revealed, media and literary representations of female same-sex relations, which tended to focus on schoolgirl romances and other adolescent experiences of homoeroticism, including double suicides *(chŏngsa)*, trace their modern origins to the colonial period (1910–45).[14] By contrast, popular discussions of same-sex cohabitation and marriage between adult women began in earnest in the wake of the Korean War.[15] This cataclysmic event caused the death of millions, many of them male soldiers, and left numerous widowed women, to say nothing of orphaned children.[16] Given that many of their male husbands perished in battle, some women abandoned the perils (and comforts) of heterosexual marriage, also escaping the surveillance and control of their in-laws.[17] Oral histories of war widows suggest that some did so by becoming breadwinning household heads *(ka-jang)*. Less well known but equally important is that others sought to establish independent lives by presenting themselves in masculine ways, if not as men. For these women, their official sex protected them from the possibility of injury or death due to military service, although gender nonconformity did occasionally lead to accusations of posing as North Korean spies.[18] Of these masculine-presenting women, some decided to cohabit with other female partners, usually feminine in demeanor, and unofficially marry them. Beset by internal struggles and a pugnacious enemy across the 38th Parallel, the new South Korean state did not extend legal sanction to these queer couples, nor has its democratic successor done so since the early 1990s. However, even such informal arrangements may, ironically, have given these queer women more financial security and emotional sustenance than their heterosexual counterparts. As discussed later, that such women sought symbolically to express their love for one another in wedding rites indicates a remarkable urge to stabilize and dignify their relationships through hetero-marital customs. Although homosexual and unconventional, their ceremonial appearance in sartorial and tonsorial forms that gestured at gender-normative "husbands" and "wives" likely lent an air of respectability to their families and local communities, at least some of whom reportedly attended their wedding and banquet ceremonies in joyful celebration.[19]

At first glance, such dyadic couples appear to succumb passively to heteropatriarchal expectations and were occasionally presented that way in media accounts concerned with the socially and culturally disruptive effects of recent military battles.[20] For example, in one of the first extended reports of postwar gynocentric subcultures, the author simplistically referred to female "husbands" as inferior replacements for their biological male counterparts, graphically describing the use of artificial penises (e.g., dildos) to pleasure their "wives" in what problematically reads as a Freudian expression of penis envy.[21] Despite such claims of cultural conformity and pornographic descriptions of heterosexual mimicry, popular representations of "husbands" and "wives" in same-sex relationships are more fruitfully understood within the lesbian and queer subcultures of working-class women during the mid- to late twentieth century. As Elizabeth Kennedy and Madeline's Davis's detailed ethnography of interwar Buffalo shows, similar pairs of "butches" and "femmes" creatively manipulated the basic ingredients of the dominant gender system in the U.S. They also convincingly argue that such dichotomous gender pairings were not tantamount to heteronormative mimicry. Instead, they allowed female subjects to express their sense of autonomy in public space while simultaneously demonstrating romantic interest in one another.[22] Understood from this auto-ethnographic perspective, South Korean women who coupled as Ms. Pants and Ms. Skirt also came to subtly critique their country's dominant gender system rather than simply imitating mainstream models of heteropatriarchy. They did so by creating an intimate subculture in which proletarian women could escape the potentially unstable, unfulfilling, and dangerous conditions of male subordination and heterosexism.[23]

Public knowledge about gynocentric practices remained relatively limited until the mid-1950s, when the mass media began to introduce their non-normative stories to the national community as part of state-led efforts to rebuild family life after the Korean War.[24] Published primarily in newspapers and monthlies before the rise of weeklies during the mid- to late 1960s, these accounts sought to demarcate cultural boundaries between acceptable, heteropatriarchal practices and their dangerous, nonconforming counterparts. Such epistemological interventions into the everyday lives of South Koreans aimed to restore the stabilizing function of prewar kinship structures. They also formed the social basis on which postwar leaders hoped to resuscitate a devastated economy, albeit with only limited success. To these ends, journalists took great pains to heteronormalize queer relationships by designating one female partner as the male-dressed "husband" and the other as the female-dressed "wife." Having reduced their unruly subjectivities into recognizable pairs, media reports sought to integrate them as nonthreatening members of a nation still at war with North Korea. However, their unassimilable practices—for example, that Ms. Pants presented herself as masculine but typically not as a transgender man, and that Ms. Skirt tended to desire masculine women but not biological men—also enabled heterosexual readers to consider queer women as deviating from social norms. Through these accounts, readers, even poorly educated members of the male proletariat, could imagine themselves as more thoroughly embodying idealized notions of (re)productivity and patriotism, thus allowing them to assume a position of domination in relation to their "deviant" female compatriots.

A good example of these heteronormalizing efforts appears in an account published in the *Tong'a Ilbo* in 1958, exactly five years after the conclusion of an armistice that suspended but did not end military hostilities between North Korea and South Korea.[25] This salacious report chronicled the court proceedings of a homicide committed by a thirty-year-old woman, Yim Hŭi-suk (b. 1928), against her female "husband," the thirty-four-year-old Ch'oe Myŏng-im (b. 1924). According to Yim's testimony, the two women had first meet in Taejŏn (a city located ninety miles south of Seoul) just before the official outbreak of the Korean War in 1950. Early accounts of their relationship suggested that they had both served as sex-working "comfort women" *(wianbu)* for American soldiers around the U.S. military base in P'aju, which sat just south of the 38th Parallel.[26] While continuing to reside in this camp town, Yim and Ch'oe were reported as having lived harmoniously as a "married couple" and did not experience spousal discord *(namnyŏ ga kyŏlhap hadŭt tallan han [?] "pubu saenghwal" ŭl yŏngwi haewattanŭn kŏt).* Although rhetorically circumscribed by the insertion of a question mark (more on this later), this expression of amity likened their non-normative relationship to the idealized marriages of heterosexual couples. However, their long-lasting partnership ended abruptly in early 1958, when Yim murdered her "husband" at their home. What sparked the homicide was a drunken conversation in which Ch'oe professed her deep affection for a female concubine (Kim Hŭi-ji, b. 1928), a historical practice of male privilege that was still common among married Korean men. Her expression of love ultimately led a jealous Yim to vindictively kill her adulterous "husband," stabbing her heart with a knife left by an American GI who had been stationed at P'aju, a clear indication of the hot war still enveloping the Korean Peninsula.[27]

Although reportedly unaware of homosexuality hitherto, Yu Sŭng-jin, the male judge, perceived the intense affection between the female couple as exceeding that of their heterosexual counterparts, a view frequently voiced by social critics in the mass media. Indeed, one account launched its discussion of this homicide by quoting a neighbor who conveyed his/her intense fear of lesbian couples, toward whom the alarmist report encouraged readers to exert greater vigilance.[28] Also partial in his opinion of queer women as impassioned, the presiding judge explicitly cited a purported difference between homosexuals and heterosexuals, even when considering the "straight-acting" members of this love triangle. However, much as the *Tong'a Ilbo* reporter described this sensational story as a typical case of male adultery, the judge could not but explain this difference as a matter of degree rather than as one of kind. Downplaying the singular dimensions of their relationship, he repositioned the case within the heterosexist and androcentric parameters of jurisprudential practice. Thus, when adjudicating this crime of passion, the judge reduced Yim's penal servitude to five years, a ruling that displayed remarkable sympathy for her jealousy toward Kim and love for Ch'oe.[29]

Even after the threat of a major invasion by North Korea subsided in the early 1960s, newspaper and magazine accounts of female same-sex relationships continued to highlight their lurid qualities rather than consider the subcultural dynamics of such gynocentric practices. Publicizing crime, death, and other "perverse" details of their everyday lives, these scandalous stories reminded readers of non-(re)productive and potentially disruptive forces then under the anticommunist and developmentalist command of Park Chung Hee. To promote heteropatriarchy and ethnonationalism (often articulated as racial purity) under a new program of mass dictatorship, reporters framed female partnerships as a danger to the health and wealth of South Korean society. Even as they signaled a collective threat to the social order, instrumental representations of queer lives also aimed to contain the life paths of nonconforming subjects who, ironically, could read about one another with increasingly frequency in newspapers, magazines, and, soon, weeklies as well. To this end, popular accounts of coupled women highlighted individual sentiments of misery and regret that they allegedly experienced from same-sex intimacies. In the epistemological purview of the mass media, a long-lasting relationship between two women did not exist, especially after marrying one another. Nor could it produce happiness despite the reality that some female-female relationships undoubtedly flourished and survived the test of time.[30]

In one such account published in 1963, the *Tong'a Ilbo* reported that Yi Kang-suk (b. 1929), the thirty-four-year-old, male-dressed "husband," was missing after she failed to follow the fate of her thirty-five-year-old "wife," Pak Min-ja (b. 1928), who had both agreed to commit suicide by overdosing on pills.[31] The morbid details of their married life underscored the purportedly unstable nature of same-sex relationships more generally, exacerbated in this case by their social standing as ex-convicts. The couple met in May of 1962 while serving sentences for larceny and narcotics, respectively, and, after bonding in prison, decided to live together shortly after their release. Having recently divorced her third male husband, Pak even brought her two daughters (ages three and twelve) from one former marriage into their new, queer household. However, within less than a year, Yi had lost her "wife" amid an ongoing investigation into what the police suspected was a deceptive plan of murder, an accusation implicating Yi in an even more heinous crime. Another account, however, suggests that the two women struggled to earn enough money to raise Pak's two daughters and, like Yim mentioned above, Yi reportedly experienced a severe case of Othello syndrome *(ŭich'ŏjŭng)*, driving them to engage in a double suicide that, in the end, only managed to take the life of Pak.[32] Whatever the case, female same-sex relations served as the dramatic backdrop for injurious behavior inflicted on one another and, in the angst-ridden context of the Cold War, perpetuated by those who allegedly threatened South Korean society at large.

Other reports similarly spotlighted the illicit activities of dangerous female couples rather than acknowledge the precarious conditions they faced in refusing to depend on men for their material and emotional well-being. In the sanctimonious eyes of the newspaper and magazine journalists, such refusals, almost by implication, turned them into petty criminals. Although comparatively free from filial responsibilities, nonconforming women were thus regularly accused of posing a security threat to local communities and, by extension, to the heteropatriarchal order of the nation. As an example of these epistemological interventions, take Han Su-mi (b. 1944), a twenty-one-year-old woman from Pusan who was arrested in 1965 for leading a larcenous gang that included her same-age "wife," Pak Min-ok (b. 1944). In one crime covered by the *Kyŏnghyang Sinmun*, this queer gang even broke into a heterosexual neighbor's home while the bourgeois couple attended a theatrical performance, stealing possessions valued at 12,000 wŏn.[33] Through police arrest and media scrutiny, readers thus became acquainted with the purported danger of non-normative subjects who, like procommunist infiltrators, were said to lurk within South Korean society as political subversives.[34] With newspaper and magazine accounts selectively framing female homoeroticism as an internal threat, heterosexual readers could thereby reaffirm their own gender and sexual normativity while imagining and perhaps even responding to queerness as an immoral disruption and assailable impediment to their nation's path of capitalist development.

Although they took pains to depict queer women as abnormal and criminal, most reporters refused to consider the inner workings of their relationships and the complex subjectivities of individuals who invariably constituted them. Such was the case even when a female "husband" engaged in gendered practices that approximated those of men but who, because of her biological sex, failed to access male privilege in the public sphere. The popular denunciation of female masculinity and the subcultural power of Ms. Pants can perhaps be best seen in the nuanced punctuation of the mass media, especially in terms of its interrogative voice. Through frequent use of question marks, journalists regularly cast doubt on otherwise heteronormalized terms separating married men (husbands) from women (wives) and their rigidly determined associations with patriarchal masculinity and submissive femininity, respectively. To return to the report on Han Su-mi and Pak Min-ok mentioned earlier, even the headline, "Same-Sex Married Couple (?) Commits Thievery Together," refused to admit that two women could constitute a legitimate partnership. Nor did the report acknowledge the role played by a gendered labor market that, under a male-dominated regime of capital accumulation, relegated lower-class women to poorly paid, dangerous, and sexualized work.[35]

As before, the heteronormalizing gaze of this reporter led him to presuppose that one woman—in this case, Su-mi—served as the "husband" in the couple. He based this assumption on the fact that, after arriving in Seoul, Su-mi had cut her hair and masculinized her name to Sang-kyun, but she likely did this to acquire higher-paying jobs typically assumed by men. Adopting the protective role of a male patriarch, Sang-kyun (Su-mi) expressed concern for the miserable plight of her "wife" upon their imprisonment for theft, pleading with police officials that she be released. However, in response to these entreaties, the reporter once again cast doubt on the legitimacy of their partnership by referring to Sang-kyun (Su-mi)'s ersatz status as "husband" with yet another question mark. As this episode suggests, the erotic system enacted by Sang-kyun (Su-mi) and Min-ok likely functioned as "a powerful personal code of behavior and an organizing principle for community life" among Korean women who chose to partner with one another.[36] But police officials, already suspicious of the couple based on their criminal behavior, rejected Sang-kyun (Su-mi)'s role as the patriarchal protector of her "wife."[37] Although desperately in search of wealth and security enjoyed by biological men to provide for their female partners, masculine women such as Sang-kyun (Su-mi) were thus disempowered in the public sphere. In this way, media reports facilitated a secondary form of queerspolitation insofar as they encouraged male readers to reassert their authority over "wayward" women through heteropatriarchal and sexist forms of domination.

In their efforts to heteronormalize queer kinship practices, the mass media even extended its epistemological reach to extremely male-presenting women, some of whom may have identified as men. In today's parlance, we might describe these nonconforming individuals as transgender rather than simply as masculine women who, by contrast, struggled to pass as biological men.[38] These individuals' gendered sense of self notwithstanding, newspaper and magazine journalists often collaborated with local police officers and medical professionals to monitor and control transgender men. Through these efforts, the mass media exposed these queer subjects as social threats to a normative system of sex dimorphism and gendered labor on which authoritarian development depended for its (re)productive efficiency. Such was the case of Yu Sang-ch'un (b. 1937), a twenty-eight-year-old woman who, according to a report published in the *Tong'a Ilbo* in 1965 as part of the entertaining series "Topics of the Day," had passed as a young man since her parents decided to raise and even register the birth as a boy, the sex preferred by most Korean families.[39] As in the case of Han Su-mi and Pak Min-ok, Yu's story became a sensational source of public discussion in the context of police surveillance, including suspicions that this individual had entered a neighbor's home in the southern port city of Chinhae (South Kyŏngsang Province) and engaged in thievery. However, in this case, Yu's female sex was determined only during a medical examination conducted by a local doctor, who curiously noted that the person's low voice and flat chest resembled the physical appearance of most men. Supporting this pseudoscientific judgment of secondary sex characteristics, the newspaper reporter reiterated the social "fact" of Yu's female masculinity by similarly noting a discernibly male voice.[40] Although willing to acknowledge this individual's masculine presentation, the account deployed such observations to confirm an even more disturbing subcultural reality—namely, that Yu was sexually attracted to women and had acted on these carnal desires in the recent past. This account then linked Yu's gendered and sexual "deviance" to a proletarian background. That Yu had masqueraded as a man and performed manual work at a coal briquette factory during the early 1960s also converted this person into a suspect of social disruption at a time when protests by male laborers were on the rise.[41] To provide visual evidence of aggressive behavior as a cross-dressed homosexual agitator, the report also included a captivating photograph of Yu in a tough pose, wearing pants, a shirt, and boots and sporting a closely cropped haircut—in sum, the sartorial and

Figure 6.1 Police, media, and medical discovery of Yu Sang-ch'un's female masculinity.

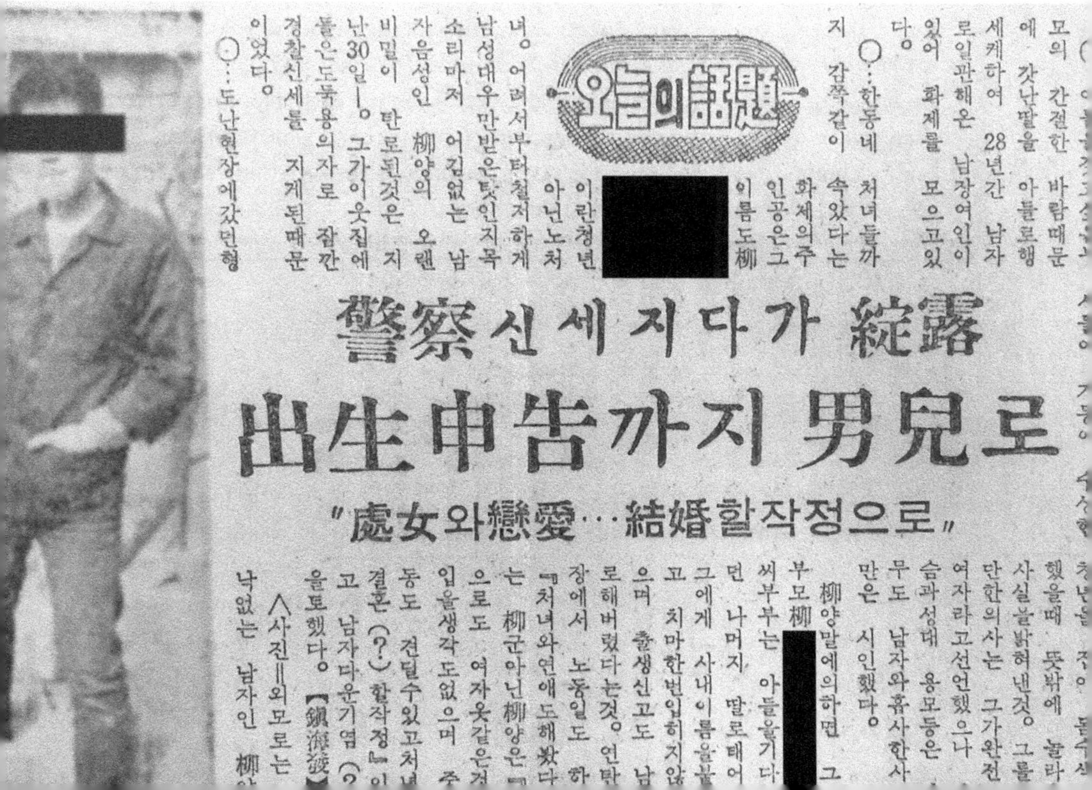

tonsorial practices that had come to define the queer subcultures of extreme female masculinity and transgender men in postwar South Korea (figure 6.1).

Overlooking the physical, social, and cultural signs of Yu's masculinity, this spectacular "outing" by police, media, and medical professionals aimed to reposition this person as a heteronormative woman, whom they expected to engage in reproductive and filial practices befitting one's biological sex. To return to the media's nuanced grammar, this report "re-gendered" Yu by negating its initial use of the distinctly male suffix *kun* (mister or unmarried man) and instead referred to Yu using the gender-specific female pronoun *yang* (miss or unmarried woman). Such forceful attempts to interpolate Yu as a "wise mother and good wife" ran in the face of this person's decision to refrain from wearing women's clothes and to continue enduring heavy labor in the style of working-class men. Even as the reporter quoted these nonconformist words, he ultimately limited Yu's ability to define a sexual and gendered sense of self by, yet again, placing two question marks around the article's concluding sentences.

One question mark was used to cast doubt on Yu's intention to eventually marry another woman, while the other ignored the female masculinity undergirding this desire—two queer practices that the mass media, in cooperation with police officials and medical doctors, had so painstakingly sought to tame. Newspaper and magazine accounts thus came to function as an entertaining apparatus of moral suasion, encouraging the reading public to look askance or laugh at women's partnerships and non-normative embodiments while simultaneously consuming their sexual excesses. By the early 1960s, reporters had thus come to recognize the subcultural existence of alternative kinship arrangements, if only for sensationalistic purposes. Moreover, they repeatedly demeaned these "deviations" from heteropatriarchy as a social danger that, if not properly controlled by mainstream society, might undermine the nation's path toward economic recovery and global notoriety.

Capitalistic Voyeurism and the Accommodation of Female Same-Sex Weddings in Newspaper Weeklies

From the second half of the 1960s, newspaper companies began to expand their readership by experimenting with weeklies, published under the patronage of an authoritarian state and its censorship apparatus. That the regime supported these publications (and vice versa) can be seen in the career of Chang Ki-yŏng (1916–77).[42] A high-ranking economic adviser to Park Chung Hee,

Chang became the founding president of *Chugan Han'guk*, South Korea's first commercial weekly; later, he served as an assemblyman in Park's Democratic Republican Party. In contrast to daily newspapers, this new media form contained much more content (approximately seventy-five pages in the late 1960s and three hundred pages by the 1980s) and far longer stories (ranging from an average of two to a maximum of about ten pages). And whereas dailies tended to focus on high politics and social concerns, weeklies took advantage of increasing the media's cultural content. In addition to publishing stories on (in)famous entertainers, they capitalized on their niche by including articles about abject figures, including sex workers, mixed-race children, and queer subjects. In every year of its existence from 1968 until 1991, *Sŏndei Sŏul* (Sunday Seoul), the most popular weekly by the 1970s, published accounts on the perceived threat of female homoeroticism, including the oft-cited practice of same-sex weddings. Aimed at an expanding but still moderate-size middle class, such profitmaking reports first appeared in late 1964 with the inauguration of *Chugan Han'guk*. This racy publication was quickly followed by its newspaper competitors, which between 1968 and 1969 released their own versions of the weekly.[43] Market competition was so intense that the pioneering *Chugan Han'guk* even decided to release a sister publication that focused on women's issues in 1969. In the early 1980s, other newspaper companies followed suit, releasing their own women's weeklies to cater to this growing consumer market and, in the process, increase their own profit margins.

To be sure, some journalists writing in these publications mentioned the personal difficulties faced by working-class queer women as they eked out a living outside officially sanctioned kinship structures. However, most weekly reporters, hired specifically for their ability to entertain readers with engrossing topics, tended to exploit their life choices as a voyeuristic method of capital accumulation under mass dictatorship.[44] As commoditized products for routine consumption, non-normative bodies appealed to a national readership of more than one million by 1970, the slight majority of whom were working-class men and mostly of a heterosexual proclivity. Sold on the street and by subscription but also widely available at public places, weeklies offered compensatory pleasures to a range of consumers, more than half of whom were residents of Seoul.[45] These psychic rewards allowed middle-class men (and some women) to reassert their bourgeois privilege over working-class persons represented in media exposés. For their part, blue-collar workers could enhance their status as gender- and sexually normative citizens by consuming stories about queer subjects. A response to gynocentric subcultures that furtively thrived despite heteropatriarchal dictates, coverage of women's same-sex weddings in particular came to function as misogynistic and transphobic entertainment aimed at softening the corrosive effects of deepening inequalities between the bourgeois and proletariat classes.[46]

In addition to a growing domestic market for middlebrow culture, the popularity of newspaper weeklies should also be considered in the context of "sexual revolutions" that spanned much of the capitalist world by the early 1970s.[47] Under the Park regime, political leaders modeled development plans after more advanced economies while adapting them to fit the military exigencies of confronting their northern rival.[48] These transnational and Cold War contexts help explain why weeklies featured carefully crafted stories of non-normative practices, such as "free sex," homosexuality, and sex change operations. However, scandalous accounts of queer lifestyles at home often appeared in strategic comparison with their overseas counterparts, particularly the liberal societies of the West. Japan, Korea's former colonizer and the primary inspiration for the emergence of national weeklies during the mid- to late 1960s, also figured in the comparative imagination of sexual and gender emancipation under an illiberal regime of capital accumulation.[49] For example, the South Korean press closely followed the gay power movement in the United States and Western Europe, which, by the 1970s, began to advocate for the legal recognition of same-sex relationships. Although politicized in different ways in the southern half of the peninsula, domestic publications also covered the purportedly novel phenomenon of nonconforming women, whom they accused of partnering with one another in defiance of heteropatriarchal (but not legal) conventions. Shortly after its creation in late 1968, *Chugan Kyŏnghyang*, for example, published its first report on female homoeroticism in which it conveyed to new readers that foreign magazines had taken the lead in introducing coverage of scandalous topics.[50] These historical precedents paved the way for South Korea's own weeklies to more fully exploit queer bodies as a form of capitalistic voyeurism.

In addition to the latest gossip on performers working in the entertainment industry and graphic photographs of seminude women (aimed at heterosexual men but likely also consumed by female shadow readers attracted to other women),[51] sales of weeklies depended on invasive reporters obtaining scoops of such shocking stories as female same-sex weddings. To some degree, these profit-driven stories followed the investigative techniques of newspaper journalists, with whom weekly reporters shared a constant flow of information and a common workspace.[52] Indeed, their accounts contain a considerable level of

detail aimed at substantiating the facticity of eccentric topics, especially to describe the bodies and practices of queer subjects. However, weekly reporters
took a comparatively higher degree of authorial license than daily journalists.
As a result, the content of investigative reports published in weeklies often dif-
fered across newspaper companies, whereas dailies tended to resemble one another. As discussed later, even a weekly that released a story about one female
same-sex wedding in the recent past could claim in a similar report published
just a few years later that two women seeking symbolic recognition of their relationship was the first of its kind.[53] To provide regular shock value to readers,
newspaper weeklies recycled many narrative strategies, a profit-oriented tactic
that aligned with popular efforts (e.g., in homes, schools, and workplaces) to
contain the disruptive potential of gynocentric practices. To this end, they also
reprinted intrusive photographs of South Korean women (or used unrelated
foreign women) that had appeared in earlier accounts of same-sex weddings.
Although it is unclear whether readers recalled these earlier cases, entrepreneurial journalists acted as if stories and images of queer subjects had indeed
receded from the memory of media consumers, just as media consumers
tended to blithely dispose weekly publications as soon as a new issue appeared.
Mirroring the disavowal of non-normative subjects, this repeated practice of
disposal coincided with the numbing pace of South Korean capitalism itself.

Such media strategies and consumption patterns can be seen in a pioneering exposé published in *Chugan Han'guk* about two women who chose to tie
the knot at a Seoul nunnery in late 1965.[54] Intent on selling this story as the
country's first same-sex wedding, the journalist began his report by introducing the newlywed couple to enthusiastic readers: Pak Suk-hŭi (b. 1932),
the thirty-three-year-old "husband," and her thirty-two-year-old "wife," Yi
Myŏng-ji (b. 1933). After conveying their legal names with aliases, he proceeded to divulge the exact address of their home in Yŏngdŭngp'o—an area
in western Seoul that was filled with industrial factories and home to many of
the city's (lumpen) proletariat.[55] At the time, newspaper companies regularly
printed the addresses of criminals and other "deviants" as matters of public
concern rather than respecting their right to privacy (for this reason, in the
photos I have placed black bars over their eyes, an anonymizing practice not
usually followed by the mass media during the authoritarian period).[56] After
Chugan Han'guk made its debut in late 1964, journalists writing for other commercial weeklies built on such invasive techniques. In these queersploitative accounts
of female homoeroticism, intrepid reporters shamelessly publicized lurid
details about the lives of nonconforming women. In this way, they sought

to capitalize on their "exotic" relationships, expanding each company's readership, and, ultimately, increasing their own profits. To return to the abovementioned exposé as an example, the account recalled the reporter's intrusive style, likening his unsolicited visit to the home of Pak and Yi to a graphic scene from an erotic film, a topic about which weeklies frequently reported. As he wrote in the main body of the report, "I risked improprieties by attempting to visit the bridal chamber" (sillye rŭl murŭp ssŭgo sinbang ŭl t'ambang hebonda). Although a stranger to the newlyweds, the invasive journalist exploited popular postnuptial practices to position himself as a nosy family member intent on confirming that the couple had consummated the marriage. To further describe working-class couples such as Yi and Pak, he drew on historical traditions of elite Koreans—using the term maetdol pubu, for example, to refer to their romantic lives. Literally translated as "millstone couples," this expression described the circular orifices that characterize these agricultural tools while simultaneously evoking the genitalia of Korean court ladies (kungnyŏ) who were known to have engaged in sexual relations with one another during the Chosŏn Dynasty (1392–1910).[57] Through such lurid allusions, the reporter thus invited readers to participate vicariously in the ceremonial and everyday lives of queer women as voyeuristic spectators, even as he admitted that Pak and Yi's own neighbors remained indifferent (mugwansim) to the newlyweds.

While first visiting their home in search of an interview, the reporter found the couple's pet dog, Johnny, protecting their bedroom door, another detail evoking the erotic aftermath of solemn matrimonial rites. A creative media that combined textual and visual representations, newspaper weeklies sought to document investigative "facts" by providing pictorial evidence to intrigued consumers. Adopting this evidentiary technique, Chugan Han'guk printed an image likely taken by the meddlesome reporter himself or by an accompanying cameraman. Although a curtain hung to conceal the bedding of the bridal chamber, as one scandalous subtitle read, the reporter eventually pried his way into this private site of queer intimacy, exposing it to the gaze of heterosexual men while perhaps also inadvertently stoking the homoerotic desires of "shadow-reading" women. Whatever the case, the intrusion allowed him to describe the contents of the couple's bedroom, including new bedclothes and pillows they had received as wedding gifts.

On a second visit to their home, the reporter entered the kitchen, where he finally met Pak's "wife." This "surprise attack" (sŭpgyŏk), as he unapologetically called it, led a startled Yi to close the kitchen door in self-defense, as the reporter proceeded to make another raid on their sleeping quarters. Having

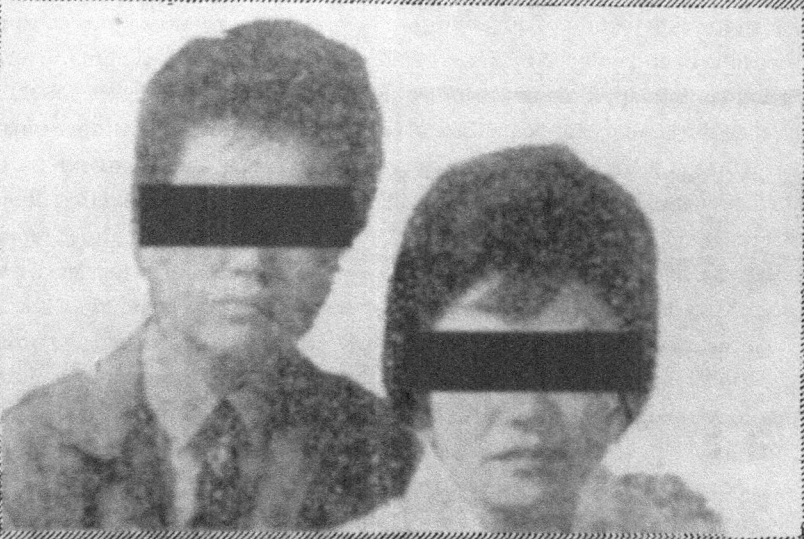

◇지난20일 「탑골」 僧房에서 올린결혼식—어엿한 新郎·新婦지만
新郎⊖은 女子다。

Figure 6.2 South Korean wedding between "millstone couple." Caption reads:
Wedding ceremony conducted on November 20, 1965, at T'apgol Nunnery. Full-fledged
bride and groom, but groom (left) is female.

already published their address, the article also revealed that journalists from
other weeklies continued to hound the couple to obtain further details about
their unusual relationship.[58] One zealous reporter even claimed to have been
dispatched from a police station and proceeded to use this mantle of official
sanction to indiscriminately take a picture of their faces, not unlike the photograph that appeared in the *Chugan Han'guk* exposé (figure 6.2).

It is worth noting the unknown origin of this image and others like it. Did
the reporter convince Yi and Pak to shoot this wedding picture, or did they

provide it to him? Although unlikely, at least some same-sex couples may have agreed to publicize their relationships, perhaps as a way of dignifying them in the eyes of profit-driven weeklies and their voyeuristic readers.

Whatever the case, reporters of same-sex relationships tended to frame the subcultural dynamics of queer kinship practices in normative terms comprehensible to and enjoyed by heterosexual men, even as their accounts also targeted (potentially) "deviant" women. For example, the 1965 exposé sought to realign the gendered appearance and personality of Yi and Pak within a binary structure of man/husband and woman/wife. The bright and active character of Pak, the male-dressed partner, was thus described as exceeding that of biological men, a comparative gesture that compensated for her presumed female anatomy. She reportedly possessed a high-pitched voice and lacked facial hair, secondary sex characteristics indicating femaleness, but her gaunt face resembled that of most laboring men. In mirrorlike fashion, this part of Pak's physical appearance matched her lower-middle-class background as an agricultural hand in her hometown of Sosa (Kyŏnggi Province), where she managed a successful shop before it burned down in 1962. By contrast, Yi wore womanly attire consisting of a pink skirt and chestnut brown sweater when the intrusive journalist found her washing dishes, housework expected of a "wise mother and good wife." The owner of a hair salon, she was also described as possessing a bashful and humble nature, characteristically feminine traits useful in catering to female clients. Yi, a native of Yesan (South Ch'ungch'ŏng Province), first met Pak when Pak visited Blonde Hair Beauty Salon in the summer of 1965. Pak quickly become Yi's most admiring client.

Coverage of their wedding, a public ceremony likely aimed at proving their love for one another in a society with a strong marriage imperative, formalized but did not ossify the binary opposition already captured by the depiction of their personalities and physical attributes. The clothing worn by female newlyweds dramatically underscored this dichotomy, especially in the hetero normalizing framework of weekly journalists. The "groom," Pak, thus appeared in a Western-style suit, while Yi donned the Korean-style dress *(hanbok)* typically worn by brides of her day. This sartorial dyad was likely the only way in which two women could present their relationship to family members and friends, more than one hundred of whom they reportedly convinced to attend their wedding. However, Pak and Yi did not simply wear masculine and feminine wedding attire as a form of heteronormative mimicry or even to pass as a straight couple, although some people may have mistaken them as such. Rather, they redeployed these aesthetic conventions to develop a unique style of queer self-fashioning, one central to an erotic system premised on women publicly recognizing one another *as women*. Such sartorial complementarities occasionally came to light in weeklies' photographs that sought to visualize the intimate lives of these women rather than focus on their matrimonial rites. A report published in 1970 (discussed later) reveals considerable differences between the dichotomous sartorial style of the couple's formal wedding portrait (figure 6.3) and a far less binary image of the newlyweds, as they both relax at home in Western-style clothing (figure 6.4).[59]

Figure 6.3 Dyadic sartorial practices. Caption reads: Posing side by side in front of camera after (1970) wedding ceremony attended by approximately 400 guests (sightseers). *Figure 6.4* Their nondichotomous counterparts. Caption reads: Same-sex couple seated at home after their (1970) wedding ceremony. Photograph taken by the reporter, Ch'oe Kap-sik.

◇4百여하객 (구경꾼) 속에결혼식을마치고 카메라앞 에나란히 포즈를취하고있다。

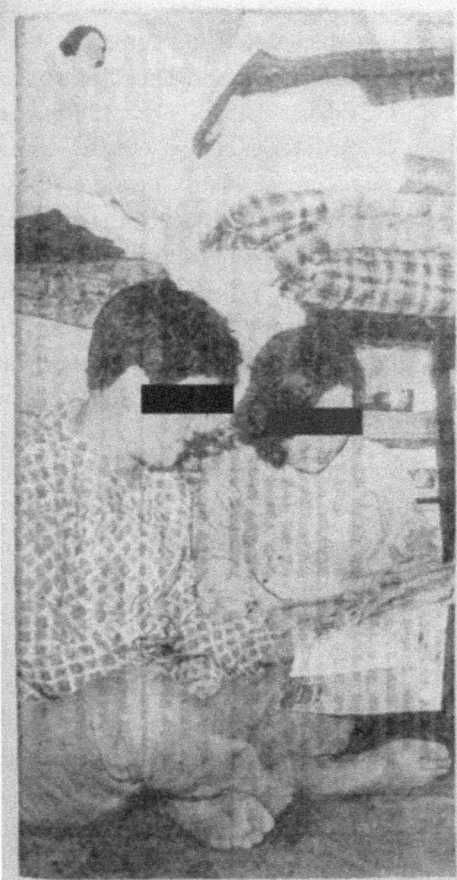

◇결혼식을 마치고 보금자리에앉은同性夫婦。
【崔甲植記者찍음】

Although same-sex weddings were sensationalized as an entirely new phenomenon in 1965, this was not the first time that Korean women formalized their love for one another.⁶⁰ Even as *Chugan Han'guk* touted its own account as historic, Pak managed to refute this disingenuous claim, reminding readers that similar ceremonies had recently taken place at various wedding halls across Seoul. In addition to explicitly downplaying their novel character, she offered a rare critique of weeklies' reporters for capitalizing on their efforts to dignify female same-sex love with and against Korean traditions of hetero-matrimony. Despite Pak's bold critique, newspaper weeklies continued to exploit these profitmaking stories, repeatedly dramatizing a seemingly new queer union as the country's first while ultimately rendering their protagonists as abnormal and thus in need of biopolitical management.⁶¹ As one early account of Seoul's lesbian community admitted, "A woman marrying a man and living together cannot possibly become the subject of a news report, but if a woman weds another woman and enjoys a sexual life like a married [heterosexual] couple, that is a story."⁶²

As if forgetting their earlier exposé and similar accounts that appeared during the late 1960s, *Chugan Han'guk* and its sister publication, *Chugan Yŏsŏng*, ran two stories in 1970 with the catchy, if apocryphal, title "South Korea's First Same-Sex Wedding Ceremony."⁶³ Even before these sensationalistic reports hit newsstands on September 27, the ceremony, held a week earlier at a wedding hall in rural Kangwŏn Province, reportedly attracted more than four hundred enthusiastic onlookers in addition to more than one hundred invited guests. According to one account, this record-breaking number exceeded that of any other marital service ever performed at the provincial wedding hall. This statistical claim, its accuracy notwithstanding, lent an air of popularity to wedding rites, much as previous descriptions of same-sex weddings had sought to induce the vicarious participation of voyeuristic readers. To a nationwide audience of media consumers, the rural location of the union also suggested that female homoeroticism extended well beyond the urban enclaves of South Korea, reaching its most remote villages. Capitalizing on the spurious logic of firsts, one particularly hyperbolic and nationalistic account indicated the historic meaning of same-sex weddings by claiming that the union in 1970 of Sŏ Ch'i-sŏng (b. 1938), a thirty-two-year-old woman, and her thirty-one-year-old partner, Ch'oe Ch'ŏl-hwa (b. 1939), was "the [most] shocking [news] since Tan'gun," the mythical godfather of the Korean people. Defining female weddings by their dangerous ubiquity, reporters undercut such gynocentric unions by questioning their social legitimacy under a Cold War regime of capitalist accumulation. They did so by describing these noncon-forming practices as outlandish manifestations of venerated kinship practices and thus worthy of homophobic and misogynistic laughter by weekly readers. To return to the 1970 case, the journalist highlighted the unusual relationship of Sŏ and Ch'oe, recalling that the wedding officiant had beseeched the couple to produce many offspring, a heteropatriarchal expectation that they obvi-ously could not fulfill. It is unclear whether the reporter witnessed this joke firsthand, heard about it from someone else after the fact, or invented it for comic effect. Whatever the case, the officiant's congratulatory remark report-edly generated intense laughter among a crowd who already knew the couple's anatomical secret, notwithstanding their gender-normative appearance as "bride" and "groom."

Even as their relationship led to scandalous rumors that shadowed them at the wedding ceremony and beyond, this unusual love story was "straight-ened" out for popular consumption, crafted into an account about idealized practices of Korean kinship under authoritarian development. To this end, the reporter created collective feelings of sympathy for the lower-class stand-ing of Sŏ and Ch'oe and their remarkable history of struggle. While references to their queerness likely appealed to the gender-normative and heterosexual status of working-class readers (mostly men, but some women, too), they also enhanced the class privilege of bourgeois consumers. Filtered through an unlikely tale of romance, their history of mutual poverty likely resonated with the reading public because the mass media presented it as a compelling account of postwar success. It thus offered hope to the material aspirations of the proletariat, even as the exploitation of its labor power only further en-riched the middle and upper classes under mass dictatorship. Although profit-driven weeklies often hypersexualized female unions, a focus on lower-class solidarities led to countervailing narratives that, by contrast, described non-conforming women in platonic terms of economic survival. The story about Sŏ and Ch'oe exemplify these desexualizing interventions, which aimed to accommodate their queer kinship practices into the heteropatriarchal imagi-nation of the reading public. According to several reports, the couple met on April 8, 1970, the Buddha's birthday. On that auspicious day, Sŏ, a hair-dresser, journeyed to a neighboring town, where she met her future "wife," Ch'oe, a shaman. Mesmerized by Ch'oe's singing and dancing at an exorcism, Sŏ decided to travel every week to visit Ch'oe before quickly moving in to-gether in May of the same year. Although perhaps sexually attracted to one another, what reportedly brought them together was the common experience of penury, a theme mentioned in many accounts of female couples during the postwar period. Sŏ, for example, was the youngest of seven children. When poverty hit, she decided to leave her hometown of P'ohang (North Kyŏngsang Province) for Kangwŏn Province, where she styled hair at a local beauty salon, a reputable profession that gave many hardworking women the chance to earn a decent living wage. Unlike the tomboyish Sŏ, who remained single and childless, Ch'oe married a man when she was twenty-five and even bore two children, according to one account. However, her stigmatized profession as a shaman dissatisfied her husband, who insisted on a divorce, thus leaving her as a single mother. Even as her abandonment revealed the vagaries of heteropatriarchy and the suffering caused by irresponsible husbands/ fathers, such stories likely appealed to the material and emotional struggles of postwar South Koreans, especially working-class women. Even a masculine woman such as Sŏ could, ironically, come to function as a model of compassionate love for men to follow in conjugal relations with women. Extolling the virtues of mutual respect, the 1970 account foregrounded the desirability of a lifelong commitment to hetero-matrimony and patriarchal duties. However, it also underscored the social abnormality of female homoeroticism insofar as kinship practices adopted by queer women prohibited them from "naturally" producing a male heir, even if they could raise adopted children. Although unable to access the material rewards of becoming a "good mother and wise wife," Ch'oe committed herself to supporting Sŏ in an alternative, gynocentric arrangement. Using this decision to downplay the sexual nature of their relationship, the reporter quoted Sŏ as saying, "I needed someone to support me, [someone] who gives me her heart while I lend mine to her. . . . I believe that we can offer one another emotional comfort even if I cannot provide [her] physical pleasure."[64] Their relationship was thus rhetorically accommodated within the country's system of heteropatriarchy, but they occupied a precarious position on its economic and cultural margins. This predicament was perhaps best underscored by their efforts to obtain legal recognition of their matrimony, a highly uncommon practice among same-sex couples during the authoritarian period.[65]

Equally remarkable was Sŏ's own attempt to communicate with the reading public by writing her own account of their relationship, thus responding to media sensationalism that came to shadow their nonconforming relationship.[66] Published in a woman's magazine in early 1971, this first-person account is extremely rare for the authoritarian period insofar as it gave voice to a queer subject to tell her own story in her own words. As the title ("Don't Ask about

Our Erotic Life") suggests, Sŏ strategically sought to de-sexualize and thus normalize her partnership with Ch'oe, dignifying herself as a masculinize woman and their same-sex relationship in ways that heterosexual and gender-normative readers might understand. To gain their sympathy and respect, she crafted an emotionally moving story of class struggle and family sacrifice, positioning herself as a filial daughter of an under-developed nation. Given Korea's rigid and dimorphic systems of gender and sex, Sŏ initially defined herself as a man, likening her social position to her male counterparts who had also married women. The only difference between them, she insisted, was the obvious inability of two women to give birth to a male heir according to heter-opatriarchal dictates. Having defined her social maleness in terms of marrying another woman, Sŏ was forced to explain the couple's reproductive challenges based on their female bodies, which she contrasted to those of intersex and transgender persons. Although Sŏ did not explicitly mention infertile men or women, readers familiar with this common condition may have imagined their own social predicament in ways that connected to this same-sex couple's own childlessness.

Having pragmatically used binary definitions of gender and sex to position herself in terms of normative boundaries, Sŏ explained how she came to live as a social man in the body of a biological woman, itself a bold act that destabilized these very dichotomies. Her tearful account also forced readers to reconsider how mass-mediated representations exploited queer persons and subjected them to further pain. Sŏ's personal history focused on how class-based poverty and gendered duties led her to cross-dress and engage in male forms of labor for her family's survival. In defining her social maleness in terms of filial piety, she distanced herself from transgender identification or even one of gender nonconformity. Rather than focusing on an atomized subjectivity, she underscored her low-class position as one of ten children in a fishing family. Agonizingly reliving a childhood tragedy, Sŏ highlighted this destitution by revealing the early 1950 death of her three younger brothers, whom she herself buried not far from P'ohang. Desperately seeking to support her family, she took the extreme measure of becoming a rough-and-tumble farmhand *(mŏsŭm'ae)* while assuming female jobs, such as washing the laundry of so-called Western whores during and after the Korean War. At seventeen, Sŏ even disobeyed her own parents who wanted her to attend high school, escaping to nearby P'ohang in search of a professional skill. After amassing 10,000 wŏn during a year of work at a knitting mill, she attended a six-month course to become a hair designer, a position then popular among women. However, continuing to live as a woman would subject her to lower wages than her male counterparts, some of whom had also begun to work in the beauty industry.[67] Articulated as an economic choice to support her family while her brothers completed their schooling and military service, she strategically chose to cross-dress as a man to obtain a higher salary. According to Sŏ's account of filial success, this decision ultimately paid off, allowing her to return home for her father's sixtieth birthday party (*hwangap chanch'i*), the expenses for which she reportedly shouldered in the conventional mold of a filial son.

By twenty-six, her gradual "assimilation into [becoming] a complete male" (*wanjŏn han namsŏng ŭro tonghwa*), as Sŏ described it, finally led her to consider marrying another woman. But only after ensuring the economic survival of her family and promoting the professional success of her older brothers did she begin to pursue her own romantic interests. In describing her sexuality, Sŏ minimized the purported deviance of female homoeroticism which, as discussed earlier, the mass media had so salaciously foregrounded in reports about their relationship. While admitting that, as a teenager, she had found beautiful women more attractive than handsome men, Sŏ explained that her same-sex desires only took root when she learned of female couples from her boss at the P'ohang beauty salon, where she also witnessed firsthand such nonconforming women. Sŏ's familiarity with lesbianism was further developed after watching the 1960 film *Chilt'u* (Jealousy), the first South Korean film to portray female homoeroticism on screen.[68] It is possible that she took advantage of such gynocentric representations to rewrite earlier memories of her own same-sex desires which, at this time, were virtually unspeakable, especially as an unmarried adult. In the film, the female protagonist's psychiatric treatment for a deep-seated hatred of men finally allows her to abandon lesbianism, which doctors had (mis)diagnosed as schizophrenia. By contrast, Sŏ's invocation of this pivotal film became an empowering source of legitimacy for romantic relations with other women, intimate bonds that she also managed to de-pathologize. Although voyeuristic readers may have been disappointed by her muted reference of same-sex intimacy, Sŏ's relation to heteropatriarchy as a marginalized woman and her poor upbringing as a masculine farmhand (and, later, as a male-dressed hair designer) came to define her queer selfhood as a social man. In this way, she followed her own wish to marry another woman while seeking to gain the respect of family members and national readers. Protecting the couple's sexual life from the voyeuristic gaze of the mass media also allowed Sŏ to shift public attention away from lesbians-as-atomized individuals and toward a critical focus on the collectivized subordination of women to androcentric families. Meanwhile, the creation of her own gynocentric family—an arrangement that, by its very definition, could not produce a biological male heir—created new kinship connections that extended beyond normative confines that restricted but did not control queer women. Sŏ concluded her remarkable account by urging readers to sympathize with the couple's predicament and journalists to refrain from exploiting their lives, but neither group ultimately heeded her earnest request.

Queer Romance as Tragic Tales and Their Heteronormative Endings

Although primarily functioning to further empower heterosexual men (especially the proletariat) at the expense of queer women, voyeuristic accounts of female homoeroticism ironically tended to depict male readers as unreliable and sometimes even violent, particularly in their roles as husbands. When explaining the driving force behind same-sex weddings, journalists often alleged that such mistreatment problematically led otherwise normative women into one another's arms for emotional and economic support as well as for erotic pleasure. Even as reporters hypersexualized gynocentric practices to capture male readers' attention and thereby ensure profit margins, their androcentric framework downplayed queer women's own desires for romantic intimacy and material stability, focusing instead on the allegedly wayward but reformable qualities of men. Weeklies' accounts of same-sex weddings thus functioned as cautionary tales directed at men, whose misogyny resulted in the proverbial loss of "their" women to other South Korean women or, worse yet, to American GIs stationed throughout the country as an anticommunist bulwark. At a time of rapid social change and cultural flux, these male-centered representations worked to reinforce heteropatriarchy and ethnonationalism as normative principles of capitalist development, especially under the repressive Yusin system (1972–79) but also beyond the dictatorial reign of Pak Chung Hee.[69]

As suggested earlier, a critical reading of newspaper weeklies suggests that women who symbolically married each other experienced a complex mixture of childhood poverty, negative experiences with men, non-normative gender embodiments, and same-sex desires. For these reasons, they often expressed hope that a relationship with another woman would fulfill their desires to pursue a personally satisfying and economically sustainable livelihood, one outside more stable but potentially unfulfilling relations of hetero-matrimony. Although they chose to live on the margins of South Korean society, their decisions to perform wedding rites were likely aimed at proving their moral respectability to family and friends who pressured them to (re)marry. However, even when same-sex couples made such public proclamations, their loved ones did not necessarily accept them, especially because they could not produce biological heirs, which, in turn, produced an associative blight on the family. While amusing male readers with sensational entertainment, media accounts of queer kinship practices, which reappeared throughout the 1970s and 1980s, thus also served as implicit warnings to other (potentially) "deviant" women. Deploying heteropatriarchal and ethnonationalist ideologies of cultural conformity under Hot War developmentalism, reports of same-sex weddings tended to demean their relationships as unfilial and even unpatriotic. These epistemological interventions further trivialized gynocentric unions as unsustainable and thus likely to unravel, often in uncomfortable and violent ways. Meanwhile, weekly accounts of queer romance refused to explain these outcomes in terms of the authoritarian state's unwillingness to sanction or protect their relationships, instead placing sole blame on female actors themselves. As such, the mass media assumed that the alleged wretched nature of queer women's lives could be improved only through (re)unification with Korean men, albeit as ongoing objects of patriarchal control and sexual subordination.

Two weekly reports published in 1974 reveal the insidious nature of these epistemological interventions. Like other working-class couples, both Kim Chin-mi (b. 1933), a forty-one-year-old woman, and her thirty-year-old "wife," Yim Ae-ja (b. 1944), had overcome a long history of suffering at the expense of men. In a formula common in Buddhist philosophy, Kim explained their painful experiences in the present as the result of wrathful karma from a former life.[70] Born in the port city of Inch'ŏn, Kim was one of four children raised by a poor family whose father worked as a day laborer. Only able to graduate from middle school, Kim drifted onto a nearby base occupied by the U.S. military. Following a path commonly taken by downtrodden women, she worked as a housemaid for an American GI stationed at Pup'yŏng (formerly, Kyŏnggi Province). The job allowed her to accumulate enough money to leave the camp town in search of an independent livelihood. However, her fortune soon vanished when, at twenty-four, she began dating an unfaithful Korean man who squandered her savings on a costly gambling habit. Worse yet, he regularly assaulted her—an offense that, although infrequently prosecuted, landed him in jail. Unable to marry a Korean man and bear him an heir, Kim then turned to William, an American sergeant. She reportedly found herself more satisfied as his live-in wife, but their relationship provoked the scorn of family members and close friends who berated her as a "Western whore."[71] Kim's attempted escape from poverty through interracial intimacy, a situation enabled by South Korea's subordination as a Hot War ally of the U.S., was thus stymied by an ethnonationalist ideology of racial purity. This ideology belittled lower-class individuals like Kim who were forced to rely on American soldiers but whose neo-imperial presence tended to reward bourgeois elements of South Korean society that supported state goals of capitalist accumulation. Such dependencies ultimately led to the traumatic end of their relationship. Not long after William ended his tour and returned to the U.S., he reportedly died in a car crash. This tragic accident left a twice-abandoned Kim without the material support of a man to overcome her enduring poverty, even when she depended on the perceived wealth of American camp towns.[72]

At this very moment of intense suffering, Kim met her future "wife" who, according to one account, was working as a hairdresser in a beauty salon near It'aewŏn, where Kim had been residing since William's transfer to the nearby U.S. military base at Yongsan (Seoul).[73] A native of San'gol (North Ch'ungch'ŏng Province), Yim also grew up in poverty. Her low-paid father, a cotton worker, died when she was just four, leaving the family without a stable source of income. To make ends meet, Yim accompanied her mother to the capital in search of work. After finishing primary school, Yim served as an apprentice at a beauty salon and, after years of hard labor, finally became an independent hairdresser. Like Kim, she reportedly tried her lot with men, but when she discovered that her fiancé was already married and had young children, she left him. Although unable to consummate a hetero-marital union, she finally met Kim, with whom she could commiserate about their miserable lives. So close did the bond between these two women become that they decided to hold a wedding ceremony in Kim's hometown of Inch'ŏn, where the couple eventually settled in a modest house and ran a small store selling Western imports. They even raised a young girl, a two-year-old orphan who mysteriously appeared on their doorstep. Although the girl was from the bloodline of another family, they reportedly raised her as their own child, giving her Yim's last name and entering her into her family registry. Although not always as successful in their efforts, many other female couples expressed strong desires to adopt children from local orphanages or produce offspring with male friends (figures 6.5 and 6.6).[74]

To be sure, these accounts acknowledged queer women such as Yim and Kim as homosocial beings and thus honorary members of the nation by dint of their unofficial matrimony and, in this case, child-rearing practices. However, even voyeuristic reports about their romantic life tended to negate the possibility of couples' homosexuality, explained away either as a psychological abnormality or an insignificant part of their relationship. Providing evidence to substantiate this disavowal of same-sex desire, one journalist even quoted Kim, who had sought to dignify their relationship by describing it as "platonic love" rather than as another racy story of lesbianism.[75] It is quite possible that such expressions of one's intimate subjectivity, which refused to establish a stable identity based primarily on orientation, existed as a social practice during this era. It may even have been prevalent among women who

Figure 6.5 Child-rearing by female same-sex couples. Caption reads: Devoted couple spends weekend afternoon [with child] at Namsan Park. Groom is on left; bride is on right (1969).
Figure 6.6 Caption reads: Holding son, Tae-hyŏn, two parents found photo studio one day. [Playing] wife's role (?), Yun (right) asserts their happiness as family (1969).

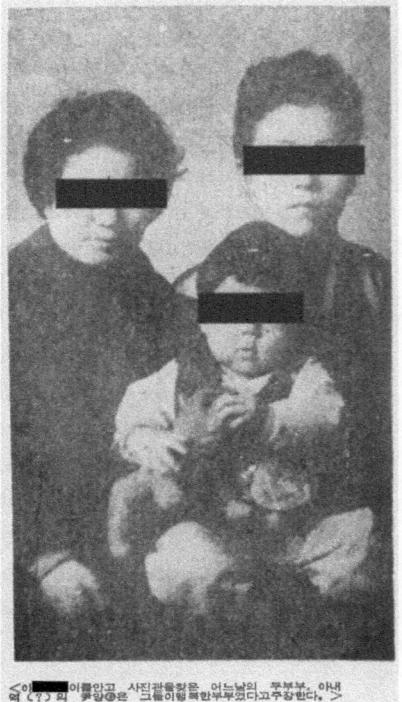

challenged social norms as a means of economic survival or emotional ful-fillment but who did not consider themselves "sexual minorities" or agitate for human rights. Although this liberal framework has become increasingly dominant since the 1990s, it still does not encompass every queer community in South Korea (and elsewhere) today.[76] Whether mentioned in weeklies' ac-counts or articulated by women themselves (whose words were also mediated through the sensational gaze of the mass media), repudiations and affirma-tions of female homosexuality during the authoritarian era usually appeared in the limited contexts of heteropatriarchy and ethnonationalism. Otherwise subversive reports about women such as Kim and Yim who decided to tie the knot (regardless of whether they were lesbian) thus tended to surface in refer-ence to the predicament of heterosexual Korean men. In this way, they came to function as cautionary tales about the consequences of men not marrying and impregnating South Korean women, who, as a result, allegedly flirted with interracial and same-sex love. Read in this way, disavowals of female homo-eroticism worked to recursively contain a national community that, although increasingly prosperous in general terms by the 1980s, remained rife with class tensions and racial fissures. Although not necessarily named as such, non-conformity to gender conventions and sexual norms perhaps most dramati-cally indexed these internal divisions and marked the normative boundaries of femininity, especially in its idealized bourgeois form of "wise mother and good wife."

Such dynamics can be seen in the tumultuous relationship between Kim Sun-mi (b. 1949), a thirty-six-year-old woman, and her "husband," the forty-six-year-old Kim Sun-hwa (b. 1939) in 1985.[77] According to reports in various weeklies, this couple tied the knot in May of that year at Taeansa, a Buddhist temple on the outskirts of Wŏnju (Kyŏnggi Province). Born in Mokp'o (South Chŏlla Province), Sun-mi, the second daughter from a family of four children, grew up in poverty, having lost both parents at a young age. She was only able to complete primary school and subsequently worked as a housemaid to support her siblings. Sun-mi was especially dedicated to her elder brother, who, according to a social system that privileged older siblings, she hoped would attend college and thereby elevate the socioeconomic standing of her family. In 1969, at age twenty, Sun-mi relocated to Wŏnju, where, after working several odd jobs for three years, she amassed enough money to open a restau-rant specializing in pork ribs. She thus became known as a *ttosun'i*, a "head-smart" woman who became economically independent. However, in this queer version of an iconic figure popular in film and literature, the ingenious woman remained unmarried until her mid-thirties.[78] Luckily, Sun-mi soon met her future "husband," Sun-hwa. After graduating high school in her hometown of Kwangju (South Chŏlla Province), Sun-hwa spent several decades working as a taxi driver, a male-dominated occupation often associated with lesbianism.[79] According to several accounts, Sun-hwa had once wed another woman but decided to end their four-year marriage to date Sun-mi. In 1980, at forty-one, Sun-hwa reportedly received a revelation from God and began studying destiny philosophy (unmyŏng ch'ŏlhak), a field in which she excelled. Several years later, she moved to Wŏnju, where she became known for her healing skills. Those skills impressed Sun-mi, who visited Sun-hwa as a client in the fall of 1984. Only seven months later, they tied the knot.

Unfortunately, the postnuptial life of many same-sex couples remains obscure because weeklies usually featured them only once, quickly moving on to yet another "new" story about female homoeroticism. However, the union between the Kims continued to garner public attention throughout the 1980s as the women's foundering relationship came to signify the insecurity of queer kinship practices more generally. At their wedding ceremony, Sun-hwa and Sun-mi had reportedly vowed to live together more harmoniously than their heterosexual counterparts. This overcompensating gesture of love likely was aimed to dignify their bond in the eyes of a skeptical public. However, the lofty promise of their wedding ceremony lasted less than two years due to disagreements over financial matters. According to one account that took perverse joy in chronicling their crumbling relationship, Sun-hwa, although a successful soothsayer, relied on her "wife's" restaurant for their income, thus becoming an unreliable "husband." Shortly after their wedding, Sun-hwa became deeply involved in charity work, seeking to help poor children through education. Having reportedly offered her ex-"wife" a hefty alimony payment when they separated, she was thus in need of financial support and even confessed to having chosen a wealthier partner in order to raise less fortunate youngsters.[80] Although altruistic, this enterprise lacked financial acumen, causing friction with her more conservative "wife." Spousal relations quickly soured thereafter, and just eighteen months later the couple separated. Although they settled their relationship without further discord, Sun-mi allegedly became an object of neighbors' pity as she continued to struggle with loneliness, to say nothing of her idealistic but less independent ex-"husband" whose whereabouts remained unknown after the couple's separation.

Subsequent media reports similarly highlighted queer partnerships that, even when they benefited from an income characteristic of the bourgeoning middle classes, ended distastefully and, at times, with violent consequences. In these normalizing accounts, relationships between women were predictably resolved using heteropatriarchal endings, thus containing female homoeroticism as unsatisfyingly temporary and woefully unrealistic. Just months after Sun-hwa and Sun-mi separated in 1987, for example, *Chugan Kyŏnghyang* published a report on two women whose jobs contributed to a substantial income. However, their relationship still went terribly awry after a relatively long six-year period of dating one another. The report featured Yi Min-suk (b. 1949), a thirty-eight-year-old woman who, after divorcing a Korean man, became the manager of a café in 1981. Her future "husband," Kim Sang-su (b. 1952), twenty-nine years old at the time, worked at a nearby company and frequently visited Yi's café. Two years after they became romantically involved, the couple decided to purchase a twenty-three million wŏn apartment in Kangnam, a rapidly expanding district in southern Seoul. They also opened a store to sell fish in nearby Togok-dong, establishing themselves as a relatively prosperous couple. However, within a few years Yi reportedly began to regret her decision about what the mass media pathologized as an "abnormal" life, and eventually demanded a separation to marry a man. Meanwhile, Kim found herself annoyed by Yi's smoking and drinking, which negatively affected their fledgling business; these complaints further provoked Yi to terminate her relationship with Kim.

Having served as the "husband," Kim generously offered her "wife" 2.5 million wŏn in alimony—a practice described as mirroring that of heterosexual divorcées, but one that failed to satisfy Yi's avariciousness. Earlier images of queer women as passionate, violent, and even criminal thus resurfaced in the context of containing their nonconforming kinship practices. In this case, Yi barged in on her ex-"husband" as she was sleeping in the Togok-dong apartment, which had remained registered in Kim's name. Arguing that the apartment was common property—a claim that would have been difficult, if not impossible, to prove under civil law at the time—Yi grabbed Kim's neck and demanded a ten million wŏn payment, causing a ruckus that awoke their (heterosexual) neighbors. In response, Kim emphasized the unofficial nature of their relationship—namely, that it was recorded neither in the family registry nor in the marriage registry. Although she was clearly seeking to maintain control over their assets, this highly publicized instance of financial and legal precarity served as a measured warning to other women, who, before reading the story, might have considered opting out of hetero-matrimony. One report's self-aggrandizing, if specious, claim that Yi was the first member of a same-sex couple to demand an alimony payment (recall the case of Sun-hwa and her ex-spouse) only further dramatized the allegedly impassioned and volatile nature of female homoeroticism.[81]

Even relatively successful women who signed oaths to prove their love for one another were vulnerable to the vicissitudes of nonconforming arrangements, suggesting to male readers the need to "rescue" them. Using the same heterosexist logic, the message conveyed to their female counterparts was never even to consider a same-sex union. Such was the case of the thirty-three-year-old Kim Suk-jin (b. 1938) and her lover, Yim Min.[82] Born and raised in North Chŏlla Province, Suk-jin managed to graduate from high school and later served eight years in the army, a highly unusual career for South Korean women and one that the mass media thus described as an "eccentric occupation" (isaek chigŏp).[83] Returning to civilian life in late 1962, she took advantage of her experience driving a military jeep to become a taxi driver, also a non-normative occupation for women of the time. After crisscrossing the streets of Seoul for nearly six years, Suk-jin met Min, a hairdresser who was born in Mokp'o (South Chŏlla Province) and was also working in the capital. After dating for several months, Min, who became Suk-jin's "wife," quit her job, and the couple moved in together on July 14, 1968, a date that came to serve as their anniversary. To formalize their relationship, the two women signed an oath, promising before Buddha to support one another until death parted them. To substantiate this gynocentric practice, Chugan Yŏsŏng even published a hand-written copy of their oath. They lived together happily for several years, but the promise evaporated when Min disappeared in March 1971. Having liquidated the couple's lease money (300,000 wŏn) for an apartment, Suk-jin not only was left to bereave her loved one, but she also struggled to make ends meet as a taxi driver. According to this disheartening account, their passionate pledge to love each other proved woefully misguided—a predicament that could, by implication, be remedied only by marrying a man.

Recalling a longer tradition of representations that began during the colonial period but remained popular after 1945, still other accounts focused on the disintegration of same-sex relationships through suicide. Under the ideological management of weeklies' reports, the tragic deaths of female lovers reestablished accepted norms of filial piety and heteropatriarchy rather than implicating these practices of social conformity as sources of institutional violence.[84] For example, in 1975, Sunday Seoul published a dramatic story on the pitiful fate of two lower-class women, both factory workers at a company in Inch'ŏn.[85] Yi Pun-suk (b. 1954), a primary-school graduate who grew up in

South Kyŏngsang Province, was only twenty-one when, in 1973, she met Kang (b. 1953), a twenty-two-year-old native of Kyŏnggi Province. The two women quickly formed an intimate bond, which included regular sleepovers at Yi's home. The couple always worked together on the factory floor and thus became an object of surveillance by company managers, who quickly learned about their relationship. To avoid persistent badgering, Yi and Kang escaped to Pusan, where they hoped to live and work in a more anonymous setting. Although they managed to repay their rent, debts, and other expenses, the young couple struggled to establish a stable existence. To make ends meet, Yi temporarily returned to her hometown with Kang. While staying with her parents, Yi pawned a broken radio that belonged to a younger sibling to pay for return tickets to Pusan. The media excoriated this theft as an unfilial act, one for which she would later apologize in a suicide note. When the couple returned to Pusan, their life remained volatile. Yi landed a job as a hostess, a common occupation for uneducated women, but her salary was insufficient to support Kang.[86] In a predictable shift presaging a heterosexual denouement, her lover began to date a man, perhaps in pursuit of a more financially stable and morally acceptable existence. In the end, Kang's new liaison soured her already strained relationship with a now despondent Yi, who decided to end an unrequited love with a fatal dose of poison. This short-lived experiment with same-sex love and cohabitation thus ended tragically, warning female readers not to follow Yi and Kang's horrifying example.

One final example reveals how weeklies boldly presented female relationships as pathologically suicidal, likening their nonconforming unions to deadly practices of kinship that could not survive outside a normative system of heteropatriarchy. Rather than implicating the pauperizing polices of an authoritarian state or the conservative nature of Korean culture as contributing factors in female suicides, the mass media framed such desperate acts of public recognition as the most dramatic indication that their queer lives had ended in social failure. According to a bourgeois logic of self-reform, the pitiful outcomes of female unions could be prevented if women agreed to fulfill their heteropatriarchal duties as "wise mothers and good wives." The relationship between Pak Pok-bun (b. 1944), a thirty-three-year-old woman, and her twenty-seven-year-old "wife," Chang Min-suk (b. 1950), painfully exposed these epistemological (and practical) interventions. According to an account published in 1977, the two women first met in Taejŏn, where Chang managed a boutique and Pak worked as her employee. Born to a poor family, Pak had attended primary school in her hometown of Kŭmsan (South Ch'ungch'ŏng

Province) before moving to Seoul, where she, like many poor immigrants in the city, toiled as a housemaid until 1971. At the time, she was married to a man from Ŭlsan (South Kyŏngsang Province) who in 1967 had relocated to work in a nearby factory. However, when his company fired him, he could no longer afford to support his already impoverished wife, whom he abruptly abandoned. Although now a divorcée, Pak embarked on a new relationship—this time with a woman—and after she and Chang dated for several years, the couple began to cohabit in 1975. However, soon the (heterosexual) neighbors, at least some of whom had likely read about female homoeroticism in weeklies, began to gossip about the unusual relationship. These malicious rumors, a common effect of yellow journalism, eventually reached Chang's family. Her older brothers, whose guidance she was expected to follow, were especially embarrassed by their sister's same-sex relationship. Undeterred, Chang continued to live with her female lover, a decision one moralizing reporter portrayed in Confucian terms of filial irresponsibility. Her parents finally intervened, forcing her to separate from Pak. Reiterating the values of the weekly's reporter, they especially worried that Chang was endangering her chances of marrying a man, the prescribed duty of Korean women her age. Although aimed at protecting their daughter, this intervention led a now distraught Pak to take her life by imbibing poison. In the end, *Sunday Seoul* did not even consider the subjective logic behind her tragic decision, including the possibility that she might have chosen this path as a desperate act of defiance against heteropatriarchal domination. Instead, the reporter drew attention to a note Pak had left in which she apologized to her parents for her unfilial act, which journalist further dramatized by concluding that the women's same-sex relationship was indeed a "regretfully tragic story" (*huhoe han pigŭk ŭi sayŏn*).[87]

Conclusion

As suggested earlier, female homoeroticism was an important, if underrecognized, topic of popular debate during South Korea's authoritarian era. Sensational accounts of nonconforming women from this period simplified the complex dynamics of queer kinship practices for highly instrumental purposes. Even as journalists entertained laboring audiences with eccentric stories about these women, their well-worn narratives of deviance, crime, and tragedy helped promote heteropatriarchal and ethnonationalist cohesion at a disorienting time of social change and cultural flux. In the process, working women, already burdened with supporting an androcentric system of kinship and a rapacious program for anticommunist development, came to signify the deep fissures accompanying South Korea's formula of industrial capitalism and illiberal politics. A middlebrow genre that spotlighted the wretched nature of nonconforming women for a male-oriented readership of consumer-citizens, commercial weeklies, which drew on but expanded the voyeuristic practices of newspaper dailies and magazine monthlies, actively engaged in a secondary form of queersploitation aimed at enhancing their own profitmaking potential while supporting and advancing the state's developmentalist ideology.

Reflecting a perceived sense of threat to the stabilizing forces of heteropatriarchy and ethnonationalism, popular representations of queerness exposed the undeniable emergence of gynocentric subcultures in and beyond the cities of postwar South Korea. Writing on behalf of nation and capital, concerned reporters deployed realistic techniques of investigative journalism to substantiate the existence of nonconforming women but almost always exaggerated the corrosive effects of their presence. For this reason, readers regularly encountered stories about lower-class women who allegedly became violent criminals or committed suicide, almost as if they had been born with such antisocial tendencies. Meanwhile, consumer-citizens of the mass media rarely witnessed same-sex couples who found happiness and support from each other or who thrived in the cracks of the country's restrictive formula of heteropatriarchal capitalism. Despite their derogatory tone, stories about women's homoeroticism likely also attracted "shadow-reading" women who—whether because of economic concern, a gender-variant self, a non-normative sexual object choice, or a negative experience with men—found courageous female figures with whom they could readily identify. That the mass media regularly featured pathologically "deviant" but undeniably formidable women from weeklies' rise to popularity during the late 1960s until their demise in the early 1990s suggests this subversive possibility and the perceived need to routinely tame such dissident energies through what I have called epistemological interventions.

The pervasiveness of unruly bodies in the popular imagination of the authoritarian era stands in stark contrast to academic and urban legends that champion South Korean society in mythical terms of its heteropatriarchal and cisgender "purity." Until at least 2000 it was not uncommon to hear defensive claims that non-normative sexuality and gender variance simply did not exist as part of this postcolonial, Cold War nation or that queerness was a recent transplant from a decadent West. But frequent coverage of nonconforming citizens contradicts this powerful myth, which, ironically, was enabled by homophobic, transphobic, and misogynistic views of queerness as virtually unthinkable. Spuriously reporting each same-sex union as if it was the country's first, enterprising journalists trained regular readers and secondhand consumers to misremember and, ultimately, forget the actual lives of queer subjects represented in disposable weeklies. We must also recall that anxious claims about the purportedly foreign origins of non-normative kinship practices were themselves products of a comparative imaginary generated in and through the mass media. Indeed, stories about same-sex couples and weddings emerged in South Korea at the very moment that Japanese and Western queers were seeking self-representation and legal recognition amid sexual revolutions that spanned the globe. These worldwide precedents, which weeklies regularly cited as cautionary tales for domestic readers, informed ideological narratives of cultural pollution aimed at minimizing the native origins and dissident power of female unions. Invariably, individual consumers of media accounts under mass dictatorship also participated in the perpetuation of what might be called the "no gays myth." Although comparatively less convincing today, this collective image of heteropatriarchal and cisgender selves persists as a powerful legacy of the authoritarian era.

Even after the emergence of procedural democracy and civil society in South Korea in the early 1990s, culturally conservative persons and institutions have repeatedly deployed this entrenched national image while actively minimizing alternative views that challenge it. In response, LGBTI activists and filmmakers, also important products of postauthoritarian democracy, have targeted the profitmaking practices of the mass media and the instrumental agendas of other institutions—schools, courts, the police, and the military, for example—that have misrepresented queer subjects and thereby subordinated them to the (re)productive goals of a developmentalist state.[88] That printed and online publications written by and about non-normative subjects as well as myriad activist and social groups have flourished despite ongoing censorship (e.g., internet sites with adult content, including non-pornographic material) by the government is one sign that efforts at self-representation may finally dismantle the no gays myth. But at present, LGBTI activists are battling the disingenuous but influential claims of fundamentalist Christians, themselves preoccupied with the real and imagined dissolution of the nuclear family in recent years, that sexual minorities sympathize with North Korea and infect fellow citizens with the AIDS virus. These nationalists thus continue to exploit queer subjects (in addition to believers of Islam and other social minorities) to perpetuate Hot War ideologies of domestic subversion in a ultra-conservative formula of heteropatriarchy under the (mis)guidance of Jesus Christ.

Unsurprisingly, one of the most contentious of these culture wars in present-day South Korea revolves around the legalization of same-sex marriage and other protections for sexual minorities. As discussed in the introduction to this volume, Kim/Cho Kwang-su and his partner, Kim Sŭng-hwan, a high-profile gay couple active in the LGBTI movement, have emerged as the most visible advocates of this possibility. Clearly, the ways that these middle-class cisgender men articulate their personal politics today differ significantly from those of the proletarian women who experienced the disempowering forces of the authoritarian era. As discussed earlier, symbolic weddings between female couples aimed to solidify their precarious relationships, but only rarely did nonconforming women seek legal recognition from an authoritarian state on which they could hardly rely for protection and sustenance. In my view, it would be historically inaccurate and ethically dangerous to equate these two politicized moments of queerness in any direct or seamless way. Doing so would flatten the past and might empty the present of its revolutionary potential. However, what we might call a "politics of dignity" is one dimension of non-normative relationships that we should pause to compare, especially as people in South Korea and across the world contemplate the current (or future) desirability of same-sex marriage. As several media reports analyzed earlier suggest, women who decided to wed each other did so in ways that tended to conform to marital conventions. When viewed from the perspective of mainstream readers under mass dictatorship, this choice was thus dignified (though not necessarily accepted) insofar as it contravened neither the expectations of adult partnerships nor the dimorphic presentation of gender that typified (but did not mimic) their heterosexual counterparts. However, even when they raised children (or attempted to do so), female partners necessarily failed to fulfill the heteropatriarchal expectations of South Korean society, which legally sanctioned neither their wedding ceremonies nor their care for orphaned youngsters. Despite or, perhaps better put, because of these important differences with their heterosexual counterparts, nonconforming women could still view their relationships as personally dignified, having used a form of social domination to create new modes of intimacy and freedom as a means of survival for the most precarious. In sum, women's same-sex weddings and the queer lives that followed in their wake thus formed a politicized realm in which a collective dignity of cisgender heteropatriarchy may have been reinforced, even as its individual expressions were actively rearticulated and thus contested in creating new, queer kinship practices about which scholars and activists still know far too little. In many ways, the dual nature of such unions continues to characterize rapidly globalizing debates about the national and personal politics of same-sex marriage today. Just as these partnerships seek to widen the meaning of matrimony to include individuals whose sexual orientation is non-normative, the public faces of marriage equality (largely, middle-class gay men) are quickly becoming assimilated to capitalist and heteropatriarchal structures that, at least in South Korea, continue to subordinate less powerful actors, especially the poor, women, transgender, and migrants from the global South. In this critical sense, the current practice of same-sex marriage resonates with the histories charted in this chapter and should encourage us to reflect critically on the past before we embrace this institution of power as our only dignified option for connection and sustenance.[89]

Notes

Due to late 2020 legal developments in South Korea and out of an abundance of caution for the people discussed in this chapter, I have chosen to anonymize most published names, even if printed as pseudonyms in original sources.

Epigraph: Kath Weston, *Families We Choose: Lesbians, Gays, Kinship* (New York: Columbia University Press, 1991), 40.

1   For a historical overview of film, see Pil Ho Kim and C. Colin Singer, "Three Periods of Korean Queer Cinema: Invisible, Camouflage, and Blockbuster," *Acta Koreana* 14, no. 1 (June 2011): 115–34. On one artist's engagement with all-female theatrical troupes that thrived after 1945, see An So-hyŏn, *Chŏnhwan kŭkjang* (Seoul: P'orŏm Aei, 2016). Exceptional, relevant scholarship on the queer aspects of contemporary South Korea is cited later.

2   On the movement, see Youngshik D. Bong, "The Gay Rights Movement in Democratizing Korea," *Korean Studies* 32 (2009): 86–103; Hyun-young Kwon Kim and John (Song Pae) Cho, "The Korean Gay and Lesbian Movement 1993–2008: From 'Identity' and 'Community' to 'Human Rights,'" in *South Korean Social Movements: From Democracy to Civil Society*, ed. Gi-Wook Shin and Paul Chang (London: Routledge, 2011), 206–23. For the role of film, see Jeongmin Kim, "Queer Cultural Movements and Local Counterpublics of Sexuality: A Case of Seoul Queer Films and Videos Festival," *Inter-Asia Cultural Studies* 8, no. 4 (2007): 617–33; Chris Berry, "My Queer Korea: Identity, Space, and the 1998 Seoul Queer Film and Video Festival," *Intersections* 2 (May 1999), April 29, 2019, http://intersections.anu.edu.au/issue2/Berry.html.

3   On this and other pathbreaking queer films that appeared before 2000, see Jooran Lee, "Remembered Branches: Towards a Future of Korean Homosexual Film," *Journal of Homosexuality* 39, nos. 3–4 (2000): 273–81.

4   By heteropatriarchy, I want to highlight how a system of male domination in reproduction-oriented households and in androcentric models of state governance and capitalist production works in tandem with an equally normative system that marginalizes alternative kinship arrangements, which are deemed abnormal and worthy of censure, if not erasure. For more on historical manifestations of this multifaceted system of control, see Francisco Valdes, "Unpacking Hetero-patriarchy: Tracing the Conflation of Sex, Gender and Sexual Orientation to Its Origins," *Yale Journal of Law and Humanities* 8, no. 1 (May 2013): 161–211; Maile Arvin, Eve Tuck, and Angie Morrill, "Decolonizing Feminism: Challenging Connections between Settler Colonialism and Heteropatriarchy," *Feminist Formations* 25, no. 1 (Spring 2013): 8–34; Jongwoo Han and L. H. M. Ling, "Hypermasculinized State: Hybridity, Patriarchy and Capitalism in Korea," *International Studies Quarterly* 42, no. 1 (March 1998): 53–78.

5   After releasing this short, So attempted to make a longer film on the history of gay cruising at South Korean movie theaters, but failed to uncover sufficient archival materials to complete this project. On this aborted attempt, see the segment focused on So in the documentary *Chongno ŭi Kijŏk* (Miracle on Jongno Street), dir. Yi Hyŏk-sang, Yŏngbunhong ch'ima, Seoul, 2010.

6   For these writings, see Yi Hŭi-il, "Sŏ innŭn saramdŭl: Kŭkjang ŭi yŏksa," *Buddy*, vol. 3, May 1998, 44–48; Yi Hŭi-il, "Kilnyŏ, Penisŭ e kada: T'ŏminŏl, kongwŏn kwa Namsan ŭi yŏksa," *Buddy*, vol. 4, June 1998, 49–53; Yi Hŭi-il, "Homo sajŏl: Sauna wa jjimjilbang ŭi yŏksa," *Buddy*, vol. 5, July 1998, 49–53; Yi Hŭi-il, "Pakkkot hŭdŭrŏjin White Saturday Night: Geiba ŭi yŏksa," *Buddy*, vol. 6, August 1998, 49–53. For the historical experiences of female homoeroticism, see Han Ch'ae-yun, "Han'guk rejŭbiŏn k'ŏmyunit'i ŭi yŏksa," *Chinbo P'yŏngnon* 49 (Fall 2011): 100–28.

7   Although not necessarily read by mainstream scholars, important work is being conducted by graduate students and non-tenure-track researchers. See, e.g., Öiron Munhwa Yŏn'gu Moim, ed., *Chendŏ ŭi ch'aenŏl ŭl tollyŏra* (Seoul: Saram Saenggak, 2008); Kwŏn/Kim Hyŏn-yŏng, Chŏng Hŭi-jin, Na Yŏng-jŏng, Ruin, and Ŏm Ki-ho, eds., *Namsŏngsŏng wa chendŏ* (Seoul: Chaŭm kwa Moŭm, 2012); Kwŏn/Kim Hyŏn-yŏng, Han Ch'ae-yun, Ruin, Yu Chin-hŭi, and Kim Chu-hŭi, eds., *Sŏng ŭi chŏngch'i, sŏng ŭi kwŏlli* (Seoul: Chaŭm kwa Moŭm, 2012); Ruin, "Kaemp'ŭ T'ŭraensŭ: It'aewŏn chiyŏk t'ŭraensŭjendŏ ŭi yŏksa ch'ujŏk hagi, 1960–1989," *Munhwa Yŏn'gu* 1, no. 1 (2012): 244–78.

8   On the role of film during this period, see Kim in this volume. For the place of queer media in post-1987 South Korea, see Pak Chi-hun, "Han'guk k'wiŏ midiŏ ŭi yŏksa wa paljŏn," in *Han'guk, sahoe midiŏ wa sosuja munhwa chŏngch'i*, ed. Han'guk Pangsong Hakhoe (Seoul: K'ŏmyunikeishŏnbuksŭ, 2011), 321–64.

9   Christina Klein, *Cold War Orientalism: Asia in the Middlebrow Imagination, 1945–1961* (Berkeley: University of California Press, 2003).

10   This approach draws on the work of Petrus Liu, *Queer Marxism in Two Chinas* (Durham, NC: Duke University Press, 2005); Rosemary Hennessy, *Profit and Pleasure: Sexual Identities in Late Capitalism* (New York: Routledge, 2000); Kevin

Floyd, *The Reification of Desire: Towards a Queer Marxism* (Minneapolis: University of Minnesota Press, 2009); Jordana Rosenberg and Amy Villajero, "Introduction: Queerness, Norms, Utopia," GLQ 18, no. 1 (2012): 1–18.

11　Jie-Hyun Lim, "Mapping Mass Dictatorship: Towards a Transnational History of Twentieth Century Dictatorship," in *Gender Politics and Mass Dictatorship: Global Perspectives*, ed. Lim Jie-Hyun (London: Palgrave, 2011), 1–22. On the contours of this paradigm, see Namhee Lee, "The Theory of Mass Dictatorship: A Re-examination of the Park Chung Hee Period," *Review of Korean Studies* 12, no. 3 (September 2009): 41–69. For a feminist critique, see Chŏng Hŭi-jin, "Han'guk sahoe ŭi chisik saengsan pangbŏp kwa taejung tokjaeron," in *Kŭndae ŭi kyŏnggye esŏ tokjae rŭl ikkda: Taejung tokjae wa Pak Chŏng-hŭi ch'eje*, ed. Chang Mun-sŏk and Yi Sang-nok (Seoul: Kurinbi, 2006), 403–19.

12　For a cultural study emphasizing the necropolitical underside of authoritarian development, see Jin-kyung Lee, *Service Economies: Militarism, Sex Work, and Migrant Labor in South Korea* (Minneapolis: University of Minnesota Press, 2010).

13　I thank Han Sang Kim for suggesting this concept to me. Although gay men were typically described as an immoral blight on South Korean society under Park and his successors, anecdotal evidence suggests that they repurposed weekly reports on cruising spots as tour guides that provided information on where and how to seek sex with other men.

14　See, e.g., Sin Chi-yŏn, "1920–30 nyŏndae 'tongsŏng(yŏn)ae' kwallyŏn kisa ŭi susajŏk maengnak," *Minjok Munhwa Yŏn'gu* 45 (2006): 265–92; Pak/Ch'a Minjŏng, *Chosŏn ŭi k'wiŏ: Kŭndae ŭi t'ŭmsae e sumŭn pyŏnt'aedŭl ŭi ch'osang* (Seoul: Hyŏnsil Munhwa Yŏn'gu, 2018); Ha's chapter in this volume. For early postliberation accounts that echoed colonial period precedents, see "Yŏsŏng namjang ŭi sibiron," *Pusan Sinmum*, November 10, 1946; "Tongsŏng yŏn'ae ro chasal?," *Chung'ang Sinmun*, October 31, 1947; "Tongsŏng'ae ro chŏngsa, Kyŏngbang yŏgong tumyŏng i," *Kong'ŏp Sinmun*, November 1, 1947.

15　Although it is impossible to verify numbers, one alarmist report published in early 1958 claimed that approximately 1,400 female couples inhabited the southern half of the peninsula, with about 400 of them residing in Seoul. "Yŏin: 30 dae ŭi chŏhang," *Chugan hŭimang* 116 (March 14, 1958): 4–6. According to a report published in 1969, 500 to 600 individual lesbians were said to inhabit the capital. "Sŏul ŭi rejŭbiŏndŭl," *Chugan Kyŏnghyang* 2, no. 8 (March 2, 1969): 54–56. For a Kinsey Report–like study of female couples, see "Tongsŏng pubu ŭi isaek chidae," *Chugan Yŏsŏng*, no. 444 (August 14, 1977): 42–44.

16　On the history of postwar widows in South Korea, see Yi Im-ha, *Chŏnjaeng mimang'in, han'guk hyŏndaesa ŭi ch'immok ŭl kkaeda: Kusullo p'urŏssŭn han'guk chŏnjaeng chŏnhu sahoe* (Seoul: Ch'aek kwa Hamkke, 2010).

17　Discussions of wartime love, marriage, and family life appear in *Sint'aeyang*, October 1952, 38–39, 42–43, January 1955, 142–45; *Chugan Hŭimang*, May 23, 1958, 5–6. See also Yi, *Chŏnjaeng mimang'in, han'guk hyŏndaesa ŭi ch'immok ŭl kkaeda*, 181–308.

18 See, e.g., "Namja ro haengsae [sic] hagi 6 nyŏn," *Sint'aeyang*, November 1, 1955, 66–69; "Minam weit'ŏ algoboni namjang yŏhaksa," *Sŏndei Sŏul* 11, no. 10 (March 12, 1978): 22.

19 Photographic images accompanying media reports of female-female weddings also suggest that friends and family regularly attended these ceremonies. See, e.g., "Hwaje ch'ujŏk: Yŏja kkiri chŏngsik kyŏlhonsik ollin Kim Xxx-xxx, Kim Xxx-xxx," *Yŏngneidi* 5, no. 6 (June 1985): 232–236. Although male cohabitation did take place during this period, same-sex weddings between men, especially gender-normative ones, were extremely rare. For an analysis of homoerotic relationships among pre-war men, see Pak Kwan-su, "1940 nyŏndae 'namsŏng tongsŏng'ae' yŏn'gu," *Pigyo Minsokhak* 31 (2006): 389–438.

20 After more than five years of archival research, the earliest postwar accounts of this nature that I have uncovered are "Sillang do yŏja sinbu do yŏja," *Silhwa* 5, no. 4 (April 1957): 190–94; "Tongsŏng pubu ŭi ihon sodong naemak," *Yadam kwa Silhwa*, vol. 2, no. 4 (April 1958): 266–267. For an early report on lesbianism, see "Yuhan madamdŭl ŭi tongsŏng'ae," *Chinsang* 2, no. 6 (June 1957): 25–27.

21 "Yŏin: 30 dae ŭi chŏhang," 5. To support its view, this voyeuristic account cited a doctor who predictably described lesbians as "sexual perverts" *(pyŏnt'ae sŏng'yokja)*. But this same medical expert contested the reporter's heterosexist analysis of their erotic life by highlighting the common practice of tribadism which did not require penetration. "Yŏin: 30 dae ŭi chŏhang," 6. A similarly (porno)graphic account of lesbian sex practices appears in "Tongsŏng pubu ŭi aejŏng mallo," *Yadam kwa Silhwa*, vol. 4, no. 11 (November 1963), 177.

22 Elizabeth Lapovsky Kennedy and Madeline D. Davis, *Boots of Leather, Slippers of Gold: The History of a Lesbian Community* (New York: Routledge, 1993). For a similar analysis (but situated in the late 1980s), see Kath Weston, *Render Me, Gender Me: Lesbians Talk Sex, Class, Color, Nation, Studmuffins* (New York: Columbia University Press, 1996).

23 For more on the meaning of "Ms. Pants" and earlier genealogies of cross-dressing in contemporary South Korea, see Han Ch'ae-yun, "Sŏlik ŭn rejŭ, ch'imassi wa pajissi rŭl mannada," *Buddy*, vol. 6, August 1998, 16–17; Kim Il-lan, "Tarŭn sesang ilki: 1960 nyŏndae ŭi yŏjang namja wa namjang yŏin," in Ŏiron Munhwa Yŏn'gu Moim, *Chendŏ ŭi ch'aenŏl ŭl tollyŏra*.

24 On how wartime disruptions found their way into literary representations of non-normative relationships, including female same-sex intimacies, and weakened forms of hegemonic masculinity, see Hŏ Yun, "1950 nyŏndae chŏnhu namsŏngsŏng ŭi t'alch'uk kwa chendŏ ŭi pisuhaeng undoing," *Yŏsŏng Munhak Yŏn'gu* 30 (2013): 43–71. For a related study on the postwar rebuilding of South Korean society through demarcations of heterosexuality and homosexuality, see Hŏ Yun, "1950 k'wiŏ chang kwa bŏpjŏk kyuje ŭi chŏpsok: 'Pyŏngyŏkbŏp,' 'kyŏngbŏmbŏp,' ŭl t'ong han sekshuŏllit'i ŭi t'ongje," *Pŏp Sahoe* 51 (April 2016): 229–50. On heteropatriarchy's post–Korean War revival as it relates to the rise and

fall of South Korea's all-female theatrical troupe, see Kim Chi-hye, "1950 nyŏndae yŏsŏng kukgŭk ŭi tanch'e hwaldong kwa soet'oe e tae han yŏn'gu," *Han'guk Yŏsŏnghak* 27, no. 2 (June 2011): 1–33.

25 Unless otherwise noted, the following discussion is based on "Pŏbjŏng p'omal 6: Tongsŏng'gan ŭi ch'ijŏng sarin sakkŏn," *Tong'a Ilbo*, July 17, 1958.

26 "Yomojomo," *Kyŏnghyang Sinmun*, February 22, 1958; "Tansang tanha," *Tong'a Ilbo*, February 22, 1958. These reports identify the "wife" with the last name of Yin, not Yim.

27 On how the Korean War and other anticommunist struggles in Asia resulted in deadly violence and kinship trauma, see Heonik Kwon, *The Other Cold War* (New York: Columbia University Press, 2010).

28 "Yomojomo," *Kyŏnghyang Sinmun*, February 22, 1958. Less than two months later, a popular weekly published an extended report on these allegedly dangerous couples and included several photographs that encouraged readers to more effectively identify these defiant women. "Yŏin: 30 dae ŭi chŏhang," 4–6.

29 "Yim Hŭi-suk e 5 nyŏn ŏndo," *Chosŏn Ilbo*, July 6, 1958. For the court's decision on this case, see BA0079706, National Archives of Korea, 1958, 286–88. I thank Kim T'ae-ho for obtaining this rare document for me. For a later debate about female-female sex crimes of revenge, see "Yŏja ga yŏja rŭl pŏmhan yŏja ŭi poksu," *Chugan Yŏsŏng*, no. 145, October 20, 1971, 84–85.

30 The mass media did occasionally admit the undeniable fact of long-lasting female partnerships. See, e.g., "Adŭl naa kirŭn rejubiŏn 10 nyŏn e," *Chugan Yŏsŏng*, no. 50 (December 10, 1969): 78–79; "T'ong do k'ŭgo t'ip do mani chudŏra," *Chugan Han'guk*, no. 459 (July 15, 1973); "Yŏja kkiri sillang sinbu," *Chugan Kyŏnghyang* 8, no. 2 (January 19, 1975): 28; "Tongsŏng pubu . . . kŭmsil chŏŭn 15 nyŏn 'mŏ ka isang hae?,'" *Chugan Kyŏnghyang* 10, no. 13 (April 10, 1977): 28–29; "Tongsŏng pubu ŭi isaek chidae," 42–44; "Ch'unggyŏk rŭp'o: Anae do yŏja, namp'yŏn do yŏja," *Yŏngneidi* 2, no. 12 (December 1982): 192–95.

31 Unless otherwise noted, the following discussion is based on "'Tongsŏng pubu' ŭmdok," *Tong'a Ilbo*, August 5, 1963; "'Namp'yŏn' e wigye sarin hyŏm'ŭi," *Tong'a Ilbo*, August 6, 1963; "Namjang hago pŏjŏsi namp'yŏn," *Kyŏnghyang Sinmun*, August 6, 1983.

32 "Tongsŏng pubu ŭi aejŏng mallo," 174–77.

33 "Tongsŏng pubu (?) kkiri todukjil," *Kyŏnghyang Sinmun*, March 8, 1965. Newspaper reports of this variety appear repeatedly throughout the authoritarian period.

34 One exceptional woman featured in the mass media was the male-dressed politician Kim Ok-sŏn. On her early career, see "Namjang yŏin ipfuboja," *Tong'a Ilbo*, July 8, 1960; "'Nekt'ai' maen namjang apdo," *Tong'a Ilbo*, May 25, 1965. Research on this important but neglected figure is needed.

35 On the precarity of these forms of labor and their representation in popular culture, see Lee, *Service Economies*, esp. 79–123.

36 Kennedy and Davis, *Boots of Leather, Slippers of Gold*, 152.

37 "Tongsŏng pubu (?) kkiri todukjil."

38   For a wide-ranging study on intellectual approaches to transgender studies, see
      Susan Stryker and Aren Z. Aizura, *The Transgender Studies Reader*, vol. 2 (New
      York: Routledge, 2013).

39   Unless noted otherwise, the following discussion is based on "Adŭl paradŏn
      pumo," *Tong'a Ilbo*, April 2, 1965. For other accounts of gender-nonconforming
      women from the early 1960s, see "Namjang 10 nyŏn ch'ŏnyŏ ŭi hoso," *Tong'a
      Ilbo*, March 5, 1961; "Namjang simnyŏn ŭi ch'ŏnyŏ," *Yadam kwa Silhwa*,
      June 1961, 250–55; "Pyŏn'ae ŭi namjang yŏin," *Yadam kwa Silhwa*, Decem-
      ber 1965: 376–81.

40   On the history of transgender practices and sex reassignment surgery in early
      South Korea, see Han Yŏng-hŭi, "Ŭihakhwa ŭi kwajŏng sok esŏ ŭi sŏngjŏnhwan
      yongmang, sŏngjŏnhwan susul, sŏngjŏn hwanja," in Ŏiron Munhwa Yŏn'gu
      Moim, *Chendŏ ŭi ch'aenŏl ŭl tollyŏra*, 48–83. For an account of biological women
      who engaged in male-like practices in the West, see Judith [Jack] Halberstam,
      Female Masculinity (Durham, NC: Duke University Press, 1998).

41   A similar outing of a male-dressed female miner appears in "T'angwang e p'in
      hyŏndaep'an Simch'ŏng," *Tong'a Ilbo*, February 12, 1961. For more on labor protests
      from this period, see Hagen Koo, *Korean Workers: The Culture and Politics of Class
      Formation* (Ithaca, NY: Cornell University Press, 2001); Hwasook B. Nam, *Build-
      ing Ships, Building a Nation: Korea's Democratic Unionism under Park Chung Hee*
      (Seattle: University of Washington Press, 2009).

42   On the intimate relationship of the press to the Park regime, see Yi Chŏng-hun,
      "Apch'ukjŏk sang'ŏphwa: 1960 nyŏndae han'guk sinmun ŏllon ŭi sang'ŏp kwa
      kwajŏng," *K'ŏmyunik'aeshon Iron* 10, no. 2 (June 2014): 242–83.

43   On the early development of newspaper weeklies, see Chŏn Sang-gi, "1960
      nyŏndae chuganji ŭi maech'ejŏk wisang: 'Chugan han'guk' ŭl chungsim ŭro,"
      Han'gukhak Nonmunjp 36 (2008): 225–58; Kim Chi, "1960 nyŏndae sang'ŏp
      chuganji *Chugan han'guk* yŏn'gu" (master's thesis, Yonsei University, 2015). For
      their treatment of gender and sexuality, see Pak Sŏng-a, "'Sŏndei sŏul' e nat'anan
      yŏsŏng ŭi yuhyŏng kwa p'yosang," *Han'guk Yŏn'gu* 22 (May 2010): 159–90; Yim
      Chong-su and Pak Se-hyŏn, "'Sŏndei sŏul' e nat'anan yŏsŏng, sekshuŏllit'I kŭrigo
      1970 nyŏndae," *Han'guk Munhak Yŏn'gu* 44 (June 2013): 91–136; Chŏn Wŏn-
      gun, "1980 nyŏndae 'Sŏndei sŏul' e nat'anan tongsŏng'ae tamnon kwa namsŏng
      tongsŏng'aejadŭl ŭi kyŏnghŏm," *Chendŏ wa Munhwa* 8, no. 2 (December 2015):
      139–70.

44   This information on the background of weekly reporters was conveyed to me
      through an interview with Pak Mu-il (b. 1941). After working for two monthly
      entertainment magazines (*Arirang* and *Myŏngnang*) during the mid-1960s, this
      talented journalist was hired to write for *Chugan Han'guk* after its inauguration in
      late 1968. On the development of professional identity among Park era journal-
      ists, see Pak Yong-kyu, "Pak Chŏng-hŭi sigi ŏllonin ŭi chigŏpjŏk chŏngch'esŏng ŭi
      pyŏnhwa," *Ŏllon Chŏngbo Yŏn'gu* 51, no. 2 (August 2014): 34–76.

45   Kim, "1960 nyŏndae sang'ŏp chuganji *Chugan han'guk* yŏn'gu," 34.

46 On the consumption practices of newspaper readers during the Park era, see Ch'ae Paek, "Pak Chŏng-hŭi sidae sinmun dokja ŭi sahoe munhwasa," *Ŏllon Chŏngbo Yŏn'gu* 51, no. 2 (August 2014): 5–33.

47 On this global phenomenon, see Eric Schaefer, ed., *Sex Scene: Media and the Sexual Revolution* (Durham, NC: Duke University Press, 2014); Gert Hekma and Alain Giami, eds., *Sexual Revolutions* (New York: Palgrave, 2014).

48 On these strategies, see Eun Mee Kim, *Big Business, Strong State: Collusion and Conflict in South Korean Developments, 1960–1990* (Albany: State University of New York Press, 1997); Gregg A. Brazinsky, *Nation Building in South Korea: Koreans, Americans, and the Making of a Democracy* (Chapel Hill: North Carolina University Press, 2009); Byung-Wook Kim and Ezra Vogel, eds., *The Park Chung Hee Era: The Transformation of South Korea* (Cambridge, MA: Harvard University Press, 2011).

49 See, e.g., "Chae 3 ŭi sŏng sidae," *Chugan Han'guk*, vol. 116, December 11, 1969, 22; "Resŭbiŏndŭl ŭi 'pam kwa nat' ŭi saneghwal chinsang," *Chugan Yŏsŏng*, vol. 129, June 30, 1971, 36–37; "Han'gukp'an 'resŭbiŏn'dŭl kwangnan," *Chugan Chung'ang*, vol. 217, October 22, 1972, 26; "'Ton do kŭgo, t'ip do mani chudŏra,'" *Chugan Han'guk*, no. 459, July 15, 1973, 10–11. A similar transnational dynamic was at work between the U.S. and Europe and within Europe itself. On these comparative frames, see Eric Schaefer, "'I'll Take Sweden': The Shifting Discourses of the 'Sexy Nation' in Sexploitation Films," in Schaefer, *Sex Scene*, 207–34; Hekma and Giami, *Sexual Revolutions*. On the postwar development of Japanese weeklies, see Kageyama Kayoko, *Sei, media, fūzoku: Shūkanshi "Asahi genō" kara miru fūzoku toshite no sei* (Tokyo: Hābestosha, 2010); Asaoka Takahiro, "Kōdo keizai sechō no torai to shūkanshi dokusha: Sōgō shūkanshi to sono dokusha dearu sarariiman o chūsin ni," in *Zasshi media no bunkashi: Henyō suru sengo paradaimu*, ed. Yoshida Noriaki and Okada Akiko (Tokyo: Shinwasha, 2012), 129–62.

50 "Sŏul ŭi rejŭbiŏndŭl," *Chugan Kyŏnghyang*, vol. 2, no. 8, March 2, 1969, 54–56. See also "Chae 3 ŭi sŏng sidae," 22.

51 In a scene from *Uncle "Bar" at Barbershop* (*Ibalso ŭi Issi*, dir. Kwŏn Chong-gwan, Indiespace, Seoul, 2000), the short film mentioned in the introduction of this volume as an example that is based on the director's story, the female protagonist, a male-presenting barber, gazes awkwardly at a poster of a semi-nude white woman, thus seeking to imitate the sexist practices of her male customers.

52 Journalists at weekly publications typically scoured the social columns of daily newspapers in search of inspiring information on which they expanded in creating their own articles. They crafted other stories from their own investigations or based on tips from the local police and other informants.

53 See, e.g., "Yŏja kkiri kyŏlhonsik," *Kyŏnghyang Sinmun*, June 13, 1963; "Ilbon ŭi 'resŭbian,'" *Chugan Chung'ang*, no. 28, March 9, 1969, 22; "Tongsŏng kyŏlhon hŏga yogu," *Kyŏnghyang Sinmun*, February 20, 1970; "Mi tu yŏin kyŏlhon sinch'ŏng," *Kyŏnghyang Sinmun*, July 10, 1970; "Tongsŏng yŏn'ae kyŏlhon injŏng," *Kyŏnghyang Sinmun*, September 28, 1970; "Tongsŏng pubu pŏbjŏng t'ujaeng,"

Kyŏnghyang Sinmun, September 9, 1971; "Tabang sŏ tongsŏng kyŏlhon," *Maeil Kyŏngje*, March 21, 1972; "Kŭpjŭng hanŭn 'resŭbiŏn kajŏng,'" *Kyŏnghyang Sinmun*, September 22, 1973; "Nŭrŏnanŭn resŭbiŏndŭl ŭi aejŏng, chilt'u, chŏngsa," *Chugan Yosŏng*, no. 289, August 4, 1974, 22–23; "Miguk esŏ tongsŏng kyŏlhon yuhaeng," *Kyŏnghynag Sinmun*, April 24, 1975; "Ch'ak oro tongsŏng kyŏlhon kong'in," *Tong'a Ilbo*, July 4, 1975; "Yŏsŏng kkiri kyŏlhon ŭn muhyo," *Tong'a Ilbo*, April 23, 1977.

54 The following account is based on "Tu noch'ŏnyŏ ga tongsŏng kyŏlhon hettanda," *Chugan Han'guk*, no. 65, November 28, 1965, 10–11.

55 On the colonial origins of Yŏngdŭngp'o as an industrial center, see Kim Ha-na, "1930 nyŏndae chŏnhu kong'ŏp tosi tamnon kwa Yŏngdŭngp'o ŭi Sŏul p'yŏnip," *Tosi Yŏn'gu* 11 (June 2014): 37–68.

56 I thank Han Sang Kim for suggesting this ethical response to media practices of queersploitation.

57 For an early reference to and explanation of millstone couples, see "Yŏin: 30 dae ŭi chŏhang," 4–6. The contemporaneous film *Pijŏn* (1970) would remind audiences of this historic practice. For accounts of this film's shocking "lesbian" bed scene, see "Mudŏwŏ sok tongsŏng yŏnae pedŭ'ssin," *Chugan Yŏsŏng*, no. 74 (August 26, 1970): 74; "Tongsŏng'ae kat'ŭn kŏn sangsang to mot'eabwassŏyo," *Chugan Chosŏn*, no. 13 (August 30, 1970): 13. Another Chosŏn period expression used by the mass media to denote female homoeroticism was *taesik*. Literally, "to eat across from one another," this term referred to sexual relations between court women. For one invocation, see "Kyŏrhon do ŏyŏt hage homŏseksŭ," *Chugan Chosŏn*, no. 152 (September 19, 1971): 22–23.

58 Such intrusions so infuriated another member of a same-sex couple that she forced the reporter to find other subjects willing to expose to the public a lesbian world that, to her, remained a private affair: "Sŏul ŭi rejŭbiŏndŭl," 54–56.

59 It is unclear from this photograph whether the "wife" is wearing pants like her male-dressed "husband": "Yŏ'miyongsa wa yŏ'mudang i han'guk ch'ŏt tongsŏng kyŏlhonsik," *Chugan Han'guk* 313, September 27, 1970, 12.

60 The earliest postwar account I have located dates to 1957. This report conveys that the couple chose not conduct a formal ceremony, but did shoot a commemorative wedding picture and hosted a home reception. "Sillang do yŏja sinbu do yŏja," 190–94.

61 While normalizing their respective gender roles as "husband" and "wife," the 1965 account drew on the opinions of two medical professionals to explain the undeniable reality of female homosexuality, which both experts predictably pathologized.

62 "Sŏul ŭi rejŭbiŏndŭl," 54–56.

63 The following discussion is based on "Yŏ'miyongsa wa yŏ'mudang i han'guk ch'ŏt tongsŏng kyŏlhonsik," 12–13; "Han'guk ch'oech'o ro tongsŏng kyŏlhonsik," *Chugan Yŏsŏng*, no. 92, October 7, 1970, 18–19.

64 "Yŏ'miyongsa wa yŏ'mudang i han'guk ch'ŏt tongsŏng kyŏlhonsik," 70.

65 Public debate to legalize same-sex marriage rarely surfaced before the 1990s. For one exception, see "Tu noch'ŏnyŏ ga tongsŏng kyŏlhon hettanda," 11. Brief references also appear in "Tongsŏng pubu . . . kŭmsil choŭn 15 nyŏn 'mŏ ka isang hae?,'" 28–29; "Hwaje ch'ujŏk," *Yŏngneidi* 5, no. 6 (June 1985), 236.

66 Unless noted otherwise, the following discussion is based on "Uri sŏngsaenghwal ŭl mulji mara dayo," *Yŏsŏng Chung'ang*, January 1971, 332–37.

67 Unlike masculine women who assumed male-dominated jobs (e.g, as taxi drivers or professional soldiers) and were viewed as social threats, feminine men who became hairdressers or chose other female-oriented positions (e.g., as nurses or fashion designers) became the subject of comic ridicule but were seen as relatively powerless. On filmic representations of female-identified men, see Kim's chapter in this volume.

68 In the film (Han Hyŏng-mo, dir.), Chae-sun suffers from schizophrenia, which is attributed to a pathological abhorrence of men (arrhenophobia). Having been raped during the Korean War, she believes that marriage turns women into slaves of men. Chae-sun thus prefers women, and she becomes passionately attached to her foster sister, Kŭm-i, who was orphaned during the war. Chae-sun is so smitten with Kŭm-i that she even tries to prevent her from marrying a male suitor and a hometown friend, Kwang-ho. But, by the end of the film, psychiatric treatment allows Chae-sun to recover from the temporary "deviance" of arrhenophobia and, one also assumes, of lesbianism as well. Unfortunately, a copy of this film is currently missing, preventing a more detailed analysis. The screenplay, the basis for this summary, can be viewed at the Korean Film Archive's reference library. Photographic stills of the two female protagonists awkwardly embracing one another adorn the cover and opening page of *Queer Korea*.

69 The Yusin (lit., "restoration") system installed a new constitution that allowed Park Chung Hee and his Democratic Republican Party to monopolize executive, legislative, and juridical power. Park used this dictatorial arrangement to promote heavy industries and military defense, while suppressing the demands of laborers and students. These repressive forces led to the Kwangju Uprising (1980) and subsequent protests for wealth redistribution and political freedom. For more on this era, see Kim and Vogel, *The Park Chung Hee Era*; Namhee Lee, *The Making of Minjung: Democracy and the Politics of Representation in South Korea* (Ithaca, NY: Cornell University Press, 2007).

70 The following discussion is based on "'Namja nŭn sirŏ . . . ,'" *Chugan Chung'ang*, March 10, 1974, 29; "29 sal yŏin kwa 38 sal yŏin i tongsŏng kyŏlhon!," *Chugan Yŏsŏng*, no. 269 (March 17, 1974): 18–19. That many women who wed one another sought out monks to preside over their marriage rites suggests a strong connection to Buddhism. Further research is needed to clarify this important linkage to religion.

71 For the place of this stigmatized figure in contemporary Korean culture, see Lee, *Service Economies*, 125–84. On the overseas meanings of the Western whore, see

Grace M. Cho, *Haunting the Korean Diaspora: Shame, Secrecy, and the Korean War* (Minneapolis: University of Minnesota Press, 2008).

72 As suggested earlier, many accounts presented conflicting information, underscoring their partially fabricated, but *not* culturally irrelevant, nature. In this case, the March 17 report suggested that Kim married William and followed him to the United States, where he died in an automobile crash two years later. Either way, Kim's fate as abandoned remained the same. For other reports of female homoeroticism involving the base economy, see "Soegorang ch'an namjang yŏin," *Chosŏn Ilbo*, March 3, 1964; "K'alburim ŭro soegorang ch'an 'namjang agassi,'" *Chugan Han'guk*, no. 459, September 7, 1975, 21; "Yŏja kkiri ŭi kyŏlhonsik e hagaek 200 myŏng," *Sŏndei Sŏul*, vol. 11, no. 1, January 1, 1978, 26–27.

73 On the post-1945 development of Yongsan as a queer space, see Ruin, "Kaemp'ŭ T'ŭraensŭ." For a first-person story with remarkably similar themes of male betrayal, U.S. military prostitution, and eventual lesbianism, see "Tasi 'namja' rŭl sarang halsuman ittamyŏn," *Yŏngneidi* 7, no. 10 (October 1987): 298–303.

74 Artificial insemination was also occasionally discussed, but not yet practiced. See, e.g., "Tambang: Tongsŏng'ae pubu," 234–37; "Adŭl noa kirŭn resŭbiŏn 10 nyŏn e," 78–79; "Ŭihakkye kwŏnidŭl ŭi imsang not'ŭ (30)," *Kyŏnghyang sinmun*, March 26, 1975; "Yŏja kkiri moyŏ salmyŏ 'yŏbo,' 'tangsin,'" *Arirang*, April 1976, 100–103; "Tongsŏng pubu ŭi isaeak chidae," 43. On the history of South Korea's domestic adoption, see Hŏ Nam-sun, "Kungnae ibyang saŏp ŭi hyŏnghyang punsŏk e kwan han yŏn'gu: Han'guk kidokkyo yangjihoe rŭl chungsim ŭro" (master's thesis, Ehwa Womans University, Seoul, 1973).

75 For other accounts emphasizing spiritual comfort over physical pleasure, see "Yŏja kkiri sillang sinbu," 28; "Sanjŏn sujŏn ta kyokkun yŏja kkiri kyŏlhonsik," *Sŏndei Sŏul*, vol. 18, no. 20, May 24, 1985, 32–33. For exposés of Seoul's lesbian community, see "Sŏul ŭi rejŭbiŏndŭl," 54–56; "Namja nŭn chilsaek ŭi 'rejŭbiandŭl,'" *Chugan Kyŏnghyang*, vol. 2, no. 36, September 17, 1969, 90–91; "Han'gukp'an 'resŭbiŏndŭl kwangnan," *Chugan Chung'ang*, no. 217, October 22, 1972, 26; "Ton do kŭgo, t'ip do mani chudŏra," 10–11; "Nŭrŏnanŭn resŭbiŏndŭl ŭi aejŏng, chilt'u, chŏngsa," 22–23; "Yŏja kkiri moyŏ salmyŏ 'yŏbo,' 'tangsin,'" 100–3; "Yumyŏng yŏyu do sangjŏngmo do tongsŏng pubu ŭi isaek chidae," *Chugan Yŏsŏng*, no. 444, August 14, 1977, 42–43; "Kŭmnam chidae: Sŏul e rejŭbiŏn k'ŭrrŏp," *Chugan Kyŏnghyang*, vol. 15, no. 39, October 3, 1982, 22–24; "Sŏbangnim haldden ŏnjego ije wasŏ paesin inya: Rejŭbiŏn sangdae pyŏnsim e haengp'ae purin namjayŏk ŭi sarrongnyŏ," *Sŏndei Sŏul*, vol. 16, no. 48, December 8, 1985, 128–29.

76 Oral histories suggest that at least some women did feel a stable sense of lesbian identity throughout this era. However, this identity may have been retroactively produced from the perspective of the present and through the process of memory making. Moreover, the formation of a historically entrenched lesbian identity was likely aided by the intervening activities of a generation of feminists who came of age during the post-1990s era of sexual minorities and human rights discourses. For one such account in which the activist seeks to document the subjectivity of

an older Korean "lesbian," while simultaneously (re)interpreting it in identitarian terms, see Pak/Kim Su-jin, ed., *50 dae rejŭbiŏn: Ch'oe Myŏng-hwan iyagi* (Seoul: Rejŭbiŏn Kwŏlli Yŏn'guso, 2003). For other oral histories with self-identified lesbian women, see Sŏng Chŏng-suk, "'Pulwanjŏn han mom' ŭi chilgok ŭl nŏmŏ: 50 dae rejŭbiŏn ŭi saeng'ae iyagi," *Han'guk Sahoe Pokjihak* 64, no. 2 (May 2012): 85–109; Pak/Kim Su-jin, ed., *Nŏ nŭn oe rejŭbiŏn ini? Chogŭm ŭn oeroun uridŭl ŭi reinbou int'ŏbyu* (Seoul: Imaejin, 2014).

77 Unless otherwise noted, the following discussion is based on "Sanjŏn sujŏn ta kyokkun yŏja kkiri kyŏlhonsik," 32–33; "Noch'ŏ kkiri tongsŏng kyŏlhon," *Chugan Chung'ang*, no. 860, May 26, 1985, 23; "Tongsŏng'ae yŏja pubu ilho p'agyŏng," *Chugan Kyŏnghyang*, vol. 20, no. 18, May 10, 1987, 42–44.

78 See, e.g., Pak Sang-ho's film with the same name (adapted from a radio drama): Pak Sang-ho, dir., *Ttosun'i*, Sejong Yŏnghwa Chusik Hoesa, Seoul, 1963. A version with English subtitles has been released as *A Happy Businesswoman* by the Korean Film Archive. An intrusive reporter conveyed Sun-mi's own explanation as a filial spinster who was so dedicated to supporting her family that she lacked the time to wed. But her worry about a future as a normative housewife could also have masked or doubled as an unspeakable desire for other women. "Hwaje ch'ujŏk," 235–36.

79 On the connection between taxi driving and queer women, see "Tongsŏng yŏja unjŏnsa," *Chugan Chung'ang*, no. 722, September 12, 1982, 35; "Samogwandae ŭijŏt i yŏja kkiri kyŏlhonsik,'" *Sŏndei Sŏul*, vol. 16, no. 44, November 6, 1983, 24–25; "Yŏja unjŏnsa kkiri kong'gae tongsŏng kyŏlhonsik ollyŏtta!," *Chugan Kyŏnghyang*, vol. 16, no. 49, December 18, 1983, 26–27.

80 One report mentions a payment of twenty million wŏn. "Hwaje ch'ujŏk," 236.

81 "Tongsŏng'ae 'yŏja pubu' kkiri wijaryo ssaum," *Chugan Kyŏnghyang*, vol. 30, no. 37, September 20, 1987, 58–59. For an earlier account mentioning the possibility of an alimony payment, see "Ton do kŭgo, t'ip do mani chudŏra," 10–11.

82 Unless noted otherwise, the following is based on "Tong'gŏ saenghwal 4 nyŏn man e pa'gyŏng," *Chugan Yŏsŏng*, no. 130, July 7, 1971, 24–25. For a similar account from a later period, see "Pam i turyŏwŏ," *Sŏndei Sŏul* 21, no. 2 (January 17, 1988): 46–47.

83 For other exceptions of women as soldiers, see "Yŏgun agassidŭl kuhon handaeyo," *Myŏngnang*, May 1964, 176–80; "18 se myoryŏng yŏgun," *Chugan Chung'ang*, no. 2, August 31, 1968, 10–11. On the privileged position of South Korean men due to the country's compulsory military system, see Seungsook Moon, "Imagining a Nation through Differences: Reading the Controversy Concerning the Military Service Extra Points System in South Korea," *Review of Korean Studies* 5, no. 2 (December 2002): 73–109.

84 On the colonial history of this queer practice, see Pak Chŏng-ae, "Yŏja rŭl sarang han yŏja: 1931 nyŏn 'tongsŏng'ae' ch'ŏldo chasal sakkŏn," in *20 segi yŏsŏng sakkŏnsa: Kŭndae yŏsŏng kyoyuk ŭi sijak esŏ saibŏ p'eminijŭm kkaji*, ed. Yŏsŏngsa Yŏn'gu Moim Kilbakk Sesang (Seoul: Yŏsŏng Sinmunsa, 2001), 100–8. On the

case of Korea's colonizer, see Jennifer Robertson, "Dying to Tell: Sexuality and Suicide in Imperial Japan," *Signs* 25, no. 1 (Autumn 1999): 1–35.

85 Unless noted otherwise, the following discussion is based on "Yŏja kkiri sarang hada silae ŭi chasal," *Sŏndei Sŏul*, vol. 8, no. 17, May 4, 1975, 28–29. For more on female factory laborers, including their queer sexual practices, see "Ch'ŏnyŏ egen 'hyŏngbu' wa 'yŏrŭm' kwa 'san' i kangjŏk ida: Yŏgong ŭi sŏng pogosŏ," *Chugan Han'guk*, no. 178, February 18, 1968, 14–15; "Yumyŏng yŏyu do sangjŏngmo do tongsŏng pubu ŭi isaek chidae," 42–43.

86 On cultural representations of what she calls "domestic prostitution," see Lee, *Service Economies*, 79–124.

87 "Yŏja tongsŏng'ae 4 nyŏn pigŭk ŭi chongmal," *Chugan Kyŏnghyang*, vol. 10, no. 6, February 13, 1977, 94–95. For similar accounts of heterosexuality's triumph through lesbian tragedy, see "Tongsŏng yŏja unjŏnsa," 35; "Rejŭbiŏn namp'yŏn'yŏk pyŏngsim chasalgi to," 133.

88 For an activist's analysis of current issues, see Tari Young-Jung Na, "The South Korean Gender System: LGBTI in the Contexts of Family, Legal Identity, and the Military," *Journal of Korean Studies* 19, no. 2 (Fall 2014): 357–77.

89 As Kath Weston has argued, "A focus on state recognition can undermine kinship practices that have no hope of gaining legal standing and narrow the range of intimacies that people create": Kath Weston, "Families in Queer States: The Rule of Law and the Politics of Recognition," *Radical History Review* 93 (Fall 2005): 135. For a similar argument that considers the South Korean case, see Sŏ Tong-jin, "K'wiŏ kajok?: Kajok, sahoe, kukka sai ŭi kŏri rŭl ŏttŏkke ch'ukjŏng hal kŏt inga," *Chinbo P'yŏngnon* 48 (June 2011): 88–119.

Works Cited

NEWSPAPERS AND MAGAZINES

Arirang
Buddy
Chinsang
Chosŏn Ilbo
Chugan Chosŏn
Chugan Chung'ang
Chugan Han'guk
Chugan Hŭimang
Chugan Kyŏnghyang
Chugan Yŏsŏng
Chung'ang Sinmun
Kong'ŏp Sinmun
Kyŏnghyang Sinmun
Maeil Kyŏngje

Myŏngnang
Pusan Simun
Sŏndei Sŏul
Silhwa
Sint'aeyang
Tong'a Ilbo
Yadam kwa Silhwa
Yŏsŏng Chung'ang
Yŏngneidi

KOREAN- AND JAPANESE-LANGUAGE SOURCES

An So-hyŏn. *Chŏnhwan kŭkjang.* Seoul: P'orŏm Aei, 2016.

Asaoka Takahiro. "Kōdo keizai sechō no torai to shūkanshi dokusha: Sōgō shūkanshi to sono dokusha dearu sarariiman o chūsin ni." In *Zasshi media no bunkashi: Henyō suru sengo paradaimu*, ed. Yoshida Noriaki and Okada Akiko, 129–62. Tokyo: Shinwasha, 2012.

Ch'ae Paek. "Pak Chŏng-hŭi sidae sinmun dokja ŭi sahoe munhwasa," *Ŏllon Chŏngbo Yŏn'gu* 51, no. 2 (August 2014): 5–33.

Chŏn Sang-gi. "1960 nyŏndae chuganji ŭi maech'ejŏk wisang: 'Chugan han'guk' ŭl chungsim ŭro." *Han'gukhak Nonmunjp* 36 (2008): 225–58.

Chŏn Wŏn-gun. "1980 nyŏndae 'Sŏndei sŏul' e nat'anan tongsŏng'ae tamnon kwa namsŏng tongsŏng'aejadŭl ŭi kyŏnghŏm." *Chendŏ wa Munhwa* 8, no. 2 (December 2015): 139–70.

Chŏng Hŭi-jin. "Han'guk sahoe ŭi chisik saengsan pangbŏp kwa taejung tokjaeron." In *Kŭndae ŭi kyŏnggye esŏ tokjae rŭl ikkda: Taejung tokjae wa Pak Chŏng-hŭi ch'eje*, eds. Chang Mun-sŏk and Yi Sang-nok, 403–19. Seoul: Kurinbi, 2006.

Han Ch'ae-yun. "Han'guk rejŭbiŏn k'ŏmyunit'i ŭi yŏksa." *Chinbo P'yŏngnon* 49 (Fall 2011): 100–28.

Han Yŏng-hŭi. "Ŭihakhwa ŭi kwajŏng sok esŏ ŭi sŏngjŏnhwan yongmang, sŏngjŏnhwan susul, sŏngjŏn hwanja." In *Chendŏ ŭi ch'aenŏl ŭl tollyora*, ed. Ŏiron Munhwa Yŏn'gu Moim. Seoul: Saram Saenggak, 2008.

Hŏ Nam-sun. "Kungnae ibyang saŏp ŭi hyŏnghyang punsŏk e kwan han yŏn'gu: Han'guk kidokkyo yangjihoe rŭl chungsim ŭro." Master's thesis, Ehwa Woman's University, Seoul, 1973.

Hŏ Yun. "1950 k'wiŏ chang kwa pŏpjŏk kyuje ŭi chŏpsok: 'Pyŏngyŏkbŏp,' 'kyŏngbŏmbŏp,' ŭl t'ong han sekshuŏllit'i ŭi t'ongje." *Pŏp Sahoe* 51 (April 2016): 229–50.

Hŏ Yun. "1950 nyŏndae chŏnhu namsŏngsŏng ŭi t'alch'uk kwa chendŏ ŭi pisuhaeng undoing." *Yŏsŏng Munhak Yŏn'gu* 30 (2013): 43–71.

Kageyama Kayoko. *Sei, media, fūzoku: Shūkanshi "Asahi genō" kara miru fūzoku toshite no sei.* Tokyo: Hābestosha, 2010.

Kim Chi. "1960 nyŏndae sang'ŏp chuganji *Chugan han'guk* yŏn'gu." Master's thesis, Yonsei University, Seoul, 2015.

Kim Chi-hye. "1950 nyŏndae yŏsŏng kukgŭk ŭi tanch'e hwaldong kwa soet'oe e tae han yŏn'gu." *Han'guk Yŏsŏnghak* 27, no. 2 (June 2011): 1–33.

Kim Ha-na. "1930 nyŏndae chŏnhu kong'ŏp tosi tamnon kwa Yŏngdŭngp'o ŭi Sŏul p'yŏnip." *Tosi Yŏn'gu* 11 (June 2014): 37–68.

Kim Il-lan. "Tarŭn sesang ilki: 1960 nyŏndae ŭi yŏjang namja wa namjang yŏin." In *Chendŏ ŭi ch'aenŏl ŭl tollyŏra*, ed. Ŏiron Munhwa Yŏn'gu Moim, 170–207. Seoul: Saram Saenggak, 2008.

Kwŏn/Kim Hyŏn-yŏng, Chŏng Hŭi-jin, Na Yŏng-jŏng, Ruin, and Ŏm Ki-ho, eds. *Namsŏngsŏng wa chendŏ*. Seoul: Chaŭm kwa Moŭm, 2012.

Kwŏn/Kim Hyŏn-yŏng, Han Ch'ae-yun, Ruin, Yu Chin-hŭi, and Kim Chu-hŭi, eds. *Sŏng ŭi chŏngch'i, sŏng ŭi kwŏlli*. Seoul: Chaŭm kwa Moŭm, 2012.

Ŏiron Munhwa Yŏn'gu Moim, ed. *Chendŏ ŭi ch'aenŏl ŭl tollyŏra*. Seoul: Saram Saenggak, 2008.

Pak/Ch'a Min-jŏng. *Chosŏn ŭi k'wiŏ: Kŭndae ŭi t'ŭmsae e sumŭn pyŏnt'aedŭl ŭi ch'osang*. Seoul: Hyŏnsil Munhwa Yŏn'gu, 2018.

Pak Chi-hun. "Han'guk k'wiŏ midiŏ ŭi yŏksa wa paljŏn." In *Han'guk, sahoe midiŏ wa sosuja munhwa chŏngch'i*, ed. Han'guk Pangsong Hakhoe, 321–64. Seoul: K'ŏmyunikeishŏnbuksŭ, 2011.

Pak Chŏng-ae. "Yŏja rŭl sarang han yŏja: 1931 nyŏn 'tongsŏng'ae' ch'ŏldo chasal sakkŏn." In *20 segi yŏsŏng sakkŏnsa: Kŭndae yŏsŏng kyoyuk ŭi sijak esŏ saibŏ p'eminijŭm kkaji*, ed. Yŏsŏngsa Yŏn'gu Moim Kilbakk Sesang, 100–8. Seoul: Yŏsŏng Sinmunsa, 2001.

Pak/Kim Su-jin, ed. *50 dae rejŭbiŏn: Ch'oe Myŏng-hwan iyagi*. Seoul: Rejŭbiŏn Kwŏlli Yŏn'guso, 2003.

Pak/Kim Su-jin, ed. *Nŏ nŭn oe rejŭbiŏn ini? Chogŭm ŭn oeroun uridŭl ŭi reinbou int'ŏbyu*. Seoul: Imaejin, 2014.

Pak Kwan-su. "1940 nyŏndae 'namsŏng tongsŏng'ae' yŏn'gu." *Pigyo Minsokhak* 31 (2006): 389–438.

Pak Sŏng-a. "'Sŏndei sŏul' e nat'anan yŏsŏng ŭi yuhyŏng kwa p'yosang." *Han'guk Yŏn'gu* 22 (May 2010): 159–90.

Pak Yong-kyu. "Pak Chŏng-hŭi sigi ŏllonin ŭi chigŏpjŏk chŏngch'esŏng ŭi pyŏnhwa." *Ŏllon Chŏngbo Yŏn'gu* 51, no. 2 (August 2014): 34–76.

Ruin. "Kaemp'ŭ T'ŭraensŭ: It'aewŏn chiyŏk t'ŭraensŭjendŏ ŭi yŏksa ch'ujŏk hagi, 1960–1989." *Munhwa Yŏn'gu* 1, no. 1 (2012): 244–78.

Sin Chi-yŏn. "1920–30 nyŏndae 'tongsŏng(yŏn)ae' kwallyŏn kisa ŭi susajŏk maengnak." *Minjok Munhwa Yŏn'gu* 45 (2006): 265–92.

Sŏ Tong-jin. "K'wiŏ kajok?: Kajok, sahoe, kukka sai ŭi kŏri rŭl ottŏkke ch'ukjŏng hal kŏt inga." *Chinbo P'yŏngnon* 48 (June 2011): 88–119.

Sŏng Chŏng-suk. "'Pulwanjŏn han mom' ŭi chilgok ŭl nŏmŏ: 50 dae rejŭbiŏn ŭi saeng'ae iyagi." *Han'guk Sahoe Pokjihak* 64, no. 2 (May 2012): 85–109.

Yi Chŏng-hun. "Apch'ukjŏk sang'ŏphwa: 1960 nyŏndae han'guk sinmun ŏllon ŭi sang'ŏp kwa kwajŏng." *K'ŏmyunik'aeshon Iron* 10, no. 2 (June 2014): 242–83.

Yi Im-ha. *Chŏnjaeng mimang'in, han'guk hyŏndaesa ŭi ch'immok ŭl kkaeda: Kusullo p'urŏssŭn han'guk chŏnjaeng chŏnhu sahoe*. Seoul: Ch'aek kwa Hamkke, 2010.

Yim Chong-su, and Pak Se-hyŏn. "'Sŏndei sŏul' e nat'anan yŏsŏng, sekshuŏllit'I kŭrigo 1970 nyŏndae." *Han'guk Munhak Yŏn'gu* 44 (June 2013): 91–136.

ENGLISH-LANGUAGE SOURCES

Arvin, Maile, Eve Tuck, and Angie Morrill. "Decolonizing Feminism: Challenging Connections between Settler Colonialism and Heteropatriarchy." *Feminist Formations* 25, no. 1 (Spring 2013): 8–34.

Berry, Chris. "My Queer Korea: Identity, Space, and the 1998 Seoul Queer Film and Video Festival." *Intersections* 2 (May 1999). Accessed April 27, 2019. http://intersections.anu.edu.au/issue2/Berry.html.

Bong, Youngshik D. "The Gay Rights Movement in Democratizing Korea." *Korean Studies* 32 (2009): 86–103.

Brazinsky, Gregg A. *Nation Building in South Korea: Koreans, Americans, and the Making of a Democracy*. Chapel Hill: North Carolina University Press, 2009.

Cho, Grace M. *Haunting the Korean Diaspora: Shame, Secrecy, and the Korean War*. Minneapolis: University of Minnesota Press, 2008.

Floyd, Kevin. *The Reification of Desire: Towards a Queer Marxism*. Minneapolis: University of Minnesota Press, 2009.

Halberstam, Judith [Jack]. *Female Masculinity*. Durham, NC: Duke University Press, 1998.

Han, Jongwoo, and L. H. M. Ling. "Hypermasculinized State: Hybridity, Patriarchy and Capitalism in Korea." *International Studies Quarterly* 42, no. 1 (March 1998): 53–78.

Hekma, Gert, and Alain Giami, eds. *Sexual Revolutions*. New York: Palgrave, 2014.

Hennessy, Rosemary. *Profit and Pleasure: Sexual Identities in Late Capitalism*. New York: Routledge, 2000.

Kennedy, Elizabeth Lapovsky, and Madeline D. Davis. *Boots of Leather, Slippers of Gold: The History of a Lesbian Community*. New York: Routledge, 1993.

Kim, Byung-Wook, and Ezra Vogel, eds. *The Park Chung Hee Era: The Transformation of South Korea*. Cambridge, MA: Harvard University Press, 2011.

Kim, Eun Mee. *Big Business, Strong State: Collusion and Conflict in South Korean Developments, 1960–1990*. Albany: State University of New York Press, 1997.

Kim, Jeongmin. "Queer Cultural Movements and Local Counterpublics of Sexuality: A Case of Seoul Queer Films and Videos Festival." *Inter-Asia Cultural Studies* 8, no. 4 (2007): 617–33.

Kim, Pil Ho, and C. Colin Singer. "Three Periods of Korean Queer Cinema: Invisible, Camouflage, and Blockbuster." *Acta Koreana* 14, no. 1 (June 2011): 115–34.

Klein, Christina. *Cold War Orientalism: Asia in the Middlebrow Imagination, 1945–1961*. Berkeley: University of California Press, 2003.

Koo, Hagen. *Korean Workers: The Culture and Politics of Class Formation*. Ithaca, NY: Cornell University Press, 2001.

Kwon, Heonik. *The Other Cold War*. New York: Columbia University Press, 2010.

Kwon Kim, Hyun-young, and John (Song Pae) Cho. "The Korean Gay and Lesbian Movement 1993–2008: From 'Identity' and 'Community' to 'Human Rights.'" In *South Korean Social Movements: From Democracy to Civil Society*, ed. Gi-Wook Shin and Paul Chang, 206–23. London: Routledge, 2011.

Lee, Jin-Kyung. *Service Economies: Militarism, Sex Work, and Migrant Labor in South Korea*. Minneapolis: University of Minnesota Press, 2010.

Lee, Jooran. "Remembered Branches: Towards a Future of Korean Homosexual Film." *Journal of Homosexuality* 39, nos. 3–4 (2000): 273–81.

Lee, Namhee. *The Making of Minjung: Democracy and the Politics of Representation in South Korea*. Ithaca, NY: Cornell University Press, 2007.

Lee, Namhee. "The Theory of Mass Dictatorship: A Re-examination of the Park Chung Hee Period." *Review of Korean Studies* 12, no. 3 (September 2009): 41–69.

Lim, Jie-Hyun. "Mapping Mass Dictatorship: Towards a Transnational History of Twentieth Century Dictatorship." In *Gender Politics and Mass Dictatorship: Global Perspectives*, ed. Lim Jie-Hyun, 1–22. London: Palgrave, 2011.

Liu, Petrus. *Queer Marxism in Two Chinas*. Durham, NC: Duke University Press, 2005.

Moon, Seungsook. "Imagining a Nation through Differences: Reading the Controversy Concerning the Military Service Extra Points System in South Korea." *Review of Korean Studies* 5, no. 2 (December 2002): 73–109.

Na, Tari Young-Jung. "The South Korean Gender System: LGBTI in the Contexts of Family, Legal Identity, and the Military." *Journal of Korean Studies* 19, no. 2 (Fall 2014): 357–77.

Nam, Hwasook B. *Building Ships, Building a Nation: Korea's Democratic Unionism under Park Chung Hee*. Seattle: University of Washington Press, 2009.

Robertson, Jennifer. "Dying to Tell: Sexuality and Suicide in Imperial Japan." *Signs* 25, no. 1 (Autumn 1999): 1–35.

Rosenberg, Jordana, and Amy Villajero. "Introduction: Queerness, Norms, Utopia." *GLQ* 18, no. 1 (2012): 1–18.

Schaefer, Eric. "'I'll Take Sweden': The Shifting Discourses of the 'Sexy Nation' in Sexploitation Films." In *Sex Scene: Media and the Sexual Revolution*, ed. Eric Schaefer, 207–34. Durham, NC: Duke University Press, 2014.

Schaefer, Eric, ed. *Sex Scene: Media and the Sexual Revolution*. Durham, NC: Duke University Press, 2014.

Stryker, Susan, and Aren Z. Aizura. *The Transgender Studies Reader*, vol. 2. New York: Routledge, 2013.

Valdes, Francisco. "Unpacking Hetero-patriarchy: Tracing the Conflation of Sex, Gender and Sexual Orientation to Its Origins." *Yale Journal of Law and Humanities* 8, no. 1 (May 2013): 161–211.

Weston, Kath. "Families in Queer States: The Rule of Law and the Politics of Recognition." *Radical History Review* 93 (Fall 2005): 122–41.

Weston, Kath. *Families We Choose: Lesbians, Gays, Kinship*. New York: Columbia
University Press, 1991.

Weston, Kath. *Render Me, Gender Me: Lesbians Talk Sex, Class, Color, Nation, Studmuffins*.
New York: Columbia University Press, 1996.

Part II

CITIZENS, CONSUMERS, AND ACTIVISTS IN POSTAUTHORITARIAN TIMES

Chapter Seven

THE THREE FACES OF SOUTH KOREA'S MALE HOMOSEXUALITY

POGAL, IBAN, AND NEOLIBERAL GAY

John (Song Pae) Cho

> At nighttime, the park changes into a different face. Men who have been waiting for darkness wander and wait for someone. After meeting someone, they put their arms across the shoulders of the men that they have just met and disappear into the darkness.
>
> —SBS News Investigation, "Homosexuals Who Have Come Out into the Sun"

In recent years, postcolonial nations worldwide have been the site of vigorous new LGBT movements that both mimic and challenge Euro-American models of identity, sexuality, and citizenship.[1] Dubbed "queer globalization," this phenomenon has provoked debates over whether or not these Westernized projects herald an accelerated Americanization, the homogenization of gay culture, and the rise of the "global gay."[2] Yet a contradiction characterizes this process of queer globalization: its detour through "Queer Asia." Defying the thesis of queer globalization as Westernization, the processes of global queering in the early twenty-first century have led to an expanding regional network that links gay, lesbian, and transgender communities in China,

Hong Kong, Singapore, Taiwan, South Korea, Indonesia, and the Philippines, as well as in other rapidly developing societies in East and Southeast Asia.[3]

Observers of these LGBT identities in Asia have attributed the proliferation of new gender/sex categories and erotic cultures to the intersection of multiple influences, including globalizing market capitalism, intensifying hybridization of local and Western cultures and discourses, increasing rates of human movement through tourism and migration, and expanding international cooperation on issues such as HIV/AIDS prevention and human rights of gender/sex minorities. The Internet, cinema, and other technologies have also been seen as critical in unmooring these categories from their static and sedentary locations in the "West" and transplanting them to "Asia."[4]

Building on this emerging literature on Queer Asia, this chapter seeks to elucidate the three discursive constructions, or "faces," of male homosexuality within South Korea's modern history: *pogal, iban*, and *neoliberal gay*.[5] Given the abrupt and sometimes confusing change in sexual categories, I do not use the term "gay" to refer to transsexuals or transgender people, as was done until the mid-1990s; instead, I use it to describe men with a normatively "masculine" gender who are attracted to other men. Moreover, while both "pogal" and "iban" are emic terms used by different generations of gay men to describe themselves, "neoliberal gay" is an etic term that I have coined to describe the latest and most contemporary manifestation of being gay. As I argue, these three faces of male homosexuality can be mapped onto three equally distinct periods of South Korea's economic development—late developmentalist, liberal, and neoliberal—when the substantive elements of queer citizenship were negotiated in a reciprocal and noncontingent dialectic with the changing geopolitical identity and future of the nation.[6] In particular, they have emerged in dialectical interaction with a contradiction at the heart of the South Korean state's contemporary nation-building project: the simultaneous valorization of both "individual" and "family" (along with "company" and "nation") as the basic units of society.

In focusing on the three faces of South Korea's male homosexuality, this chapter contributes to the emerging scholarship on Queer Asia that has begun to articulate a counterdiscourse to the hegemonic Western queer scholarship anchored in post-Stonewall tropes of the "closet" and "coming out." According to the "classic" model of gay identity that emerged in the United States during the long period of economic prosperity under the social welfare state of Fordism, homosexuality involves (1) escaping the structure of the dominant heterosexual kinship system; (2) identifying with an exclusive gay identity; (3) forging same-sex bonds; (4) creating a large-scale social network; and (5) possessing self-awareness and group identity.[7] In contrast, within South Korea and other parts of Asia, as the film scholar Chris Berry points out, many queers refuse to exit the family in order to be gay. Moreover, although there are many marginal, elusive, and tacit homoerotic spaces that are generally invisible to the public, there are few structured gay communities with established roles, relationships, and hierarchies for them to define their identity.[8]

Rather than interpreting their refusal to come out of the family in order to be gay as tantamount to "being in the closet," scholars of Queer Asia have sought to identify the particular sociocultural and historical contexts that have made homosexuality a key site of ongoing contradiction and cultural hybridity within East Asia. For instance, contesting the assumption that capitalism and its system of wage labor liberate homosexuals to construct lifestyles centered on their non-normative sexuality, John Erni and Anthony Spires note how industrial modernity in Taiwan did not agitate cultural traditions such as familialism but has, instead, worked in conjunction with them.[9] As a result, while Taiwanese queers remain caught between the state and family, emerging queer consumer spaces provide "an opportunity to work out the relationship between gay and lesbian visibility and the cultural politics of family-centeredness in Taiwan."[10] Using the term "family politics," Erni and Spires have sought to distinguish the family-based cultural politics faced by Taiwanese queers from the class- (and race-)based identity politics that have characterized the Westernized gay and lesbian movement in the United States. In this volume, Layoung Shin also demonstrates the impact of family politics on the choices that young queer women in South Korea make in terms of their gendered self-presentation and partner selection. Following their lead, this chapter identifies the substantive meanings of Korean homosexuality—which are inflected by age, class, gender, and marital status—as they are shaped by the family governmentality of what I term "Confucian biopolitics." Confucian biopolitics can be considered the primary form of governance within communitarian and nonliberal societies in Asia, where the notion of (neo)liberal individualism remains an exception.[11]

Considering the "asocial individual" within liberalism to be a fundamentally alien concept, Confucian biopolitics has, instead, prioritized the collectivity of the family (and nation) as the primary manifestation of the social, to which individuals are expected to submit their personal will and desires. Such familialism not only inhibits the expression of homosexuality, except in highly discreet ways; it also creates the very shape and texture of queer lives in terms of space, temporality, and affect. Meanwhile, such Confucian influences can arguably be seen most vividly within South Korea, which takes pride in being the vanguard of Confucianism as "the foundational culture of everyday life of East Asians."[12]

This chapter also contributes to Korean studies. In recent years, feminists have contested the androcentric nature of South Korea's postcolonial nationalism that has constructed the nation as a homosocial bonding of hypermasculine men in response to the emasculating process of colonialism.[13] While critical in trying to recover the gendered figure of the subaltern, much postcolonial feminist scholarship on South Korea, in focusing almost exclusively on the opposing and asymmetrical forms of masculinity and femininity, has unwittingly reproduced the hetero-gendering of the postcolonial nation, which erases the lives and subjectivities of sexual minorities. Drawing on a queer critique of the postcolonial nation-state and "post-Orientalist" treatments of sexualities in Queer Asia, this chapter provides a detailed ethnography of Korean gay men's symbolic-political discourses of sex, nation, and citizenship.[14] It argues that even as Korean gay men contest the androcentric notion of Korean nationalism and citizenship in many ways, they reproduce it in other ways.

Korean gay men's contradictory stance toward heteronormative patriarchy may be seen to stem from their ambivalent position within Korean society, where "their access to 'normal life' is guaranteed" as long as "they do not cross the boundary of ghettos set by invisible rules in the society."[15] Interrogating the ways in which they become complicit with the dominant hypermasculinist and heteronormative system as they struggle to avoid a stigmatized sexual identity provides a unique window into the contradictory processes of subject formation within a technologically advanced and hyperconsumerist yet culturally conservative Korean society.

Following the work of Sharon Heijin Lee on cosmetic surgery, one could say there are no "average Third World gay men." According to Lee, there is a tendency on the part of "First World" feminists to homogenize "Third World" women as an oppressed group. However, Korean women confound this binary. Even as they embrace "traditional" roles such as motherhood, they also engage in "late modern" practices such as cosmetic surgery. Similarly, even though Korean gay men are oppressed by the heavily patriarchal nature of Korean society and its family-based heteronormative structures, they are simultaneously at the forefront of new consumerist and technology-based identities and lifestyles. Thus, rather than relying on simplistic binaries such as traditional-modern or First World–Third World, it is necessary to situate their lives within the sociohistorical and economic-technological circumstances of South Korea in particular, and Asia more generally.

This chapter is based on research that I conducted for my doctoral dissertation between 2007 and 2009 in Seoul. During the research, I conducted more than one hundred interviews with gay men, lesbians, and transgender people and conducted participant observation in gay chat rooms, queer political rallies, and Internet-based recreational clubs. This research was designed to investigate how the so-called first generation of gay men in South Korea refuse compulsory marriage to women, employing the Internet to flexibly navigate issues of emotional intimacy, sexual morality, and financial (in)security during a period of resurgent heteronormative familialism and extensive neoliberal restructuring. It also draws on the interviews and archival research that I conducted for my master's thesis on gay consumer spaces at Yonsei University in Seoul in 2001–2003, as well as my own personal experiences of living through a tumultuous period of South Korea's rapid transition from a late developmentalist to a liberal and then abruptly neoliberal socioeconomic environment from 1995 to 2003.[16]

The interviews were conducted with self-identified men whom I recruited online in Ivancity, a cyber-city of 150,000 gay netizens, and Daum, a mainstream portal that hosts more than 2,500 gay, lesbian, and transsexual groups. During these interviews, which were conducted within the privacy of my office-tel or in the semi-privacy of a coffee shop, I elicited personal narratives of how the gay men viewed and interpreted their lives vis-à-vis issues such as marriage and family. With the exception of one man, they spoke freely about their lives.[17] Some saw me as a mouthpiece for the community that they wanted to use to voice thoughts and feelings that they could not share publicly otherwise. For instance, one man stated a desire to write a book about his life "not from a political perspective, but to simply show the world that this is how gay men live, and that we are all human beings."

After transcribing the interviews, I engaged in the inductive process of building grounded theory by looking for keywords, tropes, and patterned narratives.[18] Thus, recognizing the intersubjectivity of ethnographic research, this research sought less to establish timeless truths than to theorize how certain forms and aesthetics of language arose within the flow of social life as conditioned by larger structures of capitalism, nationalism, and patriarchy.[19] For instance, one key trope that Korean men rely on to describe their experiences of being homosexual is being "in the dark." This trope can be seen to emerge from the socially ostracized nature of homosexuality, which is excluded from the state-sanctioned space of social recognition. It can also be seen to arise from gay men's experience of meeting one another in dimly lit or literally dark spaces, where their social identities are mutually protected. In other words, while recognizing the subjective nature of such narratives, this chapter also recognizes their character as "social facts" that are phenomenologically based, intersubjectively produced, and ultimately constrained by larger social structures and historical processes.[20] Following gay men's own usage, I have thus relied on these tropes to distinguish, for instance, the "dark" late developmentalist period from the "sunny" liberal democratic one.

The "Dark Period" of South Korea's Homosexuality during the Late Developmentalist Period (1970s to mid-1990s)

South Korea is considered the prototypical "hypermasculine developmentalist state" in East Asia.[21] After Japanese colonial rule (1910–45) and U.S. military occupation (1945–48), the Republic of Korea was established in 1948. Following the Korean War (1950–53)—the last armed confrontation between the two Cold War blocs, which left the peninsula the most heavily fortified line in the world— the postcolonial state engaged in a project of compressed modernization that mimicked the masculine process of colonization by denigrating anything that smacked of the "feminine."[22] In the process, the country became envisioned as a patrilineal community of hypermasculine men and hyperfeminized women.[23]

A key plank of this postcolonial nationalism was the ideology of economic development, which urged individuals to sacrifice for the building of a prosperous and strong Korean nation while excluding the Western values of liberal democracy and individualism. For instance, President Park Chung Hee (1917–79), credited with engineering South Korea's economic takeoff as one of the "Four Asian Tigers," was highly suspicious of such Western values, which he believed led not only to "social disorder but also [to] the weakening of Korean national consciousness."[24] Rejecting Western ideologies such as individual rights and freedom of expression, he exploited the hierarchical metaphor of familial relationships embodied in "Confucian Parental Governance" to mobilize the population for rapid economic development. In this mode of governance, the state was depicted "as father or husband, corporations as its first son, society as mother or wife, and factory workers as filial daughters."[25]

As a result of this authoritarian ideology of the family-state, official information about non-normative sexualities such as homosexuality was highly restricted during the developmentalist period of South Korean history, from the 1970s to the early 1990s.[26] For instance, during the height of the AIDS epidemic in the West in the 1980s, when it was first figured as a disease of foreigners residing in South Korea, a Korean news anchor stated, "South Korea has nothing to worry about since we have no homosexuals."[27] As indicated in the introduction of this volume, much of the history of homosexuality during the late developmentalist period (and earlier) is still being excavated—hence, the vagueness with which my discussion of homosexuality during this period begins. Nonetheless, as the contributions in this volume by Todd A. Henry and Chung-kang Kim demonstrate, the suppression of homosexuality during this period did not mean that unofficial and popular representations of non-normative sexualities were absent. In fact, both reports in weekly newspapers and in gender comedy films were rife with such representations, of which queer populations were shadow readers and viewers. Take, for instance, the account of "Mr. A," a successful, forty-seven-year-old married man and the owner of four after-school institutes, who engaged in homosexuality after visiting a theater where same-sex lovers gathered:

> Mr. A was watching a movie when a man fumbled for his hand. For some reason, the words "I don't like it" did not come out of his mouth. After the movie, when the two men talked, there was a certain connection. Wondering whether he might not be a same-sex lover, he had sex with the other man. Afterward, Mr. A stated, "Ah!" That "thing" that had always felt like a duty with his wife even after having two kids felt different with a man.[28]

In this quote, Mr. A comes to discover the carnal pleasure of homosexuality and his non-normative status as a "same-sex lover" through the affective connection of a fumbling hand in a dark theater. This pleasure is radically different from the heterosexual sex he has performed as a duty with his wife. Still, not only is homosexuality represented as something that one should not like; it is also represented as a chance happening. That is, in contrast to the Westernized medico-scientific view of homosexuality that—starting in the late nineteenth century and early twentieth century—began to view those with homoerotic interests as a distinct species of human beings, homosexuality within South Korea was seen as a perverted desire that ordinary men "fell" or were "seduced" into (*ppajida*), especially in the absence of female partners.[29] In other words, there appeared to be a complex process of the simultaneous representation, disavowal, and containment of homosexuality as a collective social identity during the late developmentalist period of South Korea.

Of course, the fact that Westernized notions of homosexuality as a social identity did not exist in South Korea during this period does not mean that Korean men did not harbor homoerotic desires for other men or actively seek out opportunities to enact them. For instance, with the country's strong division of the sexes (*namnyŏ yubyŏl*) into the outer, or public, space (*pakkat*) for men and the inner, or domestic, space (*an*) for women, both sexes had ample opportunities for homoerotic liaisons within sex-segregated institutions such as middle and high schools (for more, see Shin-ae Ha's chapter in this volume).[30]

The hypermasculine institution of the military, responsible for "creating citizens, and creating men," also provided a key setting for homoerotic experimentation.[31] As one gay man, "Sang-su," recalled, "Since the military is a place where hot-blooded youth gather, even if you engage in a little skinship, then it soon develops into a hand job." A Korean-English expression, "skinship" refers to the affectionate touching that often occurs between members of the same sex without necessarily being construed as sexual. Much of this behavior was understood not as homosexuality but as a natural form of intimacy between "younger and older brothers" or juniors and seniors at work or in school.[32] As one gay man, In-jae, noted, "Homosexuality is not something that can be easily pinned down in South Korea because there is a widespread belief that men can be intimate with each other, especially while intoxicated."

Finally, some gay men were likely to have had regular contact with gay American soldiers and other foreigners, such as gay Japanese and Asian businessmen, who had very different understandings of homosexuality, in spaces such as gay theaters during this period. Upon meeting these foreigners, some Koreans even traveled to foreign countries, including United States, Europe, and Southeast Asia, where they were further exposed to competing models of homosexuality. However, such men appear to have been in the minority, with the majority of Koreans—including gay Koreans—kept in the dark about the meaning of homosexuality as anything but a temporarily aberrant behavior. In fact, raising the fundamental question of whether homosexuality can be experienced as an identity without the discursive construction of it as such, many men during this period were confused and morally torn about their desires.

Meanwhile, without access to information about homosexuality, and with the widespread belief about homosexuality as dirty, immoral, and unnatural, many men during this period simply acceded to the pressures of the dominant heteronormative lifestyle. As another gay man, "YS," now married to a woman, put it, "Before marriage, I had no idea about homosexuality. Even though I engaged in skinship with other men, I did not realize that I was erotically attracted to them. All I thought was, 'Oh, he's a nice guy.' That was the extent of my understanding of my desires." Especially as they got older, many men of this period, known as the "386 generation," were swept up in the "chrononormativity" of South Korea's economic developmentalism.[33]

Following Dana Luciano, I define chrononormativity as "the "sexual arrangement of the time of life of entire populations."[34] That is, if the Confucian Parental Governance of the late developmentalist state installed the heterosexual nuclear family as the grounding of the postwar nation in South Korea, then this heterosexual nuclear family served to regulate the population not only spatially, in terms of a gendered division of labor between the public and private, but also temporally in terms of a heteronormative life course involving the "proper time" to get a job, get married, and have children. As Sang-su put it, "At the time, with the [per capita] GDP at $3,000, everyone's dream was not to enjoy themselves in terms of sex or leisure but to save enough money to buy a house. That was what distinguished the poor from the rich—whether they owned their own home or not."

So for most ordinary people, the biggest goal was to prepare a home to raise their family. During this period, so many men temporarily forgot about their homoerotic desires and got married that it would not be an exaggeration to say that the vast majority of this 386 generation now lead double lives as married gay men.[35]

As I discuss later, it was not until the Internet gained popularity in the late 1990s that many of these men would rediscover the "dark secret" of homosexuality that had been deeply buried within their hearts. Once again, following the trope of living in the dark, the men's figuration of homosexuality as a dark secret spoke to their understanding of sexuality as something deeply essential and innate but that nonetheless needed to be hidden and repressed. By breaking the state monopoly on information and "rupture[ing] the implied integrity of normative family and work life," the Internet would interpellate a growing number of men ensconced within the heart of the patriarchal nation—the heterosexual family—into Westernized subject positions as "homosexuals."[36]

Homosexuality of Pogal Such as Kim Kyŏng-min

While the majority of men during the period of South Korea's late developmentalism were pressured by hetero-family norms to marry women and lead ostensibly "normal" lives as heterosexual, patriarchal men, the tiny minority who did not were left to wander the hidden, homoerotic spaces of Seoul and other large cities as "ghosts."

Among these ghosts was Kim Kyŏng-min, the author of South Korea's first, and perhaps only, autobiography by a self-identified homosexual.[37] According to Kim, he had never once in his life suffered as a pogal. A reversal of the term *kalbo*—"the most vulgar term for a prostitute in Korea"—"pogal" was often used by same-sex lovers to refer to themselves before the democratizing and globalizing phase of the gay community in the mid-1990s, when "pogal" was replaced by "gay" and "iban."[38] Kim says, "Of course, in order not to suffer, I have had to engage in painstaking effort to build a careful wall of secrecy around my homosexuality and to live hiding behind that wall with my teeth clenched like a fugitive."[39]

Given the state of emergency following the Korean War, the trope of "refugee" is a well-worn one in Korean studies.[40] Less analyzed have been the tropes of "sexual refugee," "affective alien," and "internal exile."[41] Without a heterosexual nuclear family to anchor their desires or secure their social faces, homosexuals—like other social outcasts, including the main character in Yi Sang's *Wings* (see the chapter by John Whittier Treat in this volume)—became internal exiles estranged from mainstream society and its "reproductive futurism" based on marriage and children.[42] Experiencing not material but affective deprivation, they were forced to wander the urban landscape "to find sexual gratification and build social networks" even while hiding from their families and society at large to avoid sexual persecution.[43]

As Kim Kyŏng-min writes, while hiding behind a wall of secrecy meant safety, it also meant an intolerable sense of isolation: in being excluded from the web of sociality woven around the heterosexual nuclear family and its reproductive futurism, they were coerced into remaining as nonsocial subjects with "no future." Unable to withstand a sense of loneliness as "big as a mountain," Kim—like Mr. A—ventured into a theater in Chongno, Seoul, where same-sex lovers were reported to be gathering. Part of a subterranean pogal community in Nakwŏn-dong, Chongno had many gay bars where middle-aged and often married middle- and upper-middle-class gay men often gathered. It also had the infamous "P-Theater" (Pagoda Theater), a small theater that attracted more than one thousand pogal on holidays and weekends during its heyday in the 1970s and 1980s. The Pagoda Theater was often reported about in *Sunday Seoul* and other tabloids. "Chaplin," a man I interviewed in 2003, debuted in this homoerotic scene in 1977, when he was fifteen. He said, "On rainy days when there was a sad atmosphere, men would circle inside the dark theater looking for their partners."

This was Kim's "debut" (*tebwi*) on the Chongno pogal scene. Evoking the image of a debutante making her first entrance into high society or an actress making her first appearance onstage, South Korean gay men used the term "debut" to refer to their first appearance in homosexual society. Compared with the Westernized concept of "coming out," "debuting" was a "smaller form of coming out" to a limited audience of other pogal.[44] This notion of debuting, I argue, has instilled a very different meaning and logic in the act of coming out. In the inability to come out to their families and broader society, South Korean gay men—and activists—have instead prioritized the act of voluntarily revealing themselves to other gay men. Such debuting, therefore, discloses the oppressive nature of Korean society in which "only orphans are seen to come out." It also illuminates the South Korean gay and lesbian movement's particular historical and political mandate of fostering intimate ties between gay men as part of the larger task of creating a *hidden* community of support that I have termed "lifestyle politics."

In debuting, Kim Kyŏng-min established an alternative form of social recognition denied to him by Korean society. As he writes, "Was it because I went there knowing that it was a pogal theater? For some reason, everyone looked both like and unlike a pogal. Pushing aside my feeling of unease, I looked around the 'salon' of the Pagoda Theater when everyone suddenly turned around and directed their gazes at me."[45] Evoking the spaces of public civility and sociability that Jürgen Habermas credits with having created the public sphere of early modern and revolutionary France, gay men called the lounges within the theaters where they chatted and socialized "salons."[46] In gay men's case, however, these salons inaugurated an alternative space of sociality organized around stigmatized desires that Michael Warner elsewhere has termed a "queer counterpublic."[47]

Yet, if such spaces afforded stigmatized and invisible sexual subjects such as Kim Kyŏng-min with an alternative site of pogal identity, they also produced their own forms of sexual abjection. Without the affective anchor of heterosexual family or normative ideas of love to restrain their desires, same-sex lovers found themselves "forced to resort to repeated chance sexual encounters" to fulfill their sexual and affective needs.[48] As Kim writes, "Even though I inhaled and exhaled hot breaths of pleasure every time that I was in other men's embraces, the men were always like the wind."[49] To describe the liminality and contingency of gay desire that flowed underneath and through the crevices of institutionalized heteronormative life without a social anchor, gay men often employed the metaphors of "water" and "wind." As Sŏ Tong-jin, the country's first out gay activist, notes, "pogal" is thus a term of "self-degradation" for same-sex lovers "forced to live an overeroticized [and rootless] existence."[50] The reduction of gay men's relationships to the sexual may be seen as the most pernicious effect of the Korean state's suppression of homosexuality.

The "Sunlight" of South Korea's Democratization and Globalization from the Mid- to Late 1990s: Iban

With the democratization of South Korea in 1987 and its globalization drive (*segyehwa*) in 1993, South Korea experienced dramatic changes in how it understood homoerotic desires and homosexuality. From being seen as a foreign phenomenon confined to a few "perverted" individuals in South Korea, homosexuality would increasingly be recognized as part of Korean society. In particular, what I have termed the "historical coalition" of three organizations—the gay and lesbian movement, the gay bulletin board services (BBSes), and the gay consumer scene in I'taewŏn—provided the crucial factors of discourse, technology, and space for the growing institutionalization of homoerotic desire as a gay identity and community, as captured in the term "iban." Depending on how the Chinese character "*i*" in "iban" is written, it can mean a "different" or "second-class" class of people from *ilban*—or heterosexuals—who are viewed as a "general" or "dominant/universal" class of people.

Mirroring the development of gay and lesbian movements in other Asian countries (notably, Taiwan), Korea's first gay and lesbian organization, Ch'odonghoe, was founded in 1993, after the onset of democracy in 1987. Although Ch'odonghoe disbanded within weeks of its founding due to internal conflicts between gay men and lesbian women, it was quickly replaced by the gay men's Ch'ingusai (Between Friends) in February 1994 and the lesbian organization Kkiri Kkiri (Among Ourselves) in November 1994.

Nonetheless, due to the reluctance of the members of both organizations to reveal their faces to the public, it was not until the coming out of the gay activists Sŏ Tong-jin, in March 1995, and Yi Chŏng-u, in May 1995, that the South Korean public caught its first glimpse of self-avowed homosexuals. Unlike "same-sex lovers," these gay men began to view their homosexuality as a core essence of their personal and public identities. As Sŏ put it, "I feel that it is necessary that I, and many other homosexuals, must speak of homosexuality—the reason for our unhappiness—if we are ever to overcome this unhappiness."[51] In focusing on the issue of individual happiness, Sŏ joined feminists and youth during this liberalizing period in "strongly contesting the nationalist discourse of economic development that has repressed the individual as the subject of civil rights."[52]

With the coming out of Sŏ and Yi—students at the elite institutions of Yonsei University and Seoul National University (SNU), respectively—the trickle of news stories about homosexuality, which had been mostly restricted to tabloids such as *Sunday Seoul*, became a flood. The host of an episode of the Korean Broadcasting Station program *Tokjŏm Yŏsŏng*, titled "Another Type of Love: Homosexuality," which aired on December 9, 1995, commented:

> Within our society, there are those who cannot show their faces. They are the "faces in the shadow." Now, however, homosexuals have started organizing themselves with the founding of Ch'ingusai, the country's first gay group, and the formation of homosexual groups on college campuses, including SNU and Yonsei. As they begin to proudly show their faces and raise their voices, what are the stories they want to tell? And how should we view their homosexual love? They say that theirs is "another type of love" and that they just want to live proudly as members of our society.

With the flood of discourses about homosexuality, the number of gays and lesbians calling the hotline at Ch'ingusai and Kkiri Kkiri also spiked. Many of their questions were directed less at the issue of coming out than at the issue of how to meet other homosexuals and, in some cases, how to become straight. Thus, for many homosexuals, the most important issues were those of identity and companionship: how to understand their "deviant" sexuality and meet other people for love, sex, and friendship.

Playing a key role in addressing these concerns were the technological services of the BBSes—simple text-based chat rooms and discussion boards on the servers of South Korea's three largest personal computer communication providers, Hait'el, Ch'ŏllian, Naunuri—and "153," a national telephone answering service run by Korea Telecom where people could leave one another one- to two-minute messages. Both services played a key role in enabling hidden gay men and lesbians to communicate and to circulate large volumes of forbidden information that previously had been confined to the dark.

They also enabled these newly interpellated "gay men and lesbian women" to create a nationwide community infrastructure. According to one gay man, Hyŏn-kyu, whom I interviewed in 2002 about his experiences with BBSes, when he overcame his initial fear of other homosexuals and entered the chat rooms to chat with them, he was surprised by their ordinariness. As he stated, "Talking to the people in the chat room, my stereotypes of them as strange people came crashing down. I found out that they could not be more like me. They were *just like me*, having gone through the same worries that I had when I was young and living the same *ordinary lives* that I was living now." The term "ordinary" (*p'yŏngbŏm*) was one that I often heard gay men use when I lived in South Korea from the mid-1990s to the early 2000s. For instance, many of them commented on how their most cherished dream was to meet a man who was "ordinary" in appearance (*p'yŏngbŏm han oemo*), had an "ordinary" job (*p'yŏngbŏm han chikjang*) and an "easygoing" personality (*munanhan sŏnggyŏk*), with whom they could settle down to a "quiet life" (*choyonghan salm*) of domestic bliss away from the sex- and consumer-oriented gay life.

On one hand, Hyŏn-kyu's comment about other gay men's and lesbians' ordinariness spoke to the same process of homogenization that they had undergone within the totalitarian culture of South Korea under the successive military dictatorships, when it was "dangerous for an individual to think or act from different subject positions other than that of one's national or familial identity."[53] On the other hand, it spoke to their *normality*. In contrast to the state-sponsored media portrayals of gay men as strange people with perverted desires who existed only in the West, they were ordinary, if invisible, members of Korean society. In other words, if Western scholars have emphasized gender/sexual nonconformity as the radical end point of queer politics, then for Korean men who had been excluded from the very category of humanity, simply existing as ordinary members of society can be considered the most transgressive act of all.[54]

At first, the organizers of the gay BBS chat rooms were content to let these individuals chat among themselves and discover their ordinariness. Later, however, they began to organize these gays and lesbians into off-line groups through regular meetings known as *chŏngmos*. If gay men were like "wind" or "water" that slipped invisibly through the crevices of heteronormative society, then these regular off-line meetings provided them with a social and temporal structure to tie them together. Such acts of gathering spatially dispersed men and giving them a structure to forge ties of sociality and conviviality are, once again, what I have termed the lifestyle politics of East Asian queers. These lifestyle politics can be seen to both fall short of *and* exceed the narrow scope of rights-based activism through which Western scholars have envisioned gay empowerment and queer future.[55]

In organizing these chŏngmos, BBS groups needed a space that could accommodate the large crowds of 100–150 people who eventually showed up. As noted earlier, there was already a hidden scene of pogal theaters and gay bars in Nakwŏn-dong, Chongno. However, not only was it dominated by married gay men, but it was also heavily oriented toward sex. In contrast, the newly emergent gay space of It'aewŏn provided a nonsexualized alternative within the queer counterpublic. Thus complicating Warner's conceptualization of the term, Korean gay men felt compelled to create a space of public civility and sociality *within* an overly sexualized queer counterpublic to create their own "quasi-intermediary civil society."[56] Due to its close proximity to the U.S. military base in Yongsan and its large deployment of American soldiers, who provided a painful reminder of South Korea's politically divided status, It'aewŏn was formerly known as an "alien" and "abandoned" space in South Korea.[57] As an alien space less subjected to the discipline of the state and the surveillance of its neighbors, it provided an ideal setting for the emergence of Westernized gay bars and dance clubs where the growing membership of gay BBS organizations, along with other gay organizations, could gather and socialize.

Kki and the Expression of an Inner Homosexual Self

Coming off-line for the first time, many gay men were cautious and afraid. As one gay man, "Yukino," put it, "Since I had much prejudice about homosexuality, it was, at first, scary coming off-line into this night culture associated with taboo subjects. For instance, I worried about falling into this gay lifestyle and becoming like these people who I heard were dirty, engaged in group sex, and transmitted diseases." Interacting with other men, gay men like Yukino found the gay culture to be much "healthier" (*kŏnjŏn hada*) than they had initially imagined. As they began to explore "bodily pleasures" within these consumer spaces, they also learned to liberate themselves from "the rigid bodily habits and dogmatic fashion codes" of the older generation.[58] As one gay man, Bun-dang, put it, "I do not look like it, but I really like going to clubs. When I listen to loud music and shake my body, I get this uncanny feeling, as if my eardrums are about to burst and my internal organs are going to explode." To describe this "uncanny feeling," gay men often used the word *kki*. Partly derived from *ki* (life force), *kki* signified a unique talent, creativity, or energy within a given person.[59] Within the gay culture, it was often used in the expression *kki tulda* (to act in an exaggerated feminized manner or to be campy). During the community-building phase of the gay and lesbian movement, gay organizations such as Ch'ingusai often frowned on this type of behavior, believing that it expressed the internalized homophobia of gay men who thought they were women rather than men. In Bun-dang's comment, however, it referred to the feeling being alive as a gay individual despite the sadness and loneliness of being symbolically excluded from the imaginaries of the Korean family and nation.

As the English-language copy of a poster for "All About Sex, Dance, and Music," a celebration of the first anniversary of the gay dance club "G," in It'aewŏn, put it:

> Have you ever had it?
> We are family
> What is [sic] that mean being GAY?
> I had enough but I want more
> Are you ready to open?
> Something inside of you
> Take that, would you do what I ask you to do
> Feel free cuz I'm ready for it
> Cum on in and Enjoy
> Get Me!—Do Me—Fuck Me
> Those three words you need to ask me to be free tonight!

Thus, while gayness once meant loneliness and unhappiness by reducing homosexuality to pleasurable but highly individualized and transient sexual encounters, these collective displays of gay sociality—which subordinated overt sexual acts to public rituals of gay courtship and friendship—provided "a radical vision of intimacy, sexual identity, and belonging that deviates from the normative model of the privatized conjugal couple and nuclear family."[60]

According to gay men who lived through this liberalizing period of South Korean history, with the formation of the gay consumer scene in It'aewŏn, the countenances of Korean gay men became brighter. There was also a growing sense of community energy as captured in the term "iban." As Sŏ writes, iban "indicate[d] a new consciousness of the homosexual community as a social group only vaguely differentiated from heterosexuals."[61]

The IMF Crisis and the "Neoliberal Gay" (from 1998 to Present)

South Korea saw a radical transformation in the conditions for gay men's negotiation of their desire after the Asian financial crisis, which began in 1997–1998. This cataclysmic event is more popularly referred to as the "IMF Crisis" in South Korea. On one hand, the crisis prompted a radical transformation in the country's mode of governance. From a late developmentalist mode of capital accumulation based on state-directed manufacturing, the engine of economic growth shifted to a neoliberal mode of capital accumulation based on finance and individual enterprise and creativity.

At the same time, the mass layoff of male heads of middle-class households provoked widespread panic about the collapse of the patriarchal family and nation. In response, the Korean state revived the older ideology of "family as nation," prompting the retreat and reprivatization of progressive movements such as the women's movement, which had "enjoyed a liberalizing social environment during the decade leading up to the crisis."[62] As Jesook Song notes, during this period "newspaper editorials [also] took note of families of same-sex couples (tongsŏng'ae kajok) and divorce among 'silver' (or elderly) couples (hwangho ihon) as signs of family breakdown."[63]

Caught in the crosshairs of these contradictory changes was the emergent gay and lesbian community. While the valorization of entrepreneurial individualism helped to fuel the dramatic growth of the Korean gay and lesbian community, particularly as a sexual consumer market, the renewed valorization of the ideology of family as nation ensured that this community and market would remain privatized and hidden from the mainstream public. Deploying the metonym of family as nation, the South Korean state used family, employment, and other social benefits to discriminate against non-married members of society and discipline non-normative populations who did not belong to the heterosexual nuclear family.

Adding a further layer of complexity to these contradictory trends was the growing transformation of South Korea into an Internet "powerhouse." Intended to catapult South Korea into the ranks of "advanced" countries and open up new markets for postindustrial capitalistic competition, the Internet did that and more. It also spawned new online gay communities both on gay platforms such as Ivancity and on mainstream platforms such as Daum. Much of this particular cyberculture (i.e., chat rooms, bulletin boards, and instant messaging), however, remains hidden from the Korean public—calling into question the significance of this thriving online form of sociality for the everyday lives of gay men in South Korea.

During my field research in Seoul from 2007 to 2009, I discovered that Ivancity and Daum provided two very different pathways to being gay in post-IMF South Korea. One pathway involved Korean gay men exploiting the anonymous freedom of Ivancity to experiment with diverse identities, desires, and activities, including sexual hookups known as *pŏnseksŭ* (lit., lightning sex). Modeled after the flexible economy of part-time contractual labor that characterized the broader transformation of Korean economy, these activities helped to assuage feelings of loneliness and boredom and transform sexual abjection into pleasure. With the passage of time, gay men often found that there was a heavy price to be paid for this Internet-based sexual freedom. The very ability to log on and off and to engage and disengage at will was precisely what made these online interactions highly unstable and contingent.[64] In other words, if the flexibility of part-time contractual labor made the lives of workers highly precarious, then the flexibility of pŏnseksŭ made the lives of gay men more socially insecure, emotionally unsatisfying, and often physically draining, given the need to constantly seek out new partners. Viewed through the hetero-norms of long-term and binding personal relationships, they also could not "but stand out as something purely negative, an absence and an evil."[65] As Ivancity became increasingly an erotic market, gay men ultimately found themselves "alone together" within a body- and class-stratified online space, where they continuously had to develop themselves and their bodies to remain marketable as sexual subjects.[66]

Another pathway involved Korean gay men responding to the seeming sexual immorality and social immaturity of gay men on Ivancity by establishing on Daum hundreds of gay Internet-based clubs called *tonghohoes*, with hundreds of thousands of *mini-hompys* (personalized web pages). Oriented around a shared hobby or interest, such as swimming or skiing, these gay tonghohoes met off-line, once a week on the weekend, in a discreet public setting. Within a physical setting where the gay men were readily identifiable as an "ethico-legal subject" with a unique body and social identity, they were forced to exercise self-restraint and be properly respectful to others.[67] In turn, such civility allowed the men to fashion a gay lifestyle and queer future beyond the reproductive futurism of the heterosexual family and its children as the cornerstone on which the South Korean state had staked its own uncertain future.

Nonetheless, the intensification of neoliberal reforms after the IMF Crisis brought about a challenge of a different kind: financial insecurity. Facing open discrimination within South Korea's hypermasculinist and family-oriented workplace and a bleak future without the imagined support of wives and children, many single gay men in their thirties and forties were forced to retreat and retire from the gay community to focus on self-development and financial security. This retreat and retirement of single gay men in post-IMF South Korea, which occurred at the same time that married gay men known as "bats" (a transliteration of the Korean word *pakch'wi*) were emerging as a powerful sexual constituency within the Korean gay community, highlighted the paradoxical importance of the heterosexual family as a primary source of affective, social, and financial support during a time of heightened neoliberal individualism.[68] It also disclosed the fragility of South Korea's sexual democracy against the excesses of neoliberal capitalism.

The Retreat and Retirement of Single Gay Men in Post-IMF South Korea

Best exemplifying this retreat and retirement of single gay men into the heterosexual fold of their blood families was "Ka-in," a South Korean gay man who had debuted into the gay community in the late 1980s, around the time of the 1988 Olympics in Seoul, when terms such as "pogal" and "homo" were more popular than "gay" and "iban." During my interview with Ka-in, I discovered that his name was actually derived from the English name "Cain"—as in Cain and Abel. Illustrating the moral ambivalence that many gay men felt toward their homosexuality, Ka-in said that he had chosen the name because he felt caught between the "worlds of good and evil"—the heterosexual world that he was loathe to leave and the homosexual world that he found himself drawn to in spite of himself. Ka-in also illustrated the increasingly powerful desire for marriage and family—as the primary seat of intimacy and economic security during neoliberal restructuring—among gay men, even as his own working-class background foreclosed his access to it.

Like many gay men I spoke to, Ka-in was shy and reserved at home and in school. His gay life, however, was an entirely different matter. With his soft, feminine demeanor and youth, he attracted instant attention at gay bars from other gay men, to a point that he said that he thought that he was the "best" (*ch'oego*). As he recalled:

> At home and in school I was quiet and reserved—one of those children whose heads the teachers counted during roll call but otherwise ignored. In gay bars, however, I was completely different. The student whom no one paid any attention to in school became an object of attention in the bars. While the madams bought me drinks so I would visit their bars often, older men offered me spending money. From being an extra in a movie, I had become its star.

With Chongno only thirty minutes from his home, Ka-in said, he soon became immersed in the world of gay bars. Arriving home just before midnight when the last bus stopped running, he would either knock on his younger brother's window or quietly climb through his bedroom window using a garbage bin and then go to bed. However, Ka-in was approaching forty and felt increasingly insecure about his future. "There are probably many gay men who share my thoughts," he said. "I am the eldest son in my family. As I watch my parents get older and people around me—both gay and straight—get married, I wonder whether there is anything that I have done properly. There is nothing. Even though I think that I have worked hard, there is nothing left."

Ka-in said that he had actually become what he had once despised and dreaded, an older gay man: "Before, I could not understand ajŏssis (middle-aged men) who offered me spending money to be with them. But in the blink of an eye, I also became older. What will happen if I continue to be alone like this? My forties will quickly pass, followed by my fifties. At least my parents are still alive now. But I do not think I can keep living the way that I have been living." With his greatest fear that of becoming a "pathetic (ch'ora han) white-haired grandfather who chased after young men," Ka-in said that his biggest goal now was to get married so he would have a wife to look after him in his old age. He said that he also wanted the "fun" of raising children: "With only one life to live, I would feel bitter (ŏgul hada) if I died without having lived an ordinary life like other people."

As with the wholesale application of the term "homonormativity" to local contexts (as critiqued in Layoung Shin's chapter in this volume), it is easy to conflate this desire for ordinariness as embodied by the heterosexual nuclear family and its normative life course with the "aspirational normalcy" of neo-liberal life as discussed by Lauren Berlant.[69] According to Berlant, "aspirational normalcy" is "the desire to feel normal and to feel normalcy as a ground of dependable life, a life that does not have to keep being invented" during a period of intensive economic restructuring in which the "tattered family" has become "the only institution of reciprocity remaining for fantasy to attach itself to."[70] To do so, however, would elide the postcolonial history of South Korea, especially immediately after the Korean War, when in the absence of any stable institution, including the state or family, the desire for an ordinary life became deeply implanted in the minds of all Koreans as a widely shared postcolonial fantasy. Like all fantasy structures, this desire seemed to be most powerful among those denied access to it by virtue of their sexuality and economic background.

If gay men like Ka-in sought to retreat into the fold of the heterosexual family in order to secure a sense of normalcy but were prevented from doing so by virtue of their low economic status, other men turned toward money as the only form of security in a neoliberal world. As one gay man put it:

> In this community, there are no restraints (*kusok*). Even though one might call someone one's boyfriend, there's no legal commitment. No matter how much you might like the other person, the relationship can break up anytime, leading to a potential crisis. If the relationship breaks up, who can you believe? The money that you have saved is the only thing you can believe. In any case, because you are a minority, the world is unfair. Money can supplement some of the things you seek. It can help alleviate some of the social injustice.

Indeed, in the absence of faith in human relationships, many gay men turned to money as the only form of financial and affective security, leading to the creation of what I have termed the "neoliberal gay man" in post-IMF South Korea.

Conclusion

In this chapter, I have painted a portrait of the three "faces" of South Korea's homosexuality, a metaphor that Koreans undoubtedly will find odd to describe the LGBT population within the country. Despite the efflorescence of gay consumer spaces in It'aewŏn and Chongno, the tens of thousands of online groups and off-line Internet-based clubs, and the recent boom in cinematic depictions of homosexuality, "ordinary" homosexuals remain invisible within Korean public life. As the title of one short film by the gay filmmaker Kim Kyŏng-muk states, they remain *Faceless Things* (2005).[71]

Perhaps the metaphor of "faces" indexes what Korean gay men thus far have been denied: access to social recognition as human beings within a society based on the heterosexual nuclear family. Within such a social order governed by what I have called Confucian biopolitics and its moral system of family values, their existence becomes an impossible perversity. They are seen not only as disrupting the binary gender system and interrupting the reproduction of the patrilineal family on which the state bases its own viability as a nation-state, but also as upsetting the natural social order, causing chaos, and leaving the nation-state exposed to "foreign" diseases such as AIDS. In other words, despite its social invisibility, male homosexuality has the symbolic power to represent all of the moral hazards and social ills of globalization, thus rupturing the collective fantasy that "Koreans can globalize their economy but not themselves, nor their relationships."[72]

As this chapter has demonstrated, however, homosexuality is not a "foreign Other" that has been imported only recently into the country as part of the phenomenon of globalization. It likely has always existed as a "proximate Other" within the nation itself. As Jonathan Dollimore notes, "Within metaphysical constructions of the Other what is typically occluded is the significance of the *proximate*—i.e., that which is (1) adjacent and *there-by* related temporally or spatially, or (2) that which is approaching . . . and thus (3) the opposite of *remote* or *ultimate*."[73] In other words, in contrast to "distant Others," such as foreign laborers and marriage migrants who have more recently challenged "the 'pure blood' ideology . . . in [South] Korea," homosexuality—as a shadowy and faceless Other—can be viewed as likely having always existed in close proximity to and tension with the heterosexual family ever since, if not before, the founding of the modern Korean nation.[74] Hence, the hysterical blindness that has accompanied the hyper (in)visibility of homosexuality as a complex system of *"permissions and prohibitions, presence and absence."*[75] For if homosexuality is Other, through its proximity, then it also threatens to "trackback into the 'same,'" thereby revealing the sexual alterity and other forms of difference that have always been present but suppressed by the homogenizing discourses of nationalism.[76]

Seizing on these contradictions, queer activists in South Korea have relied on the Westernized discourses of gay and lesbian identity to try to interpolate diverse sexual practices and identities formerly known as pogal into a Westernized form of community. Although they briefly succeeded during the community-building phase of the gay and lesbian movement from the mid-1990s to the early 2000s, their efforts quickly were undermined by the family-based restructuring that accompanied South Korea's transition from a late developmentalist to a liberal, then a neoliberal, economy from the late 1990s onward. As a result, even as the ghostly apparition of the consuming gay subject is now being incorporated into the legal order as a sexual citizen, older and formerly middle-class members of the gay community are being forced to retreat and retire from the gay culture as insecure neoliberal actors without the real and imagined protection of wives and children. As Henry writes within this volume, the family-state of South Korea thereby seeks to contain the insurrectionary potential of sexuality to disrupt family and national life.

Within this context, it is more imperative than ever to understand, alongside the broader wave of social conservatism, the role of heteronormative familialism in redisciplining both normative and non-normative populations into the world of work, self-discipline, and frugality. How is it that many in

South Korea dream of social change, including leading different lives, but are unable to follow their ideals due to their sense of family loyalty and responsibility as parents or children? How is it that the institution of family creates feelings of warmth and safety but also demands unconditional sacrifice? How is it that gay men—without wives and children—experience not only abject feelings of loneliness but also the giddiness of dizzying possibilities? Perhaps therein lies the paradoxical nature of homosexuality in South Korea: the ability of queers to craft new forms of intimate and social life beyond the heterosexual nuclear family by virtue of their estrangement *and* partial freedom from the normative constraints of the family.

Finally, with the ongoing clashes between gay activists and the Christian right mentioned by Henry (see the introduction in this volume) and the recent use of gay dating apps by the Korean military to root out and entrap gay military personnel, one might wonder whether the moment of (neo)liberal community building enacted by the Internet in South Korea is decisively ending, ushering in a new period of neofascism in Korean history.[77] Given that "no hegemonic discourse or master narrative" of homosexuality has been able to develop within South Korea, it is more likely that individual and collective performances of (neo)liberal community building via sex, affect, and consumption will coexist with neofascist acts of "hunting gays" by the Korean military, even as other branches of the government gesture toward gentler forms of homophobia.[78]

Notes

Epigraph: SBS News Investigation (*Nyusŭ Ch'ujŏk*), "Homosexuals Who Have Come Out into the Sun" (*Yangjiro naon tongsŏng'ae*), June 9, 1998.

1   Elizabeth A. Povinelli and George Chauncey, "Thinking Sexuality Transnationally," GLQ 5 (1999): 439–50. I take inspiration for the title of this chapter from Pil Ho Kim and C. Colin Singer, "Three Periods of Korean Queer Cinema: Invisible, Camouflage, and Blockbuster," *Acta Koreana* 14, no. 1 (2011): 115–34. Kim and Singer break the history of Korean queer cinema into three distinct chronological periods—the Invisible Age (1976–98), the Camouflage Age (1998–2005), and the Blockbuster Age (2005–present)—according to the manner in which queer content was displayed and received by the public and government authorities.

2   Dennis Altman, *Global Sex* (Chicago: University of Chicago Press, 2001).

3   See, e.g., Evelyn Blackwood, *Falling into the Lesbi World: Desire and Difference in Indonesia* (Honolulu: University of Hawai'i Press, 2010); Fran Martin, *Situating Sexualities: Queer Representation in Taiwanese Fiction, Film and Public Culture*

(Hong Kong: Hong Kong University Press, 2003); Mark McLelland, *Queer Japan from the Pacific War to the Internet* (Oxford: Rowman and Littlefield, 2005); Ara Wilson, *The Intimate Economies of Bangkok: Tomboys, Tycoons, and Avon Ladies in the Global City* (Berkeley: University of California Press, 2004).

4   Chris Berry, Fran Martin, and Audrey Yue, eds. *Mobile Cultures: New Media in Queer Asia* (Durham, NC: Duke University Press, 2003).

5   Gerard Sullivan and Peter A. Jackson, eds., *Gay and Lesbian Asia: Culture, Identity, Community* (New York: Routledge, 2001).

6   I follow Petrus Liu in formulating this conception of homosexuality as a historically constituted discursive artifact: see Petrus Liu, "Queer Marxism in Taiwan," *Inter-Asia Cultural Studies* 8, no. 4 (2007): 517–39. These three distinct periods are, more than anything, heuristic devices. Though there is a clear historical break between the discursive categories of *pogal* and *iban*, the category of *iban* currently coexists alongside Westernized terms, such as *gay* and *queer*, as "little whirlpools, each with their own centripetal force" within a society where no hegemonic discourse or master narrative of homosexuality has been able to develop: Dong-Jin Seo [Sŏ Tong-jin], "Mapping the Vicissitudes of Homosexual Identities in South Korea," *Journal of Homosexuality* 40, nos. 3–4 (2001): 65–78.

7   Peter Drucker, "The Fracturing of LGBT Identities under Neoliberal Capitalism." *Historical Materialism* 19, no. 4 (2011): 3–32; Barry D. Adam, *The Rise of a Gay and Lesbian Movement* (Boston: Twayne, 1987), quoted in Martin Manalansan, "In the Shadows of Stonewall: Examining Gay Transnational Politics and the Diasporic Dilemma," *GLQ* 2 (1995): 428.

8   Chris Berry, "Asian Values, Family Values: Film, Video, and Lesbian and Gay Identities," in Sullivan and Jackson, *Gay and Lesbian Asia*, 211–32.

9   John D'Emilio, "Capitalism and Gay Identity," in *Powers of Desire: The Politics of Sexuality*, ed. Ann Snitow, Christine Stansell, and Sharan Thompson (New York: Monthly Review, 1983), 100–114.

10   John N. Erni and Anthony Spires, "The Formation of a Queer-Imagined Community in Post-Martial Law Taiwan," in *Asian Media Studies: Politics of Subjectivities*, ed. John Erni and Chua Siew Keng (Malden, MA: Blackwell, 2005), 227.

11   Younghan Cho, "The National Crisis and De/constructing Nationalism in South Korea during the IMF Intervention," *Inter-Asia Cultural Studies* 9, no. 1 (2008): 82–96; Beng Huat Chua, *Communitarian Politics in Asia* (London: Routledge, 2004); Aihwa Ong, *Neoliberalism as Exception: Mutations in Citizenship and Sovereignty* (Durham, NC: Duke University Press, 2006). In this volume, Todd A. Henry and Layoung Shin also reiterate the limits of neoliberal individualism as the primary locus of queer agency and politics within South Korea.

12   Chua, *Communitarian Politics in Asia*, 202; Sea-ling Cheng, "Assuming Manhood: Prostitution and Patriotic Passions in Korea," *East Asia* 18, no. 4 (2000): 40–78.

13   Hae-joang Cho Han, "'You Are Entrapped in an Imaginary Well': The Formation of Subjectivity within Compressed Development—A Feminist Critique of Modernity and Korean Culture," *Inter-Asia Cultural Studies* 1, no. 1 (2000): 49–69;

Chungmoo Choi, "Nationalism and Construction of Gender in Korea," in *Dangerous Women: Gender and Korean Nationalism*, ed. Elaine H. Kim and Chungmoo Choi (New York: Routledge, 1998), 9–31; Hyun-Mee Kim, "Work, Nation and Hypermasculinity: The 'Woman' Question in the Economic Miracle and Crisis in South Korea," *Inter-Asia Cultural Studies* 2, no. 1 (2001): 53–68; Frantz Fanon, *Black Skin, White Masks* (New York: Grove, [1967] 2008); Ashis Nandy, *The Intimate Enemy: Loss and Recovery of Self under Colonialism* (Oxford: Oxford University Press, [1983] 2010).

14 Ara Wilson, "Queering Asia," *Intersections* 14 (2006), http://intersections.anu.edu.au/issue14/wilson.html.

15 Youngshik D. Bong, "The Gay Rights Movement in Democraticizing Korea," *Korean Studies* 32 (2008): 86–103.

16 I suggest that South Korea is an exemplary site to understand the contradictions among politics, economy, family, gender, sexuality, space, information, and technology, whose articulation constitutes what Judith [Jack] Halberstam terms the "queer time and place" of gay life: see Judith [Jack] Halberstam, *In a Queer Time and Place: Transgender Bodies, Subcultural Lives* (New York: New York University Press, 2005). One reason for this is the highly compressed nature of its gay history; another is the densely populated and hyperconnected nature of this country. Together, they render starkly visible the dynamics between the aforementioned elements that might otherwise remain naturalized and invisible in other parts of the world.

17 This one man expressed impatience with the interview and my questions to issues that he said were ones that "everyone already knew"—"everyone" meaning gay men. Thus there appeared to be the assumption of the homogenous and self-evident nature of gay experiences that did not need any further interrogating. In this case, I promptly ended the interview.

18 Kathy Charmaz, *Constructing Grounded Theory* (London: Sage, 2014).

19 Vincent Crapanzano, *Hermes' Dilemma and Hamlet's Desire: On the Epistemology of Interpretation* (Cambridge, MA: Harvard University Press, 1992); Johannes Fabian, "Ethnography and Intersubjectivity: Loose Ends," *HAU: Journal of Ethnographic Theory* 4, no. 1 (2014): 199–209.

20 Émile Durkheim, "What Is a Social Fact?" in *The Rules of the Sociological Method*, ed. Steven Lukes (New York: Free Press, 1982), 50–59.

21 J. W. Han and L. H. M. Ling, "Authoritarianism in the Hypermasculinized State: Hybridity, Patriarchy, and Capitalism in Korea," *International Studies Quarterly* 42, no. 1 (1999): 53–78.

22 Bruce Cumings, *Korea's Place in the Sun: A Modern History* (New York: W. W. Norton, 1997), quoted in Cheng, "Assuming Manhood," 63.

23 Seungsook Moon, "Begetting the Nation: The Androcentric Discourse of National History and Tradition in South Korea," in *Dangerous Women: Gender and Korean Nationalism*, ed. Elaine H. Kim and Chungmoo Choi (New York: Routledge, 1998), 33–66.

24 Moon, "Begetting the Nation," 37. The "Four Asian Tigers" refers to Hong Kong, Singapore, South Korea, and Taiwan, which were able to achieve exceptionally high economic growth between the 1960s and 1990s.

25 Kim, "Work, Nation and Hypermasculinity," 1.

26 It is unclear when gay culture emerged during the developmentalist period of Korean history. One account dates it to the mid-1980s: see Seo, "Mapping the Vicissitudes of Homosexual Identities in South Korea." However, one of my informants, "Chaplin," recalls participating in a Seoul gay culture organized around theaters and bars since 1978.

27 Pak/Ch'a Min-jŏng, "AIDS p'aenik hogŭn kwaedam ŭi chŏngch'i," *Mal kwa Hwal* 12 (Summer 2016): 35–48; Ch'aeyun Han, "Chronicle," *Buddy*, April 26, 2002, 20.

28 Eun-young Park, "The Country's First 'Men's Room': What Are They Like?" *Sunday Newspaper*, June 8, 1997, 39.

29 Pyong-choon Hahm, *Korean Jurisprudence, Politics, and Culture* (Seoul: Yonsei University Press, 1986).

30 Hae-joang Cho, "Male Dominance and Mother Power: The Two Sides of Confucian Patriarchy in Korea," in *Confucianism and the Family*, ed. Walter H. Slote and George A. De Vos (Albany: State University of New York Press, 1998), 187–207.

31 Cheng, "Assuming Manhood," 53.

32 Koreans use these biological terms for intimate intergenerational male relations, not just for biological siblings, reflecting the broader conception of South Korea as a network of kin-based relationships.

33 Popularized in the early 2000s during the administration of Roh Moo-hyun, a former human rights lawyer elected president of South Korea (2003–2008), the term "386 generation" referred to people then in their thirties who were educated in the 1980s and born in the 1960s.

34 Dana Luciano, *Arranging Grief: Sacred Time and the Body in Nineteenth Century America* (New York: New York University Press, 2007).

35 I emphasize the membership of this older generation of married gay men within the 386 generation to highlight how their intimate lives were sacrificed at the altar of South Korea's economic development, based on strict binary notions of gender and strong heteronormative ideas of happiness and success, even as they were active in overthrowing the South Korea's military dictatorship as part of the Pro-Democracy Movement. In other words, the sexual or affective politics of the gay and lesbian movement, while deepening the legacy of the Pro-Democracy Movement, also run along different political tracks.

36 William Frederick Schroeder, "An Anthropology of the Weekend: Recreation and Relatedness in Gay and Lesbian Beijing" (PhD diss., University of Virginia, Charlottesville, 2009).

37 Kyŏng-min Kim, *Kyŏul hŏsuabi do sanŭn il e nŭn yŏnsŭp i p'ilyo hada* (Seoul: K'oat'ŭ Sent'ŏ, 1993).

38 Seo, "Mapping the Vicissitudes of Homosexual Identities in South Korea."

39 Kim, *Kyŏul hŏsuabi do sanŭn il e nŭn yŏnsŭp i p'ilyo hada*, 24.

40 Cho Han, "'You Are Entrapped in an Imaginary Well.'"

41 Sara Ahmed, *The Promise of Happiness* (Durham, NC: Duke University Press, 2010).

42 Lee Edelman, *No Future: Queer Theory and the Death Drive* (Durham, NC: Duke University Press, 2014).

43 Wei Wei, "'Wandering Men' No Longer Wander Around: Production and Transformation of Local Homosexual Identities in Contemporary Chengdu, China," *Inter-Asia Cultural Studies* 8, no. 4 (2007): 572–88.

44 Nonetheless, given the tightly knit and overlapping networks of family, clan, classmates, and colleagues that formed the basis of Korean sociality and on which the gay men were reliant to secure both their sense of identity and economic livelihood, gay men were necessarily cautious of meeting even other men.

45 Kim, *Kyŏul hŏsuabi do sanŭn il e nŭn yŏnsŭp i p'ilyo hada*, 88.

46 Jürgen Habermas, *The Structural Transformation of the Public Sphere: An Inquiry into a Category of Bourgeois Society* (Cambridge: Polity, 1989).

47 Michael Warner, *Publics and Counterpublics* (New York: Zone, 2002).

48 Seo, "Mapping the Vicissitudes of Homosexual Identities in South Korea," 69.

49 Kim, *Kyŏul hŏsuabi do sanŭn il e nŭn yŏnsŭp i p'ilyo hada*, 96.

50 Seo, "Mapping the Vicissitudes of Homosexual Identities in South Korea," 69.

51 Seo, "Mapping the Vicissitudes of Homosexual Identities in South Korea," 66.

52 Kim, "Hypermasculinity," 53.

53 Cho, "'You Are Entrapped in an Imaginary Well,'" 60.

54 In this volume, both Todd Henry and Layoung Shin raise a similar point in relation to their respective discussions of the "politics of dignity" and "homonormativity."

55 Schroeder, "An Anthropology of the Weekend."

56 Schroeder, "An Anthropology of the Weekend."

57 Eun-shil Kim, "Itaewon as an Alien Space within the Nation-State and a Place in the Globalization Era," *Korea Journal* 44, no. 3 (2004): 34–64.

58 Jesook Song, *South Korea in the Debt Crisis: The Creation of a Neoliberal Welfare Society* (Durham, NC: Duke University Press, 2009).

59 Yi Hŭi-il, "Ŭn'ŏ nŭn ŭn' ŏŭi segye: Chongno ŭn'ŏ sajŏn," *Buddy*, April 1, 1999, 17.

60 Jennifer Elizabeth Moon, "Cruising and Queer Counterpublics: Theories and Fictions" (PhD diss., University of Michigan, Ann Arbor, 2006), 7.

61 Seo, "Mapping the Vicissitudes of Homosexual Identities in South Korea," 69.

62 Song, *South Korea in the Debt Crisis*, 51.

63 Song, *South Korea in the Debt Crisis*, 52.

64 Don Slater, "Consumption without Scarcity: Exchange and Normativity in an Internet Setting," in *Commercial Cultures: Economies, Practices, Spaces*, ed. Peter A. Jackson, Michelle Lowe, Daniel Miller, and Frank Mort, 123–42 (Oxford: Berg, 2000).

65 Henning Bech, *When Men Meet: Homosexuality and Modernity* (Chicago: University of Chicago Press, 1997), 112, quoted in Schroeder, "An Anthropology of the Weekend."

66 Sherry Turkle, *Alone Together: Why We Expect More from Technology and Less from Each Other* (New York: Basic, 2011).

67 Slater, "Consumption without Scarcity."

68 Married gay men are referred to as "bats" for blurring the temporal, spatial, and affective boundaries that single gay men have used to demarcate their "weekend gay" lives from their "weekday heterosexual" lives. In other words, just like the category "gay," which transcended clear categories, memberships, and allegiances, they occupied an ambiguous position within the gay world. Meanwhile, in transgressing the boundaries of the heterosexual and homosexual worlds, they have become a key vector of sexual hybridization and, therefore, one of the most intense sites of public anxiety and interest.

69 Lauren Berlant, "Nearly Utopian, Nearly Normal: Post-Fordist Affect in *La Promesse* and *Rosetta*," *Public Culture* 19, no. 2 (2007): 273–301.

70 Berlant, "Nearly Utopian, Nearly Normal," 28, 278.

71 The discrepancy between the online visibility of gay men as a group and off-line invisibility is also reflected in the growing representation of homosexuality in popular films including the blockbuster, *The King and the Clown* (2005), depicting a love triangle between Yeonsangun, a king during the Chosŏn Dynasty (1392–1910), and a court clown. Such discrepancies reflect the commercialization of homosexuality as a theme that introduces narrative tension into a film without directly challenging the culture of heteronormative familialism that continues to force ordinary queers to hide and remain faceless.

72 Josephine Ho, "Is Global Governance Bad for East Asian Queers?" *GLQ* 14, no. 4 (2008): 457–79; Fred C. Alford, *Think No Evil: Korean Values in the Age of Globalization* (Ithaca, NY: Cornell University Press, 1999), 151.

73 Jonathan Dollimore, *Sexual Dissonance: Augustine to Wilde, Freud to Foucault* (Oxford: Oxford University Press, 1991), quoted in Martin, *Situating Sexualities*, 182.

74 Hyun Mee Kim, "The State and Migrant Women: Diverging Hopes in the Making of 'Multicultural Families' in Contemporary Korea," *Korea Journal* 47, no. 4 (Winter 2007): 100–122. Moreover, through the cultivating of intense emotional bonds between men, homosocial institutions like the military may be also seen as factories for the active production of homoeroticism and homosexuality.

75 Avery F. Gordon, *Ghostly Matters: Haunting and the Sociological Imagination* (Minneapolis: University of Minnesota Press, 1997), 17.

76 Martin, *Situating Sexualities*, 182.

77 Roseann Rife, "South Korea: Soldier Convicted in Outrageous Military Gay Witch-Hunt" *Amnesty International*, May 24, 2017, https://www.amnesty.org/en/latest/news/2017/05/south-korea-soldier-convicted-in-outrageous-military-gay-witch-hunt.

78 Seo, "Mapping the Vicissitudes of Homosexual Identities in South Korea," 78. In her chapter in this volume, Layoung Shin notes the emergence of a new type of homophobia, which claims to be "tolerant" of homosexuality.

Works Cited

NEWSPAPERS AND MAGAZINES

Buddy
Nyusŭ Ch'ujŏk
Sunday Newspaper

KOREAN-LANGUAGE SOURCES

Kim, Kyŏng-min. *Kyŏul hŏsuabi do sanŭn il e nŭn yŏnsŭp i p'ilyo hada.* Seoul: K'oat'ŭ Sent'ŏ, 1993.
Pak/Ch'a Min-jŏng. "AIDS p'aenik hogŭn kwaedam ŭi chŏngch'i." *Mal kwa Hwal* 12 (2016): 35–48.

ENGLISH-LANGUAGE SOURCES

Adam, Barry D. *The Rise of a Gay and Lesbian Movement.* Boston: Twayne, 1987.
Ahmed, Sara. *The Promise of Happiness.* Durham, NC: Duke University Press, 2010.
Alford, Fred C. *Think No Evil: Korean Values in the Age of Globalization.* Ithaca, NY: Cornell University Press, 1999.
Altman, Dennis. *Global Sex.* Chicago: University of Chicago Press, 2001.
Bech, Henning. *When Men Meet: Homosexuality and Modernity.* Chicago: University of Chicago Press, 1997.
Berlant, Lauren. "Nearly Utopian, Nearly Normal: Post-Fordist Affect in *La Promesse* and *Rosetta.*" *Public Culture* 19, no. 2 (2007): 273–301.
Berry, Chris. "Asian Values, Family Values: Film, Video, and Lesbian and Gay Identities." In *Gay and Lesbian Asia: Culture, Identity, Community,* ed. Gerard Sullivan and Peter A. Jackson, 211–32. New York: Routledge, 2001.
Berry, Chris, Fran Martin, and Audrey Yue, eds. *Mobile Cultures: New Media in Queer Asia.* Durham, NC: Duke University Press, 2003.
Blackwood, Evelyn. *Falling into the Lesbi World: Desire and Difference in Indonesia.* Honolulu: University of Hawai'i Press, 2010.
Bong, Youngshik D. "The Gay Rights Movement in Democraticizing Korea." *Korean Studies* 32 (2008): 86–103.
Charmaz, Kathy. *Constructing Grounded Theory.* London: Sage, 2014.
Cheng, Sea-ling. "Assuming Manhood: Prostitution and Patriotic Passions in Korea." *East Asia* 18, no. 4 (2000): 40–78.
Cho, Hae-joang. "Male Dominance and Mother Power: The Two Sides of Confucian Patriarchy in Korea." In *Confucianism and the Family,* ed. Walter H. Slote and George A. De Vos, 187–207. Albany: State University of New York Press, 1998.
Cho Han, Hae-joang. "'You Are Entrapped in an Imaginary Well': The Formation of Subjectivity within Compressed Development—A Feminist Critique of

Modernity and Korean Culture." *Inter-Asia Cultural Studies* 1, no. 1 (2000): 49–69.

Cho, Younghan. "The National Crisis and De/constructing Nationalism in South Korea during the IMF Intervention." *Inter-Asia Cultural Studies* 9, no. 1 (2008): 82–96.

Choi, Chungmoo. "Nationalism and Construction of Gender in Korea." In *Dangerous Women: Gender and Korean Nationalism*, ed. Elaine H. Kim and Chungmoo Choi, 9–31. New York: Routledge, 1998.

Chua, Beng Huat. *Communitarian Politics in Asia*. London: Routledge, 2004.

Crapanzano, Vincent. *Hermes' Dilemma and Hamlet's Desire: On the Epistemology of Interpretation*. Cambridge, MA: Harvard University Press, 1992.

Cumings, Bruce. *Korea's Place in the Sun: A Modern History*. New York: W. W. Norton, 1997.

D'Emilio, John. "Capitalism and Gay Identity." In *Powers of Desire: The Politics of Sexuality*, ed. Ann Snitow, Christine Stansell, and Sharon Thompson, 100–113. New York: Monthly Review, 1983.

Dollimore, Jonathan. *Sexual Dissonance: Augustine to Wilde, Freud to Foucault*. Oxford: Oxford University Press, 1991.

Drucker, Peter. "The Fracturing of LGBT Identities under Neoliberal Capitalism." *Historical Materialism* 19, no. 4 (2011): 3–32.

Durkheim, Émile. "What Is a Social Fact?" In *The Rules of the Sociological Method,* ed. Steven Lukes, 50–59. New York: Free Press, 1982.

Edelman, Lee. *No Future: Queer Theory and the Death Drive*. Durham, NC: Duke University Press, 2014.

Erni, John N., and Anthony Spires. "The Formation of a Queer-Imagined Community in Post-Martial Law Taiwan." In *Asian Media Studies: Politics of Subjectivities*, ed. John Erni and Chua Siew Keng, 225–52. Malden, MA: Blackwell, 2005.

Fabian, Johannes. "Ethnography and Intersubjectivity: Loose Ends." *HAU: Journal of Ethnographic Theory* 4, no. 1 (2014): 199–209.

Fanon, Frantz. *Black Skin, White Masks*. New York: Grove, (1967) 2008.

Gordon, Avery F. *Ghostly Matters: Haunting and the Sociological Imagination*. Minneapolis: University of Minnesota Press, 1997.

Habermas, Jürgen. *The Structural Transformation of the Public Sphere: An Inquiry into a Category of Bourgeois Society*. Cambridge: Polity, 1989.

Hahm, Pyong-choon. *Korean Jurisprudence, Politics, and Culture*. Seoul: Yonsei University Press, 1986.

Halberstam, Judith [Jack]. *In a Queer Time and Place: Transgender Bodies, Subcultural Lives*. New York: New York University Press, 2005.

Han, J. W., and L. H. M. Ling. "Authoritarianism in the Hypermasculinized State: Hybridity, Patriarchy, and Capitalism in Korea." *International Studies Quarterly* 42, no. 1 (1999): 53–78.

Ho, Josephine. "Is Global Governance Bad for East Asian Queers?" *GLQ* 14, no. 4 (2008): 457–79.

Kim Eun-shil. "Itaewon as an Alien Space within the Nation-State and a Place in the Globalization Era." *Korea Journal* 44, no. 3 (2004): 34–64.

Kim, Hyun-Mee. "The State and Migrant Women: Diverging Hopes in the Making of 'Multicultural Families' in Contemporary Korea." *Korea Journal* 47, no. 4 (2007): 100–122.

Kim, Hyun-Mee. "Work, Nation and Hypermasculinity: The 'Woman' Question in the Economic Miracle and Crisis in South Korea." *Inter-Asia Cultural Studies* 2, no. 1 (2001): 53–68.

Kim, Pil Ho, and C. Colin Singer. "Three Periods of Korean Queer Cinema: Invisible, Camouflage, and Blockbuster." *Acta Koreana* 14, no. 1 (2011): 115–34.

Liu, Petrus. "Queer Marxism in Taiwan." *Inter-Asia Cultural Studies* 8, no. 4 (2007): 517–39.

Luciano, Dana. *Arranging Grief: Sacred Time and the Body in Nineteenth Century America.* New York: New York University Press, 2007.

Manalansan, Martin. "In the Shadows of Stonewall: Examining Gay Transnational Politics and the Diasporic Dilemma." GLQ 2 (1995): 425–38.

Martin, Fran. *Situating Sexualities: Queer Representation in Taiwanese Fiction, Film and Public Culture.* Hong Kong: Hong Kong University Press, 2003.

McLelland, Mark. *Queer Japan from the Pacific War to the Internet.* Oxford: Rowman and Littlefield, 2005.

Moon, Jennifer Elizabeth. "Cruising and Queer Counterpublics: Theories and Fictions." PhD diss., University of Michigan, Ann Arbor, 2006.

Moon, Seungsook. "Begetting the Nation: The Androcentric Discourse of National History and Tradition in South Korea." In *Dangerous Women: Gender and Korean Nationalism*, ed. Elaine H. Kim and Chungmoo Choi, 33–66. New York: Routledge, 1998.

Nandy, Ashis. *The Intimate Enemy: Loss and Recovery of Self under Colonialism.* Oxford: Oxford University Press, (1983) 2010.

Ong, Aihwa. *Neoliberalism as Exception: Mutations in Citizenship and Sovereignty.* Durham, NC: Duke University Press, 2006.

Povinelli, Elizabeth A., and George Chauncey. "Thinking Sexuality Transnationally." GLQ 5 (1999): 439–50.

Rife, Roseann. "South Korea: Soldier Convicted in Outrageous Military Gay Witch-Hunt." Amnesty International, May 24, 2017. https://www.amnesty.org/en/latest/news/2017/05/south-korea-soldier-convicted-in-outrageous-military-gay-witch-hunt.

Schroeder, William Frederick. "An Anthropology of the Weekend: Recreation and Relatedness in Gay and Lesbian Beijing." PhD diss., University of Virginia, Charlottesville, 2009.

Seo, Dong-Jin [Sŏ Tong-jin]. "Mapping the Vicissitudes of Homosexual Identities in South Korea." *Journal of Homosexuality* 40, nos. 3–4 (2001): 65–78.

Slater, Don. 2000. "Consumption without Scarcity: Exchange and Normativity in an Internet Setting." In *Commercial Cultures: Economies, Practices, Spaces*, ed. Peter

Jackson, Michelle Lowe, Daniel Miller, and Frank Mort, 123–42. Oxford: Berg, 2000.

Song, Jesook. *South Korea in the Debt Crisis: The Creation of a Neoliberal Welfare Society.* Durham, NC: Duke University Press, 2009.

Sullivan, Gerard, and Peter A. Jackson, eds. *Gay and Lesbian Asia: Culture, Identity, Community.* New York: Routledge, 2001.

Turkle, Sherry. *Alone Together: Why We Expect More from Technology and Less from Each Other.* New York: Basic, 2011.

Warner, Michael. *Publics and Counterpublics.* New York: Zone, 2002.

Wei, Wei. "'Wandering Men' No Longer Wander Around: Production and Transformation of Local Homosexual Identities in Contemporary Chengdu, China." *Inter-Asia Cultural Studies* 8, no. 4 (2007): 572–88.

Wilson, Ara. *The Intimate Economies of Bangkok: Tomboys, Tycoons, and Avon Ladies in the Global City.* Berkeley: University of California Press, 2004.

Wilson, Ara. "Queering Asia." *Intersections* 14 (2006). http://intersections.anu.edu.au /issue14/wilson.html.

Chapter Eight

AVOIDING T'IBU (OBVIOUS BUTCHNESS)

INVISIBILITY AS A SURVIVAL STRATEGY AMONG YOUNG QUEER WOMEN IN SOUTH KOREA

Layoung Shin

The Reduced Popularity of Masculine Queer Women

My connection with young queer women, or *ibans*, in South Korea began in 2002 when I studied *fancos* for my master's thesis.[1] "Fancos," which is short for fan costume play, emerged among young women in the late 1990s when boy bands produced by the commercial star system, such as H.O.T., gained enormous popularity among teenage women. Instead of just cheering for their favorite stars, some young women began cutting their hair short, wearing young men's clothing to emulate the boy bands' male singers, and creating performance festivals where they even staged the singers' performances.

It is a kind of drag show, therefore, highlighting female performance of masculinity, since about 80 percent of fancos teams performed as boy groups. In imitating popular boy-band singers onstage, young women embodied male singers' public images through hairstyles, clothing, gestures, speaking styles, and word choices (which in Korean are sometimes assigned according to gender). Cutting one's hair short, in the so-called *k'al mŏri* (blade hair), is the first step to performing as a male singer. Fancos members also borrow male singers' "hip-hop" style, which includes oversize T-shirts and pants, a popular style among boy groups during fancos's heyday. They take on fictive masculine names that match their appearance. Many adopted Hyŏk and Min, which are frequently used in men's names—for example, Chŏng-hyŏk and Si-hyŏk and Chŏng-min and Kyu-min, to mention a few names of my informants. Some male-singer fancos members also used appellations for men such as *hyŏng* or *nuna* and other masculine ways of speaking and linguistic expressions.

At the same time, some fancos participants began dating their same-sex friends and identifying as ibans. As a result, in the early to mid-2000s, fancos came to be considered an iban community among some young women who were familiar with pop culture and fandom. Thus, driven by the remarkable development of the pop music industry during the late 1990s and early 2000s, some young women created new forms of queer culture and community through the consumption of pop culture.[2] Also, masculinity performed by young iban-identified women was popular and a regular part of the subculture at that time.

Ten years later, in 2012 and 2013, I again conducted fieldwork research with queer-identified young women, who were then involved in queer subcultural activities. In meeting with them, I found certain changes had occurred in the intervening ten years. For instance, among young queer women discrimination against or social avoidance of masculine butch-style lesbians had increased. This trend stands in stark contrast to the early to mid-2000s, when masculine young women who appropriated male singers' styles were common and even popular. Sinch'on Park, where young queer women used to hang out, was filled with that kind of masculine young women.[3]

Neologisms such as *t'ibu* and *kŏlk'ŏ*, which were popularly used among my interviewees during 2012 and 2013, highlight this important shift. "T'ibu" is a shortened form of *t'inanŭn* (easily noticeable) butch, thus referring to butch women with short hair and a masculine style. These masculine women are also called "kŏlk'ŏ," a combination of *kŏrŏdaninŭn* and *"coming out,"* which can be translated literally as "walking around while coming out." It means their persona as lesbian or gay is so strong that even heterosexuals would recognize them as such. This expression also refers to lesbian women and gay men who are easily recognizable because their styles, manners, and attitudes appear stereotypically lesbian and gay. The terms "t'ibu" and "kŏlk'ŏ" have often been used in denigrating or disparaging ways, although at times the terms were used humorously. The development of such new terms demonstrates the increasing negative sentiments toward female masculinity among queer-identified young women.

Another example comes from a casual meeting with one of my informants, a seventeen-year-old named So-yu. She told me she was introduced to someone who had shown interest in her after seeing her picture on her friend's phone. But So-yu was reluctant to go out with this girl, saying, "But she [the girl who showed interest in So-yu] is t'ibu." So-yu did not want to go out with the girl just because the girl had a masculine style. To my question about why did she not like t'ibu, So-yu was not quite sure, saying, "Just because." Then after a while she added, "They [t'ibu] usually cheat more." Based on stereotypes tied to their masculine appearance, young queer women's animosity toward t'ibu was new to me.[4]

Such an increase in negative stereotypes about certain groups within the LGBT community can result in exclusion and discrimination of those gender-nonconforming subjects, including transgender people. How did this change in attitude, an increased level of discrimination, and avoidance of t'ibu arise in the intervening ten years? In this chapter, I contextualize this change in queer women's subculture in relation to transformations in South Korean society, including the increased social recognition of homosexuality and the growth of homophobia; increased unemployment and a lack of job security among youth; and the retreat of the state from social welfare and its concomitant promotion of heterosexual families as the basis of economic security and survival.

By revealing the specific conditions of young queer women in South Korea, I engage with the concept of "homonormativity" developed by scholars of queer studies in the West.[5] I argue that this term is insufficient to grasp the specific conditions of South Korea. For young working-class queer women in South Korea, the shift toward avoiding masculinity that I observed in 2012 and 2013 does not simply signify assimilation into "normative" categories of citizenship. Instead, by understanding local contexts—such as increased public visibility and recognition of homosexuality and the institutionalization of homophobia at school, the lack of legal protection for LGBT people, and cultural and economic meanings of family—the necessity of reconceptualizing the very notion of "normativity" will be revealed.

Questioning the equation between "normativity" and "homosexuality" itself in the Korean context, this chapter seeks to find alternative explanations for increasing gender conformity among young queer women in recent years. First, I examine the reasons for young women's avoidance of masculinity in relation to the consequences of recognition and association as queers in straight society. Second, I provide examples of avoiding visibility in both online and off-line settings to show how the fear of visibility was prevalent in the early 2010s.

The third section reveals how the choice of invisibility is related to intensified institutionalized homophobia at school. Fourth, through a critique of queer politics based on "visibility" and "out and proud," I show that in South Korea the meaning of coming out is different from that in the West. However, instead of relying on a preexisting notion of "Asian" values of family, I emphasize the economic function of family as crucial for young queer women's survival amid economic hardship and a retreat of the social welfare system.

Neoliberalism and Homonormativity

The specific characteristics of the transformation of queer youth subculture in South Korea can be understood better when compared with Western examples, particularly in terms of the development of capitalism. First, John D'Emilio suggests that in the U.S., the formation of gay identity and communities among urban young people happened during the 1920s in relation to the development of capitalism. He especially emphasizes the growth of "free labor," which provided new sources of income and living situations that made young people independent of their families.[6] As Peter Drucker has written, "It is by now nothing new to link the rise of what might be called classic lesbian/gay identity to the rise of a 'free' labour-force under capitalism."[7] By comparison, the development of identity and community among young urban queer women in South Korea was less connected to a rise in "free" labor as in Fordist capitalism than to the rise of consumption in late/neoliberal capitalism during and after the International Monetary Fund (IMF) economic crisis of 1997.

Second, Drucker argues that in the U.S. and other Western contexts there is a correlation between the shift to neoliberal capitalism and the increasing tendency toward "gender conformity" within LGBT communities. He argues that amid this transformation, middle-class lesbian women and gay men prospered while constructing and stabilizing their identities and community. He also suggests that by embracing gender conformity, many LGBT people incorporated "a neoliberal social and sexual order," thus marginalizing other sexual minorities who do not conform to such logics of capital.[8]

In recent decades, queer studies has addressed this critique of middle-class white gay and lesbian movements. Using the concept of homonormativity, Lisa Duggan, for example, identifies gay and lesbian movements that do not challenge fundamental "norms" of heterosexual society under neoliberal politics.[9] She labels this phenomenon "the new homonormativity," which she defines as "a politics that does not contest dominant heteronormative assumptions and institutions, but upholds and sustains them, while promising the possibility of a demobilized gay constituency and a privatized, depoliticized gay culture anchored in domesticity and consumption."[10]

Following Duggan, many scholars have since studied different types of homonormativity in LGBT communities across the world, exploring how this system reinforces preexisting discrimination and hierarchies of race, class, and gender as well as nationality and ethnicity.[11] Thus, only "nationally acceptable queers" or "top gays" are acknowledged as qualified citizens in a straight world, while other queers of color or working-class queers are excluded.[12] In the East Asian context, Denise Tang, Lisa Rofel, and John Cho have examined the influence of neoliberalism in reconstructing homosexuality in Hong Kong, China, and South Korea, respectively.[13] They effectively reveal how neoliberalism produces "desire" and how it introduces an opposition between those gays who embody "right," "respectful," and "creative" desire and those who do not.

In some ways, the avoidance of t'ibu corresponds to following norms of gender. However, mechanistically applying the concept of homonormativity, which has been used to critique middle-class gay men and lesbians attempting to assimilate into straight societies, does not fit well with my informants' situations. Many of my informants who started to avoid t'ibu come from "the particular sector of working class" that, as Drucker points out, includes "the younger, less skilled, less organized and lower-paid."[14] After ten years of economic restructuring that resulted in an increased gap between rich and poor, youth unemployment, and the irregularization of employment, young Korean queer women in my research have become "the younger, less skilled, less organized and lower-paid," as well as queer.

The working-class young queer women with whom I have been meeting used to call themselves or others in their group ing'yŏ.[15] Although originally signifying "surplus" in Korea, ing'yŏ was used among young people to refer to themselves as "leftover" people or "losers" who failed in their jobs or did not contribute to society. They used the word in a self-mocking way to describe their unemployed status and overall lack of value or to point out others' uselessness.[16] This word choice reflects and expresses the widespread frustration among youth in South Korea under job insecurity.

In actual numbers, the unemployment rate of youth in South Korea was about 8 percent in 2013 and 12.3 percent in February 2017.[17] This figure is almost two or three times higher than the overall unemployment rate, which was 3.1 percent and 5 percent, respectively. However, the report has some flaws since it does not include the part of the youth population that is preparing for employment or that gave up employment after a series of trials. Yun Chin-ho, an economist, argues that the actual unemployment rate is about 18 percent, while Yang Ho-kyŏng, a policy development team leader at the Youth Community Union, estimates that the actual unemployment rate among youth is 21 percent.[18] In addition to increased unemployment, the irregularization and flexibilization of labor are not captured as unemployment in these statistics, which are constructed along the lines of age and gender.[19]

This means that almost all young women in their teens and twenties are part-time contract workers in service jobs, especially if they are not college-educated. Most of my informants between the ages of nineteen and twenty-two were experiencing this kind of job insecurity and fear of an unknown future. These young women do not have the same "luxurious" concerns as middle-class queers who want to gain admission to "normative" societies. Thus, they cannot simply be said to be avoiding masculinity or conforming to gender standards out of a desire for inclusion in heteronormative society or for job security, when they never belonged to "normative" society in the first place.

In addition, in Korean society, the inclusion of middle-class gay men and lesbians in the commercialized market system and in neoliberal categories of citizens has not yet occurred. As Cho shows in his contribution to this volume and elsewhere, with the case of Korean gay men in their thirties and forties, many of whom could be considered middle class, some are actually choosing to "retreat" from "homosexuality" while encountering economic crisis and neoliberal reestablishment of the society. Choosing to retreat for economic reasons would be even more appropriate, then, for lesbian women, who have much less economic power in this gender-unequal society. Kim Sun-nam also shows that economic instability among LGBT people varies based on gender, class, and age, making lesbians more vulnerable. As an example, according to a survey conducted with Korean LGBT people in 2007, 73.8 percent of lesbians earn less than 1.5 million wŏn (about $ 1,300) per month, while 8.5 percent earn more than 2.5 million wŏn (about $2,171). By contrast, 51.3 percent of gay men earn less than 1.5 million wŏn, while 19.8 percent earn more than 2.5 million wŏn.[20]

Likewise, there is a clear difference between the Korean and Western contexts in terms of the relationship between the transformation of capitalism and the development of LGBT identity and community. Anglo-American gay men and lesbian women stabilized their economic position through the development of Fordism (free labor, full employment, and independence from family, even among students and the working class) during the 1940s and 1950s and increased their social standing through the gay rights movement and its legal successes in the 1970s. Through this long process, they at least had the chance to solidify the grounds of gay and lesbian rights, although the community later fractured and moved toward "homonormativity" or "homonationalism."[21] By contrast, South Korean queers have not had a similar history of economic stability, the solidification of LGBT movements, or the achievement of legal rights. Although there has been growth in LGBT organizations, their membership, and participation in political activities, legal and institutional achievement protecting LGBT rights has not been accomplished. In addition, employment opportunities and economic survival among marginalized populations, especially female queer youth, deteriorated as the neoliberal economy intensified during the ten years between my two research periods.

Given these differences, this chapter explores other possibilities for explaining the increase in gender conformity among young queer-identified women that go beyond homonormativity. Applying the critique of homonormativity to lesbian women and gay men in South Korea does not have the same connotations as in the Western context. As Yau Ching argues, "Normativity as a relative ideal might not be accessible for many people in most parts of the world."[22] That is, if we question the concept of "normativity" itself and contextualize it in South Korean history, we need to ask whether cisgender lesbians and gay men were ever tolerated and accepted in Korean society.

Avoiding Masculinity: The Choice of Invisibility

The reason for discrimination against or avoidance of masculine queer women in South Korea is the desire to avoid being recognized as lesbian. Seventeen-year-old Chun-hŭi, one of my informants, said:

> I used to hang out with handsome [masculine] girls in the park. It was fun, and they were handsome. But these days, I am reluctant to spend time with t'ibu and prefer *ilbansŭt'ŭ* [ilban style; straight women's style]. If I hang out with them [t'ibu], there are more eyes on us and more risks of being recognized. If I take a picture with them and post it, people ask, "Who is that? Is it a girl or a boy?"[23]

As this interview shows, the reason that Chun-hŭi began to avoid hanging out with t'ibu was increased attention and the related risk of being recognized as iban rather than because she specifically developed a negative stereotype and dislike of t'ibu.

As the term itself shows, t'ibu are easily recognizable as lesbian. Because homosexuality as an identity has become more familiar to mainstream society, masculine women are now more easily identified as lesbian, much as feminine men are identified as gay. That is, gender nonconformity became a common way to signify one's sexual identity among South Koreans. If a young woman has short hair, classmates at school began to gossip about her, speculating that she is a lesbian. Even teachers and social workers in youth centers came to acknowledge such associations. This association became increasingly common during the mid- to late 2000s, after my first research period in the early 2000s. My informant Chin-sil, a fancos member with a masculine style, told me about her experience at age fifteen, when she was going to a Youth Center in Seoul to practice fancos: "The teacher [a social worker at the Youth Center] asked me, 'Why is your hair so short?' I just answered, 'Because it is uncomfortable to dance with long hair.' Then he continued to ask, 'Why is it uncomfortable?' Then he directly asked me, 'Are you rejŭ [lesbian]?' I was upset and answered, 'Yes, I am. So what?' Then all the teachers came out to see me."[24] This incident shows that the recognition of sexual identity in association with gendered expression has increased and, at the same time, teachers and social workers are also discriminating against queer-identified students, not protecting them. As I elaborate more in the next section, schools became sites of institutionalized homophobia during the mid-2000s. Therefore, young queer women who feel the need to protect themselves have found ways to avoid being seen as queer. The first step is to avoid masculinity or avoid being friendly with or dating queer women who are easily noticeable as homosexual, butches, or t'ibu.

Thus, the dating customs of young iban women have also changed. While t'ibu became less popular, ilbansŭt'ŭ—straight-looking cisgender lesbians—became more desirable as dating partners in 2012 and 2013. While butch-and-femme couples or butch-butch couples were most common in the early 2000s, the number of ilbasŭt'ŭ, or femme-femme couples, was rising ten years later. In my first meeting with Chu-hŭi and Ko-ŭn, an ilbansŭt'ŭ couple who styled themselves in the female office worker look, with long hair and high heels, they told me about these changes. Although they later broke up, they dated on and off for about three years. They said that when they started dating in 2010, other lesbian friends were surprised and asked how one femme could date another femme.[25] Dating between women without a butch was uncommon even until 2009–10. Chu-hŭi said, "It was really rare. We were the only couple I know of at that time who dated like this [as two feminine girls]."

Ye-rim and Sŭng-ho, a butch-butch couple in fancos, said, "There were butch-and-femme and b-to-b [butch and butch], but there was no femme-femme relationship at all. I have never seen that case in fancos." In other words, even until recently, ilbansŭt'ŭ couples were not common, and t'ibu were not shunned. These days, however, ilbansŭt'ŭ is the preferred dating style, and these couples are becoming the norm. In these cases, it is the desire not to be noticed as a lesbian that comes first, rather than a sudden change in taste in women in the lesbian community or because of an intention to discriminate against masculine women.

Female Same-Sex Sexuality Disappearing from the Public Scene

In addition to reluctance to date t'ibu to avoid being identified as iban, fear of visibility was widely expressed among my fieldwork informants. For example, some fancos teams do not post their videos on portal sites because they are afraid they will be associated with lesbians. According to Ch'o-hŭi, a longtime active member in fancos, when blogs and social networking sites became popular, one fancos team posted a performance video on a portal site, and many comments and responses followed that discussed their gender and sexual identity, such as, "Are they boys or girls?" "Why do girls do men's dance?" and "Are they lesbians?" Because of such responses, fancos teams started to avoid Internet publicity, which had been one of the most crucial ways they recruited members, attracted audiences, and promoted events.

In addition, government policies on Internet regulation and surveillance, as well as increased online bullying and scamming using personal information, contributed to increased fear about exposing oneself in online communities, and led to increased self-protective measures among young queer women. As an example, there have been some cases of scammers who threaten to reveal young queer women's sexual identities to their schools and parents. To prevent this, some lesbian websites and online community cafés have implemented strict regulations for joining their communities out of fear of unknowingly allowing in straight or homophobic members. For instance, the M community online café was a popular site for some of my informants, but one could join only by invitation from an existing member, which made it difficult for outsiders to find out about the community. One also had to answer specific questions (answers were known exclusively by the members) and, to maintain membership, follow strict regulations in terms of writing styles and word choices. These measures have been developed over time among queer youth to protect themselves against a homophobic society, both online and off-line. At the same time, however, such regulations have been restrictive even for existing members, and the sites' resulting invisibility has made it hard for young queer women to find and join these communities.

Fear of being recognized online is especially severe among young women who live in a digital-media society where there is a "possibility of unimaginably wide publicity."[26] As danah boyd has written, "A mediated public could consist of all people across all space and all time."[27] This factor of digitally mediated society makes young queer women concerned about exposure of any kind; their pictures and other posts and messages that can relate them to queer identity are searchable, persistent, and replicable. They also cannot control who can read and see online materials related to them, causing a fear of "unimaginable" audiences.

This theme of the avoidance of public scrutiny also occurred in off-line settings. Many fancos teams began performing only at fancos events and skipping other events, such as youth festivals sponsored by the Seoul City Youth Centers or on open stages in front of department stores such as Miliore and Doota.[28] Until 2006 and 2007, fancos teams performed on these stages. However, by 2012 and 2013, fancos now hesitated to do so because they had experienced negative responses. The members of one fancos team, Mirotic, complained about those venues: "First of all, people usually do not like women with short hair. There is prejudice. So if we dance with short hair, they do not like it." The masculine-style female fancos members were not welcomed because they confused the audiences' gender expectations, and they sometimes experienced harsh commentary. In response, fancos members avoided performing in public more than ever.

Such concern about visibility was highlighted at a fancos event sponsored by the M Youth Center. Unlike many Korean youth centers, the M center was very supportive of fancos—Se-mi, a social worker there and a longtime idol group fan herself, in particular, was very close to many fancos members. The problem arose, however, when the center sent out a press release. Since the center is part of the city government's institute, it regularly announced upcoming events. Thus, the publicity about the fancos event was part of its normal routine, from the perspective of the youth center. After the M Center–sponsored event in November of 2012, pictures of fancos were published on some digital news sites. Se-mi, who was in charge of the event, received many calls and messages from the fancos members who had performed, asking her to remove the pictures because they were afraid that their families, friends, or classmates would recognize them; fancos members were very sensitive to being exposed in the media in any form. Se-mi was put in an awkward position when the news site did not want to remove the pictures.

Another example of these dynamics occurred at the Korean Queer Culture Festival (KQCF) in 2013. I invited Hǔi-ch'ǒl and her team members, who were my informants during a year of fieldwork, to the festival. Hǔi-ch'ǒl, who was more interested in queer politics than any of my other informants, used to tell me that she had always wanted to see the KQCF but had never had the chance to attend. Other team members had also shown interest in LGBT activism, though to a lesser degree than Hǔi-ch'ǒl, so I expected that they would enjoy the festival's crowd, performances, speeches, and diverse booths.

The day of the KQCF and the Queer Parade, the team showed up in the middle of the event. But aside from Hǔi-ch'ǒl, the other team members quickly left without enjoying the festival. Only Hǔi-ch'ǒl spent the rest of the day with me watching performances on stage and exploring booths from diverse LGBT communities and organizations. Later, Hai, one of the members who left the KQCF without enjoying it with us, told me that they had gone early because they were afraid of being in an open space at a festival of "queers." They were afraid they might accidentally encounter their classmates or someone they knew at the festival and be identified as queer. I thought it would have been okay to be seen there, since the festival is open to everyone and includes heterosexuals. However, for these young queer women, the fear of being perceived as lesbian because they attended a queer festival was a real issue.

Together, these anecdotes reveal young queer women's intensified fear of being recognized as iban in current South Korean society. Preference for ilbansǔt'ǔ while shunning t'ibu and kǒlk'ǒ and avoiding any kind of public exposure, both online and off-line, are all part of their effort to stay "invisible" as queers in a heteronormative society. This is different from the U.S. case, where gender conformity increased after the decline of Fordism in the 1980s, and LGBT people did not necessarily hide their sexuality, though they lived "preferably without 'flaunting' it."[29] By comparison, young queer women's avoidance of masculinity in South Korea was aimed at hiding their sexuality completely. In short, they refuse to be recognized as lesbian. Hiding one's sexual identity itself from the public is different from striving to appear "normal" while admitting to straight society that one is a lesbian or gay man.

As mentioned earlier, the difference in meaning of invisibility and gender conformity between South Korea and the U.S. is also the result of place-specific gay rights laws and sentiments toward homosexuality. In the U.S., since gaining legal protection in the 1970s, at least the baby-boom generation middle-class lesbians and gay men were protected by their economic success and the growth of social tolerance. However, in South Korea, gay rights protection under the law does not yet exist, even after a lot of demands for an antidiscrimination bill by LGBT organizations and some liberal legislators. Legal prevention of discrimination does not necessarily mean the eradication of discrimination in reality. However, it would provide at least some grounds for queers to protect themselves or fight against official or overt discriminatory policies at school or at work, which is important, since even teachers and youth social workers have fomented discrimination and hate speech toward homosexuality in classrooms. Instead of preventive laws, however, the Military Punishment Law still exists, which officially discriminates against homosexuality.[30] Although the Ordinance on Students' Human Rights (OSHR) was passed in 2011 by some local governments to prevent discrimination at schools, including discrimination based on sexual orientation, it has not yet been applied in practice.[31]

Here we can witness the imbalance between an increase in homophobia, on the one hand, and a lack of legal, physical, and psychological protections for queer youth, on the other. Although there was no law protecting the rights of LGBT people in South Korea until the early 2000s, there were no regulations at schools that punished masculine female students or those who were suspected of being queer, either. However, with the increased visibility and the proliferation of mainstream discourse on homosexuality since the mid-2000s, discrimination against homosexuality has been on the rise at schools and in official forms.

Some schools instituted disciplinary policies in the mid-2000s, the so-called Iban Inspection, which consists of regulations prohibiting behavior deemed "homosexual" among female students. For instance, administrators at a girls' school issued penalties for activities such as holding hands, hugging, wearing short hairstyles, hanging around together in hallways, going to the restroom together, and sending and receiving letters.[32] Some schools have also singled out students suspected of being homosexuals (*tongsŏngaeja*). For instance, figure 8.1 shows a survey conducted at a girls' school for the purpose of creating a "healthy environment." It asks respondents whether they know anyone who "does" "homosexuality" (*tongsŏngae rŭl hanŭn saram*) and, if they do, to report them. The following is one example of such disciplines at school:

My middle school, which was a girls' school, had so-called Iban Inspection. Teachers asked students to point out who are iban (lesbians). They also used to say "don't hold hands," "don't hug each other," "don't go to the restroom together." I am not sure if it was officially documented as their school's principles, but teachers spoke as if they were the rules. The girls who were known as iban were dragged to the office and forced to write "memorandum" promising "they would never do that [the prohibited behaviors]." I didn't experience that myself, but I saw they were dragged to the office held by their hair and wrists. I heard from them later that the teachers threatened them, saying, "Tell me who else [are iban], otherwise I will call your parents to school." . . . Those who were designated iban were ignored by teachers and bullied by classmates. I was not revealed because only a few friends know about my sexual identity, but it was close. I was so scared seeing what other friends were going through. I thought it would be the end of the world if I was exposed. . . . Since then, I never talked about my serious concern and stories to any of [my] other classmates and teachers at my school.[33]

All of these cases show how school administrations assume homosexuality to be misbehavior requiring punishment. This bodily discipline and inspection created a homophobic school environment during the mid-2000s.

These discriminatory cases reflect the increased recognition of homosexuality and institutionalized surveillance of young queer women at schools, rather than the prevention of such discrimination. Feelings of fear about being associated with lesbians among young queer women thus arise out of this difficult environment. Control over their visibility—choosing to whom they come out and knowing how to hide their orientation under other conditions—is critical to their safety from discrimination and bullying, as well as to their avoidance of punishment and discipline.

Some young women drop out of school due to such discrimination and harsh reactions. Among my informants, almost 20 percent had left secondary school without finishing, although the reasons were not only limited to their sexual identity and issues of bullying. However, junior high and high school dropouts are severely stigmatized as "delinquents" in Korean society. As Jung-ah Choi (Ch'oi Chung-a) mentions, the high school diploma is a symbol of being "normal."[34] When school is a necessity, young girls end up staying in classrooms that are hostile toward them.

Survey

* This survey is anonymous and confidential. The goal of this survey is to create healthy and wholesome environment at School. Please answer honestly.

1. What do you think about homosexuality?
   a) I don't care much.
   b) I can understand.
   c) I can't understand.
   d) I have not thought about it.

2. Do you think there are homosexuals in our school?
   a) Yes, there are.
   b) No, there aren't.
   c) I don't know
   d) I have heard about it.

3. If so, which grade do you think has the most number of them?
   a) Freshman
   b) Junior
   c) Senior

4. What do you think school needs to do about homosexual students?
   a) Counseling
   b) Service work at school
   c) Infinite suspension
   d) Expulsion of the student

5. If you know students who do homosexuality, please write down the students' year, class and name.

   Year: Class: Name:

Figure 8.1 Survey of "homosexuality" at a girls' school.

Su-hyŏn, who had just graduated from high school when I interviewed her, reflected painfully on her high school years. As soon as she entered the school, teachers and classmates identified her as a lesbian. She wanted to quit school because she was afraid of bullying and discrimination, but her father was strict about it. Her father told her, "At least you should finish school to be able to live like a human." She could not leave or change schools due to her father. Instead, whenever she went to school, she just put her head down on her desk to avoid talking with anyone at school. Her only friends and communication were outside the school and in online communities.

Likewise, young queer women struggle to stay invisible, seeing it as a preferable alternative to all the traumatic experiences they could encounter when identified as queer. Thus, while homonormativity in the West concerns white middle-class lesbians and gay men trying to assimilate into middle-class straight society, while excluding working-class queers, queers of color, and gender-nonconforming queers, in the South Korean case, gender conformity and the desire to blend in with straight society is a protective measure designed to safeguard those who are weakest in terms of gender, age, class, and sexuality.

Different Meanings of "Visibility" and "Coming Out"

The issue of visibility also needs to be considered in the South Korean cultural context, where coming out has different meanings from those in Western societies. Chris Tan argues, "After all, coming out arguably constitutes the central ritual in the process of Anglo-American gay-identity formation."[35] In the rhetoric of coming out, those who come out are seen as "being truthful to themselves."[36] This focus on the politics of visibility and "out and proud" campaigns in the West have the potential to exclude those who are not visible, labeling them "not truthful" or "backward." This occurs in the case of Palestinian queers, queer rural youth, and queers in non-Western contexts. Jason Ritchie, for example, criticizes depoliticized mainstream Israeli gay activism, which depends on the politics of visibility, recognition, and coming out of the closet and is supportive of Israeli nationalism, thus maintaining "the political, economic, and social subordination of Palestinians."[37]

In her study of rural queer youth in the U.S., Mary Gray finds a similar use of the rhetoric of visibility when comparing urban and rural areas. Citing Eve Kosofsky Sedgwick, she argues, "Visibility operates as a binary: in order for someone to be visible, to 'come out,' there must always be a closet someplace where others clamor or struggle to get out."[38] Therefore, the politics of visibility can lead to the "privileging of some queer identities over others."[39] In this case, rural queers have been described as "pre-existing, yet alienated" and "'lacking' or 'incomplete.'"[40]

Likewise, Asian queer studies criticize the visibility-based Western framework as the primary standard measuring development of LGBT progressiveness. In comparing the context of Confucian Singapore with Anglo-American society, Tan argues that the ideals of "coming-out" and "visibility" do not make sense in Singapore. In an Anglo-American context, coming out begins with coming out to one's parents; however, gay men in Singapore, as in other Confucian countries in Asia, "refrain from coming out to their parents to avoid shaming their families."[41] They do not even feel obliged to do so. Therefore, "Coming out does not occupy the same central position in the everyday lives of Singaporean gay men as it does in Anglo-American gay rights discourses."[42]

When it comes to South Korea, John (Song Pae) Cho also notes the different context in terms of visibility and coming out by challenging the binary approach itself:

> The issue of coming out was a complicated issue for Korean gays and lesbians, involving subtle feelings such as empathy, guilt, and worry, which could not be reduced to the binaries of "pride versus shame" or "knowledge versus ignorance." . . . [T]herefore, some gay men choose a deferred gay future where they would come out and live their lives openly as fulltime gay men once their parents passed away. . . . Korean gay men imagined their "closet" as only a temporary holding pad, from which they would emerge to become fulltime gays once their parents passed away.[43]

As he explains, in South Korea gay men and lesbians do not feel the necessity of coming out to their parents. They consider hiding or "deferring" gay life or temporarily staying in the "closet" out of respect for their parents natural.

In the case of young queer women in South Korea, most of my informants made every effort to hide their sexual identities from their parents and relatives to protect themselves from punishment or backlash. Some of them said they would never come out to their parents, even after they become adults. However, others consider not coming out to their parents as a way of "protecting" them from the shock of their daughter's sexual identity, rather than filial duty or adherence to Confucian principles. Some of my informants used to say, "Oh, my parents would be shocked. They might die from the shock. I would never tell them that that I'm a lesbian." Likewise, in a culture where family ties are strong, keeping one's identity private has different meanings and implications, including "protecting" parents.

This does not mean all queers in Asia or South Korea are reluctant to come out or refuse the politics of visibility, just as not all queers in Western urban societies are willing to come out and are supportive of out and proud politics. Actually, similar (but different) tensions and debates on the issue of coming out were prevalent among activists in the early 2000s in South Korea. Some activists argued that coming out was the "prerequisite" for activism, while others argued against the equation between activism and coming out. Indeed, there are some in South Korea who come out and pursue visibility as a political strategy, and the number who are doing so seems to be increasing among young activists in recent years. Thus, I am not trying to generalize that all queers in South Korea or Asia are reluctant to come out, but my intention is to show the general cultural sentiments and attitudes toward coming out and visibility in the Korean context. The shift toward invisibility among young queer women needs to be considered in this cultural context to avoid stigmatizing them as "backward" or following a teleological trajectory of "normativity."

Meaning of Family: Not Just an "Asian" Value but an Economic Unit

I argue that the family-oriented culture of (South) Korea based on Confucianism and filial duty explains only part of the reason that young queer women try to avoid coming out to their parents. Kwon Kim Hyun-young and John Cho show the close relationship between job security and heterosexual family. They list the benefits available to company employees who are members of heterosexual nuclear families and argue that, because they cannot obtain employment at such companies, lesbians and gay men face discrimination in the areas of taxes, mortgages, inheritances, hospital visitation rights, and so on.[44] Jesook Song further shows that, after the IMF Crisis of 1997, the South Korean government promoted the heterosexual nuclear family as "the primary unit responsible for individual security" and "the core of social well-being."[45] The economic crisis thus resulted in the reinforcement of the ideological prominence of the family—specifically, heterosexual marriage and the normative family.

In addition to this general privilege of heterosexual family, when it comes to less privileged, working-class queer youth, the situation becomes worse.

As mentioned in the previous section, employment rates for youth and women of all generations were low throughout the ten-year period of my research. Young queer women from working-class backgrounds without mainstream education fell under the category of the most marginalized in terms of gender, age, and education. Under these conditions, young queer women cannot but depend on their families for economic survival. Therefore, the importance of the family for queer youth also results from the family's ability to provide economic stability, especially in these times of job insecurity, increased youth unemployment, and a welfare system that privileges heteronormative families.

In addition, dependence on heterosexual marriage for economic survival is also found among older generations of lesbians, even, according to Song, among single women who have strong and independent spirits and are willing to live outside conventional patriarchal norms. Even lesbian-identified women came to consider marriage an option. "Because of insecurity of employment and financing," Song writes, "marriage may be the only option for women who do not have a sufficient income or financial security."[46] Some of her informants seriously considered "getting married in order to survive."[47] One, for instance, said, "I was paranoid that I would die of hunger when I was outed at work and to my parents. I was contemplating marriage, seriously. If I suppress my bodily suffering, choosing to marry and live with a guy, at least my body won't starve to death."[48] Likewise, for some working-class queer women who have few economic resources, heterosexual marriage and the heteronormative family appear to them to be the only "choices" for survival, less in terms of symbolic belonging to a family norm than in terms of financial and physical survival.

This reliance on family for survival can also be found among other East Asian queer women, as well as among queer immigrants in the U.S. Lucetta Yip Lo Kam, for example, shows that economic self-sufficiency is very important for *lalas* (lesbian, bisexual, and transgender) in urban China because economically dependent lalas are hard-pressed to "convince their families that they can support themselves without marrying an economically better off man."[49] Similarly, due to high rents and dense living conditions, dependence on family for lesbians in Hong Kong is not optional but necessary. As Denise Tse-Shang Tang also argues, "Sexualities are tightly constrained with the family structure and the living space."[50] David Eng further shows that, for multiply marginalized working-class queer immigrants of color in the United States, dependence on family and kinship, and the related expectation of heteronormativity, have become stronger rather than weaker in late capitalism.[51]

My informants' interviews support this line of analysis. Since my informants were younger than marriage age (they were teenagers and in their early twenties), their discussion about family did not yet involve marriage. Instead, it focused on maintaining relationships with their natal families. Chun-hŭi, who was seventeen at the time of her interview in 2012, reported having run away from home when her father beat her after finding out she was lesbian. She stayed with friends for a week, then was contacted by family and asked to return, so she went home. After talking about the experience, she told me about her dream of becoming a computer engineer. Her career choice was not, however, based on interest in this type of job; instead, it was related to her desire for economic stability. "I don't know when my family will discard me, though now we are staying together 'in peace' without talking about what happened," she said. "So I need to have a good job in case I cannot have any [financial] support from my family." Once her parents found out about her sexual identity and responded harshly to it, Chun-hŭi came to understand that her future might not include relying on her family for financial support. That is to say, becoming a professional would be her way to secure financial security. This shows that in South Korea, negotiation with families is related not only to emotional support and traditional values of family and kinship, but also to financial support.

There are those like Chun-hŭi who pursue professional careers as a strategy for economic survival and an alternative to heteronormative family, but most of my working-class, queer women informants are already far removed from such a career track, as they quit school at an early age or showed low achievement in education. Many of them continue to work in low-paying part-time jobs. In such cases, they have few options; depending on their families, even though their parents earn low incomes, is actually a safe way to survive. Drawing on Ching, I therefore argue that this trend of queer women in South Korea moving toward avoiding the appearance of or association with masculinity—that is, avoiding visibility and recognition as queer—is not just about the desire to assimilate into straight society but to maintain financial stability. We need to reflect on how young women's struggle not to be identified as lesbian is therefore consistent with "the complex processes of construction of and negotiation with normativity *within* subjects who are deprived of the right or the option or resist to be normal to start with."[52]

Conclusion: Beyond Visibility and the Critique of Homonormativity

Compared with the early 2000s, when young queer women had their own, active subcultures around Seoul, where they showed off their masculine styles and gathered in public communities such as Sinch'on Park, many of the same women seemed to be in hiding by the early 2010s. The general shift was from visibility to invisibility, from a general approval of female masculinity to a preference for "straight-looking" queer women. These trends resulted in a decrease in off-line queer subcultures and communities, eradicating opportunities for young queer women to easily and freely meet face-to-face. By this time, masculine queer women were experiencing a new form of discrimination and stereotypes, one that spread among lesbians themselves. This change might be interpreted as an effect of Western-style homonormativity—namely, that these young women were focusing more on being accepted in straight society by reducing their chances of being seen as "abnormal" in public spaces. However, I argue that this shift cannot be explained simply in terms of homonormativity.

Over the last ten years of my research, while LGBT activism has become more dynamic and diverse, a basic antidiscrimination bill has not yet been passed, and the number of antihomosexuality rallies led by conservative groups has increased. Economic hardship brought about by unemployment and the irregularization of work has affected many young people, including queer young women, making their desire for independence from family more difficult. Together, these phenomena caused an imbalance insofar as Korean society was not prepared to offer queer youth protection from discrimination at school, home, or the workplace. The burden of surviving the effects of discrimination rests entirely with queer women themselves. Therefore, in a society that does not provide any alternatives, the young women focus on hiding. The choice of staying invisible as lesbian, which has resulted in the avoidance of masculinity among young queer women in South Korea, is therefore related to the need to survive rather than to desires for class mobility or assimilation into "normal" society. The phenomenon of gender conformity, in this case, signifies a desire for survival. Therefore, both young queer women's subculture and the meaning of "normativity" need to be contextualized.

This finding also contributes to queer scholars' critiques of "visibility" and "out and proud"–based LGBT movements, which often label those who do not follow the path of visibility inferior and even backward. As other scholars have already argued, and as my research suggests, visibility does not always have to be the signifier of agency. Depending on local meanings and situations, the choice to stay invisible could be strategic. Through an examination of the transformation of queer subcultures, this chapter has further revealed that young queer women are affected by unequal socioeconomic change, as well as by the development of state welfare focused on the heterosexual family. Therefore, their survival strategy of avoiding masculinity and thus being invisible as sexual subjects to heterosexual society can be read as a necessary response to deepened socioeconomic inequality during the past ten years.

Although strategic, these tactics have started to exclude others, such as t'ibu and kŏlk'ŏ and transgender individuals, creating hierarchies within South Korea's queer communities. These changes may result in the similar effects of homonormativity, about which scholars like Duggan have warned in terms of mainstream lesbians and gay men in Western contexts. As progressive intellectuals and activists, we await fundamental changes in South Korean society. Meanwhile, we cannot blame young queer women's avoidance of masculinity. Rather, our criticism may offer them the courage to not fear punishment and harassment or bullying at school, which an antidiscrimination bill would remedy. By highlighting youth unemployment and gender inequality in the job market, we also hope to help them feel more secure in their ability to survive the current economic downturn without such dependence on the heterosexual family.

Notes

1   *Iban* (lit., "second class") is a term coined by queer subjects in South Korea to refer to their marginalized status, emphasizing "difference" rather than "second" citizen. It became popular in the early to mid-2000s and was also used by my informants to refer to themselves. In 2012, another term, *tting* (lesbian or bi), came to be used more frequently among them. In this chapter, I use "queer," "iban," and "tting" interchangeably, depending on where and how the terms were used and respecting the preferences of my informants. In general engagements with theory, and depending on the context of interviews, I also use the terms "lesbian women" and "gay men."

In 2002–2003, I met twenty-one young iban-identified women who were between age fifteen and twenty, and in 2012–13, I met with eighty-eight more queer-identified young women between sixteen and thirty-two. Many of my informants are from underprivileged groups and working-class families; their parents were unskilled, many of them irregularly hired workers living on the outskirts of Seoul.

2   Ji-eun Lee, who, like me, conducted her research on teenage queer women in the early 2000s in South Korea, found that identity, sexuality, and popular culture were interrelated and concluded that popular culture has opened spaces to "experiment" with sexualities that are not included in the "normal": see Jie-un Lee [Yi Chi-ŭn], "Sipdae yŏsŏng iban ŭi k'ŏmyunit'i kyŏnghŏm kwa chŏngch'esŏng e kwanhan yŏn'gu"(master's thesis, Yonsei University, Seoul, 2005).

Though I am more cautious than Lee about using the term "experiment," since it can reinforce the stereotype that teenagers' identification as queer is thoughtless, temporary, and insincere, I also argue that K-Pop and fandom, especially fancos, became a space for young female fans to explore gender and sexual identity. I discuss this in more detail in Layoung Shin, "Queer Eye for K-Pop Fandom: Popular Culture, Cross-Gender Performance, and Queer Desire in South Korean Cosplay of K-Pop Stars," *Korea Journal* 58, no. 4 (2018): 87–113.

3   Located in downtown Seoul, Sinch'on Park is a public park and was well known as a "lesbian park" in the early 2000s. Some young queer women used to hang out at this park and even called it their "home."

4   So-yu, however, met this *t'ibu* girl and dated her for a couple of months. When they broke up, the reason was not cheating but just because they found they had little in common.

5   Lisa Duggan, *The Twilight of Equality? Neoliberalism, Cultural Politics, and the Attack on Democracy* (Boston: Beacon, 2003).

6   John D'Emilio, "Capitalism and Gay Identity," in *Powers of Desire: The Politics of Sexuality*, ed. Ann Snitow, Christine Stansell, and Sharon Thompson (New York: Monthly Review, 1983), 100–113.

7   Peter Drucker, "The Fracturing of LGBT Identities under Neoliberal Capitalism," *Historical Materialism* 19, no. 4 (2011): 3–32.

8   Drucker, "The Fracturing of LGBT Identities under Neoliberal Capitalism," 16.

9   Duggan, *The Twilight of Equality?*

10   Duggan, *The Twilight of Equality?*, 50.

11   Maxime Cervulle, "French Homonormativity and the Commodification of the Arab Body," *Radical History Review* 100 (2008): 170–79; Fred Fejes, *Gay Rights and Moral Panic: The Origins of America's Debate on Homosexuality* (New York: Palgrave Macmillan, 2008); Roderick A. Ferguson, "Administering Sexuality or, the Will to Institutionality," *Radical History Review* 100 (2008): 158–69; Sandra Jeppesen, "Queer Anarchist Autonomous Zones and Publics: Direct Action Vomiting against Homonormative Consumerism," *Sexualities* 13, no. 4 (2010): 463–78; Martin F. Manalansan, "Race, Violence, and Neoliberal Spatial Politics in the Global City," *Social Text* 23, no. 3 (2005): 141–55; David Murray, *Homophobias: Lust and Loathing across Time and Space* (Durham, NC: Duke University Press, 2009); Jasbir K. Puar, *Terrorist Assemblages: Homonationalism in Queer Times* (Durham, NC: Duke University Press, 2007); Margot D. Weiss, "Gay Shame and BDSM Pride: Neoliberalism, Privacy, and Sexual Politics," *Radical History Review* 100 (2008): 86–101.

12 On "nationally acceptable queers," see Puar, *Terrorist Assemblages*. On "top gays," see Fejes, *Gay Rights and Moral Panic.*

13 John (Song Pae) Cho, "Faceless Things: South Korean Gay Men, Internet, and Sexual Citizenship" (PhD diss., University of Illinois, Urbana-Champaign, 2011); Lisa Rofel, *Desiring China: Experiments in Neoliberalism, Sexuality, and Public Culture* (Durham, NC: Duke University Press, 2007); Denise Tse-Shang Tang, *Conditional Spaces: Hong Kong Lesbian Desires and Everyday Life* (Hong Kong: Hong Kong University Press, 2011).

14 Drucker, "The Fracturing of LGBT Identities under Neoliberal Capitalism," 24. Drucker says not all working-class gays and lesbians and gays and lesbians of color are non-homonormative. They are also cautious about visibility, since it could jeopardize their work.

15 Paek So-yŏng, "Chamjaesŏng ŭl ing'yŏ ra purŭnŭn sesang," in *Ing'yŏ ŭi sisŏn ŭro pon konggongsŏng ŭi inmunhak*, ed. Paek So-yŏng et al. (Seoul: Ip'arŭ, 2011), 13–43; Ŏm Ki-ho, "Se ch'ŏngnyŏn ŭi iyagi," in Paek So-yŏng et al., *Ing'yŏ ŭi sisŏn ŭro pon konggongsŏng ŭi inmunhak*, 44–70.

16 Ch'oe Hyŏn-jŏng, "Ch'ŏngnyŏnch'ŭng ŭi chajo sŏkkin yuhaeng'ŏ 'ing'yŏ ingan,'" *T'onga Ilbo*, March 10, 2009, accessed July 7, 2014, http://news.donga.com/3/all/20090310/8706013/1.

17 Korean Statistics, "Ch'wiŏpja su, sirŏpnyul chui," *E-nara Chip'yo*, June 15, 2017, accessed September 27, 2017, http://www.index.go.kr/potal/main/EachDtlPage Detail.do?idx_cd=1063.

18 Yun Chin-ho, "Sinjayujuŭi sidae ŭi koyong pulan kwa ch'ŏngnyŏn sil'ŏp," *Hwanghae Munhwa* 67, no. 6 (2010): 240–58; Yang Ho-kyŏng, "Chohŭn iljari hyanghan 'ch'wiŏp kyedan' mandŭrŏya," *The Hankyoreh*, February 4, 2013, accessed February 5, 2013, http://www.hani.co.kr/arti/society/society_general/572768.html.

19 Working-class unskilled workers are mostly female, and these positions make up the highest proportion of irregular jobs, 66.3 percent: Shin Kwang-Yeong. "Globalization and Social Inequality in South Korea," in *New Millennium South Korea: Neoliberal Capitalism and Transnational Movements*, ed. Jesook Song, 11–28 (New York: Routledge 2011), 19. Irregular workers earn an income that is 50–70 percent that of regular workers; they also lack job stability due to yearly contracts and do not share the welfare benefits that regular workers receive. For more, see Shin Kwang-Yeong, "Economic Crisis, Neoliberal Reforms, and the Rise of Precarious Work in South Korea," *American Behavioral Scientist* 57, no. 3 (2013): 335–53; Yoonkyung Lee, "Labor after Neoliberalism: The Birth of the Insecure Class in South Korea," *Globalizations* 12, no. 2 (2014): 184–202.

20 For more detail, see Kim Sun-nam, "Isŏng'ae kyŏrhon kajok kyubŏm ŭl haech'e chaegusŏng hanŭn tongsŏng'ae ch'inmilsŏng," *Han'guk Yŏsŏnghak* 29, no. 1 (2013): 85–125.

21 Duggan, *The Twilight of Equality?*; Puar, *Terrorist Assemblages*.

22 Yau Ching, "Dreaming of Normal while Sleeping with Impossible: Introduction," in *As Normal as Possible: Negotiating Sexuality and Gender in Mainland China and Hong Kong*, ed. Yau Ching (Hong Kong: Hong Kong University Press, 2010), 3.

23 "Ilbansŭt'ŭ" is a shortened form of "ilban style," referring to lesbians who look ilban (heterosexual)—that is, ilbansŭt'ŭ appear feminine, or like "normative" girls, so they can "pass" as heterosexual in straight society. The term is similar to "femmes"—lesbians who style themselves in normatively feminine ways.

24 *Rejŭ* is the shortened form of *rejŭbiŏn*, the Korean pronunciation of lesbian, and used in a disparaging way.

25 Here femme was used similarly to *ilbansŭt'ŭ*, who is feminine.

26 danah boyd, "Why Youth (Heart) Social Network Sites: The Role of Networked Publics in Teenage Social Life," in *Youth, Identity, and Digital Media*, ed. David Buckingham (Cambridge, MA: MIT Press, 2008), 126. As many scholars have discussed, while (digital) media provide new avenues for intimacy, desire, and sexuality in non-heteronormative and non-cisgender ways, these media are not positive or negative for queer people, communities, and activism in themselves. They have the potential to be subversive by providing information and resources to create queer communities through online connectivity but can also cause one to become a target of surveillance and human rights violation because they are interconnected with multiple social constraints and possibilities of the off-line world. On the relationship between digital media and the off-line world, see Daniel Miller and Don Slater, *The Internet: An Ethnographic Approach* (New York: Berg, 2000); Tom Boellstorff, *Coming of Age in Second Life* (Princeton, NJ: Princeton University Press, 2008). On the use of digital media in queer Asian cultures, see Chris Berry, Fran Martin, and Audrey Yue, eds., *Mobile Cultures: New Media in Queer Asia* (Durham, NC: Duke University Press, 2003).

27 boyd, "Why Youth (Heart) Social Network Sites," 126.

28 These are well-known shopping malls in Tongdaemun, downtown Seoul, with twenty-four-hour shopping. The malls have open stages in front with events such as dancing or singing competitions to attract customers.

29 Drucker, "The Fracturing of LGBT Identities under Neoliberal Capitalism," 17.

30 In Article 92–6 of the Military Penal Code, Sodomy and Various Harassment Crime, *kyeganjoe* (which can be translated as "sodomy"), is designated a crime to be punished. The law allows punishment for sex between servicemen regardless of consent and whether it was conducted within or outside a military base. Based on this law, military officials investigated their soldiers to identify supposedly gay men, and in May 2017 a soldier was sentenced at a military trial to six months in prison and suspension for one year.

31 The OSHR was passed by the Seoul city government in 2011 in following similar measures in Kyŏnggi Province and Kwangju City. The OSHR in all three regions included "sexual orientation" as one of the factors that should not be the basis for discrimination in schools. Different from the conservative central government, a majority of City Council members in those areas represented a more liberal

Democratic Party. With a lot of effort from activists in education and youth and LGBT movements, and supported by the liberal City Council, the OSHR was passed despite strong objections from conservatives.

32 A school penalty system was introduced to junior high and high schools in 2005 as an alternative to physical punishment as a way to discipline students. The penalties are given to students who violate school regulations; those who exceed a certain number of points can be punished or transferred to another school, or they may leave school. On the punishment of young queer women at school, see Hyŏn/Yi Yu-bin, "Son chabŭmyŏn chinggye hanŭn hakkyo, pyŏrang kkŭt e nae mollinŭn ch'ŏngsonyŏn tongsŏngaejadŭl," NGO News, February 20, 2006, accessed June 30, 2009, http://www.ngo-news.co.kr/sub_read.html?uid=509&section=sc9&section2=.

33 Haksaeng Inkwŏn Chorye Sŏngsosuja Kongdong Haengdong, ed., Sŏngsosuja hakkyonae ch'abyŏl sarye moŭmjip (Seoul: N.p., 2011), 85–86.

34 Jung-ah Choi, "New Generation's Career Aspirations and New Ways of Marginalization in a Postindustrial Economy," British Journal of Sociology of Education 26, no. 2 (2005): 277.

35 Chris K. K. Tan, "Go Home, Gay Boy! Or, Why Do Singaporean Gay Men Prefer to 'Go Home' and Not 'Come Out'?" Journal of Homosexuality 58, nos. 6–7 (2011): 866.

36 Tan, "Go Home, Gay Boy!," 868.

37 Jason Ritchie, "How Do You Say 'Come out of the Closet' in Arabic? Queer Activism and the Politics of Visibility in Israel-Palestine," GLQ 16, no. 4 (2010): 558.

38 Mary L. Gray, Out in the Country: Youth, Media, and Queer Visibility in Rural America (New York: New York University Press, 2009), 4.

39 Gray, Out in the Country, 4.

40 Gray, Out in the Country, 9–10.

41 Tan, "Go Home, Gay Boy!" 865.

42 Tan, "Go Home, Gay Boy!" 866.

43 John (Song Pae) Cho, "'Deferred Futures': The Diverse Imaginaries of Gay Retirement in Post-IMF South Korea," Culture, Theory and Critique 58, no. 2 (2017): 252.

44 John (Song Pae) Cho and Hyun-young Kwon Kim, "The Korean Gay and Lesbian Movement 1993–2008: From 'Identity' and 'Community' to 'Human Rights,'" in South Korean Social Movements: From Democracy to Civil Society, ed. Gi-wook Shin and Paul Chang (New York: Routledge, 2010), 206–23. They argue that this privileging of family in Korean culture can be traced from the Chosŏn period (1392–1910).

45 Jesook Song, South Koreans in the Debt Crisis: The Creation of a Neoliberal Welfare Society (Durham, NC: Duke University Press, 2009), 47.

46 Jesook Song, Living on Your Own: Single Women, Rental Housing, and Post-revolutionary Affect in Contemporary South Korea (Albany: State University of New York Press, 2014), 9.

47 Song, Living on Your Own, 33.

48 Song, Living on Your Own, 33.

49 Lucetta Y. L. Kam, *Shanghai Lalas: Female Tongzi Communities and Politics in Urban China* (Hong Kong: Hong Kong University Press, 2013), 91.
50 Tang, *Conditional Spaces*, 20.
51 David L. Eng, *The Feeling of Kinship: Queer Liberalism and the Racialization of Intimacy* (Durham, NC: Duke University Press, 2010).
52 Ching, "Dreaming of Normal while Sleeping with Impossible," 3.

Works Cited

NEWSPAPERS AND MAGAZINES

NGO News
The Hankyoreh
T'onga Ilbo

KOREAN-LANGUAGE SOURCES

Haksaeng Inkwŏn Chorye Sŏngsosuja Kongdong Haengdong, ed. *Sŏngsosuja hakkyonae ch'abyŏl sarye moŭmjip*. Seoul: N.p., 2011.

Kim Sun-nam. "Isŏng'ae kyŏrhon kajok kyubŏm ŭl haech'e chaegusŏng hanŭn tongsŏng'ae ch'inmilsŏng." *Han'guk Yŏsŏnghak* 29, no. 1 (2013): 85–125.

Korean Statistics. "Ch'wiŏpja su, sirŏpnyul chui." *E-nara Chip'yo*, June 15, 2017. Accessed September 27, 2017. http://www.index.go.kr/potal/main/EachDtlPageDetail.do?idx_cd=1063.

Lee Ji-eun [Yi Chi-ŭn]. "Sipdae yŏsŏng iban ŭi k'ŏmyunit'i kyŏnghŏm kwa chŏngch'esŏng e kwanhan yŏn'gu." Master's thesis, Yonsei University, Seoul, 2005.

Ŏm Ki-ho. "Se ch'ŏngnyŏn ŭi iyagi." In *Ing'yŏ ŭi sisŏn ŭro pon konggongsŏng ŭi inmunhak*, Baek So-yŏng et al., eds., 44–70. Seoul: Ip'arŭ, 2011.

Paek, So-yŏng. "Chamjaesŏng ŭl ing'yŏ ra purŭnŭn sesang." In *Ing'yŏ ŭi sisŏn ŭro pon konggongsŏng ŭi inmunhak*, Baek So-yŏng et al., eds., 13–43. Seoul: Ip'arŭ, 2011.

Yun Chin-ho. "Sinjayujuŭi sidae ŭi koyong pulan kwa ch'ŏngnyŏn sil'ŏp." *Hwanghae Munhwa* 67, no. 6 (2010): 240–58.

ENGLISH-LANGUAGE SOURCES

Berry, Chris, Fran Martin, and Audrey Yue, eds. *Mobile Cultures: New Media in Queer Asia*. Durham, NC: Duke University Press, 2003.

Boellstorff, Tom. *Coming of Age in Second Life*. Princeton, NJ: Princeton University Press, 2008.

boyd, danah. "Why Youth (Heart) Social Network Sites: The Role of Networked Publics in Teenage Social Life." In *Youth, Identity, and Digital Media*, ed. David Buckingham, 119–42. Cambridge, MA: MIT Press, 2008.

Cervulle, Maxime. "French Homonormativity and the Commodification of the Arab Body." *Radical History Review* 100 (2008): 170–79.

Ching, Yau. "Dreaming of Normal while Sleeping with Impossible: Introduction." In *As Normal as Possible: Negotiating Sexuality and Gender in Mainland China and Hong Kong*, ed. Yau Ching, 1–14. Hong Kong: Hong Kong University Press, 2010.

Cho, John (Song Pae). "'Deferred Futures': The Diverse Imaginaries of Gay Retirement in Post-IMF South Korea." *Culture, Theory and Critique* 58, no. 2 (2017): 243–59.

Cho, John (Song Pae), and Hyun-young Kwon Kim. "The Korean Gay and Lesbian Movement 1993–2008: From 'Identity' and 'Community' to 'Human Rights.'" In *South Korean Social Movements: From Democracy to Civil Society*, ed. Gi-wook Shin and Paul Chang, 206–23. New York: Routledge, 2010.

Choi, Jung-ah. "New Generation's Career Aspirations and New Ways of Marginalization in a Postindustrial Economy." *British Journal of Sociology of Education* 26, no. 2 (2005): 269–83.

D'Emilio, John. "Capitalism and Gay Identity." In *Powers of Desire: The Politics of Sexuality*, ed. Ann Snitow, Christine Stansell, and Sharon Thompson, 100–113. New York: Monthly Review, 1983.

Drucker, Peter. "The Fracturing of LGBT Identities under Neoliberal Capitalism." *Historical Materialism* 19, no. 4 (2011): 3–32.

Duggan, Lisa. *The Twilight of Equality? Neoliberalism, Cultural Politics, and the Attack on Democracy*. Boston: Beacon, 2003.

Eng, David L. *The Feeling of Kinship: Queer Liberalism and the Racialization of Intimacy*. Durham, NC: Duke University Press, 2010.

Fejes, Fred. *Gay Rights and Moral Panic: The Origins of America's Debate on Homosexuality*. New York: Palgrave Macmillan, 2008.

Ferguson, Roderick A. "Administering Sexuality: Or, the Will to Institutionality." *Radical History Review* 100 (2008): 158–69.

Gray, Mary L. *Out in the Country: Youth, Media, and Queer Visibility in Rural America*. New York: New York University Press, 2009.

Jeppesen, Sandra. "Queer Anarchist Autonomous Zones and Publics: Direct Action Vomiting against Homonormative Consumerism." *Sexualities* 13, no. 4 (2010): 463–78.

Kam, Lucetta Y. L. *Shanghai Lalas: Female Tongzi Communities and Politics in Urban China*. Hong Kong: Hong Kong University Press, 2013.

Lee, Yoonkyung. "Labor after Neoliberalism: The Birth of the Insecure Class in South Korea." *Globalizations* 12, no. 2 (2014): 184–202.

Manalansan, Martin F. "Race, Violence, and Neoliberal Spatial Politics in the Global City." *Social Text* 23, no. 3 (2005): 141–55.

Miller, Daniel, and Don Slater. *The Internet: An Ethnographic Approach*. New York: Berg, 2000.

Murray, David A. B., ed. *Homophobias: Lust and Loathing across Time and Space*. Durham, NC: Duke University Press, 2009.

Puar, Jasbir K. *Terrorist Assemblages: Homonationalism in Queer Times*. Durham, NC: Duke University Press, 2007.

Ritchie, Jason. "How Do You Say 'Come out of the Closet' in Arabic? Queer Activism and the Politics of Visibility in Israel-Palestine." *GLQ* 16, no. 4 (2010): 557–75.

Rofel, Lisa. *Desiring China: Experiments in Neoliberalism, Sexuality, and Public Culture*. Durham, NC: Duke University Press, 2007.

Shin, Kwang-Yeong. "Economic Crisis, Neoliberal Reforms, and the Rise of Precarious Work in South Korea." *American Behavioral Scientist* 57, no. 3 (2013): 335–53.

Shin, Kwang-Yeong. "Globalization and Social Inequality in South Korea." In *New Millennium South Korea: Neoliberal Capitalism and Transnational Movements*, ed. Jesook Song, 11–28. New York: Routledge, 2011.

Shin, Layoung. "Queer Eye for K-Pop Fandom: Popular Culture, Cross-Gender Performance, and Queer Desire in South Korean Cosplay of K-Pop Stars." *Korea Journal* 58, no. 4 (2018): 87–113.

Song, Jesook. *Living on Your Own: Single Women, Rental Housing, and Post-revolutionary Affect in Contemporary South Korea*. Albany: State University of New York Press, 2014.

Song, Jesook. *South Koreans in the Debt Crisis: The Creation of a Neoliberal Welfare Society*. Durham, NC: Duke University Press, 2009.

Tan, Chris K. K. "Go Home, Gay Boy! Or, Why Do Singaporean Gay Men Prefer to 'Go Home' and Not 'Come Out'?" *Journal of Homosexuality* 58, nos. 6–7 (2011): 865–82.

Tang, Denise Tse-Shang. *Conditional Spaces: Hong Kong Lesbian Desires and Everyday Life*. Hong Kong: Hong Kong University Press, 2011.

Weiss, Margot D. "Gay Shame and BDSM Pride: Neoliberalism, Privacy, and Sexual Politics." *Radical History Review* 100 (Winter 2008): 86–101.

Chapter Nine

MOBILE NUMBERS AND GENDER TRANSITIONS

THE RESIDENT REGISTRATION SYSTEM,
THE NATION-STATE,
AND TRANS/GENDER IDENTITIES

Ruin

TRANSLATED BY MAX BALHORN

A few years ago, I visited my local municipal government office to obtain a new national identification (ID) card. At the time, I did not think twice when a government employee took my fingerprints. It seemed like a completely natural procedure, and the only part that really bothered me were the smudges of black ink left on my fingertips. Getting my prints taken was not particularly enjoyable, but I was looking forward to getting an ID card and curious to see how it would turn out. I had put it off for quite some time and submitted the paperwork only due to my mother's incessant prodding. My hesitation, however, had nothing to do with the movement to abolish national ID cards or the campaign against compulsory fingerprinting; I had been aware of national ID cards since primary school but thought little about their significance. I only realized what the first digit of the second half of a national ID card stood for much later, and even then I did not consider it a particularly problematic issue.[1] Is this evidence of how deeply internalized the mechanisms of citizen control have become? Does getting one's prints taken for a national ID card ultimately signify complete submission to the state? Or, instead, is resistance and disavowal simply an effect of power that, in the end, affirms and upholds the domination of the state?

As this chapter's subtitle suggests, the text unpacks how the state polices gender through the use of national ID cards and numbers before discussing the ongoing struggle over the meanings surrounding national ID cards in South Korea today. The chapter forgoes a detailed history of the Chumin Tŭngnokbŏp (Resident Registration Act), instead reconstructing contemporary debates while reading the politics of the nation-state, national ID numbers, and gender from a transgender perspective. Moreover, it seeks to uncover the possible implications and meanings of changing one's legal sex in the family register (hojŏk) as a transgender person.

The Nation-State, National ID Numbers, and the Military

At eighteen, I was put in the system
Fingerprints from my ten fingers
If I disappear, will I be tracked down?
A Korean person is their ID card. . . .
Inscribed in my head, my ID number
I cannot erase it, I cannot forget it
Inscribed in my brain 'til the day I die
Because it's always with me.
—Sinawe, "Chumin tŭngnokjŭng" (National ID Card)[2]

A Brief History of the Resident Registration System and Citizen Making

South Korea's current resident registration system consists of three major components: assigning national ID numbers, recording addresses of residents, and collecting fingerprints for the issuing of ID cards. The system has changed significantly since its inception.[3] Identity tags (hop'ye) of the Chosŏn era (1392–1910) arguably could be considered the precursor to the current resident registration system. As the South Korean scholar Kim Sang-su notes, "Although the system's primary objective was to identify and record individuals' identities, in practice, the system operated to harness manpower for the military and keep track of debtors through ID card issuance and surveillance."[4] The identity tag system was a means to regulate the duties of subjects, such as forced labor and military service; to do so, it recorded in detail the identity, residence, age, and physical features of adult males. Ultimately, however, the system failed to achieve the desired result.

During the Japanese colonial period (1910–45), resident registration was not simply based on home addresses. Instead, it identified individuals according to family relations, with the male as head of each household. As war mobilization intensified and military conscription was introduced across the peninsula, detailed statistics became necessary to evaluate and categorize the male population. The result was the Chosŏn Kiryuryŏng (Korean Residence Law) of 1942, the precursor to the Resident Registration Act enacted by the Park Chung Hee government in 1962.

After liberation in 1945, the resident registration system became deeply implicated in the ideological confrontation between right and left and the circumstances surrounding the Korean War. Although the need for detailed statistics to control the citizenry quickly became apparent in the wake of founding the Republic of Korea in 1948, the process of becoming a South Korean citizen was neither natural nor without friction. Outside Seoul, and especially in rural areas, it took quite some time for the reality that a new government had been established to truly make an impression on residents. In areas where conflict between the right and the left was particularly fierce, the process of "recognizing the existence of the modern nation-state" did not take place under the direction of a central government. Instead, it unfolded within the contexts of violence and ideological censorship engendered by the conflict between *ppalgaeng'i* (a derogatory term for communists) and *sangol taet'ongnyŏng* (supporters of Syngman Rhee).[5] The process of becoming a citizen began in this context.[6] Against the backdrop of ideological polarization of communism against anticommunism and the ongoing Korean War, national ID cards were issued only after a thorough evaluation of one's political convictions. Individuals suspected of being ppalgaeng'i were excluded from receiving ID cards.[7] The process of becoming a South Korean citizen was firmly rooted in anticommunist ideology and, as a result, produced categorically "anticommunist citizens."[8] Likewise, identification cards, issued by local cities or provinces during the war, "defined South Korean national identity as complete obedience to the commands of the nation-state as necessary for survival and compelled individuals to internalize anticommunism as the official national ideology. More simply, national ID cards identified South Korean citizens as non-leftists."[9]

After the Korean War, the state attempted to discipline citizens by issuing national ID cards on the pretext of tracking down North Korean spies. Although this plan was met with considerable resistance from citizens and political opposition, it was implemented and carried out regardless. The system persisted despite criticisms of its ineffectiveness in capturing spies because it justified random searches and "assisted in tracking down draft dodgers and those who avoided properly registering their residence."[10] In terms of the need for the new state to secure its borders through the formation of a standing army, turning inhabitants into citizens and potential soldiers was, by extension, a major objective of the resident registration system. Therefore, the persistence of the resident registration system was partially due to its utility as a policing method to survey and control citizens.[11]

The resident registration system was further consolidated and fortified by the Park Chung Hee administration during the 1960s. In 1962, citing espionage as a pretext once again, the Kiryubŏp (Residence Act) and Resident Registration Act were enacted. However, this process was not without friction and difficulties. The system managed to consolidate itself in a form similar to its current iteration due largely to the international situation at the time—specifically, the military relationship between South Korea and the United States immediately before the Vietnam War and the backdrop of small armed skirmishes occurring between the North and the South in the mid- to late 1960s.[12] The reduction of U.S. troops in South Korea due to their deployment to Vietnam, border skirmishes with the North, and spy provocations all brought about a state of quasi-war on the peninsula. At this historical moment, the state deployed the resident registration system, assigning unique identifying numbers to each citizen. Writings from 1970 by government employees in charge of this system clearly demonstrate its objectives:

> The management of the citizenry and its labor power is the basis for the construction and prosperity of the nation. Moreover, if national defense is the most important objective of the nation, then the citizenry itself must fulfil its duty of national defense. To concentrate the collective force of the citizenry in one place, the labor force must also be thoroughly managed. . . .
>
> Originally, the purpose of the Resident Registration Act was to seek out impure elements that threatened the state and to facilitate investigations of unlawful activities. However, the growing centralization of information that has resulted from the registration and issuance of national ID cards is producing clear and evident benefits.[13]

Not only does the resident registration system catalog the residence and movement of citizens and provide basic information for administrative purposes, it also strengthens the nationwide initiative to eradicate Communist influence as well as establishes a system for rationally managing the country's manpower.[14]

As is clearly demonstrated in these passages written, respectively, by U Kwang-sŏn, a local section chief, and Kim Tae-ho, the resident registration director at the Department of the Interior, the national ID card and number system were implemented to realize state policies concerning the efficient use and management of citizens, although they did not rely on the resident registration system alone. As President Park stated, "There is such a thing as a 'second economy' that exists on a psychological level—by which I mean cultivating a national consciousness and a level of understanding commensurate with modernization."[15] In this sense, the Saemaŭl Undong (New Town Movement), the Kungmin Kyoyuk Hŏnjang (National Charter of Education), state-issued textbooks, and high school military drills were part of this "second economy," all of which were aimed at making forms of control more familiar to the body.

As demonstrated earlier, the national ID card system was pivotal in disciplining citizens because it standardized the citizenry and compelled them to identify with the state.

GENDER'S PECULIAR ABSENCE FROM THE DEBATE

As has been shown, debates surrounding the resident registration system thus far have focused on how the system controlled and managed citizens in the name of national security during the formation of the South Korean nation-state and on human rights violations in the form of collecting excessive personal information, such as fingerprints. This view is true of arguments both for and against the resident registration system.[16]

Criticisms of the resident registration system framed in terms of human rights easily find support and sympathy. However, human rights are not an essential or absolute category; they are constantly contested and negotiated. Who really qualifies as human in the language of universal human rights? How are the categories of human and human rights constructed? These questions are under-discussed and pose a substantial challenge to advancing discussion on human rights.

When confronted with the existence of transgender people, most individuals respond with sentiments such as, "They're human, too," and, "Even they deserve rights." However, those who (can) speak from such a position do not question their own subjectivity from a position of self-awareness, and instead otherize transgender people as "subjects to be recognized," while failing to acknowledge humanity's brutal history of dehumanization.[17] Historically, not all humans have been or currently are considered human. In modern Europe, African woman were put in cages for amusement. In South Korea, perpetrators of spousal abuse often defend themselves by saying, "I was not beating just anyone. I was beating my wife." Hunting nets are used to catch "illegal" workers, and school principals in South Korea regularly urge gay and lesbian students to transfer to other schools because of their sexuality. The question of who is categorized as human is always contested; it is an uneven and selective concept. The "universal" in universal human rights is always a matter of one's experience and positionality. If the relative nature of human rights is not interrogated, mechanisms of power remain obscured.

Another point in need of further scrutiny (and the subject of this chapter) is the relative absence of gender in these debates. Most debates concerning the resident registration system take the system's dependence on a binary division of sex for granted. Most debates also avoid addressing how the military conscription system and national security initiatives brought about the division and demarcation of sex between 1 (or 3) and 2 (or 4) on national ID cards in the formation of the modern nation-state. Finally, the possibility that someone may be at odds with a state-assigned ID number, or that someone may choose not to live in accordance with the sex printed on a national ID card, is not sufficiently recognized or discussed.

Struggle(s) Surrounding National ID Numbers

MILITARY CONSCRIPTION, REGULATING GENDER,
AND FAMILY RELATIONS

After 1968, the government launched a full-scale implementation of the national ID card system, invoking the need to root out North Korean spies and improve public administration. This "administration" took the form of random searches of citizens and was justified using the rhetoric of social cohesion and combating "communist provocation." The military system was at the heart of this logic. Although the Constitution of the Republic of Korea stipulates that all citizens have a military duty to the country, the targets of military conscription are men who have been deemed "normal" and therefore eligible. Precisely this point is absent from debates about the resident registration system and national ID numbers. The question of why citizens are divided between 1 and

2 in their national ID numbers is completely absent. This oversight could be the result of people regarding the binary division of sex and gender as straightforward and believing that those born belonging to neither sex can later be assigned an immutable sex.

Further research into the context under which bodies have been divided between 1 and 2 in national ID numbers is needed. It is unclear whether a binary understanding of gender—and the mandate to live as one's assigned gender for the rest of one's life—was a common attitude prior to the national ID number scheme being established or whether this was a consequence of the nation-state's military conscription policy, which strictly identified citizens as either male or female. For example, on South Korean birth registration forms, sex is designated as either "(1) male" or "(2) female." However, on birth certificates sex is designated as "male, female, or undetermined." Assuming that birth certificates are produced prior to registering a birth, it can be surmised that the project of citizen making demands that all South Koreans eventually be incorporated into the state as only one of two sexes, despite the acknowledgment that not all people are born to one sex. The maintenance of the sex binary solidifies maleness for the purpose of securing the manpower essential to the operation of the military conscription system, which is considered the duty of all South Korean citizens. Although relatively little is known about premodern conceptions of gender on the Korean Peninsula, the current gender binary is central to sustaining a functioning military and capitalist nation-state. The separation of public and private spheres and the gendered division of labor are possible only in a society that presumes the existence of two sexes. Accordingly, those who do not conform are considered problematic beings ("undetermined") who simply cannot exist (outside of choosing 1 or 2).

That said, the regulation of sex cannot be understood exclusively as a problem of military conscription. On the occasion of introducing the individualized national ID card system, one government official, U Kwang-sŏn, stated, "Through increasing the efficiency of the Family Register Act (Hojŏkbŏp) by the consolidation of familial ties according to the male head of each household, the act conforms to the principles of family structure necessitated by the Law of Domestic Relations (Ch'injokbŏp)."[18] In Korean, terms used to refer to family members and relatives, such as *imo* (aunt), *samch'ŏn* (uncle), *ŏnni* (older sister when used by a younger woman), *nuna* (older sister when used by a younger man), *hyŏng* (older brother when used by a younger man), *oppa* (older brother when used by a younger woman), *ŏmma* (mother), and *appa* (father) differ slightly in meaning according to place and local culture but are also firmly rooted in sex and social status. However, it is not simply the sex of the person being referred to that determines which term is used but also the sex of the speaker. For example, when someone calls another person *ŏnni* (older sister), it reveals not only that the person referred to, but also the speaker, is a woman. The term *nuna* (older sister) operates in the same way insofar as it reveals that the speaker is male. Therefore, in family relations, it is rare for someone regarded as male to use the terms *ŏnni* and *oppa* (older brother).[19]

The statement that the resident registration system and numbers "conform to the basic principles of family composition necessitated by the Law of Domestic Relations" reveals the state's intention to firmly base the family and kinship systems on the sex binary. By extension, we can also infer the state's intention to prevent the existence of "troublesome" individuals who fail to conform to this binary and who thereby challenge the Law of Domestic Relations.

CHALLENGING NATIONAL ID NUMBERS, CALLS FOR ABOLISHMENT,
AND OTHER DEMANDS AT THE MARGINS

Jacob Hale is a trans man who recounted the following episode, highlighting the issue of pronouns and sex binaries: "For example, once when my father started telling a story about one of his memories of me as a child, he said: 'When Jake was a little boy . . . , I mean a little girl . . . , I mean a little child . . . , he . . . , I mean she . . . , I mean . . . , I do not know what I mean!' There he broke off."[20]

My sex was assigned male (1 on my national ID card) at birth, but I use both *nuna* and *ŏnni*. Within the heteronormative space of the household, I say *nuna* to refer to my older sister, but outside the house I use *ŏnni* or a nickname to refer to her. Am I male when I say *nuna* and female when I say *ŏnni*? Rather than using the term "male-to-female" or "trans woman," I usually identify myself as trans. In this situation, should I be referred to as "he" or "she"? I use the term "trans" to refer to myself rather than "trans male" or "trans female," and occasionally I refer to myself as a female-to-male trans woman. Disregarding the number on my national ID card, what pronouns or family terms can others use to call me? Calling my older sister *nuna* is a habit that has formed over the past twenty years. Although I have never identified as male, if the term "son" is used to refer to me during the time before I identified as trans, then what words are possible to refer to me now? In the case of a trans woman who says she was not born male and has always been female, what words in our existing lexicon can accommodate her experience of attending an all-male middle and high school? As regards trans women who experience enlisting in the army and being subjected to physical exams, do the words "woman" and "daughter" really capture the entirety of their lived experiences? When referring to transgender people, words that "clearly" reveal sex always encounter these problems. Transgender people are constantly a moving target under the current binary of sexed language; when words attempt to fix them in language, various contextual nuances and personal experiences are inevitably erased. When I am called a "man," this term refers to me, while at the same time it does not; the same is true when I am represented in language as a woman. When the word "woman" is used to refer to me, the parts of my male life and experiences as a son until now are erased or concealed.

Nevertheless, these experiences do not mean that transgender people are completely irrelevant to the sex binary and heterosexuality; nor are they beings who transcend gender altogether. The idea that transgender people simply traverse or transcend the boundaries of gender is a dangerous one.[21] In fact, many transgender people are currently demanding revisions to their family registers and wish to change the first digit in the second half of their national ID numbers. Are these desires tantamount to conforming to the control mechanisms of the nation-state and therefore in conflict with the campaign for completely dissolving the resident registration system?

As demonstrated earlier, most discussions surrounding the resident registration system focus on the issue of human rights. As a result, "the obligation to always carry identification and prove one's identity is now being seriously questioned."[22] Although I agree with the implications of this statement, it rests on the problematic assumption that the speaker's state-issued national ID card can and does properly represent their identity.

In South Korean society, proof of resident registration (*chumin tŭngnok ch'obon*) and other personal information is unnecessarily demanded for employment and other everyday processes. Government records concerning sex-reassignment surgery remain on one's proof of resident registration (recently, as a temporary measure, individuals are allowed to erase such records, but in principle a record remains). Therefore, applying for a job forces transgender people to out themselves and declare, "Yes, I'm transgender." In an environment where employees frequently end up resigning or "resigning as a result of strong suggestion" after being outed in the workplace, such records on one's resident registration convey to employers the following message: "Just do not hire me."

Many transgender people who elect to receive hormone therapy or other medical treatments often speak of having experienced suspicion and rejection, especially when asked, "Are you really who you say you are?" When registering for a credit card or mobile phone membership card over the phone, they must give their national ID number and date of issuance to prove their identities, to which operators often respond, "Please don't try to register with someone else's information." Calls often end with the phrase, "We can't verify your identity." Does this mean that one's identity and sex can be verified by the sound of one's voice? What exactly does my national ID card prove about me? After one's voice changes as a result of hormone treatment, the act of revealing one's national ID number over the phone is no longer to confirm identity but, rather, to prove that one is not a spy or a criminal. One transgender person reported being stopped at a sobriety checkpoint. Upon presenting their ID to police, the officers claimed to be unable to verify their identity and demanded to fingerprint them. According to another individual, they hated the inevitable rejection and suspicion when using their national ID card so much that, even when involved in a car crash that was the other driver's fault, they did not file a complaint rather than involve police. While these examples indicate problems when national ID cards serve as the exclusive method of verifying one's identity, they also highlight the necessity of considering how transgender people navigate the current system to conduct their lives. In such situations, what does the resident registration system prove about a person and under what circumstances? Does it prove anything at all? In this context, can demanding to change one's sex in the family register really be criticized as strengthening and upholding the legitimacy of the nation-state? Changing one's national ID number can be seen as (re-)integrating oneself into the existing system, but it is also a self-affirming act for transgender people because it can guarantee that a transgender person will no longer be denied selfhood by the society that surrounds them.

One trans male stated that if he were able to change his sex in the family register and change the first digit of the second half of his national ID number to a 1, he would no longer have to over-represent his masculinity and could pay proper attention to his femaleness. This statement demonstrates how intensely national ID numbers regulate gender expression. That is to say, the efforts of transgender people to change their legal sex in the family register and the number on their national ID cards reveal the strength of national ID numbers as a mechanism of control. Transgender people living as if they never changed their national ID number, having sex-reassignment surgery, or changing their sex in the family register are often interpreted as simply desiring to assimilate into the existing system. Such a judgment risks missing the context that informs this decision. Instead, this decision must be read for what it reveals about how power operates in South Korean society.

When talking with people who do not identify as trans, they often ask my opinion about the legality of transgender people strategically changing national ID cards, which they likely heard about on the news. Questions about whether changing IDs should be punished or not, or whether one considers changing IDs as an understandable choice, conceals the operation of deeper social systems that force transgender people to exchange IDs in order to conduct their lives in the first place. Upholding the illegality of the act while still debating whether it should be punished or not ignores inherent problems of the law itself and, on a social and cultural level, overlooks the excessive demands placed on individuals to continuously identify themselves. (Regardless, for transgender people national ID cards deny rather than affirm their identity.) If we fail to talk about the cultural and structural aspects of the law, such as having to submit a copy of one's family register when being hired or showing one's ID at a bar, we inevitably condemn certain individuals to the status of "illegal sojourners." Transgender people swapping national ID cards demonstrates that these cards operate as the strongest proof in forming and guaranteeing one's status and identity in South Korean society.

Compared with non-trans-identified people, there is a certain tendency for transgender people to internalize an excess of maleness or femaleness; only then can they be recognized as "a real man" or "a real woman." However, the process of being deemed "real" is also a process of disavowal, such as when people comment, "You may be transgender, but you really do seem like a guy/girl." Changing one's legal sex in the family register as well as one's national ID number allows transgender people to assert their identity without the need for excessive gender representation and demonstrates that the meanings held by national ID cards are not so simple after all. This is precisely because affirmation can erase the process of disavowal. Therefore, the act of transgender people changing their legal sex and swapping national ID cards should not be condemned as upholding accepted legal and state apparatuses. Instead, it should be understood as an opportunity to interrogate the context in which the resident registration system exercises its excessive control over citizens in the first place.

LAWMAKING AND MEDICAL DISCOURSE: "ILLEGAL" HUMANS

In this context, passage of the currently pending Sŏngjŏnhwanja Sŏngbyŏl Pyŏnggyŏng Tŭng e Kwan Han Tŭkpyŏlbŏp (Special Law on Transgender Gender Reassignment) would be a significant development.[23] However, this law will also place transgender people within the language of legal statutes and risks defining certain transgender people as legal and others as illegal. The law also risks forcing transgender people to undergo unwanted medical treatments or surgeries to conform to new legal requirements for changing the legal status of one's sex.

In fact, the activism surrounding the Special Law on Transgender Gender Reassignment and the meanings of the Special Law itself are as ambiguous as those of the resident registration system. The most visible aspects of present-day transgender activism are legal reform efforts aimed at passing the Special Law. However, it is possible to criticize the limitations of legal reform while also questioning the priority of legal reform itself.[24] Current activism focused on legal reform has its limits, such as calling for more regulatory measures and potentially neglecting to debate the problems of existing laws. Although not all activism aimed at legal reforms suffers from these problems, the Special Law requires revising family registers to change one's legal sex status and therefore forces transgender people to either conform to certain legal conditions or be excluded entirely. The law has the effect of creating and expanding stricter conditions and criteria for determining who is a "true transgender person."

Relying on the proposed Special Law and other legal reforms to resolve issues concerning the legal status of sex entails obvious limitations when considering the lived experiences of transgender people. The current system, under which a doctor assigns a baby's sex as either 1 (or 3) or 2 (or 4) at birth, and is henceforth known and managed by the state accordingly, creates the fundamental conditions that compel transgender people to demand the right of changing their legal sex. Therefore, this problem cannot be solved by legal reform; on the contrary, abolishing these legal structures altogether may be a more fundamental and effective solution. Calls for legal reform do not problematize existing legal structures and, instead, create new laws that conform to current legal discourse. This does little to problematize current thinking (and even when it does, it takes place within existing legal discourse) and does not necessarily guarantee further victories for transgender people in the future.

Nevertheless, efforts to abolish these legal structures are not necessarily preferable. In some regards, the difference between abolishing and reforming laws is negligible. Arguments for abolishment and reform both operate on the assumptions of legal discourse and ascribe to law a privileged position. Legal reform movements propose that new laws can solve existing problems, whereas movements to abolish such laws argue that the law itself is the problem and therefore appear to challenge legal discourse. However, a politics based on an "if there were no law" logic sustains and strengthens the authority of the law itself and is the desired effect of law and discourse. Legal reform and abolishment movements are not very different insofar as they assume law to be the main determinant in solving our problems.

This is not to say that we should stop pursuing legal reform or that we should not abolish persecutory laws. Both efforts are needed and they depend on the situation. Nevertheless, if we want to avoid adopting laws as our sole analytical criterion, how can we conduct our activism in such a way that current laws and discourses are understood as relative concepts among many and not as the singular criterion of action? How can we recognize the usefulness of the law while still regarding it as relative? Even here, such concerns conceal the fact that gender and sexuality are products of discourse and presume that gender and sexuality exist outside the law and discourse. Gender in contemporary society conceals its status as "either male or female, and immutable from that which a doctor assigns at birth." Therefore, the belief that abolishing legal statutes would result in more free expressions of gender and sexuality is also an effect of law and discourse.

Another issue to consider is why the state, through the medium of gynecologists and doctors, is endowed with the authority to determine each citizen's sex and compel them to live according to that assigned sex. People are not always born strictly male or female, and the distinctions among male, female, and intersex are always ambiguous.[25] Regardless of this fact, the assignment of an immutable sex is enforced by the nation-state and realized through the resident registration system. Furthermore, requirements informing sex-confirming surgery make it such that doctors ultimately decide whether patients correctly conform to norms associated with each sex. For example, if a trans woman communicates that she is female, but a doctor decides otherwise, what is to be done? In an example from the United States, after a trans woman finished a period of counseling, the psychologist judged that, because the woman wore pants to the session, she was not a "real woman" and needed to receive further counseling. When one's idea of femininity (or masculinity) fails to correspond to a doctor's definition of femininity (or masculinity), the determination of who is a "true" transgender person is made by a doctor according to normative standards fixed in discourse. However, regardless of whether one is transgender or not, few people manage to conform perfectly to ideal gender norms prevalent in South Korean society. We all lead our lives in constant tension with these gender norms, constraining our freedom in turn.

If that is the case, instead of individual practices such as fingerprinting and the resident registration system, should we not instead criticize the entire system that incorporates subjects as only one of two genders and that excludes individuals who refuse to live by those terms? Moreover, we should not criticize the demands of transgender people to change the legal status of their gender as integrating themselves into the regulatory mechanisms of the nation-state. Instead, we should ask why people feel compelled to do so and consider the meanings that can be extrapolated from this action.

What Does Your National ID Number Say about You?

I once heard a woman say that because she is a woman, she has both testicles and ovaries. A different woman (a "biological female") stated that because she is a woman, she regularly administers the "male hormone," testosterone. Another man indicated that he is a man with a clitoris, and another woman said that she is a woman who has a penis. A trans man I know suggested that even if he received breast reduction surgery, he wants to keep his vagina. Another lesbian/asexual transgender person said that she has a penitoris and can get an erection.[26]

Although most people interpret bodies in ways similar to how a national ID number strictly assigns a fixed sex to a corresponding body, the methods by which we interpret our own bodies are not so simple. There are trans women who, in the past, had "straight" or lesbian relationships that produced children. Are erections and ejaculation experiences only of men? Why is it taken as common sense that pregnancy and birth are impossible in a relationship between two women? Is it not a product of constant disciplining in a system that tells us there are only two genders and that pregnancy and birth are possible only between a man and a woman? Moreover, why is the common response that a pregnancy was possible only because the woman used to be a "straight guy" considered such powerful evidence to deny the validity of transgender lesbian women? Does a trans man who gives birth prove that he is not "really transgender" and can always "return to his previous sex"?[27] In a relationship between a trans man and trans woman who decline surgery for the sake of having a baby, a trans man can get pregnant. The person who gives birth to this child is both a trans man and the father; the mother is a trans woman who did not bear the child. In this context, the words of the poet Chŏng-ch'ŏl are more applicable than ever: "Because my father birthed me and my mother raised me."[28] The belief that a women can never become a father and a man can never become a mother, as well as the presumption that a father is *always* a father and a mother is *always* a mother, not only informs opposition to same-sex marriage and homophobic rhetoric, but also upholds the notion, enforced by national ID numbers, that all people belong to one of two genders.

I have a penitoris, and I am a female-to-male trans woman, but when someone meets me and comes to know the first number in the second half of my national ID number, what is it that they know about me? When one knows what genitals someone possesses, or the first digit of the second half of someone's national ID number, what does that purport to say about them, and what is one really knowing about them? The simplest method for forging a national ID card is simply changing the photograph. What this means is that the information on a national ID card does not exactly correspond to me; rather, it is only temporarily linked. The belief that one corresponds exactly to the content of one's national ID card is simply an act of adjusting me to conform to the contents of the card. Therefore, just because someone says my outward appearance is that of a man, in no way does that correctly identify me as male.[29] I suspect that saying one knows is tantamount to the desire to think one knows about a body, and the subsequent desire to control and regulate that body.[30] I believe that this suspicion constitutes a fruitful point of departure for debates surrounding transgender people and national ID numbers.

Notes

This chapter was originally published in Korean as Ruin, "Pŏnho idong kwa sŏngjŏnhwan: Chumin tŭngnok chedo, kungmin kukka kŭrigo t'ŭrensŭ/chenjdŏ," in Kwiŏ Iron Munhwa Yŏn'guso Moim, ed., *Chendŏ ŭi ch'aenŏl ŭl tollyŏra* (Seoul: Saram Saeng'gak, 2008): 26–46. Copyright © English, by Max Balhorn. All rights reserved.

1   South Korean national ID numbers are composed of thirteen digits. The first six digits reflect the holder's date of birth. The seventh digit is determined according to the holder's assigned sex. Men and women born before 2000 were assigned 1 or 2, respectively, and those born after 2000 were assigned 3 or 4.

2   Sinawe, "Chumin tŭngnokjŭng," track 9 on *Ŭnt'oesŏnŏn*, Toremi, 1997, compact disc.

3   For more on this discussion, see Hong, "Chumin tŭngnok chedo nŭn p'asijŭm ida"; Hwang, "Uri nara chumin tŭngnokjŭng hyŏnhwang kwa kaesŏn panghyang"; Kim, "Chumin tŭngnok chedo idaeron an toenda"; Kim, "Kukka ŭi kungmin kwalli ch'egye wa inkwŏn"; Kim, "Chumin tŭngnokjŭng ŭn wae saenggyŏnna"; Kim, "20 segi han'guk esŏ ŭi 'kungmin'"; Kim, "Chumin tŭngnok chŏngpi wa chibang haengjŏng t'onggye samu"; Mun, "Sinbun tŭngnok chedo kaep'yŏn nonŭi

e issŏ kaein chŏngbo ŭi poho wa chumin tŭngnok pŏnho ŭi yŏkhal"; Pak, "1960
nyŏndae chungban anbo wigi wa che 2-kyŏngjeron"; U, "Chumin tŭngnok kwa
hojŏkbŏp kaesŏn pangan"; Yi Sŭng-hun, "Kanch'ŏ i aniranŭn kŏl chŭngmyŏng
hae pwa."

4   Kim, "Chumin tŭngnokjŭng ŭn wae saenggyŏnna," 140.

5   No, "Haebang ihu kukka hyŏngsŏng kwajŏng e taehan chibangmin ŭi insik," 82.

6   For more on this process see, Kim, "20 segi han'guk esŏ ŭi 'kungmin'"; Kim, "Chumin tŭngnokjŭng ŭn wae saenggyŏnna"; No, "Haebang ihu kukka hyŏngsŏng
kwajŏng e taehan chibangmin ŭi insik."

7   Kim, "Chumin tŭngnokjŭng ŭn wae saenggyŏnna," 145.

8   Kim, "20 segi han'guk esŏ ŭi 'kungmin,'" 36.

9   Kim, "Chumin tŭngnokjŭng ŭn wae saenggyŏnna," 146.

10 Kim, "Chumin tŭngnokjŭng ŭn wae saenggyŏnna," 147.

11 Kim, "Chumin tŭngnokjŭng ŭn wae saenggyŏnna"; U, "Chumin tŭngnok kwa
hojŏkbŏp kaesŏn pangan."

12 For more background concerning the situation at the time, see Moon, *Sex among
Allies*; Pak, "1960 nyŏndae chungban anbo wigi wa che 2-kyŏngjeron."

13 U, "Chumin tŭngnok kwa hojŏkbŏp kaesŏn pangan," 65–67.

14 Kim, "Chumin tŭngnok chŏngpi wa chibang haengjŏng t'onggye samu," 80.

15 Pak Chŏng-hŭi, "There is such a thing . . . ," in Pak, "1960 nyŏndae chungban
anbo wigi wa che 2-kyŏngjeron," 267.

16 For a list of scholarly articles central to the debate surrounding the resident registration system, see the sources cited above in note 3.

17 Ch'ae, "Sŏngjŏnhwan cheguk-empire, sŏngjŏnhwan hŭpyŏlgwi-vampire,
sŏngjŏnhwan simp'an-umpire."

18 U, "Chumin tŭngnok kwa hojŏkbŏp kaesŏn pangan," 55.

19 Although such usage is rare, it does occur. In South Korean gay culture, men often
refer to each other using the term *hyŏng* (older brother), but also use the term *ŏnni*
(older sister). Also, among a group of siblings in which the majority are female, a
male sibling might use the term *ŏnni* (older sister) to refer to his older siblings.

20 Hale, "Tracing a Ghostly Memory," 113.

21 For further discussion, see Ruin, "Chendŏ rŭl tullŏssan kyŏnghapdŭl (gender
dysphoria)."

22 Kim, "Kukka ŭi kungmin kwalli ch'egye wa inkwŏn."

23 This section is based on a presentation I gave at the Graduate Student Conference on Law and Society (Pŏp kwa sahoe taehagwŏnsaeng moim chipdanhoe) on
April 21, 2007, titled, "Pŏp ŭrosŏ ŭi chendŏ/seksyuŏlrit'i."

24 At the time of writing this chapter, the conditions for changing the legal status
of one's sex set forth by the Special Law were as follows: "(1) Receive written
opinions from two doctors as defined per the second statute of the Medical Service Act (*Ŭiryobŏp*), including one psychiatrist. (2) Unable to reproduce (3) Not
married." There are various opinions concerning how these conditions should
be interpreted. Some say that the conditions are insufficient and overly flexible,

making it possible for anyone to easily change the legal status of their sex in the family register, while others criticize the law for being excessively regulatory and restrictive. My opinion agrees with the latter, and I am quite critical of the law. For example, the second condition demands one be "unable to reproduce," but does this mean that taking hormones for a set amount of time is sufficient, or is receiving sex-confirming surgery required? If one is sterile or infertile, does this mean the person does not need to take hormones? What about a female-to-male trans man who has not taken hormones but has gone through menopause and therefore is "unable to reproduce"? As one can see, there are many ambiguities, meaning the final decision would likely be decided by a judge. (I am not arguing here that the law should be stricter with additional regulations.)

25   For more on this discussion, see Hong, "Sŏng chŏnhwanja ŭi sŏngbyŏl kyŏljŏng e taehan pŏpjŏk chŏpgŭn"; Fausto-Sterling, "The Five Sexes"; Hegarty, "Intersex Activism, Feminism and Psychology"; Kessler, "The Medical Construction of Gender"; Kessler, *Lessons from the Intersexed*; Turner, "Intersex Identities"; Wilchins, *Queer Theory, Gender Theory*.

26   The neologism "penitoris" (*p'ellit'orisŭ*) combines the words penis and clitoris, and can be used by both trans women and trans men. See also Ruin, "Uri nŭn ŏdi ro kanŭnga: T'ŭraensŭ' chendŏ hogŭn 'to' e kwanhan tansang," *Idae Taehagwŏn Sinmun*, November 15, 2006.

27   This language comes from the criterion to change one's legal sex put forward by the Supreme Court of South Korea.

28   Chŏng-ch'ŏl was a Korean scholar, poet, and statesman who lived during the sixteenth century of the Chosŏn Dynasty.

29   Such claims are often met with the response, "That could be used to avoid prosecution for a sexual crime," or "That is concerning because it could be used to avoid military service." The first statement rests on the assumption that only men commit sex crimes and that sex crimes only occur in heterosexual relationships. This statement not only conceals the reality of sexual violence in same-sex relationships (that is to say, it idealizes and romanticizes same-sex relationships), but is also oblivious to the fact that there is no validity to the claim that a sex offender could claim to be a woman as a way to avoid prosecution for a sex crime. In the latter case (although I do not know why avoiding military service would be an issue in the first place), this is covered by the criminal code and military law. What is more, this sort of reaction is similar to those who opposed the Special Law on Sexual Crimes (Sŏngp'oknyŏk T'ŭkpyŏlbŏp), claiming it would be abused by women in order to extort money from men.

30   To continue, what does it mean to make assumptions about another's gender based on appearance? A trans woman who decides against hormone treatment or other medical treatments is often read by others as male, but what do one's assumptions about gender truly reveal about that person? What did one really know about that person? When I hear someone assume something about another's gender, I often ask them, "How do you know that person is not perhaps trans

or gay?" This question is often deflected by the listener as irrelevant and out of context. This response makes me sad because it confirms that the very existence of trans, gay, and queer people is still something that must be explicitly explained. Even when heteronormativity is questioned, it still operates as a conventional unit of analysis; trans and queer people seem to exist as complete others occupying the margins of heteronormative space. In such conversations, is outing oneself the only way for one's identity to be recognized?

Works Cited

NEWSPAPERS AND MAGAZINES

Idae Taehagwŏn Sinmun

MUSICAL RECORDINGS

Sinawe. "Chumin tŭngnokjŭng." Track 9 on *Ŭnt'oesŏnŏn*. Toremi, 1997, compact disc.

KOREAN-LANGUAGE SOURCES

Ch'ae Un-jo. "Sŏngjŏnhwan cheguk-empire, sŏngjŏnhwan hŭpyŏlgwi-vampire, sŏngjŏnhwan simp'an umpire: Rejŭbiŏn p'eminijŭm kwa t'ŭraensŭjendŏrijŭm ŭi kyŏnggye punjaeng." Paper presented at Che 13-hoe Yŏsŏng munhwa iron yŏn'guso k'ollok'ium, Seoul, South Korea, 2006.

Hong Ch'un-ŭi. "Sŏng chŏnhwanja ŭi sŏngbyŏl kyŏlchŏng e taehan pŏpchŏk chŏpgŭn." In *Sŏngjŏk sosuja ŭi inkwŏn*, ed. Han In-sŏ and Yang Hyŏn-a, 89–132. Seoul: Saram Saenggak, 2002.

Hong Sŏk-man. "Chumin tŭngnok chedo nŭn p'asijŭm ida." *Wŏlgan Mal* 171 (2000): 184–87.

Hwang Po-yŏl. "Uri nara chumin tŭngnokjŭng hyŏnhwang kwa kaesŏn panghyang." In *Han'guk haengjŏng hak'oe tonggye haksul palp'yo nonmunjip*, 519–38. Seoul: Han'guk Haengjŏng Hakhoe, 2004.

Kim Ki-jung. "Chumin tŭngnok chedo idaeron an toenda." *Wŏlgan Mal* 158 (August 1999): 142–45.

Kim Ki-jung. "Kukka ŭi kungmin kwalli ch'egye wa inkwŏn." Paper presented at Segye inkwŏn sŏnŏn 50-chunyŏn kinyŏm haksul haengsa palp'yomun, Seoul, February 26–March 1, 1999.

Kim Po-hyŏn. "Chumin tŭngnok chedo wa chibang kongmuwŏn chedo kŭrigo chibang haengjŏng yŏnsuwŏn." *Taehan Chibang Haengjŏng Kongjehoe* 47, no. 542 (1998): 116–20.

Kim Tae-ho. "Chumin tŭngnok chŏngbi wa chibang haengjŏng t'onggye samu." *Chibang Haengjŏng* 19, no. 206 (1970): 80–87.

Kim Tong-ch'un. "20 segi han'guk esŏ ŭi 'kungmin.'" *Ch'angjak kwa Pip'yŏng* 106 (Winter 1999): 30–47.

Kim Yŏng-mi. "Chumin tŭngnokjŭng ŭn wae saenggyŏnna." *Naeil Rŭl Yŏnŭn Yŏksa* 25, (September 2006): 139–49.

Mun Hong-an. "Sinbun tŭngnok chedo kaep'yŏn nonŭi e issŏ kaein chŏngbo ŭi poho wa chumin tŭngnok pŏnho ŭi yŏkhal." *Kajokbŏp Yŏn'gu* 18, no. 1 (2004): 217–47.

No Yong-sŏk. "Haebang ihu kukka hyŏngsŏng kwajŏng e taehan chibangmin ŭi insik." *Tonghyang kwa Chŏnmang* 62 (2004): 48–93.

Pak T'ae-gyun. "1960 nyŏndae chungban anbo wigi wa che 2-kyŏngjeron." *Yŏksa Pip'yŏng* 72 (Fall 2005): 250–76.

Ruin. "Chendŏ rŭl tullŏssan kyŏnghapdŭl (gender dysphoria): T'ŭraensŭ/jendŏ chŏngch'ihak ŭl mosaek hamyŏ." *Yŏ/sŏng Iron* 15 (November 2006): 289–304.

Ruin. "Uri nŭn ŏdi ro kanŭnga: T'ŭraensŭ' jendŏ hogŭn 'to' e kwanhan tansang." *Idae taehagwŏn sinmun*, November 15, 2006.

U Kwang-sŏn. "Chumin tŭngnok kwa hojŏkbŏp kaesŏn pangan." *Chibang Haengjŏng* 19, no. 205 (1970): 48–69.

Yi Sŭng-hun. "Kanch'ŏp i aniranŭn kŏl chŭngmyŏng hae pwa." *O Mai Nyusŭ*, July 18, 2003, http://www.ohmynews.com.

ENGLISH-LANGUAGE SOURCES

Fausto-Sterling, Anne. "The Five Sexes: Why Male and Female Are Not Enough." *Sciences* 33, no. 2 (1993): 20–25.

Hale, C. Jacob. "Tracing a Ghostly Memory in My Throat: Reflections on Ftm Feminist Voice and Agency." In *Men Doing Feminism*, ed. Tom Digby, 99–129. New York: Routledge, 1998.

Hegarty, Peter. "Intersex Activism, Feminism, and Psychology: Opening a Dialogue on Theory, Research, and Practice." *Feminism and Psychology* 10, no. 1 (2000): 117–32.

Kessler, Suzanne J. *Lessons from the Intersexed*. New Brunswick, NJ: Rutgers University Press, 1998.

Kessler, Suzanne J. "The Medical Construction of Gender: Case Management of Intersexed Infants." *Signs* 16, no. 10 (1990): 3–26.

Moon, Katherine H. S. *Sex among Allies: Military Prostitution in U.S.-Korea Relations*. New York: Columbia University Press, 1997.

Turner, Stephanie S. "Intersex Identities: Locating New Intersection of Sex and Gender." *Gender and Society* 13, no. 4 (1999): 457–79.

Wilchins, Riki. *Queer Theory Gender Theory: An Instant Primer*. Los Angeles: Alyson, 2004.

CONTRIBUTORS

Pei Jean Chen is an assistant professor of Taiwanese Literature at National Chengchi University in Taiwan. She received her PhD degree from the Department of Asian Studies, Cornell University, in 2016. Her current book project, *The Politics of Love: Modern Sexuality in Colonial Taiwan and Korea*, offers a new cultural history of the colonial world order by comparing Taiwanese and Korean constructions of love and sexuality and their historical responses to Western and Japanese imperialism.

John (Song Pae) Cho is a visiting assistant professor in anthropology at Davidson College. A recipient of fellowships from the Korea Foundation and the Social Science Research Council for Transregional Research, Cho writes and teaches on subjects surrounding transnational LGBT studies, Korean and East Asian studies, neoliberalism, and the Internet.

Chung-kang Kim is an assistant professor in the Department of Theater and Film at Hanyang University in South Korea. Her research considers the realms of Korean and East Asian cinema; cultural studies; gender, race, and sexuality studies; and (trans)national visual culture.

Todd A. Henry is an associate professor of history and the inaugural director of Transnational Korean Studies at the University of California, San Diego. He specializes in modern Korea, with an interest in everyday life under Japanese colonialism. He also explores mass media, sexual medicine, and state policing in the geopolitical contexts of American militarism and Cold War knowledge formations. Henry is the author of *Assimilating Seoul: Japanese Rule and the Politics of Public Space in Colonial Korea, 1910–1945* (2014) and is currently completing a book on the understudied place of queerness in South Korea's authoritarian modernity.

Merose Hwang is an associate professor of history and program coordinator for the Asian studies minor at Hiram College. She is a former research fellow at the Institute for Korean Studies, Yonsei University, and a visiting scholar at the Institute for the Study of Religion, Sogang University. Her research considers the relationship between folk and institutionalized religions.

Ruin is a lead researcher at the Institute for Trans/Gender/Queer Studies in Seoul and director of the Korean Queer Archive. Zher main research interests include tracing the history of transgenderqueer persons in South Korea and advancing critical ways of thinking about gender/sexuality and violence. Ruin's English-language research appears in *TSQ*, vol. 3, nos. 1–2 (May 2016).

Layoung Shin is the ASIANetwork-Luce Foundation Postdoctoral Teaching Fellow at Lewis and Clark University. As a sociocultural anthropologist and teacher of cultural politics, Shin examines questions of race, sexuality, and class while researching queer youth, desire, and fandom culture in South Korea.

Shin-ae Ha is a research professor at the Center for Northeast Asian Humanities and Social Sciences, Institute for Korean-Chinese Relations Studies, Wonkwang University, South Korea. Her research considers the realms of Korean and Northeast Asian literature. Her current research centers on colonialism, gender, and cultural geography revealed in modern fiction during the 1930s and 1940s. She is the author of *Asia Trouble: The Imagination of Asia's Regional Identity and Decentering Cultural Geography* (2018).

John Whittier Treat is professor emeritus of East Asian Languages and Literatures at Yale University. His publications include *Writing Ground Zero: Japanese Literature and the Atomic Bomb* (1995), *Great Mirrors Shattered: Homosexuality, Orientalism, and Japan* (1999), and *The Rise and Fall of Modern Japanese Literature* (2018). He is currently writing a study of Korean writers under Japanese rule.

Drucker, Peter, 298–99
Duggan, Lisa, 298–99, 315

East Asia Daily [Tong'a ilbo], 55–56,
    58–59, 69–70, 73
Eastern Learning [Toghak], 60
Edelman, Lee, 100–101, 111, 134
education: cultural, 71; homophobia in,
    306–9; sex, 123; war and, 168; women
    and girls and, 16, 73, 119, 154, 312–13.
    See also girls' schools
Em, Henry, 98, 109
Eng, David, 312–13
entertainers: female, 12, 55, 58; male,
    175–93
Erni, John, 265
Eunuch, A [Naesi] (Yu), 190

Faceless Things [Ŏlgul ŏmnŭn kŏtdŭl]
    (Kim), 283
failure, 111
familialism, 9, 11, 25–26, 265–67, 290n71.
    See also Confucianism; female mas-
    culinity; transgender people
families, 101, 281, 298, 311–14. *See also* filial
    piety conventions; kinship
Family Register Act, 329
Fanon, Frantz, 128
fashion, 154
female homoeroticism: *Chugan
    Kyŏnghyang* and, 220–21; depic-
    tions of, 15, 215, 226–31; depic-
    tions of male readers and, 231–40;
    Kaesalgu and, 129; weeklies and, 19,
    208–10, 219
female masculinity, 27, 215–18, 296, 314
filial piety conventions, 25, 133, 206,
    215–18, 229–30, 240, 254n78, 310–11.
    See also Confucianism
film: A-grade, 187–88; arrests of directors,
    187; contemporary South Korean,
    205–7; culture, 179; family-planning,
    179; politics of gender and sexuality

and, 175–93; state-controlled produc-
    tion, 176–80
Film Law, 179
Foucault, Michel, 177
Frankl, John, 102, 110
futurism, 100, 111, 134, 272

Garber, Marjorie, 186
gay marriage. *See* marriage
gender: assigned sex's relation to, 335–36;
    binary conceptions of, 12, 266;
    citizenship and, 327–28; colonialism's
    relation to, 17–18, 21, 56, 72, 76n12,
    84n101, 151–66; comedy films, 175–93,
    209; female masculinity and, 27,
    215–18, 296, 314; labor and, 215–16;
    nationalisms and, 120, 124–29, 133–36,
    179; queer performance of, 27, 72,
    83n82, 84n90, 215–18, 295–303, 313–15;
    sex and, 21, 29–30, 229, 335. *See also*
    intersex people; transgender people
girls' schools, 130–31, 146–52, 154, 306–7.
    See also schoolgirls
global queering, 2, 8, 263
Golden Demon [Konjiki], 121–22
Gossiping for Trifles [K'ongch'ilp'al Saesa-
    mnyuk] (play), 134–35
Grandfather's Real Estate Agency [Odae
    pokdŏkbang] (film), 187
Gray, Mary, 309

Habermas, Jürgen, 273
Halberstam, Judith [Jack], 98–100,
    110–11
Hale, Jacob, 330
Han Sang Kim, 251n56
Heartless [Mujŏng] (Yi), 129
Heavenly Church Monthly [Ch'ŏndogyo
    Hoewŏlbo], 60
Hegel, Georg Wilhelm Friedrich, 90
Henry, Todd A., 269, 284–85
heteronormativity: queer romance and,
    231–40

History Compilation Committee, 64–66
homoeroticism, 205–44
homonationalism, 24, 301; chrononormativity and, 110; definitions of, 24
homonormativity: Berlant on, 282;
  female masculinity and, 314–15;
  insufficiency of, 282, 297; Korean,
  306–9; neoliberalism and, 298–301;
  visibility and, 309–15
homophobia, 3, 10, 26–30, 209, 227, 242,
  277, 285, 290n78, 297–307, 337
homosexuality. *See* homoeroticism;
  queer; rights; visibility
Hong Ch'ŏn, 187
H.O.T., 295
Hŏ Yŏng-suk, 130–32, 147
human rights: LGBTI movement and, 24;
  resident registration system and,
  327–28, 331; sexual minorities and,
  9; students and, 306; violations, 327;
  women and, 235, 253n76. *See also*
  rights
Hwang Sin-dŏk, 130–32, 147

iban (second-class citizen), 26, 264, 272,
  274–78, 281, 295–96, 302–3, 305
Iban Inspection, 306–7
identity politics, 7–9, 11, 20, 24–26, 176,
  265
Im Chong-guk, 93
intersex people, 21, 29–30, 229, 335
intimate events, 117–36
I Prefer Being a Woman [Yŏja ka tŏ choa]
  (film), 180
Ivancity, 267, 279–80

Jameson, Fredric, 103
Japan. *See* colonialism
Japanese Buddhism, 57
Jealousy [Chilt'u] (film), 230
Jie-Hyun Lim, 208
"Journey, The" [Haengno] (Chang),
  154–69

Kam, Lucetta Yip Lo, 312
Kendall, Laurel, 57
Kennedy, Elizabeth, 211
Key, Ellen, 119–20
Kim, Chung-kang, 269
Kim, Tae-gon, 61
Kim, U-chang, 94
Kim/Cho Kwang-su, 1–5, 243
Kim Hwal-lan, 168
Kim Hyŏn-ju, 127
Kim Kyŏng-min, 271–74
Kim Myŏng-sun, 120
Kim Seong-Nae, 63
Kim Sŭng-hwan, 1–5, 243
Kim Sun-nam, 300
Kim Su-yong, 190
Kim Tae-ho, 327
Kim T'ae-ik, 55
Kim Tong-in, 119, 130
Kim Yŏ-je, 125, 150
Kim Yun-kyŏng, 124
Kinema Junpō (film journal), 109
kinship: choice and, 123; Confucian, 15,
  117; cultural purity and, 209–10;
  heteropatriarchy and, 239; identity
  and, 22; Korean War and, 5; lesbians
  and, 25; nonconforming practices of,
  5; prewar structures of, 212; queer,
  206–7, 216, 218, 224, 227–28, 231–32,
  236, 240–44. *See also* families
Kkiri Kkiri [Among Ourselves], 274–75
Klein, Christina, 208
Korea Central Daily [Chosŏn Chung'ang
  Ilbo], 73
Korean Association of Wartime Patriots,
  152–53
Korean Broadcasting Station, 275
Korean Queer Culture Festival, 305
Korean studies: in the 1920s, 62; queer-
  ing, 8; tropes in, 272
Korea Theater, 182
Kukje Theater, 181–82
Ku Pong-sŏ, 185–86, 188–98

348 | Index

women and, 27, 297–98, 301–15. *See also* coming out

Warner, Michael, 273, 277
wartime: female same-sex love during, 146–69; motherhood during, 150–69
Weaker Than a Woman (Clay), 121
weddings, 5, 19, 73, 205–44. *See also* marriage
weeklies: B-film reviews in, 183; capitalistic voyeurism in, 209, 220; criminality in, 210–18; female homoeroticism in, 205–44; gendered labor and, 215–16; same-sex weddings in, 218–31; suicide in, 238–40
Weston, Kath, 123, 255n89
Wild Apricots [Kaesalgu] (Yi), 129
Wings (film), 109
"Wings" [Nalgae] (Yi), 90–112, 272

yangbogal, 43n76
Yang Ho-kyŏng, 300
Yi Chŏng-suk, 127
Yi Chŏng-u, 274–75
Yi Kwang-su, 127–28, 132–33
Yi Nŭng-hwa, 62–69
Yi Sang, 90–112
Yi Sŏk-un, 125
Yi [Song] Hŭi-il, 206
Yi Tŏk-yo, 130
Yi Yŏng-il, 180
Yongsan Theater, 182
Yŏnhap Productions, 181
Yonsei University, 267, 275
Youth [Sonyŏn] (magazine), 121
Yu Hyŏn-Mok, 187, 190
Yu Jong-yul, 119, 131
Yun Ch'i-ho, 133
Yun Chin-ho, 300
Yun Ik-sam, 188

www.ingramcontent.com/pod-product-compliance
Lightning Source LLC
Chambersburg PA
CBHW020454270326
41926CB00008B/593